WISCH

CONTEMPORARY
NATIVE AMERICAN
CULTURAL ISSUES

CONTEMPORARY NATIVE AMERICAN COMMUNITIES
Stepping Stones to the Seventh Generation

Native American communities and people have survived through the twentieth century and are poised to embark on the twenty-first century. The survival and continuity of Native American cultures and communities has been a varied and complex path. Hundreds of communities continue to preserve many features of their religion, government, kinship organization, values, art, ceremony, and belief systems, and to maintain political relations with the United States. The series is intended to fill an existing void in the literature on Native American contemporary world experiences. While providing a historical background, the series will focus on an interpretation of contemporary life and cultures, interpreted in their broadest contexts. The series will draw from the disciplines of Native American Studies, History, Sociology, Political Science, Religion, and Social Work, and solicit treatments of treaty interpretation, sovereign rights, incorporation into global and national economic, political, and cultural relations, land rights, subsistence rights, health and medicine, cultural preservation, contemporary spirituality, multiple genders, policy, and other issues that confront tribal communities and affect their possibilities for survival. New and culturally creative possibilities have emerged in film, theater, literature, dance, art, and other fields as a result and reflection of the challenges that have confronted Native American communities over the past centuries and will again in the coming century. We believe it is essential to examine contemporary Native American life from the point of view of Native concerns and values. Manuscripts that examine any significant aspect of Native American contemporary life and future trends are welcome.

SERIES EDITORS

Troy R. Johnson
American Indian Studies and History
California State University, Long Beach
Long Beach, CA 90840
trj@csulb.edu

Duane Champagne
American Indian Studies Center
3220 Campbell Hall
Box 951548
UCLA
Los Angeles, CA 90095-1548
champagn@ucla.edu

EDITORIAL BOARD

SERIES EDITORS' ROYALTIES WILL BE DONATED TO THE UCLA FOUNDATION/YELLOWTHUNDER SCHOLARSHIP FOUNDATION

BOOKS IN THE SERIES

CONTEMPORARY

NATIVE AMERICAN

CULTURAL ISSUES

Edited by
Duane Champagne

ALTAMIRA
PRESS

A Division of Sage Publications, Inc.

Walnut Creek • London • New Delhi

For information address:

AltaMira Press
A Division of Sage Publications, Inc.
1630 North Main Street, Suite 367
Walnut Creek, CA 94596
explore@altamira.sagepub.com
www.altamirapress.com

SAGE Publications Ltd.
6 Bonhill Street
London EC2A 4PU
United Kingdom

SAGE Publications India Pvt. Ltd.
M-32 Market
Greater Kailash 1
New Delhi 110 048
India

PRINTED IN THE UNITED STATES OF AMERICA

Library of Congress Cataloging-in-Publication Data
Contemporary Native American cultural issues / edited by Duane Champagne
p. cm.—(Contemporary Native American communities; v. 3)
Includes bibliographical references and index.
ISBN 0-7619-9058-5 (cloth)
ISBN 0-7619-9059-3 (pbk.)
1. Indians of North America—Social conditions. 2. Indians of North America—Ethnic Identity.
1. Champagne, Duane. II. Series
E98.S67 C66 1999
305.897—dc21   98-40178
                              CIP

99 00 01 02 03 04 6 5 4 3 2 1

Production, Design, and Editorial Services: *Zenda, Inc.*
Editorial Management: *Jennifer R. Collier*
Cover Design: *Joanna Ebenstein*

CONTENTS

PART V
HEALTH

PART VI
ENVIRONMENTAL ISSUES

Introduction

Change, Destruction, and Renewal
of Native American Cultures
at the End of the Twentieth Century

Duane Champagne

OVER THE PAST five hundred years, Native American communities have been subjected to the drastic effects of Western colonial intrusion. While Native cultures were transforming even before the arrival of European colonists, the post-Columbian period has been one of greatly accelerated change caused by newly introduced diseases, colonial political competition and—ultimately—domination, incorporation into the increasingly globalized world economy, and changes introduced by cultural interrelations with Western education, religious conversion, language loss, and the borrowing of Western values and concepts. As a result, the contemporary state of Native cultures is very complex and diverse. Nevertheless, if one wanted to make a single statement about Native Americans, it might be that they have sought to retain their cultures and communities despite colonial domination. Unfortunately, not all have been entirely successful. Yet very subtle forms of spirituality, political culture, holistic health, and community and individual identity remain in most Indian communities, although their expression is often hidden from non-Indian view.

Native American cultures are extremely diverse in the contemporary world, certainly more diverse than in previous centuries. Today, according to the 1990 U.S. Census, over two-thirds of the country's Native Americans live in urban areas; only about 700,000 live on or near Indian reservations. While the census counted about 1.75 million Indians based on its category of race, there are an estimated 7 million Americans who claimed descent from an Indian ancestor. Many in the latter group do not have enduring or recent ties with any particular Native community or culture, but they nevertheless retain a sense of identity and interest in Native issues. Meanwhile, many Natives who live on or near reservations speak English, are well educated, practice Christianity, and aspire to professional careers. Contemporary tribal life is multicultural, and many communities manage this cultural diversity in their own way. For example, the Northern Cheyenne, whose reservation is in eastern Montana, accept a variety of religious orientations including several forms of Christianity, peyotism, the traditional Cheyenne sun dance, and

7

teachings of the prophet Sweet Medicine. For the Cheyenne, there are multiple paths to the sacred, and the Cheyenne Elders ask only that spiritual practitioners not mix the ceremonies and teachings of various sacred paths. The Iroquois nations of upstate New York have a long history of contention among Protestant Christian groups, the Handsome Lake Church, and, more recently, some Iroquois who wish to reclaim and practice traditional teachings.

Contemporary Native American cultural diversity is additionally reflected in the continued presence of hundreds of distinct tribal communities. There are at least 550 federally recognized Indian tribes, and more will be recognized in the future. About 200 nonrecognized Indian communities have petitioned for federal recognition, and there are many more who are preparing to do so. On the other hand, there are some communities who do not seek federal recognition, believing that it is not the U.S. government's place to define their own community or identity.

There are hundreds of Native nations with many distinct traditions, languages, and spiritual histories. In this way, Native communities do not form a single nationwide ethnic group, but rather a collection of many ethnic groups. For example, at the convention of the National Congress of American Indians (NCAI), each Indian Nation, regardless of population or land size, has a single vote. This method preserves the cultural and political autonomy of each tribal community. The collection of tribal nations forms a national lobbying organization, which is the main task of the NCAI. No tribal community is willing to subordinate its political sovereignty to any of the other Indian Nations. Working with tribes as the unit of political representation, the NCAI is reluctant to represent urban Indians directly; rather it suggests that urban Indians gain representation through tribal communities.

Throughout the past few centuries, most Native communities experienced the incorporation of foreign religious views, political culture, economic culture, and values. In a complex combination of colonial domination and cultural sharing, Native people have struggled with colonial impositions such as boarding schools and the discouragement of tribal language, culture, and religion, while at the same time they have selectively and strategically borrowed ideas, technologies, and religious, political, and legal concepts. Introducing these concepts into their own communities has become a means of preserving tribal sovereignty, identity and community. For example, concepts such a sovereignty are borrowed from Euro-American culture and law. Although Native concepts of territory, political power, and community organization are very different from the corresponding European concepts, the doctrine of tribal sovereignty has become a keystone to preserving tribal political and cultural independence. Learning English, developing knowledge and understanding of U.S. culture and government, and acquiring Western education and other skills have enhanced the capability of tribal members and communities to compete and protect their interests more effectively in U.S. society and in increasingly globalized political, cultural, and economic environments.

Many members of contemporary tribal cultures are engaged in upholding and preserving their specific traditions. Either through political debate or by the lifeways or life style they choose to follow, many Native Americans negotiate the meaning and place of traditional and Western cultural elements within their communities. In any particular group, these discussions and actions take a variety of paths. Because tribes have a very different cultural tradition and relatively unique colonial experience, the solutions that each settles upon are varied and community specific. For example, the Navajo Nation adopted an American-style court system in the early 1960s. Over time, however, many rural Navajo preferred their court to use more traditional methods to solve most local issues. The Navajo court system responded with peacemaker courts, which did not operate according to the competitive advocacy methods of Anglo-American courts but worked to restore good relations among the groups engaged in a dispute. This method works well in many cases. While some tribal communities are considering the inclusion of tribal law and traditional understandings of justice within their tribal court systems, the differences of traditional tribal law among the tribes will move each community toward a unique solution in creating a court system that works for the community and preserves the central features of justice and social relations.

Native communities will continue to discuss and experiment with their cultures, norms, values, and institutions, as do all cultures. Contemporary communities are dynamic in their simultaneous creation and preservation of cultures and institutions. This process of change has been going on for centuries, or perhaps from time immemorial, but contemporary communities face powerful external forces and conditions of domination that require considerable efforts among the community members who wish to preserve a specific tribal identity or culture. Under such conditions of rapid social, economic, political, and cultural change, it is not surprising that within many Native communities there are differences among community members and groups over what are the proper or best ways to proceed. Such discussions are part of the process of change and preservation. There are usually several views about how much tradition or change is acceptable. While this type of conflict is often called factionalism, such discussions are a natural aspect of community action whenever important issues of identity and community preservation and survival are at stake. This process will continue for centuries to come. While such debates may be the result of intense struggles over power and values, they are a sign of the importance of these issues and of the commitment that people and groups have to particular paths.

Again, most Native people currently live off reservation and within urban communities. Yet many urban Indians have life-long ties to their tribal communities. Intertribal powwows, urban community centers, and university Indian studies centers have contributed to preserving tribal and Indian identity among those who have less and less direct contact with their tribal community. Even in urban areas, Indians have preserved tribal identities while creating pan-Indian tribal institutions and organizations. Nevertheless, more and more Native people are emerging as second- and third-generation off-reservation people. This group may be well on their way to creating an intertribal, ethnic Native American identity and community that is organized in very different ways from tribal communities.

While Native people have been exposed to colonial imposition of nontribal cultural concepts and experiences, they have increasingly developed creative ways to express tribal issues and help preserve and extend tribal traditions by incorporating many U.S. cultural elements. Since the 1960s, Native authors writing powerful novels about Native experiences have emerged in increasing numbers. As a result, many Native American issues and experiences are more widely and deeply understood than before. Dance troupes such as the American Indian Dance Theater have presented social and instructive dances to audiences around the world. Recent Native theater and dance groups have taken up Native themes and issues that speak to broad audiences and, at the same time, support the preservation and creative extension of Native culture. Since the early 1990s, Native people have increasingly gained access to participation in movie production. Through a variety of contemporary media, Native artists, writers, and producers explore, preserve, and extend the interpretation of Native cultures.

Native cultures, like all cultures, have always been in process of change and negotiation. This process continues today. While few will argue that much Native culture has been lost, the challenge for today is to reclaim and preserve as much as possible, while upholding and maintaining cultural expression in contemporary life that will strengthen and extend the creativity of Native wisdom and culture.

PART I

NATIVE IDENTITY

Who is Indian? This is a very contemporary issue, negotiated in the context of current cultural, economic, and institutional relations. For many tribal communities of previous centuries the answer to this question was much clearer and definite than it is today. A large majority of Native American communities were matrilinial: one was born into the clan or family of one's mother. For example, among the Iroquois and Cherokee, people reckoned descent through the mother's clan. Social and legal rules were to a large extent determined by family and clan, and community members were determined by clan or family membership. Even today, the method by which one formally introduces oneself is the identification of one's family or clan. Many contemporary Navajo do this, and it is the tradition among other nations such as the Ojibwa. Native people often adopt other people, including Europeans, and introduce them into a clan or family.

Contemporary identity issues, however, are increasingly political and controversial, and they are intertwined with questions of sovereignty. Postconquest identity involves complex interactions among tribal traditions, governmental policies of recognition and resource distribution, and individual connections and identities. The Bureau of Indian Affairs, which since the 1880s has controlled much of Indian reservation life, generally provided services for all those Indians who had 25 percent or more Indian blood. This policy introduced categories of race into Indian country, whereas most tribal classifications had been based on kinship and culture. Since the 1960s, through political action and court cases, tribal communities have increasingly won the right to determine their own tribal membership and have adopted a variety of modes of doing so in the context of changing cultural, economic, and demographic circumstances.

The Cherokee Nation of Oklahoma, for example, will grant tribal citizenship to all individuals who can prove that any of their ancestors was listed on one of the Cherokee census rolls dating back to the 1830s. The rationale for this method of selecting tribal members is based in part on Cherokee nationalism, which holds that a Nation has the right to decide the rules of membership. Thus a Cherokee can enroll with a relatively small amount of Indian blood. There are other tribes, however, which have blood quanta criteria for tribal membership and often restrict voting privileges only to those tribal members who are in residence on the reservation.

For the United States government, a primary means of identifying Native American is by enrollment within a federally recognized tribe. Members of non-recognized tribes frequently have difficulty asserting their identities in legal realms but are sometimes recognized for benefits or identified as Indian for powwows and other Indian community events.

On a cultural level and within communities, tribal and community membership is often contested on a number of fronts. In some cases, ability to speak the tribal language is gaged as a criteria for Indian identity. However, since many U.S. Native communities do not have many fluent speakers, such criteria are not widely used. Community participation and close proximity of living is an informal criteria that is often central to community membership. Often those who live and participate in the local community over long periods are regarded as community members for all practical purposes. Some individuals are Native Americans culturally, but because they do not belong to any federally or state recognized tribe, they are not classified as Native Americans. On the other hand, many enrolled member of federally recognized tribes have little cultural or political contact with their communities.

Clearly, Native identity is neither homogenous nor taken for granted. Historical and contemporary realities of cultural tradition and colonial domination have made identity a complex and fundamental question for Native people as they work to create cultural, economic, and political futures for themselves and their communities. The following articles by Ward Churchill and Devon A. Mihesuah provide detailed examinations of the range of issues involved in the creation and preservation of contemporary Native identity.

1

American Indian Identities: Issues of Individual Choice and Development

Devon A. Mihesuah

 How Indianness is defined by American Indians[1] and non-Indians, who claims to be Indian and why, and the anxieties among multiheritage Indians are complex historical and present-day issues. While the politics of identity and the life experiences of Indians have been addressed more in recent years by scholars, activists, and novelists, there is little research addressing how and why American Indians make their identity choices.

Unquestionably, the diversity of opinions over what it means to be American Indian renders the issue impossible to generalize and difficult to analyze. I am a historian, not a sociologist, but after historical study, self-analysis, observation, and much interaction with people concerned about what it means to be American Indian, it is obvious that any study of Indian identity will be complicated and that there are certainly more "types" of Indians than the ones proposed in 1964 by Clyde Warrior.[2]

Not all individuals claiming to be Indian "look Indian," nor were many born into tribal environments. Many are not tribally enrolled, and others who claim to be Indian are not Indian at all. Some Indians who appear Caucasian or black go back and forth assuming Indian, white, and black identities, while others who have lived most of their lives as non-Indians decide to "become Indians" at a later age. Some individuals are Indian by virtue of biological connection but know little about their cultural mores either because of lack of interest; because there was no one to teach them; or because it was not (or is not) socially or economically profitable to pursue an Indian identity due to the time period, location, and degree of racism, prejudice, and stereotypes.

Because of assimilation, acculturation, and intermarriage with non-Indians, American Indians have a variety of references to describe themselves: full-blood, traditional, mixed-blood, cross-blood, half-breed, progressive, enrolled, unenrolled, re-Indianized, multiheritage, bicultural, post-Indian, or simply, "I'm _____ (tribal affiliation)." Reflecting internal debate over identity, many individuals will

Devon A. Mihesuah is associate professor of history at Northern Arizona University in Flagstaff, Arizona.

also say that they are secure, confused, reborn, marginal, or lost. Those who are hopeful about being accepted as Indians declare that "I just discovered my grandmother was a full-blood," or "I'm part Indian but I'm not sure what kind," and so forth.

Most research on identity development focuses on African Americans (usually referred to as black in the literature), Asian Americans, Mexican Americans, or biracial peoples in general.[3] One of the most thoughtful is the "life stages" paradigm for African Americans proposed by William Cross[4] and extended by Thomas Parham, termed "Cycles of Nigrescence" (the process of becoming black[5]). Cross posits that as blacks respond to a variety of social events, pressures, and expectations, they progress through a set of definable stages that lead to identity resolution. If we substitute American Indians for blacks and figure in social, economic, and political influences, it is possible to use the Nigrescense outline to logically consider here—albeit briefly—the various elements that influence the identity choices of persons who claim to be racially and/or ethnically American Indian.[6] For comprehensive psychological studies of American Indian identity choice and development, it is, of course, advantageous to investigate the construction of ethnic identity as studied by developmental psychologists.

One assumption of this discussion is that American Indians, like blacks, live in a white world. Historically (and presently), they have had to deal with racism, stereotypes, and oppression. Sociologist Maria P. P. Root's assessment of biracial peoples is that "it is the marginal status imposed by society rather than the objective mixed race of biracial individuals which poses a severe stress to positive identity development."[7] When Root writes "society," she is referring to white society, but it is apparent that the standards, expectations, and prejudices of tribal societies have the same impact on an Indian's identity formation. The self-image of Indian people not of mixed races (full-bloods) also are affected by white and Indian societies' influences.

In this essay, *multiheritage* Indian refers to an individual of two or more races, one being American Indian, who defines Indian as his or her primary reference group. *Racial identity* is the biological race one claims. A multiheritage person might claim all of his or her racial heritages or only one; he or she can be biologically mixed-blood or full-blood and have no exposure to the cultural mores of an American Indian tribe, being connected to their group only by virtue of genetics.

Cultural identity reflects the cultural standards of a society to which one subscribes. Michael Green describes cultural identity as an identity that "gives the individual a sense of a common past and of a shared destiny."[8] Tribes have the commonalties of having to deal with the effects of colonialism (racism; prejudice; loss of culture, land, and population) and originally having members who were exclusively indigenous peoples. Indians who only recognize this general definition of Indians' common past and who utilize a spectrum of tribal symbols and cultural mores to construct their version of an Indian, subscribe to a pan-Indian cultural identity. Green also asserts that culture "unifies and integrates the individuals, gives them a sense of belonging, and a sense of their own uniqueness as a people. Further, a culture provides the individuals within that culture a way of life that is constitutive of what it means to be a human being."[9] Using this definition of culture, Indians who practice their specific tribal traditions and are profoundly affected socially, religiously, and politically by those traditions are often referred to as *culturally Indian*. Individuals who adhere to the cultural norms of two groups may refer to themselves as bicultural.

Ethnic or *group identity* are terms often interchangeable with cultural identity. Borrowing from Rose, ethnicity is a "group classification in which the members share a unique social and cultural heritage passed on from one generation to the next."[10] It does not have a biological basis. Traditional Indians adhere to the culture of their tribe by speaking the language, practicing religious ceremonies, and living among their tribespeople. They might use the term ethnic to mean that both their racial background and cultural adherence are Indian. Other individuals who claim to be Indian but who have no cultural connection to their tribe may also refer to themselves as ethnically Indian. American Indian ethnic or cultural identities have a variety of meanings attached to them by Indian and non-Indian societies and by individuals who claim them; they are salient terms that change with the economic, political, and social tides.

LIFE STAGES

As applied to blacks, those in Cross's first stage, pre-encounter, know they are black, but they give little thought to race issues. Some see their blackness as an imposition on their lives. Exposure to racial stereotypes and miseducation may lead them to perceive blackness as negative, and some individuals may adopt a white world view, using white/mainstream standards to judge themselves and everyone else. They may devalue black culture (everything from their skin color and hair texture to African art and religion) and glorify white/mainstream culture.[11]

It is during the first part of Cross's second stage, encounter, that such persons experience a shocking event that jolts them into considering that their frame of reference for forming their identity is inadequate. Experiences such as black people being denied access to an exclusive nonblack neighborhood because of their skin color, the death of Martin Luther King, Jr., or time spent in prison—as in the case of Malcolm X—act as catalysts to initiate an exploration of the Black Power movement and to listen to different opinions on life. The second part of the encounter stage is when the person decides to develop his black identity.[12]

The third stage, immersion-emersion, is marked by an intense interest in all that is black, and everything pertaining to blackness (hairstyles, clothing, mannerisms, speech) is enthusiastically incorporated into this person's life. She attends activist meetings, studies black history, and denigrates white and "less black" people, sometimes aggressively. Feelings of insecurity about one's identity remain high, and the individual often will criticize anyone who resembles unattractive aspects of the person's old self.[13]

The forth stage, internalization, comes when the person attains a sense of inner security and self-confidence about his black identity. Defensiveness, stress, and antiwhite behavior regress in favor of "ideological flexibility, psychological openness, and self-confidence."[14] The person is at peace with himself and is able to express feelings of dissatisfaction about racism and inequality through constructive, nonviolent means.[15]

The Cross Model Indians

Upon first reading the Cross model, it was easy to insert the names of Indian acquaintances into the model, and I see myself scattered throughout. But, as Cross explains, the stages are not always clear-cut and simplistic for blacks, and neither are they for Indians. Some individuals might remain at one level, or hover between two or more stages simultaneously; or some may arrive at one stage then move back to a previous stage. Some Indians never feel the need to change or develop their identities at all and fit into the internalization stage all their lives.

Cross's model presents an adequate outline to begin discussion of identity development for Indians, but numerous factors must be taken into consideration, most of which spur confusion. First, tribes are not alike. They have different languages, religions, histories, and methods of dealing with non-Indians. Full-blood members also retain a notable degree of physiological distinctiveness. Second, many tribes incorporate members with minimal biological heritage and no knowledge of tribal culture, giving the impression to some that all one needs in order to be Indian is to prove that one has a distant Indian ancestor. Third, many tribal members look phenotypically Caucasian. Fourth, many people with little or no knowledge of Indians want to identify and to be identified as Indian. Fifth, the historical time period of the person's life must be taken into account. In the 1990s, Indians are considerably more outspoken, populous, and accepted by non-Indians than they have been historically. Their physiologies, images among non-Indians, and individual and tribal socioeconomic situations are different, as are their world views.[16] Sixth, even within a group, the personal needs, physiology, and environmental influences of each individual is different.

Cross designed his model with the idea that blacks will become more so after progressing through the stages. In regard to Indians, I posit that: (1) some Indians go through stages on their way to becoming like whites; (2) some white, black, and Hispanic individuals and mixed-heritage people of minimal Indian heritage who desire to become Indian also progress through stages on their quest for an Indian identity;[17] and (3) multiheritage individuals, especially those who do not have cultural knowledge of the group they aspire to become a member of and/or do not physically resemble other members of that group, will have more difficulty in establishing a comfortable identity.

INDIAN LIFE STAGES

Stage 1: Pre-encounter

Cross writes that black individuals at this stage may identify with white culture or focus on aspects other than blackness (such as their job), but their blackness is denied in favor of being accepted as just a human being.[18] Some Indians in the pre-encounter stage are well aware of themselves as Indians yet they know little about their tribal history and culture, much less about other Indians or the political, economic, and social state of tribes in general. They do not necessarily identify with whites, although some do. Others see themselves as racially and culturally Indians, but they also believe themselves to be inferior to whites and at fault for their economic, social, and/or political conditions. Of course, many Indians have no feelings of inferiority. They are fulfilled, satisfied with their place in the world, and never seek an identity change.

The home environment is the place where children first learn values.[19] It is during adolescence that they strive to create an identity while at the same time attempting to conform to the norms of peer groups.[20] Neighbors' ethnicities and attitudes, television, radio, movies, and literature also affect the child's world view. The parents may be full-blood, mixed-blood, or one may be white and one Indian—full or mixed—and possess a variety of values that affect their children, such as in one of the following modern scenarios:

1. The parents may possess only a white world view and are Indians by merit of blood, not by cultural connection. These individuals may be of minimal Indian blood, and they know they are Indian because of family legend (often without proof of tribal membership), or because their ancestors are indeed listed on tribal rolls. The children often hear that they are Indian throughout their childhood, but they are not taught any details about tribal life. Because of their possible connection to Indians, they often romanticize Indian culture as monolithic and inherently good, but they know nothing of tribal politics, health statistics, poverty levels, or other realities of daily tribal life. The children are essentially white in every way, including appearance. If they do pursue their Indianness, it is usually during adulthood.[21]

2. The parents may be white with no knowledge of Indians while the children are adopted Indians. Even if the parents teach the children about Indians, it is often a superficial attempt, and the children desire to find out about their heritage as they grow older. The children are taught to live as whites, but they will know at an early age that they look different from their parents and neighbors.

3. The parents may have an understanding of their tribal culture and of the white world because they are forced to interact in mainstream society. For example, some Indians during the relocation period (1950s) moved to large cities and found themselves isolated from other Indians. They either learned about white society, remained frustrated in a foreign environment, or moved back home.[22] More currently, in Flagstaff, Arizona, because of the Navajo-Hopi land

issue, numerous Navajo have moved from their reservation homes to urban areas next to non-Indians. Although they attempt to retain traditions, they must learn about and interact with white society to survive. These individuals may be surprised at the level of racism towards Indians, but because of their traditional family values and extended family on the reservation most remain confident with their Indianness. Many of the children become acquainted with the values of non-Indian society while attending white schools and playing with white children. Some grow judgmental against their tribespeople and question the value of their tribal culture.

4. The parents possess both white and Indian blood and want the children to know about both cultures. The children may attend white schools and participate in tribal activities after school and on weekends, and they have access to their extended family. They may have a confusing childhood, as Root surmises that many multiheritage people will encounter discrimination within their family from the group with higher social status.[23] The group of higher status, however, is not always white.

If a portion of the multiheritage children's family is composed of a socially dominant racial group, they may perceive that race as the superior one, especially if racist remarks and/or jokes are made about the other racial group.[24] For example, a multiheritage child with a white mother and Indian father who is never allowed to visit her father's family may begin to believe that her white blood is superior to Indian blood. Conversely, if the child were to spend time with her father's Indian relatives, he or she might hear enough negative comments about whites to believe that her white blood is inferior. This scenario could also be true of a full-blood, multicultural Indian child whose parents are representatives of two (or more) different tribes. Another cause for confusion is when the extended family refuses to accept an interracial marriage and will not visit a son or daughter who married outside the group. Children are, however, less likely to become upset and confused by their mixed ancestry if both parents and the extended families have pride in themselves and their cultures and if both have equal social status within the family unit.[25]

5. The parents may be bicultural. They appear to live like whites during the week when they work and socialize with non-Indians, and they resemble Indians on weekends or at other times when they attend powwows, sun dances, tribal activities, or other Indian social and familial functions. They are comfortable with the bicultural lifestyle, and the children have extended family members they can turn to for information about their heritage. This family will look phenotypically like Indians, some of mixed heritage.

6. One or both parents may be racially Indian and repress Indian values in the home and refuse to impart tribal knowledge to their children. Some parents may try to deemphasize Indian culture either because they think that white culture is superior to Indian cultures or because they believe that by learning only the ways of white society can their children succeed socially and economically.

An Indian's rejection of Indian culture does not necessarily lead to self-hatred. As Cross discusses, despite the reality that we live in a complex, pluralistic society, most white children usually "see the world in monoracial terms" and perceive no need to learn how to interact with other racial and/or cultural groups.[26] Most black children, on the other hand, are taught to be biculturally competent. Similarly, many Indian parents who appear to reject Indian culture do not want their children to become white. They simply want them to have equal access to the socioeconomic privileges that whites have.

7. Children with parents who possess an Indian world view exclusively are likely to live on a reservation or in an area inhabited by other traditionals. The family is mainly exposed to other Indians and their tribal cultures. The children are similar to those in the second example in that they may become alarmed at the racism they encounter if they leave the home environment. Some of the children may be similar to those who discover desirable aspects of white culture and begin to wonder about the usefulness of tribal culture. The same can be said of some Indian children who enroll in university away from their home environment and those who were forced to attend federal boarding schools in the 1800s.

8. The biological and cultural Indian family may live on the reservation or in an urban area in poverty. One or both parents and some extended family may be uneducated alcoholics in poor physical and mental health. This family identifies as Indian but they see little hope for advancement, so they do not try.

9. The family members look phenotypically black and possess Indian blood. Even if they desire to pursue an Indian identity, their appearances alert others to the reality that they are part black. Depending on the attitudes of the neighborhood and nearby tribes, the people who look black will most likely be viewed as black.[27]

There are other examples, of course, especially when the varying kinship, clan, and extended family systems among the numerous tribes are considered, but, regardless of the home arrangement, the individual will in large measure adopt the values and identities that are prevalent in the household. According to Parham, it is during late adolescence to early adulthood that the child begins to locate her place in the social environment. Indians, like blacks, realize that they are at once a part of, yet apart from, American society.[28] Not every Indian, however, becomes aware of this. Individuals who are mixed Indian and white, are Caucasian in appearance, and who were not taught any aspects of Indian culture may experience none or only minimal negative feelings about being Indian because they do not perceive themselves to be Indian and neither does anyone else. They can "pass" as white and can "stay white" if they so choose. C. Matthew Snipp's analysis of the 1980 census reveals that the majority of persons who claimed Indian ancestry did not claim to be of the Indian race and are termed "Americans of Indian descent." Most of these individuals are no different from other whites except that they have an Indian ancestor in their family tree. He proposes that socioeconomic factors account for the choices evidenced on the census. Many people become Indian only when it is economically profitable and socially desirable to be an Indian.[29]

In addition to home values, children are influenced by teachers, television, radio, books, sports mascots, and people on the street and their reaction to the children. Seemingly positive comments directed toward mixed-heritage children may cause them to realize that they are different. To illustrate, at around the age of three, children become aware of skin, hair, and eye color.[30] They also become aware that their ethnic names sound unlike those of other children.[31] My son, for example, learned to say Mihesuah at three. Several times he has been asked, "What kind of name is that?" by people not meaning anything negative. But the comments may start him thinking that despite the rich Comanche history behind his name, he is different. Root posits that it is when the child encounters negative experiences at an older age that identity conflicts—including aspects such as names—will arise.[32]

Stage 2: Encounter

Cross explains that after a black individual encounters a negative or positive event, she may be jolted into reevaluating her place in the world.[33] In regard to Indians, the person may hear a moving speech about American Indian history and culture that makes her want to know more about her tribal history. This is an encounter because the person had previously only heard a negative version of her history and is enthused enough by the new version to embark upon a quest to discover the truth. There are three basic goals of individuals who have an Indian encounter:

Becoming an Indian. Appearance may be one of the first catalysts for exploring identity possibilities. If Indian children are adopted by white parents, they wonder at an early age why they appear different from the parents. If parents attempt to keep children from exploring their Indian heritage, the children will become curious as to why their parents feel Indianness is "bad" when other people may say the opposite. The adopted children's jolt may be a discovery of their tribe. Some white parents may attempt to educate the adopted children about their Indian heritage, but, if they know nothing about Indians, they may take the children to general events such as powwows and movies dealing with Indians and read them books with Indian characters. The lack of depth in any of these activities usually proves to be unsatisfactory to the children. The parents may attempt to involve their adopted children in specific tribal functions, but usually this does not happen as most white parents keep their Indian children away from their true origins out of fear that they may be taken away from them. In a few instances, the white parents and their adopted Indian children have good relations with the children's Indian families, thus providing the youngsters with an avenue for obtaining information.

Two young men I knew when living in Texas, one a Kiowa/Muscogee and the other a Lakota, had been adopted as infants by white couples. Both sets of parents were extremely religious and discouraged either child from pursuing knowledge about their Indian heritages. In the mid 1980s when I met them, both were in their early thirties; they were angry, confused, estranged from their white parents, and were both regular patrons of a drug and alcohol rehabilitation center in Fort Worth. They were attempting to find themselves by participating in powwows and attending generic sweat lodge ceremonies. Their lack of kin relations and knowledge of tribal culture reminded them that they were marginally Indian, and their distinctive Indian appearances disallowed them from becoming white. Although they were Indians by race, they remained culturally unsatisfied.[34]

Some children raised in households that did not impart values of Indian culture but are linked to a tribe because of blood might hear positive facts about Indians at school and become increasingly interested in meeting their extended family. Often the person will explore archives to find relatives listed on tribal rolls and will enroll themselves if they have not been already enrolled.

White adults who have "always been interested in Indians" and who become disillusioned with other white people are sometimes jolted when they hear an Indian speak because they identify with put-upon peoples. Or perhaps they feel guilt for what has been done to Indians. They may especially admire radicals who garner attention through their flamboyant actions and rhetoric. These people adopt a mixed-blood Indian identity because this claim is easier to defend than a full-blood one.

A white person, after attending a "sweat lodge ceremony" conducted by white people, discovers that it can be profitable to impart the teachings of Indian religions to others so she embarks on a journey "on the red road" to gather information. The "white shamans" usually retain their knowledge of white ways, marketing, and accounting especially.[35] Still others can be seen in archives across the country attempting to locate an Indian ancestor on tribal rolls so they can receive whatever moneys they believe Indians have coming to them each month.[36]

Indians are not seen with the same prejudices in all parts of the country. Among affluent suburbanites in some cities, a person who looks white but claims to be part Indian may garner the response, "That's so neat." Being "part Indian" but not really looking it affords a form of status among some Caucasian groups. Receiving kudos for one's racial claims can jolt the individual on to garner more attention.[37]

Becoming More Indian/Rediscovering Indianness. Some Indians may never have been aware of their history or culture. Some Indians move away from their tribal area while others join a non-Indian religious group or marry a non-Indian or an Indian with little interest in Native culture and then lose their connection to their tribal cultures. They speak English exclusively and do not attend tribal ceremonies. Numerous events may jar Indians who have lost touch with their heritage into becoming Indians or "rediscovering their Indianness."

Indian people who have heard negative comments about Indians all their lives from television, radio, and teachers—while the family did nothing to correct the misinformation—then hear from an informed teacher that Indians have a rich and positive history and culture, become alert to the possibility that the negative view of themselves and their cultures are unfounded. Another Indian attends a traditional marriage, puberty, or healing ceremony and is moved enough by the event to learn more about the religion and culture.

An Indian student in an anthropology class hears the professor refer to Indians as "our" Indians. The student may visit an archives filled with skeletal remains and sacred cultural objects and become insulted, outraged, or even scared. Upon realizing that the professor is referring to his ancestors as "objects of study," the student is stirred into political activism.

A prison sentence might give the Indian person the time and impetus to learn about other tribes and cultures with similar histories of oppression. The inmate decides that an organized movement to improve conditions for oppressed peoples is in order and becomes determined to learn about her tribe and to fight for her people. This was the case with many of the original members of the American Indian Movement (AIM).[38]

Becoming Less Indian. Not all Indians desire to find an identity that stresses their Indianness. Some Indians have and still do search for an identity that is more white oriented. For example, from 1852 to 1909, Cherokee youth attended the Cherokee Male or Female Seminaries, both boarding schools established by the Cherokee tribe in an effort to acculturate their youth to the ways of white society. The Cherokee tribal council initially hired alumni from Mount Holyoke Female Seminary in South Hadley, Massachusetts, and from Yale as teachers, and, by the 1870s, graduates of the Cherokee seminaries returned to teach at their alma maters. Both seminaries were patterned after the New England schools and offered the Cherokee students a sophisticated curriculum that included courses in physics, botany, mathematics, languages, and literature. Teachers did not include information about Cherokee culture,[39] an interesting aspect considering that the schools were not established by the federal government—an entity with a reputation for devaluing tribal culture.[40] One focus of both seminaries was to teach the students to imitate white people in every way. After a hefty dose of lessons that imbued students with information about how whites were superior to Cherokees, many of the students commented in school papers and in correspondence about the need to leave the old ways behind and began to refer to their more traditional tribesmen as "backwards" and "unenlightened."[41]

By the 1850s, at least, many mixed-heritage Cherokees expressed their confusion over race and culture. They knew that biologically they were both Cherokee and white, and they knew something about both cultures. They were, however, members of the Cherokee Nation. They did not want to leave their Cherokee heritage behind, just their current Cherokee culture, which many students believed was useless to them. They strived to establish a new Cherokee identity, that of a person knowledgeable about the white world, possessing Cherokee and white blood, and often looking Caucasian. They could be members of the Cherokee tribe and culturally white at the same time.

Just as some non-Indians attempt to legitimatize their claims to Indianness by marrying an Indian, or some multiheritage Indians try to become more

Indian by marrying an Indian darker in color and with cultural knowledge,[42] some Indians may attempt to become less Indian by marrying a white person or an Indian with lighter coloring. Examples of the latter include graduates of the Cherokee Female Seminary who married either white men or Cherokee men with smaller amounts of Cherokee blood than they had.[43] Frantz Fanon's remark about men of color and white women—"I wish to be acknowledged not as Black but as white . . . who but a white woman can do this for me? By loving me she proves that I am worthy of white love. I am loved like a white man"[44]— is a statement that could be true for some Indian men and women who marry whites, but this aspect requires further, sensitive inquiry.

Identity Resolutions Considered during the Encounter Stage

Root's series of identity "resolutions"[45] for biracial peoples may be appropriate to include here because it is during Cross's encounter stage that the person considers what identities he or she can and cannot choose to pursue. Acceptance of these resolutions depend on the social, political, economic, and environmental situations the person encounters. Therefore, the person may change resolutions more than once in a lifetime, or may settle on two resolutions at once.

Resolution 1: Acceptance of the Identity Society Assigns. Root posits that multiheritage people who are part white, who do not appear to be Caucasian, and who are reared in racially oppressive parts of the United States will have little choice about their racial identity.[46] If a person looks black or Indian, she will be seen as black or Indian regardless of whether or not the person wants to identify as white. Her supposition can also be taken to mean that those Indians who look white or black may not be accepted as an Indian among Indian societies.

A problem with this resolution is that persons may feel comfortable with their chosen identity in one area of the country and may be perceived by others in another area as belonging to a different racial group. For example, a multiheritage person whose racial reference group is an Oklahoma tribe may be accepted as an Indian in the Plains states. In the Southwest, however, where Pueblo, Navajo, and other tribes have members with substantial blood quantums and distinctive Indian appearances, that same person may be viewed as barely Indian or as a non-Indian. In fact, numerous members of tribes from outside the Southwest either attending or working at Northern Arizona University complain that "Navajos think if you're not Navajo then you're not an Indian."

Indians who are enrolled in tribes but who look white often identify themselves as Caucasians in order to avoid racism. Lavera Rose writes in her thesis on biracial Lakota women that many biracial Lakota females try to hide their Indian racial heritage when moving to non-Indian society because they perceive that non-Indians view all Indians as inferior to Euro-Americans.[47] Some black or mixed-heritage Indian-black individuals identify as Indians in an attempt to escape racism against blacks. As Brewton Berry describes the mindset of many Nanticokes, Chickahominys, and Lumbees, "Most of them would doubtless prefer to be whites. But, since that goal is beyond their reach, they will settle for Indian. It is better to be red than black—even an off-shade of red."[48]

Solution 2: Identification with Two or More Racial or Cultural Groups. Root purports this to be a positive resolution only if the persons are able to retain their personality across groups and they feel welcomed in both groups. This resolution may only be possible in parts of the United States where interracial marriages and mixed-blood children are tolerated.[49] The challenge for multiheritage Indians wishing to live in two worlds is to construct strategies for coping with social resistance to their membership in both groups. A problem for many is that if they look Caucasian and/or have little knowledge of tribal culture, they may not be accepted by the Indian community they wish to be part of. This is especially true if they have inadequate background to enroll in their tribe and no kinship ties. Conversely, multiheritage Indians who look phenotypically Indian may not be considered as equals by whites.

There are numerous multiheritage individuals who identify simultaneously as Indian and non-Indian and are accepted by all sides of their family and tribe, and because of strong familial connections to all parts of their heritage, they feel secure in themselves. These people resemble McFee's proposed "150% Man" in that they are able to absorb and use both new and old ways.[50] In addition, they are able to meet the "membership" demands required by both groups.

Many Indians who are able to pass as both Indian and white use their appearances and social knowledge to their advantage. Root defines one form of identification as *tokenism*—a process by which a person's ambiguous appearance, but identification with a racial group, allows the individual to be hired to fill a minority quota because the person is seen as less threatening than a full-blood.[51] While Root asserts that the hiring agency assigns the identity for the individual, often the person of ambiguous appearance seeks employment at an institution that desires an individual of the race the person wants to be. The hire validates his or her identity desires and bestows a title that can be recorded on a resume for the future, such as Director of American Indian Programs. These people often claim Indianness as their "articulated identity," defined by Williams as the identity "one calls oneself publicly. It may or may not be in concert with one's intuitive or experiential identity."[52]

Solution 3: Identification as a New Racial Group. Although the U.S. government will allow citizens to mark more than one racial or ethnic category on the next census,[53] many mixed-heritage people identify themselves as a new race, such as the Hapa Haole in Hawaii[54] and the Métis in Canada,[55] or as multiheritage, multiracial, or biracial so they will not have to choose specific races or cultures.

Many multiheritage Indians prefer this type of classification either because they know little or nothing about their racial heritages or because they cannot decide which one to designate as the primary racial reference group. The option to choose more than one race has incurred debate from those who believe that people should make a decision about their racial choice; they argue that not choosing one's obvious heritage (because one looks black, one is black, as in the case of Tiger Woods) is a denial of self.[56]

Solution 4: Identification with a Single Racial and/or Cultural Group. This resolution is different from the first one because the person actively seeks identification with one group regardless of what society thinks, the choices made by one's siblings, or one's physical resemblance to the group. This resolution is positive if the person is accepted by the selected group, does not feel marginal to the group, and does not deny other aspects of her heritage.[57]

Numerous complicated and interwoven factors influence people when deciding what identity they can realistically pursue. For example, since contact, American Indians have been romanticized, reviled, admired, feared, and hated by Euro-Americans. These Euro-American views of Indians, and the negative and positive images of Indians that have become a part of American culture, continue to exert powerful effects on the self-image of Indian people.[58]

Indians hear and see negative stereotypes that American Indians are inferior to whites. Television, movies, cartoons, books, and teachers contribute to the ideas that Indians are heathens, savages, ignorant, and lazy. Children learn from juvenile literature that Indians are much like animals: primal, simple, and stupid. On television everyday are classic westerns that portray Indians as violent antagonists who were impediments to western civilization, and sports teams such as the Washington Redskins and the Atlanta Braves feature mascots that are warlike and ugly.[59] Movies such as Disney's *Pocahontas* (1995) portray the title character as a woman who wears minimal clothing, sings with animals, and is shaped like Barbie, a feature that angers many Indian women who argue that the character's unrealistic body image contributes to feelings of inferiority among Indian girls.[60]

On the other hand, positive stereotyping might account for some non-Indians' and mixed-heritage peoples' decision to become Indians. Individuals with little knowledge of their tribe might become enamored with images of Indians as physically attractive beings, valiant warriors, and mystical environmentalists who are "one with nature." Positive imagery of Indians in the 1960s and 1970s probably accounts in part for the dramatic increase in the numbers of Indians on the 1980 census.[61]

In their 1987 article, "Dimensions of Native American Stereotyping," Hanson and Rouse propose that stereotypes are not static, that they change "in form and prevalence" depending on "historical and socio-cultural circumstances."[62] For example, in areas of the United States where Indians and non-Indians clash over treaty hunting and fishing rights, and other economic resources, stereotypes of Indians are more negative. In a subsequent article the authors assert that "factual knowledge is not sufficient to counter status-based prejudice."[63] Indeed, those who have vested economic and social interest in images of Indians as inferior beings rarely will acknowledge Indians as equals. In areas of the country where Indians are not viewed with favor, the Indian's perceived level of discrimination plays a factor in whether or not the individuals want to pursue their Indian identity in that area or if they prefer to express their Indianness elsewhere.

A stumbling block to identifying with only one group is if the persons' self-perception differs from how others perceive them. Just because a person— mixed-blood or full-blood—desires to join a particular racial or ethnic group does not mean that he or she has a guaranteed entrance into the group. One factor that hinders a person's acceptance by Indian groups is tribal membership standards. Almost always, tribes require that proposed enrollees supply proof that they are directly related to a member of the tribe who is listed on the current tribal roll or on specified historical tribal rolls. Some tribes allow a person membership regardless of blood quantum, while others require the person be at least half-blood. Others allow entrance only if the mother is a tribal member.

Federally recognized tribes[64] are granted specified rights such as self-government; benefits, including health care; and education, housing, and resource development programs. Tribal membership bestowed by a state or federally recognized tribe is important for some Indians. The Indian Arts and Crafts Act of 1990, for example, requires that anyone producing and selling "Indian products" be a member of a recognized tribe, thus excluding numerous self-proclaimed Indian artists who have been creating "Indian" works for years. In Texas, at least, individuals who wish to use peyote legally in Native American Church ceremonies must prove that they are at least one-quarter Indian blood, which also means they must be tribally enrolled. In addition, the Bureau of Indian Affairs (BIA) and the U.S. Department of Education recognize as Indians only those who are recognized as such by a tribe.[65]

Other limiting factors for choosing Indianness is lack of cultural knowledge and residence apart from the tribe, ethnocentrism, and what I term culturalism. Root purports that all racial groups have prejudices. When these prejudices are "projected" onto the multiheritage person, the racial group becomes the "creators of marginal status."[66]

Among members of a single tribe, racism and suspicion often exist. Economics, politics, and social aspects surrounding kinship systems, clans, religion, and interaction with non-Indians are major factors affecting how tribes people feel about each other. Culturalism exists when tribal members view each other with disdain because of their cultural adherences. Mixed-heritage members may see traditionals as uncivilized and backwards. Traditionalists may believe that progressives are "less Indian" because of their cultural naiveté and that multi-heritage peoples only claim tribal membership for land and annuity purposes. As a result of this attitude among Lakotas, those who do not live on the reservation, who do not speak the language, and are "less Indian looking" do not, according to Lavera Rose, enjoy the "cultural entirety of being Lakota."[67] Other examples: Zitkala-Sa, Yankton, and Charles Eastman, Dakota, lived away from their tribes and were successful, yet they failed to retain strong kinship ties and therefore lost status among their people.[68]

Current tribal leaders often dictate how tribal membership is defined, how annuities are dispersed, and who receives tribal jobs. Indian persons out of favor with the current political tribal power, or who are successful by the whites' standards (such as completing a university degree or earning a substantial salary and accumulating material wealth) but not by tribal standards, or who marry into an "inappropriate" racial group may find it easier to live apart from the tribe or to distance themselves completely and not enroll their children.

Another limiting factor in choosing identity is the most obvious aspect of one's racial heritage: appearance. The color of one's hair, eyes, and skin are the barometers used to measure how "Indian" one is, and these characteristics either limit or broaden one's choice of ethnicity. If an individual doesn't "look Indian," she is often suspect for claiming Indian identity regardless of her cultural knowledge.[69]

The idea that a Caucasian appearance is "better" serves as a point of contention among many people of color.[70] As among blacks, darker-skinned Indians often distrust lighter-skinned ones, arguing that their non-Indian blood takes them out of touch with the realities of Indian life. Because it is assumed that light-skinned Indians have a choice as to which world they inhabit, their dedication to fighting the various social, political, religious, and economic oppressions faced by "real" Indians is questioned. A person who looks Caucasian, was raised in white society, and has little, if any, connection to his or her tribe but still claims an Indian identity will be looked at with suspicion. Why would an individual want to become Indian if he or she were not raised as an Indian? Why call oneself a "person of color" if one looks white?

Numerous white-looking people claim to be Indian and often are readily considered by many whites to be Indians. Why are they accepted as such? One answer may be that movies and television strongly influence public opinion (journalist Orville Schell comments that "Hollywood is the most powerful force in the world, besides the U.S. military"[71]), and Indian characters who look white supply a new definition of "Indian." For example, the blond, fair Mariel Hemingway is one-fourth Sioux in *Personal Best* (1982); the blond, fair Val Kilmer is one-fourth Sioux in *Thunderheart* (1992); the blond, fair Chuck Norris is one-half Cherokee in the current television series *Walker: Texas Ranger.* Indeed, many Indians and non-Indians believe that even the most tenuous biological affiliation with a tribal group is enough to qualify the person as Indian.

Multiheritage Indians with a desire to identify as Indians are well aware that light-skinned and blue-eyed individuals are viewed as white, and they fret about being accepted by Indians and by white society. In her book, *When Nickels Were Indians: An Urban Mixed Blood Story,*[72] ethnic studies professor Patricia Penn Hilden writes that in the 1970s she did not claim to be Nez Perce when applying for an Office of Economic Opportunity position because she looks phenotypically white and was fearful that people might mistake her for a wannabe.

Her repeated references to the "shovel nature" of her teeth (a feature that she claims was "that era's [1950s-1960s?] 'scientific' signifiers of Native blood") and to her cheekbones (are we to assume they are high?) illustrate her apparent need to convince readers that she does have a tribal connection.[73]

Okazawa-Rey argues that when light-skinned black women degrade darker-skinned black women their "identification with the racist oppressors is complete."[74] And this may be true for Indians in some cases. For example, progressive Cherokee women in the 1870s who were lighter in color than their tribeswomen used words like heathen to describe girls who were darker and therefore presumably inferior. During the process of preparing for one annual Shakespeare production, one light-skinned Cherokee female seminarian said to a classmate with darker skin who aspired to a certain role, "You are too dark to be an angel."[75]

Indeed, some Indians preferred to mingle only with their own color group, as reflected by the comments of a Choctaw woman reminiscing on her school days at Tuskahoma, Oklahoma, in 1910: "I have never been so scared in my life. I shake when I think about it. There were so many full-blood girls blacker than anybody you ever seen. . . . I don't believe they were all just Indian, they were mixed with this other race. . . . I cried and I cried and I cried because I was up there with them Black kids. I just don't like the looks of [those] people." She also referred to them as "that bunch of little old Black kids I tell you just looked like flies flying around."[76]

Many Indians attempt to keep their skin at a minimal darkness, presumably to distance themselves from blacks or from their own African American blood. At a powwow outside of Lawton, Oklahoma, about ten years ago, a Muscogee woman asked me to retrieve her umbrella from her truck's cab saying, "Get me my umbrella, Hon; otherwise I'll be lookin' like a nigger by supper." Cherokee female seminarians who were never without their parasols and wide-brimmed hats worried about the same thing more than a hundred years ago. On the other hand, many multiheritage Indians may be comparatively dark in color but nevertheless lie in the sun to darken their skin. Despite her Indian appearance (to most non-Indians, at least), Mary Brave Bird recalled that in her youth she "waited for the summer, for the prairie sun, the Badlands sun, to tan me and make me into a real skin."[77]

Stage 3: Immersion-Emersion

Cross and Parham agree that blacks at this stage attempt to develop a thorough black frame of reference. For Indians, like blacks, it can be a volatile stage, often causing anxiety, depression, and frustration over attempts at becoming the "right kind of Indian." In Cross's words, "the person begins to demolish the old perspective and simultaneously tries to construct what will become his or her new frame of reference."[78]

Many Indians at this stage engage in aggressive behavior. They seek information on Indians (not necessarily their own tribe) and participate in powwows and religious ceremonies. They protest against racial injustices (often violently), deny the racial and cultural non-Indian aspects of themselves, and become hostile towards non-Indians (whites, especially) and other Indians who do not conform to their ideas of Indianness. Those insecure in their economic or political worlds adopt a "redder than thou" attitude and question whether another Indian is "really Indian."

Although the founding members of the American Indian Movement were young and had been incarcerated and/or victimized by poverty, racism, and self-doubt, AIM and the Red Power movement—like the Black Power movement—touched individuals of all classes, identities, and motivations.[79] The male "radicals," however, garnered media attention and have subsequently demonstrated through rhetoric and actions that during AIM's formation many of them were indeed in the immersion stage of their life; some appear to be there still.

The aforementioned Cherokee seminarians, on the other hand, began a "whiter than thou" campaign and judged their fellow Indians (Cherokees and members of other tribes) on the basis of their degree of assimilation. Whether or not a person was Christian, educated, and striving for the white ideal played a large part in how these young men and women evaluated each other as human beings. In the encounter stage, the Cherokee students were convinced, according to one alumnus, that the "white way was the only acceptable way,"[80] and they began strategizing to become more like the whites their teachers so overtly praised and less like the Indians their teachers criticized.

Stage 4: Internalization

At this point a person develops inner security about her identity. She is able to discuss in a rational manner racial issues with members of other racial and/or ethnic groups. "In short," Parham writes, "the person becomes biculturally successful."[81] But what about those individuals who never reach an equitable solution about their identity? Do they mirror Stonequist's model of a marginal person—one who lives a life of frustration, unable to fit comfortably into any group?[82]

Whether an Indian person can be at peace with himself can only be answered by each individual. As an Ojibwa counselor at Northern Arizona University observed, "Every Indian person I know has an identity issue." As the few examples of the Cherokee seminarians, Indian adoptees of white parents, and the victims of prejudice and stereotypes illustrate, just because a person is visually recognized as an Indian does not mean that he is satisfied with his identity. In addition to the perceived level of discrimination, rejection of one's identity choice by Indians and non-Indians, unfamiliarity with tribal culture and residence away from the tribe, social status of the group, and appearance, another reason for Indian peoples' identity insecurities may be because they almost always suffer from "internalized oppression": they often reject a part of their racial heritage that is also a part of themselves.[83]

Indians may believe that in order to achieve approval from one group, they must embrace only the personal aspects that conform to that group and thus reject the other aspects. Rejected parts, as Root points out, cannot be easily forgotten. Parents, extended family, and physical attributes remain powerful reminders of what the individual is attempting to abandon.[84] Even parts that are not rejected are consistently evaluated and compared by the individual and by others. For instance, I remember distinctly that after passing my comprehensive Ph.D. exams in 1988 a professor asked me, "Have you considered that it's your white blood that makes you successful?"

Other aspects of self-identification that sociologists assume apply to all multiheritage peoples may not apply to individuals claiming to be Indians. For example, Root asserts that persons have the right to identify themselves according to how they want to be identified. She also believes that they should develop strategies for coping with resistance to their proclaimed identities so that they do not "internalize questions as inferring that there is something wrong with them."[85]

Indeed, Indians should identify themselves as Indians if they feel the need, but obviously not if their identities are fabricated. In addition, one of the most hotly contested aspects of Indian identity today concerns whether or not a person of minimal Indian blood, no tribal cultural knowledge, and lack of kinship and familial ties should identify as Indian. Not everyone who claims to be Indian agrees that they need to be tribally enrolled or even recognized by their tribe in order to identify with them. It may cause stress to the Indians whose tribe will not claim them, but tribes which must contend with unrecognized individuals may also feel stress. As voiced by a number of Indian writers, it is a violation of tribal rights not to allow tribes to determine who their members are.[86]

While the economic, political, and social forces affecting American Indians' identity choices and development often can be readily categorized, the vast differences among tribes and individual Indians, in addition to the complexities they face, disallow one empirical study to answer the myriad questions about how an individual or group maintains, alters, or loses identity. Studies focusing on specific groups of Indians at a definitive point in time and place must incorporate a host of variables the researcher may have trouble comprehending. For instance, many non-Indians are puzzled why persons of mixed-blood would call themselves Indian and not a member of another group. In response, Mohawk poet Peter Blue Cloud echoes the sentiment of many multiheritage Indians: "They wouldn't understand even if you explained it."[87]

The task of sorting out the elements that contribute to an Indian's identity choice and development, and how that person's ethnic, gender, racial, political, occupational, and religious identities intersect may appear daunting. But these studies are important because: (1) identity conflicts among Indians are critical and ongoing psychological problems; (2) definitions of American Indian differ not only among non-Indians but also among Indians; (3) an Indian may have several identities (individual, occupational, religious, social, etc.) that correspond to their allegiances (such as family, tribe, community, state, country); (4)

Indian identity constantly develops in response to the person's social, political, and economic environments; (5) the United States government has recently agreed to allow citizens to check more than one racial category on the next census, thus giving mixed-heritage people an opportunity to proclaim their mixed parentage; (6) health care and social workers, educators, and politicians, at least, need to understand that there are cultural differences among tribes and individual Indians; (7) physical appearance does not always coincide with an individual's chosen identity; (8) census surveys regarding Indian race, heritage, and ethnicity are often interpreted incorrectly;[88] (9) the number of individuals self-identifying as American Indians is growing;[89] and (10) the escalating incidences of ethnic fraud demonstrates the need for definitive guidelines for determining who is and is not Indian. Finally, any study on Indian identity, social history, acculturation, and assimilation must include Indian interpretations and debate, for Indians can best identify the forces that shape their unique self-images.[90]

Acknowledgments

Thanks to the Ford Foundation for the postdoctoral award that allowed me to gather and organize materials for my book *American Indian Racial and Ethnic Identities*, of which this article is a partial excerpt, and to Vicki Green, chair of Northern Arizona University's Department of Psychology for comments and suggestions.

Notes

1. Although it is preferable to refer to the indigenous people of this country by their specific tribal names, for the sake of space I opt for American Indian or Indian rather than Native American, which signifies anyone born in the United States.

2. Clyde Warrior, "Which One Are You?: Five Types of Young Indians," cited in Stan Steiner, *The New Indians* (New York: Dell, 1968), 305–7.

3. William E. Cross, Jr., *Shades of Black: Diversity in African-American Identity* (Philadelphia: Temple University Press, 1991); David E. Hayes-Bautista, "Becoming Chicano: A Disassimilation Theory of Transformation of Ethnic Identity," Ph.D. dissertation (University of California, Santa Barbara, 1974); Jean Kim, "Processes of Asian American Identity Development: A Study of Japanese American Women's Perceptions of Their Struggle to Achieve Positive Identities as Americans of Asian Ancestry," Ed.D. dissertation (University of Massachusetts, 1981). See also Donald R. Atkinson, George Morten, and Derald Wing Sue's "Minority Development Model," in *Counseling American Minorities: A Cross Cultural Perspective* (Dubuque, IA: Wm. C. Brown Co. Publishers, 1989), 191–200.

4. Cross, *Shades of Black*, 189-223.

5. Thomas A. Parham, "Cycles of Psychological Nigrescence," *The Counseling Psychologist* 17:2 (April 1989): 187–226.

6. It is not within the scope of this paper to encompass the history of intermarriage or acculturation; the symbols and expressions of Indianness; how cultures persist, desist, and resurrect; the politics of blood quantum; or women's identity issues. These aspects are

explored in historical perspective in my book manuscript, "American Indian Racial and Ethnic Identities" (in progress).

7. Maria P. P. Root, "Resolving 'Other' Status: Identity Development of Biracial Individuals," in L. Brown and M.P.P. Root, *Diversity and Complexity in Feminist Theory and Therapy* (New York: Haworth, 1990), 188. The idea that "race is socially and economically constructed to serve the interests of the privileged" is expounded by Zena Moore in "Check the Box that Best Describes You," in Naomi Zack, ed., *American Mixed Race: The Culture of Microdiversity* (Lanham, MD: Rowman and Littlefield Publishers, 1995), 39–51.

8. Michael K. Green, *Issues in Native American Identity* (New York: Peter Lang, 1995), 7.

9. Ibid.

10. Peter I. Rose, *They and We: Racial and Ethnic Relations in the United States* (New York: Random House, 1964), 7.

11. Cross, *Shades of Black*, 190–98.

12. Idem., 198–201.

13. Idem., 201–9.

14. Cross, "The Thomas and Cross Models on Psychological Nigrescence: A Literature Review," *Journal of Black Psychology* 4 (1978): 18.

15. Cross, *Shades of Black*, 209–16.

16. In this essay, *world view* refers to a person's value system and how one interprets events and history. There is, of course, no one Indian world view.

17. I base this assertion in part on personal observation of non-Indians in Texas who have grown from showing interest in Indians to becoming medicine people of tribes they at one time knew nothing about. One, a white man now deceased, married a Creek woman, shaved his arms ("Indians have no body hair you know"), and proceeded to hold sweats and ceremonies he claimed were Lakota. Another, a Hispanic man, followed the same routine. I met his mother at a Grand Prairie powwow where she admitted that the family was not Indian, yet her son is now a "spiritual leader of the Mescalero Apache tribe" who utilizes Lakota religious traditions.

18. Parham, "Cycles of Nigrescence," 199.

19. There are two major developmental stages of the identity process. The basic one is a simplistic category-style identity process which generally occurs in preschool. The second stage is more complex because as the children develop their cognitive capacity identity becomes more developed. See, for example, Erik H. Erikson, *Identity & the Life Cycle* (New York: W. W. Norton & Co., 1980).

20. Parham, "Cycles of Nigrescence," 195.

21. The decision to identify as a member of an ancestor's race or culture when one does not subscribe to that culture is what Howard Stein and Robert Hill term "dime store" ethnicity or "unreal" ethnicity because one shops for an identity as one would for items at a dime store. See Howard Stein and Robert Hill, *The Ethnic Imperative: Examining the New White Ethnic Movement* (University Park: Pennsylvania State University Press, 1977), 22.

22. For information about relocation, see Larry W. Burt, "Roots of the Native American Urban Experience: Relocation Policy in the 1950s," *American Indian Quarterly* 10 (1986): 85–99; Donald L. Fixico, *Termination and Relocation: Federal Indian Policy, 1945–1960* (Albuquerque: University of New Mexico Press, 1986); Jennie R. Joe, "Forced Relocation and Assimilation: Dillon Myer and the Native American," *Amerasia Journal* 13:2 (1986–87): 161–65.

23. Maria P. P. Root, "Resolving 'Other' Status," 191–93.

24. Idem., 190–92.

25. Idem., 192.

26. Cross, *Shades of Black*, 119.

27. See, for example, the letter to the editor from Orlando Tom in *Indian Country Today*, December 1–8, 1998, A5, expressing concerns over the current Miss Navajo being part black. Discerning between cultural adherence and biology as prerequisite for tribal admission, Tom writes, "Language, weaving, beading, and being able to dance is all culturally correct, but nonetheless, it is still learned behavior . . . when the Navajo people select a person to represent their nation as Miss Navajo, that person must possess the appearance and physical characteristics of the Navajo. Miss Cody's appearance and physical characteristics are black, and thus are representative of another race of people."

For information on Indian-black relations, see Vernon Bellecourt, "The glorification of Buffalo Soldiers raises racial divisions between blacks, Indians," *Indian Country Today*, May 4, 1994, A5; William Loren Katz, *Black Indians: A Hidden Heritage* (New York: Atheneum, 1986); William G. McLoughlin, "Red Indians, Black Slavery and White Racism: America's Slaveholding Indians," *American Quarterly* 26 (October 1974): 367–85; Theda Perdue, *Slavery and the Evolution of Cherokee Society* (Knoxville: University of Tennessee Press, 1979); the *American Indian Quarterly's* special issue on Indian-black relations, forthcoming in 1998.

28. Parham, "Cycles of Psychological Nigrescence," 199.

29. See Snipp, "Who Are the American Indians? Some Observations about the Perils and Pitfalls of Data for Race and Ethnicity," *Population Research and Policy Review* 5 (1986): 237–52.

30. M. E. Goodman, *Race Awareness in Young Children* (New York: Collier Press, 1968), 19.

31. Root, "Resolving 'Other' Status," 189–90.

32. Root, "Resolving 'Other' Status," 189. For discussion on the importance of names to identity and how "family surnames carry with them all the associations of the language and tradition from which they come," see Harold R. Isaacs, *Idols of the Tribe: Group Identity and Political Change* (New York: Harper and Row, 1975), 71–92.

33. Cross, *Shades of Black*, 199.

34. As Michael R. Green states, "Deculturalization can lead to severe psychological disorientation, such as, dissolution of the self, a sense of meaninglessness, aimlessness, and depression. This creates a painful situation, which the individual then may attempt to escape by the use of alcohol or drugs or by self-stupefication through pleasures." See *Issues in Native American Cultural Identity* (New York: Peter Lang, 1995), 7.

35. After an assessment of the preponderance of ethnic fraud in the United States, I propose that the majority of wannabes have assessed the economic possibilities of becoming a member of the group and have formulated a new identity for monetary reasons. Therefore, a person claiming Indianness may be perceived as trying to fit in to get a job, to gain prestige, to write a book with an authoritative voice, or to gain notoriety and fame as a medicine person. Some wannabes, however, do not necessarily desire money, but desire the attention as an Indian that perhaps they do not receive as a non-Indian. See Kara Gniewek, "The Silent Genocide," *Red Ink* 5:1 (Fall 1996): 60–71; "Plastic Indians," *Indian Country Today*, August 26–Sept 2, 1996, A3; A6; Wendy Rose, "The Great Pretenders: Further Reflections on Whiteshamanism," in M. Annette Jaimes, *The State of Native America: Genocide, Colonization, and Resistance* (Boston: South End Press, 1992), 403–21; Andrea Smith, "Opinion: The New Age Movement and Native Spirituality," *Indigenous Woman* (Spring 1991): 17–18; "White Shamans and Plastic Medicine Men," video (Native Voices Public Television, Montana State University, Bozeman, Montana).

36. Kent Carter, "Wantabes and Outalucks: Searching for Indian Ancestors in Federal Records," *Chronicles of Oklahoma* 56 (Spring 1988): 94–104; Ron Andrade, "Are Tribes Too

Exclusive?" *American Indian Journal* (July 1980): 12–13.

37. Herbert Gans describes a leisure-time form of ethnicity that some engage in as "symbolic identification" with their ethnic heritage when they are reminded of it. For example, some people claim to be Irish only on St. Patrick's Day, while others may "become Indian" when Indians are in the news and are the topic of public conversation. They become ethnic only when they want to. See Gans, "Symbolic Ethnicity: The Future of Ethnic Groups and Cultures in America," *Ethnic and Racial Studies* 2 (January 1979): 1–20.

38. Rachel A. Bonney, "The Role of AIM Leaders in Indian Nationalism," *American Indian Quarterly* 3:3 (1977): 209–24; "Interview: Vernon Bellecourt: He is the Symbol of the Most Militant Indian Group Since Geronimo," *Penthouse* (July): 58–60; 62; 64; 122; 131–3; Peter Matthiesson, *In the Spirit of Crazy Horse* (New York: Viking, 1984, 1991); Russell Means, *Where White Men Fear to Tread: Autobiography of Russell Means* (New York: St. Martin's Press, 1995); Bella Stumbo, "A World Apart: Indian Activists Dennis Banks and Russell Means . . . ," *Los Angeles Times Magazine*, June 15, 1986: 10–21; Gerald Vizenor, "Dennis of Wounded Knee," *American Indian Quarterly* 7:2 (1983): 51–65.

39. For information on the Cherokee seminaries, see Devon A. Mihesuah, *Cultivating the Rose Buds: The Education of Women at the Cherokee Female Seminary, 1851–1909* (Urbana: University of Illinois Press, 1993; 1997) and "Out of the Graves of the Polluted Debauches: The Boys of the Cherokee Male Seminary," *American Indian Quarterly* 15 (Fall 1991): 503–21.

40. For example, see David Wallace Adams, *Education for Extinction: American Indians and the Boarding School Experience, 1875–1928* (Lawrence, Kansas: University of Kansas Press, 1995); Michael C. Coleman, *American Indian Children at School, 1850–1930* (Jackson: University Press of Mississippi, 1993; Clyde Ellis, *To Change Them Forever: Indian Education at the Rainy Mountain Boarding School, 1893–1920* (Norman: University of Oklahoma Press, 1996); K. Tsianina Lomawaima, *They Called it Prairie Light: The Story of Chilocco Indian School* (Lincoln: University of Nebraska Press, 1994); Sally J. McBeth, *Ethnic Identity and the Boarding School Experience of West-Central Oklahoma American Indians* (Washington, DC: University Press of America, 1983); Robert A. Trennert, *The Phoenix Indian School: Forced Assimilation in Arizona, 1891–1935* (Norman: University of Oklahoma Press, 1988).

41. The social hierarchy at the seminaries is the focus of Mihesuah's "'Too Dark to Be Angels': The Class System Among the Cherokee at the Female Seminary," *American Indian Culture and Research Journal* 15 (1991): 29–52.

42. I base this assertion on several male acquaintances who admit that this is why they married Indian women. One, a dark skinned non-Indian, commented to me in 1985 that he purposely sought out a Cherokee woman who could speak the language, had a recognizable "Indian " name, and who "looked Indian." He found her and now claims to be a full-blood Cherokee despite the fact that he is unenrolled and was asked to remove himself from two important Indian committees in Texas by tribal leaders who believed it important that anyone claiming tribal membership should be able to prove it.

43. One full-blood Cherokee man I knew in Texas said that he was always ashamed of being Cherokee in Oklahoma so he divorced his first (full-blood) wife and married a white woman in hopes that he would be more accepted by non-Indian society. He was not, so he divorced her, moved to Texas, and proceeded to marry a non-Indian woman who at first commented that she was not Indian at all, but now proclaims that she is Cherokee, Choctaw, and a direct descendant of Quanah Parker, even though none of the Comanches in the Dallas/Ft. Worth area, or any in my husband's family, have ever heard of her. Also see D. Mihesuah, *Cultivating the Rose Buds*, 105–6.

44. Frantz Fanon, *Black Skin, White Masks* (New York: Grove Press, Inc., 1967), 63.

45. Root, "Resolving 'Other' Status," 197–201.

46. Idem., 199–200.

47. Lavera Rose, "Iyeska Win: Intermarriage and Ethnicity Among the Lakota in the Nineteenth and Twentieth Centuries," M.A. thesis (Northern Arizona University, 1994), 100.

48. Brewton Berry, *Almost White* (Toronto: Collier-Macmillan, 1963), 160.

49. Root, "Resolving 'Other' Status," 200.

50. Malcolm McFee, "The 150% Man: A Product of Blackfeet Acculturation," *American Anthropologist* 70 (1968): 1096–103. McFee writes that the "levels of acculturation" concept—the view that individuals of mixed heritage replace traditional cultural traits after exposure to different cultures—is often wrong. Many Indian Territory mixed-heritage people did just that.

51. Root, "Resolving 'Other' Status," 196.

52. Teresa Kay Williams, "The Theatre of Identity," in Naomi Zack, ed., *American Mixed Race: The Culture of Microdiversity* (Rowman and Littlefield, Inc., 1995), 79–96, 318–19.

53. "The New Sensitive Census," *American Indian Report* 8:12 (December 1997): 8; "Census changes to recognize mixed races," *The Arizona Republic*, October 30, 1997, A1, A11.

54. George Yamamoto, "Interracial Marriage in Hawaii," in I. R. Stuart and L. Edwin, eds., *Interracial Marriage: Expectations and Realities* (New York: Grossman Publishers, 1973).

55. Among the best works on the Métis include: Bruce A. Cox, ed., *Native People, Native Lands: Canadian Indians, Inuit, and Métis* (Ottawa: Carleton University Press, 1988); Olive Patricia Dickason, *Canada's First Nations* (Norman: University of Oklahoma Press, 1992); Jacqueline Peterson and Jennifer S. Brown, *The New Peoples: Being and Becoming Métis in North America* (Lincoln: University of Nebraska Press, 1985); *Report of the Royal Commission on Aboriginal Peoples, Looking Forward, Looking Back*, Vols. 1–5 (Minister of Supply and Services, Canada, 1996).

56. Itabari Njeri, "Call for Census Category Creates Interracial Debate," *Los Angeles Times*, January 13, 1991, E1, 9–11. John Leland and Gregory Beals, "In Living Colors," *Newsweek*, May 5, 1997.

57. Root, "Resolving 'Other' Status," 200–201.

58. For discussions on Euro-Americans' views on Indians, see for examples: James Axtell, *The Invasion Within: The Contest of Cultures in Colonial North America* (New York: Oxford University Press, 1985); Robert F. Berkhofer, Jr., *The White Man's Indian* (New York: Vintage Books, 1978); idem., "White Conceptions of Indians," in *Handbook of North American Indians*, Vol. 4 (Washington, DC: Smithsonian Institution Press, 1988), 522–47; Robert E. Bieder, *Science Encounters the Indian, 1820–1880* (Norman: University of Oklahoma Press, 1992, 1986); Leslie A. Fiedler, "The Indian in Literature in English," *Handbook of North American Indians*, Vol. 4, 573–81; Rayna Green, "The Pocahontas Perplex: The Image of Indian Women in American Culture," *The Massachusetts Review* 16:4 (Autumn 1975): 698–714; idem., "The Indian in Popular American Culture," in *Handbook of North American Indians*, Vol. 4, 587–606; Reginald Horsman, "Scientific Racism and the American Indian in the Mid-Nineteenth Century," *American Quarterly* 27:2 (May 1975): 152–68; Francis Jennings, *The Invasion of America: Indians, Colonialism, and the Cant of Conquest* (Chapel Hill: University of North Carolina Press, 1975); Gary B. Nash, "The Image of the Indian in the Southern Colonial Mind," *The William and Mary Quarterly* 29:2 (April 1972): 197–230; Roy Harvey Pearce, *Savagism and Civilization: A Study of the Indian and the American Mind* (Baltimore: John Hopkins Press, 1953); idem., *The Savages of America: A Study of the Indian and the Idea of Civilization* (Baltimore: Johns Hopkins Press, 1965); Bernard Sheehan, *Savagism and Civility: Indians and Englishmen in Colonial Virginia* (Cambridge: Cam-

bridge University Press, 1980); Alden T. Vaughan, "From White Man to Red Skin: Changing Anglo-American Perceptions of the American Indian," *American Historical Review* 87 (October 1982): 917–53.

59. Gretchen Bataille and Charles P. Silet, *The Pretend Indians: Images of Native Americans in the Movies* (Ames, IA: Iowa State University Press, 1980); Robert F. Hill, Glenn W. Solomon, Jane K. Tiger, and J. Dennis Fortenberry, "Complexities of Ethnicity Among Oklahoma Native Americans: Health Behaviors of Rural Adolescents," in *The Culture of Oklahoma* (Norman: University of Oklahoma Press, 1993), 84–100; Aelene B. Hirschfelder, *American Indian Stereotypes in the World of Children* (Metuchen, NJ: Scarecrow Press, 1982); Michael T. Marsden and Jack G. Nachbar, "The Indian in the Movies," in *Handbook of North American Indians*, Vol. 4, 607–16; Devon A. Mihesuah, *American Indians: Stereotypes and Realities* (Atlanta: Clarity International, 1996); Raymond William Stedman, *Shadows of the Indians: Stereotypes in American Culture* (Norman: University of Oklahoma Press, 1982).

60. "'Pocahontas': One of the best or worst films about American Indians?," *Indian Country Today*, June 1, 1995, C3, 6; "Pocahontas Rates an F in Indian Country," idem., July 6, 1995, D1.

61. William T. Hagan, "Full Blood, Mixed Blood, Generic, and Ersatz: The Problem of Indian Identity," *Arizona and the West* (Winter 1985): 317–18.

62. Jeffrey R. Hanson and Linda P. Rouse, "Dimensions of Native American Stereotyping," *American Indian Culture and Research Journal* 11:4 (1987): 33–58.

63. Idem., "American Indian Stereotyping, Resource Competition, and Status-based Prejudice," *American Indian Culture and Research Journal* 15:3 (1991): 1–18.

64. Title 25 of the Code of Federal Regulations (CFR), Part 83, "Procedures for Establishing That an American Indian Group Exists as an Indian Tribe." See also Anne Merline McCullough and David E. Wilkins, "'Constructing' Nations Within States: The Quest for Federal Recognition by the Catawba and Lumbee Tribes," *American Indian Quarterly* 19:3 (Summer 1995): 361–88.

65. "Act to Promote Development of Indian Arts and Crafts," *Public Law* (PL) 101–644 (104 Stat. 4662); "A Saint of South Texas: Retired peyote dealer remains a symbol of hope for a misunderstood faith," *The Dallas Morning News*, March 15, 1997, 1, 3G; "Congress considers Native American Church pleas on peyote use," *The Dallas Morning News*, June 20, 1994, 1, 8A.

66. Root, "Resolving 'Other' Status," 203.

67. Rose, "Iyeska Win," 69. See also H. Isaacs, *Idols of the Tribe*, for a discussion about feelings of inadequacy in the use of language, 93–114. For a comparative voice, see Sarah Min, "Language Lessons: Once I learned to speak Korean, I could finally hear my real voice," *Glamour* (November 1997): 106.

68. For information on Gertrude Bonnin (Zitkala Sa), see Dexter Fisher, "Zitkala Sa: The Evolution of a Writer," *American Indian Quarterly* 5 (August 1979): 229–38; David L. Johnson and Raymond Wilson, "Gertrude Simmons Bonnin, 1876–1938: 'Americanize the First Americans," *American Indian Quarterly* 12 (Winter 1988): 27–40; Deborah Welch, "Zitkala Sa: An American Indian Leader, 1976–1938," Ph.D. dissertation (University of Wyoming, 1985). For Charles Eastman, see C. Eastman, *From Deep Woods to Civilization: Chapters in the Autobiography of an Indian* (Boston: Little, Brown, 1916; idem., *Indian Boyhood* (New York: McClure, Phillips, 1902); Raymond Wilson, "Dr. Charles Alexander Eastman (Ohiyesa), Santee Sioux," Ph.D. dissertation (University of New Mexico, 1977).

69. Terry P. Wilson addresses appearances and blood quantum in, "Blood Quantum: Native American Mixed Bloods," *Racially Mixed People in America*, ed. Maria P. P. Root (Thousand Oaks, CA: Sage Publications, 1992), 108–25.

70. Carla K. Bradshaw, "Beauty and the Beast: On Racial Ambiguity in Racially Mixed People," in *Racially Mixed People in America*, 77–90; Edwidge Danticat, "Local Color: In Haiti, the color of a person's skin often determines whether she is considered beautiful—or not," *Allure* (September 1995): 124, 139; Itabari Njeri, "Colorism: In American Society Are Lighter-Skinned Blacks Better Off?" *Los Angeles Times*, April 24, 1988, F1, 10, 12–13; Gregory P. Stone, "Appearance and the Self," in Arnold Rose, ed., *Human Behavior and Social Processes* (Boston: Houghton Mifflin, 1962): 86–118; Julia Szaba, "The Morphing Pot," *New Woman* (January 1995): 94-95; 114, 166.

71. Quoted in Will Blythe, "Mr. Popular," *Outside* 22:11 (November 1997): 118.

72. Patricia Penn Hilden, *When Nickels Were Indians: An Urban Mixed Blood Story* (Washington, DC: Smithsonian, 1995).

73. Ibid., 16, 94, 125, 207.

74. Margo Okazawa-Rey, Tracy Robinson, and Janie Victoria Ward, "Black Women and the Politics of Skin Color and Hair," *Women's Studies Quarterly* 14: 1–2 (Spring/Summer 1986): 13–14, 16, 94, 125, 207.

75. Mihesuah, "'Too Dark to Be Angels': The Class System Among the Cherokees," 36.

76. Living Legends Collection interview #84.028, March 8, 1984, Mrs. Allie Mae Statha, Oklahoma Historical Society, Indian Archives Division, Oklahoma City.

77. Mary Crow Dog, *Lakota Woman* (New York: Harper, 1991), 9.

78. Cross, *Shades of Black*, 202.

79. Idem., 153.

80. Mihesuah, *Cultivating the Rose Buds*, 81.

81. Parham, "Cycles of Nigrescence," 201.

82. Everett Stonequist, *The Marginal Man: A Study in Personality and Culture Conflict* (New York: Russell and Russell, 1937); See also Arnold W. Green, "A Re-examination of the Marginal Man Concept," *Social Forces* 26 (1947): 167–71; Milton M. Goldberg, "A Qualification of the Marginal Man Theory," *American Sociological Review* 6 (1941): 52–58; Roy Dean Wright and Susan N. Wright, "A Plea for a Further Refinement of the Marginal Man Theory," *Phylon* 33 (1972): 361–68.

83. Root, "Resolution of 'Other' Status," 193.

84. Idem., 193.

85. Idem., 201-02, and idem., "A Bill of Rights for Racially Mixed People," in *The Multiracial Experience: Racial Borders as the New Frontier* (Thousand Oaks, CA: Sage, 1996), 3–14.

86. The debate over criteria for tribal enrollment and for identifying as an Indian is intensifying. In regard to extending tribal membership to individuals who are culturally ignorant, Jerry Bread, director of the American Indian Teacher Corps at the University of Oklahoma, commented, "It's a dilution of our identity. Many people who are culturally non-Indian will be classified as a member of that tribe, and they'll bring with them values that are not the same values that formulated the spirit of the tribe." See "Oklahomans Rush to Join Tribal Rolls," *Dallas Morning News*, June 12, 1995, 7A. See also *Indian Country Today's* series, "Indian Writers: Real or Imagined," September 8, 1993; "Indian Writers: The Good, The Bad, and the Could Be," September 15, 1993 and October 6, 1993, in addition to numerous letters to the editor; John Leville's review essay of Ward Churchill's *Indians Are Us?: Culture and Genocide in Native North America* (Monroe, ME: Common Courage Press, 1994), which addresses Churchill's notable essay, "Nobody's Pet Poodle: Jimmie Durham, An Artist for Native North America," in *American Indian Quarterly* 20 (Winter 1996): 109–18; James Clifton, ed., *Being and Becoming Indian: Biographical Studies of North American Frontiers* (Chicago: Dorsey Press, 1989); idem., *The Invented Indian: Cultural Fictions and*

Government Policies (New Brunswick, NJ: Transaction Publishers, 1990); Tim Giago, "It's time to establish guidelines for tribal enrollment criteria," *Indian Country Today*, March 10–17, 1997, A4; William W. Quinn, Jr., "The Southeast Syndrome: Notes on Indian Descendant Recruitment Organizations and Their Perceptions of Native American Culture," *American Indian Quarterly* 14:2 (Spring 1990) 147–54; William A. Starna, "The Southeast Syndrome: The Prior Restraint of a Non-Event," *American Indian Quarterly* (Fall 1991): 493–502; M. Annette Jaimes, "Federal Indian Identification Policy: An Usurpation of Indigenous Sovereignty in North America," in M. A. Jaimes, ed., *The State of Native America: Genocide, Colonization, and Resistance* (Boston: South End Press, 1992), 123–38.

87. Joseph Bruchac, ed., *Survival This Way: Interviews With American Indian Poets* (Tucson: University of Arizona Press, 1987), 34.

88. Jack D. Forbes, "The Manipulation of Race, Caste and Identity: Classifying Afroamerican, Native American and Red-Black People," *Journal of Ethnic Studies* 17 (1990): 1–51; idem., "Undercounting Native Americans: The 1980 Census and the Manipulation of Racial Identity in the United States," *Storia Nordamericana* 5 (1990): 5–47; C. M. Snipp, "Who Are American Indians? . . ."

89. "Oklahoma Indians rush to join tribal rolls," *Dallas Morning News*, June 12, 1995, 7A ; David Foster, "Tribes face conflict over who's a real Indian," *Arizona Daily Sun*, January 27, 1997, 3. Melissa Dyea, editor of the Arizona State University-based H-AmIndian Listserv website, also reports a surge in the numbers of "new Indians" who subscribe to the list. See also Stephen Cornell, *The Return of the Native: American Indian Political Resurgence* (New York: Oxford University Press, 1988); Joane Nagel, *American Indian Ethnic Renewal: Red Power and the Resurgence of Identity and Culture* (New York: Oxford University Press, 1996, 1997).

90. See Morris Foster's *Being and Becoming Comanche: A Social History of an American Indian Community* (Tucson: University of Arizona Press, 1991).

2

The Crucible of American Indian Identity: Native Tradition versus Colonial Imposition in Postconquest North America

Ward Churchill

Don't we have enough headaches trying to unite without . . . additional headaches? Why must people be categorized as full-bloods, mixed-bloods, etc.? Many years ago, the Bureau of Indian Affairs decided to establish blood quanta for the purpose of [tribal] enrollment. At the time, blood quantum was set at one-quarter degree, [a matter which] caused many people on the reservation to be categorized and labeled. The situation was caused solely by the BIA, with the able assistance of the Interior Department.

—TIM GIAGO
Lakota Times

 AMONG THE MOST vexing issues afflicting Native North America at the dawn of the twenty-first century are the questions of who does or does not hold a legitimate right to say he or she is American Indian, and by what criteria—whose definition—this may or may not be true. Such queries, and the answers to them, hold an obvious and deeply important bearing not only upon the personal sense of identity inhering in millions of individuals scattered throughout the continent, but in terms of the degree to which some form of genuine self-determination can be exercised by indigenous Nations in coming years. Conversely, they represent both an accurate gauge of the extent to which the sovereignty of North America's Native peoples has been historically eroded or usurped by the continent's two preeminent settler-states, the United States and Canada, and a preview of how the remainder stands to be eradicated altogether in the not so distant future.[1]

Ward Churchill, enrolled Keetoowah Cherokee, is associate chair of the Department of Ethnic Studies and professor of American Indian Studies at the University of Colorado, Boulder. His most recent book is *A Little Matter of Genocide: Holocaust and Denial in the Americas, 1492 to the Present.*

Defining for itself the composition of its membership (citizenry), in whatever terms and in accordance with whatever standards it freely chooses, is, of course, the very bedrock expression of self-determination by any nation or people. The ability to maintain this prerogative is thus a vital measure of its sovereign standing.[2] By the same token, intervention in or preemption of this plainly internal function by an external entity may be taken as signifying the abridgment of a nation's right to self-determination and a corresponding diminishment of its sovereignty. For that very reason, under conditions of colonialism—where one nation is directly subordinated to the politico-economic or strategic interests of another, and most especially in the kind of "internal colonial" systems prevailing in North America, where the colonizing powers have quite literally subsumed the territoriality of the colonized within their own claimed geographies[3]—such domination assumes the weight of a structural imperative.[4]

Things cannot be put so straightforwardly in contemporary practice, however, since colonialism in all forms has been flatly prohibited by international law since at least as early as 1960.[5] In these circumstances, the kinds of subterfuge designed to create false appearances are an essential aspect of maintaining and perfecting the order of colonial rule. Hence, it is necessary for the colonizer not merely to preempt the sovereignty of the colonized, but to co-opt it, inculcating a comprador consciousness among some segment of the subaltern population in which the forms of dominion imposed by colonization will be advocated as a self-determining expression of will emanating from the colonized themselves.[6]

At this point, with the codes of colonial domination embraced by many Native people as comprising their own traditions, and articulation of the latter often perceived as a contravention of indigenous sovereignty, the colonized become for all practical intents and purposes self-colonizing.[7] In this most advanced and refined iteration of imperialism, confusion accomplishes much more cheaply, quietly, and efficiently what raw force was once required to achieve.[8] In these circumstances, the kinds of subterfuge designed to create false appearances are an essential aspect of maintaining and perfecting the order of colonial rule. Meaningful resistance, never mind decolonization, among those so thoroughly indoctrinated and deluded as to accept and enforce the terms of their own subjugation in the name of liberation is, on its face, quite impossible. Yet both resistance and decolonization are not simply rights but obligations under international law and most other recent philosophical and moral schemas of justice.[9]

The situation presents a serious dilemma. Resolving it, and thereby actualizing the potential for a coherent and constructive indigenous response to the realities which now confront us, and which will confront our future generations, requires a systematic unraveling of the web of mystification through which North America's Native peoples have been bound ever more tightly into the carefully crafted mechanisms of oppression and eventual negation.[10] The purpose of the present essay is to make a contribution in this regard by sorting out that which has traditionally been part of the "Indian way" of identifying member/citizens from that which has not, and to sketch the mechanisms through which the latter has supplanted the former. From the resulting vantage point it should prove possible to ascertain with some clarity the methods that must be (re)asserted if we are ever to throw off the yoke of colonial bondage.

THE TRADITIONAL WAY

There is not, and has never been, much of a genetic ("hereditary") distinction to be drawn between indigenous peoples in the Americas. In part, this devolves upon the probability that the great proliferation of culturally distinct groups evident in the hemisphere by the time the European invasions commenced around 1500 had all evolved from three, or perhaps four, discernible gene stocks, figures correlating rather well to the evident number of root linguistic variants.[11] More to the point, Native peoples have for the most part always maintained relatively high degrees of sociocultural inclusiveness and consequent reproductive interactivity (interbreeding) among one another.

Since time immemorial, the Cheyenne (or their precursors) have intermarried with Arapaho, Ojibwa with Cree, Cayuga with Onondaga, Yaquis with Turamara, Choctaw with Chickasaw, and so on. In such instances, depending on whether the cultures in question were matrilinear or patrilinear, either the male or female spouse would become a part of the other's society, as would their offspring. Genealogy rather than genetics was the core component of societal composition, although procedures for incorporation of individuals and sometimes whole groups by adoption, naturalization, and occasional merger were similarly well established and practiced with varying degrees of scale and frequency by most peoples, either periodically or continuously.[12]

Whatever else may be said of such processes, they served over time to erase any meaningful genetic distinctions between the groups involved. Indeed, there are recorded instances—as when the Mohawk absorbed significant portions of both the Huron and the Susquahannock during the seventeenth century—in which the number of outsiders incorporated into a given society noticeably exceeded that of the original members.[13] Given these historical circumstances, the contemporary notion of somehow being Mohawk "by blood" is self-evidently ludicrous, albeit no more so than similar claims advanced with respect to the Pawnee, Cherokee, Apache, Paiute, or virtually any other Native people.[14]

Once non-Indians began to appear in substantial numbers across the hemisphere, the same time-honored principles prevailed. Probably the earliest group of English to have simply melted into a Native society were the inhabitants of Raleigh's "lost colony" of Roanoak in 1590.[15] A century later, there were literally thousands of "white Indians"—mostly English and French, but also Swedes, Scots, Irish, Dutch, and others as well—who, dis-eased with aspects of their own cultures, had either married into, been adopted by, or petitioned for naturalization as member/citizens of indigenous nations.[16] By then, the phenomenon had become pronounced enough that it had long since precipitated a crisis among the

Puritans of Plymouth Colony and figured in their waging of a war of extermination against the Pequots in 1637.[17]

The attraction of "going native" remained so strong, and the willingness of indigenous peoples to accept Europeans into their societies so apparent, that it prevailed even among those captured in Indian-white warfare.[18] During the 1770s, George Croghan and Guy Johnson, both acknowledged authorities on the Native peoples of the mid-Atlantic region, estimated that the great bulk of the several hundred English prisoners of all ages and both genders taken by the Indians had been adopted by them rather than being put to death.[19] At about the same time, Benjamin Franklin lamented that:

> [W]hen white persons of either sex have been taken prisoners young by the Indians, and lived a while among them, tho' ransomed by their Friends, and treated with all imaginable tenderness to prevail with them to stay among the English, yet in a Short time they become disgusted with our manner of life, and the care and pains that are necessary to support it, and take the first good Opportunity of escaping again into the Woods, from thence there is no reclaiming them.[20]

The literature of the period is filled with similar observations. Virginia's Lieutenant Governor Francis Fauquier, for example, noted that whites "recovered" from Indians had to be "closely watched [lest] they will certainly return to the Barbarians."[21] Colonel Henry Bouquet, who headed a 1764 expedition to take charge of "captives" returned under terms of a treaty with England by the Shawnee, Miami, and other peoples of the Ohio River Valley, issued orders that "they are to be closely watched and well Secured [as] most of them, particularly those who have been a long time among the Indians, will take the first Opportunity to run away."[22] The Reverend William Smith, chaplain and chronicler of Bouquet's foray, noted that most younger whites seemed to view their "liberators" as captors and "parted from the savages with tears."[23]

Some, like fourteen-year-old John McCullough, managed to escape Bouquet's column and quickly reunited himself with his Native family.[24] Adults often expressed the same sentiments, as with the English wife of a Native leader who shortly slipped away to rejoin her husband and their children.[25]

> Although most of the returned captives did not try to escape, the emotional torment caused by the separation from their adopted families deeply impressed the colonists. The Indians "delivered up their beloved captives with the utmost reluctance; shed torrents of tears over them, recommending them to the care and protection of the commanding officer." One young woman "cryed and roared when asked to come and begged to Stay a little longer." "Some, who could not make their escape, clung to their savage acquaintance at parting, and continued many days in bitter lamentations, even refusing sustenance." Children "cried as if they would die when they were presented to us." With only small exaggeration an observer . . . could report that "every captive left the Indians with regret."[26]

Many Indians reciprocated by refusing to surrender those they had married, adopted, or otherwise accepted, especially children, under any but the most coercive circumstances.[27] In cases where there was no viable alternative, the record is replete with examples of adoptive Native parents regularly visiting and otherwise maintaining familial relations with such children for the remainder of their own lives.[28] And, of course, children born of a union between Indian and non-Indian were almost invariably never relinquished at all (not least because whites, not Indians, tended to frown upon such mixed-blood offspring and thus made little or no effort to claim them).[29] One upshot is a marked proliferation of European surnames among indigenous peoples, not only in the East but the West as well; witness such sizable contemporary mixed-blood families as Morriseau, Robideau, Peltier, and Bellecourt among the Chippewa, and the Pourier, Garnier, Amiott, Roubideaux, Archambault, and Mousseau among the Lakota.[30]

With respect to blacks—mostly Africans brought to the southeastern quadrant of North America as chattel slaves, but the occasional free man as well—the situation was not dissimilar, albeit the imperative for them to reject a return to Euro-American society was obviously greater than for whites, and a much larger proportion of adults was involved. Escaped slaves were typically accepted among the Native peoples they encountered, marrying and producing children who were fully integrated into indigenous societies.[31] So prominent was this process of intermingling that at some point around 1750 an entire people, the Seminole, was constituted as an amalgamation of the remnants of several thoroughly decimated indigenous nations and a very substantial element, about one-third of the whole, of blacks.[32]

Hence, by 1830 at the latest, the notion of defining "Indianness" in terms of race had been rendered patently absurd. It has been reliably estimated that something approaching half of all Native people still residing east of the Mississippi River were at that point genetically intermixed not only with one another, but with "Negroid and Caucasoid racial stock," a demographic pattern which would spread rapidly westward over the next half-century.[33] There is little if any indication, moreover, that most indigenous societies viewed this increasing admixture as untoward or peculiar, much less threatening, in and of itself (this is as opposed to their often bitter resistance to the cultural, political, and material encroachments of Euro-American "civilization").

ON THE MATTER OF FIDELITY

It has become an article of faith among historical interpreters that mixed-bloods served as something of a Trojan Horse within indigenous societies during the era of Euro-American conquest, undermining their cohesion and thereby eroding their ability to resist the onslaught effectively.[34] While it is true that the colonizing powers, especially the United States, often sought to use those of mixed ancestry in precisely this fashion, the realities of mixed-blood performance were rather different. Indeed, their aggregate record in mounting a defense of Native rights is not only equal in most respects to those who were of the "pure" variety, it was plainly stronger in certain instances. Examples abound, beginning with the above-mentioned Seminole, who proved to be the U.S. army's most successful adversaries east of the Mississippi.[35]

During the twenty-year period leading up to the Cherokee Removal of 1838, it was John Ross, a man "seven-eighths Scotch-Irish and one-eighth Cherokee by descent," who served as the primary leader of his people's effort to revitalize their traditional culture, prevent the loss of their homelands in the Georgia-Tennessee area, and thereby avert mass relocation to Oklahoma Territory.[36] On the other hand, it was John Ridge—son of a full-blood leader called "Major" Ridge by whites, and himself only one-eighth white by pedigree—who headed the accommodationist ("sell-out") faction of Cherokee society. The dilution of unity that weakened Cherokee resistance, as well as the internal strife plaguing this Nation for generations after its Trail of Tears, were thus demonstrably attributable to Ridge and his generally well-blooded followers rather than the "genetically marginal" Ross.[37]

Far to the west, a comparable example may be found in Quannah (Parker), "half-breed" son of Peta Nacona, principal leader of the Quahadi Comanche, and Cynthia Ann Parker, a white captive who was his wife.[38] Beginning in the late 1860s, after his father had been killed and his mother "recovered" by white raiders, Quannah emerged as a major galvanizer of military resistance to the United States, not just among the Quahadi but with respect to all Comanche and allied Kiowa, Kiowa Apache, Southern Cheyenne, and Arapaho. After consummation of the U.S. conquest of the Southern Plains during the mid-1870s—the Quahadis were last to lay down their arms—Quannah shifted to a position of political leadership, a role which included introduction of the peyote religion, charting the Comanche course through the perilous waters of the early reservation period and on into the twentieth century.[39]

Among the Cheyenne were the brothers George, Robert, and Charlie Bent, sons of William Bent, a noted white trader, and his Cheyenne wife. While each struggled for their people's rights in his own way—George, for instance, fought briefly against the white invaders and testified on three separate occasions against perpetrators of the Colorado militia's infamous 1864 massacre of noncombatant Cheyennes and Arapahos at Sand Creek—Charlie is the better example (or at least the most reviled among mainstream commentators).[40] Accepted into the Cheyenne elite Crazy Dog Society (or Dog Soldiers), he acquired an almost legendary status because of his courage in physically defending his homeland. Ultimately, Charlie Bent gave his all, dying an agonizing, lingering death in 1868 of wounds suffered during a skirmish with Pawnees fighting for the United States.[41]

To the north, among the Oglala Lakota, there was the all but mythic figure of Crazy Horse, the man who vanquished both Crook and Custer, establishing himself in the process as perhaps the preeminent symbol of Native valor and integrity, both to his own people and to many others as well.[42] Slight, pale-complexioned, with fair, wavy hair—he was actually named Curly as a youth—the "strange man of the Oglalas" may well have been of mixed racial descent.[43] Regardless of Crazy Horse's ancestry, it is clear that men like Red Cloud, who figured most prominently in undercutting his ability to sustain the Lakota resistance, were themselves full-bloods.[44] So too was Little Big Man, the former friend who pinned Crazy Horse's arms, allowing William Gentles, a U.S. army private, to get close enough to bayonet him to death during the fall of 1877.[45]

The same could be said of Bull Head and the rest of the contingent of Indian police who murdered Sitting Bull in December 1890, the Arikara, Crow, and Pawnee scouts who guided Custer and Colonel Ranald Mackenzie on their bloody paths across the plains, and the bulk of those who finally ran Geronimo to ground in the upper Sonora Desert.[46] Nor was it a question of genetics that prompted Crow Dog, a noted "recalcitrant," to kill the government-sponsored Brûlé Lakota chief, Spotted Tail, whom the former viewed as having sacrificed his people's interest in favor of personal gain (both materially and in terms of imagined prestige).[47] The list goes on and on, with deadly repetition.

At the same time, it wasn't necessarily required that one be of any part Indian blood to assume a position of importance within an indigenous society. A salient example is that of Jim Beckwourth (variously spelled as Beckworth or Beckwith), who was by all accounts of exclusively African descent. Having been adopted by the Crow during the mid-1820s and marrying a woman named Still Water shortly thereafter, he was elevated first to the station of counselor to the headmen and eventually to serving as a headman in his own right. Although he left the Crow for a time after the death of his second wife, he remained unstinting in his defense of Indian rights and returned in 1866 to die among the people who had accepted him as a naturalized leader.[48]

On balance, then, it is both fair and accurate to observe that questions concerning the likelihood an individual might display a strong loyalty to Indian interests never devolved upon his or her genetic makeup. Unquestionably, mixed-bloods and persons lacking even the pretense of a Native gene stood among the foremost exemplars of patriotism in a number of indigenous nations during the nineteenth century (and earlier). By the same token, many Native people "untainted" by any hint of admixture with whites or blacks conducted themselves with all the fidelity of Vidkun Quisling.[49] Such matters were well understood in traditional societies, which is precisely why they never considered blood quantum to be a useful factor in determining citizenship or cultural identity.

THE RACIAL DIMENSION OF DIVIDE AND RULE

The intellectual establishment of the United States played a major role in pioneering such pseudoscientific "disciplines" as ethnology, craniometry, phrenology, and eugenics from the early nineteenth century onwards.[50] In essence, although it has evidenced a variety of offshoots and subtexts over the years, the entire project—which has lasted into the present moment—has been devoted to devising "objective" criteria by which the human species may be subdivided into races according to certain "heritable" and "empirically demonstrable" characteristics. Values are then assigned to these genetically transmitted attributes in order to create the appearance of a natural hierarchy of humanity ranging upward from Negroid at the lowest level to Caucasoid at the highest.[51]

With publication of Samuel George Morton's *Crania Americana* in 1839, it is no overstatement to suggest that the Euro-American intelligentsia stood at the cutting edge of "scholarly" efforts to lend both a patina of academic respectability and an aura of sheer inevitability to the white supremacist ideology attending European imperialism.[52] While it was put to various uses abroad, such material was utilized in the United States to justify both a domestic order of which black chattel slavery was an integral aspect and a continental trajectory of national expansion—America's "manifest destiny" to extend uninterruptedly "from sea to shining sea"—which could be consummated only at the direct expense of North America's indigenous population.[53]

It is instructive that while U.S. policymakers professed to embrace racism on both scientific and philosophical grounds, standpoints implying an at least minimal consistency in application, their implementation of its principles was at once transparently self-serving and utterly contradictory. Since blacks were considered to be property, yielding value not only in their labor but as commodities which could be bought and sold, it was profitable not only to employ but to breed them in ever larger numbers.[54] To this end, an elaborate system of quantifying their racial admixture was devised—classifications such as maroon, quadroon, and octoroon—by which to assess their relative worth.[55] The overriding premise, however, was the one drop rule: A person with any amount of "Negroid blood" could be considered black for purposes of law, even if computation of their quantum revealed them to be 127/128 white.[56]

Native people, by contrast, were legally understood to own property—mainly land, and minerals within that land—coveted by whites.[57] It followed then, as it still does, that reductions in the number of Indians at large in North America corresponded directly to diminishment of the cloud surrounding the dominant society's claims of clear title to, and jurisdictional rights over, its purported land base.[58] Hence, any racial admixture at all, especially with blacks, was often deemed sufficient to warrant individuals, and sometimes entire groups, being legally classified as non-Indians, regardless of their actual standing in indigenous society.[59] On this basis, most noticeably in the South but elsewhere as well, whole Native peoples were declared extinct via the expedient of simply reclassifying them as mulattos or coloreds.[60]

While the intermingling of Natives with blacks was invariably cast in a negative light, the mixing of Indian with white "stock" came to be viewed more favorably. As no less than Thomas Jefferson observed in 1803, a calculated policy of subsuming Native genetics within a much larger white gene pool might serve as an alternative to outright extermination in answering what he termed the "Indian Question."

> In truth, the ultimate point of rest and happiness for them is to let our settlements and theirs meet and blend together, to intermix, and become one people. Incorporating themselves with us as citizens of the United States, this is what the natural progress of things will, of course, bring on, and it will be better to promote than retard it.[61]

Completely oblivious to the reality of North America's abundant indigenous agriculture, and to the fact that whites had learned to cultivate corn and other crops from Indians rather than the other way round, America's "most admired ... slave-holding philosopher of freedom" actually urged a delegation of Munsee, Lenni Lenape, and Mohican leaders to adopt a farming way of life when they visited him in 1808.[62] "You will become one people with us," he went on to tell the astonished Indians, "your blood will mix with ours, and will spread with ours across this great land."[63]

The sentiments underlying Jefferson's "humanitarian" strategy were framed less pleasantly, but with remarkable clarity, by J. C. Nott, a racial theorist whose views were endorsed by Morton and other prominent scientists of the day. With reference to the idea that at least five southern peoples—Cherokee, Choctaw, Chickasaw, Creek, and Seminole—had become "civilized" in their own right before being forcibly evicted from their homelands during the 1830s,[64] he argued:

> It has been falsely asserted that the *Choctaw* and *Cherokee* Indians have made great progress in civilization. I assert positively, after the most ample investigation of the facts, that the pure-blooded Indians are every-where unchanged in their habits. Many white persons, settling among the above tribes, have intermarried with them; and all such trumpeted progress exists among these whites and their mixed breeds alone. The pure-blooded savage still skulks untamed through the forest, or gallops athwart the prairie. Can any one call the name of a single pure Indian of the *Barbarous* tribes who—except in death, like a wild cat—has done anything worthy of remembrance?[65]

It followed, according to the noted phrenologist Charles Caldwell, that the "only efficient scheme to civilize the Indians is to cross the breed. Attempt any other and you [will have no alternative] but to *extinguish the race* [emphasis in the original]."[66] Such views, posing the alternative of genetic and cultural absorption to literal extirpation, were avidly embraced by Lewis Henry Morgan, the "found-ing giant" of American anthropology. Indeed, Morgan was of the express opinion that the former option was preferable to the latter mainly because a blending of minute quantities of Indian blood into that of the white "mainstream" would serve to "toughen our race" even while it "painlessly" eradicated the indigenous popula-tion as such.[67]

All told, by 1860 or shortly thereafter, Euro-American academicians had forged the full range of conceptual tools necessary for their government to use the traditionally inclusive structures of Native societies in a manner that would facili-tate their rapid division, fragmentation, and, so it was thought at the time, ultimate dissipation.[68] Slowly but steadily, a national consensus was emerging to the effect that this represented the most appropriate (and final) solution to what was by then being called "The Indian Problem."[69] What remained necessary was for these tools to be applied systematically, through the design and implementation of a compre-hensive set of policies. And, to this end, experimentation had long since begun.

THE IMPOSITIONS OF U.S. POLICY

Probably the first concerted effort by U.S. officialdom to use the incorporation of whites and their mixed-blood offspring as a wedge with which to pry indigenous societies apart began in the late 1700s, when Moravian missionaries were asked to serve as de facto federal emissaries to the Cherokee Nation.[70] Imbued with the mystical notion that Aryan genetics correlated to such innate endowments as intellect and moral capacity—which in their minds corresponded with the potential to adopt "civilized" (Christian) outlooks and values—the Moravians and, after 1803, their Presbyterian colleagues "went out of their way to befriend" mixed-bloods rather than "pure" Indians while pursuing their goals of obtaining religious converts cum political allies.[71]

Predictably, this racial bias translated into a privileging of mixed-bloods in both political and material terms, regardless of their rank within the Cherokee polity and irrespective of whether they desired such "benefits," a situation which was quite reasonably resented by other Cherokees (most especially those whose authority was undermined or supplanted by such external manipulation). The result, obviously intended by the United States, was the opening of deep cleavages among Cherokees that greatly weakened them in military as well as political and cultural terms, circumstances which amplified considerably the decisive advantages the United States already enjoyed in its drive to dispossess them of their property.[72] Meanwhile, similar initiatives had been undertaken vis-à-vis the Creek, Choctaw, Chickasaw, and others.[73]

The United States largely refrained from attempting such maneuvers in a more formal sense during the first thirty years of its treaty making with indigenous nations. This interval roughly corresponds to the period in which the young republic, a veritable revolutionary outlaw state, desperately required the legitimation which could be bestowed through Native recognition of its sovereign status (indigenous sovereignty having already been recognized through treaties with the European powers).[74] Nonetheless, special provisions pertaining to mixed-bloods soon entered U.S. diplomacy with Indians, beginning with an 1817 treaty with the Wyandot and several other peoples of the Ohio-Pennsylvania region.[75] Thereafter, the performance was repeated in compact after compact, at least fifty-three times by 1868.[76]

In only a few instances—such as the 1847 treaty with the Chippewa of the Mississippi and Lake Superior, in which it is recognized by the United States that "half of mixed bloods of the Chippewas residing with them [should simply] be considered Chippewas"—is there acknowledgment of the right of indigenous nations to naturalize citizens as they saw fit.[77] In most cases, such treaty provisions are plainly designed to accomplish the opposite effect, distinguishing those of mixed ancestry from the rest of their people, almost always by unilaterally privileging them in a material fashion. Usually this followed upon the model established in the 1817 treaty, the eighth article of which provided that while the Indians themselves would hold certain lands in common, those "connected with said Indians, by blood or adoption" would receive individual tracts averaging 640 acres each.[78]

There were several variations on the theme. In one, exemplified by the 1818 treaty with the Miami, chiefs as well as mixed-bloods and intermarried whites were assigned individual parcels, one to six sections each in this case, while the rest of the people were assigned a tract in common. Thus, not only were mixed-bloods figuratively elevated to the same standing as chiefs by external fiat, but the Miamis' actual leaders were implicitly linked to them rather than to their people as a whole.[79] On other occasions, as in the 1855 treaty with the Winnebago, missionaries were substituted for chiefs.[80] On still others, as in the 1837 treaty with the Sioux, money and/or other special provisions were substituted for land.[81] Even in cases like that of the 1861 treaty with the Cheyenne and Arapaho, where full-bloods and mixed-bloods were nominally treated the same (i.e., everyone was allotted a parcel and/or monetary award), mixed-bloods were singled out to receive larger quantities.[82]

In a number of instances, as in the 1857 treaty with the Pawnee, provisions were explicitly designed to induce an outright physical separation of mixed-bloods from their people, a particularly odious practice in cases such as that addressed by the 1865 treaty with the Osage where "breeds" were the only group allowed (or coerced) to remain within a traditional homeland from which the rest of their nation was removed.[83] In the 1831 treaty with the Shawnee, the notion of blood quantum was first applied in a formal way to determine who would—or, more importantly, who would not—be recognized by the United States as a "real" Indian.[84]

And, racism aside, the treaties often employed a virulent sexist bias, tracing descent, acknowledging authority, and bestowing land titles along decidedly patriarchal lines even (or especially) in contexts where female property ownership, political leadership, and matrilinearity were the indigenous norms. When combined with the usual racial manipulations, such gender criteria represented an extraordinarily potent means of subverting the integrity of Native cultures, undermining their sociopolitical cohesion, and confusing or nullifying their procedures for identifying member/citizens.[85]

In 1871, sensing that the capacity of most indigenous nations to offer effective military resistance was nearing an end, Congress suspended further treaty making with Indians.[86] There then followed a decade of reorganization during which the government shifted from what had been primarily a policy of subjugating Native peoples to an emphasis upon assimilating what remained of them, both geographically and demographically.[87] There were a number of aspects to this transition, notably the extension of U.S. criminal jurisdiction over reserved Native territories via the Major Crimes Act of 1885.[88] Its hallmark, however, was passage of the 1887 General Allotment Act, a measure expressly intended to dissolve the collective relationship to land that was the fundament of traditional cultures by imposing the allegedly superior Anglo-Saxon system of individuated property ownership.[89]

The main ingredient of the allotment act was that each Indian recognized as such by the United States would be assigned an individually deeded parcel of land within existing reservation boundaries. These varied in size, depending on whether the Indian was a child (40 acres), unmarried adult (80 acres), or head of a family

(160 acres). Once each Indian had received his or her personal allotment, becoming a U.S. citizen in the process, the law prescribed that the balance of reserved territory be declared surplus and opened up to homesteading by non-Indians, corporate usage, or placed in some form of perpetual federal trust status (e.g., designated as national parks and forests, military installations, etc.). In this manner, about two-thirds of the approximately 150 million acres of land still retained by indigenous nations at the outset passed to whites by 1934.[90]

The bedrock upon which the allotment process was built was the compilation of formal rolls listing those belonging to each reservation-based Native people.[91] While the act itself posited no specific criteria by which this would be accomplished, responsibility for completing the task was ultimately vested in the individual federal agents assigned to preside over the reservations. Endowed as they were with staunchly racialist perspectives, and fully aware that whatever definitional constraints might be applied in determining the overall number of Indians would translate directly into an increased availability of property to their own society, it was predictable that these men would rely heavily upon the sort of blood quantum standards already evident in treaty language.[92]

In practice, it was typically required that potential enrollees or allottees be able to demonstrate that they possessed "not less than one-half degree of blood" in the particular group in which they wished to be enrolled (intertribal pedigrees were seldom accepted, even for ostensible full-bloods, and the overall standard was almost never allowed to slip below quarter-blood).[93] The upshot was that anywhere from a third to two-thirds of all those who might otherwise have been eligible to receive allotments were denied not only land but federal recognition as member/citizens of their nations.[94] In sum, government functionaries admitted to the existence of only 237,196 Native people within U.S. borders by the late 1890s, of whom only a small percentage were less than half-blood members of specific groups.[95]

To complete this racist reshaping of Indian identity, the act provided that those enrolled as full-bloods would be placed under the legal presumption of being genetically incompetent to manage their own affairs. Hence, they were issued "trust patents" for their allotments, to be "administered in their behalf by the Secretary of the Interior or his delegate" (local Indian agents) for a quarter-century.[96] Mixed-bloods, by virtue of their white genetics, were deemed to be competent and issued patents in fee simple. This, along with other blatantly preferential treatment bestowed as a matter of policy upon those of mixed ancestry, drove the final wedges into many once harmonious indigenous societies.[97] In the more extreme instances, such as that of the Kaw in Kansas, the full-bloods' visceral response was to repudiate mixed-bloods altogether, demanding their elimination from the tribal roll and seeking to expel them as a body from their society.[98]

By the turn of the century, virtually every indigenous nation within the United States had, by way of an unrelenting substitution of federal definitions for their own, been stripped of the ability to determine for themselves in any meaningful way the internal composition of their polities. The manner in which this had been accomplished, moreover, ensured that rifts even among those still acknowledged as being Indians were of a nature that would all but guarantee eventual dissolution of Native societies, at least in the sense they had traditionally understood themselves. Allotment and the broader assimilation policy of which it was part had truly proven to be, in the words of Indian Commissioner Francis E. Leupp, "a mighty pulverizing engine for breaking up the tribal mass."[99]

INTERNALIZATION

The break-up and diminishment of the reservation land base were not the only factors leading to confident predictions that there would be no Indians culturally recognizable as such in the United States by some point around 1935.[100] Beginning in the 1860s, there had been an increasing emphasis on educating Native youth in the ways of the dominant society, a trend that was consolidated in the 1880s as a key aspect of assimilationist technique.[101] While there were several other options available, all of them less expensive and more humane, the mode selected for delivery of such instruction was primarily that of off-reservation boarding schools located in places as remote as possible from Native communities.[102]

The model for what became an entire system was Pennsylvania's Carlisle Indian School, established in 1875 by Captain Richard Henry Pratt, a man whose main qualification for the task seems to have been that he had earlier served as warden of a military prison at Fort Marion, Florida.[103] Following Pratt's stated objective of "killing the Indian" in each student, Carlisle and other such facilities—Chilocco, Albuquerque, Phoenix, Haskell, Riverside (by 1902, there were two dozen of them)—systematically "deculturated" their pupils.[104] Children brought to the schools as young as age six were denied most or all direct contact with their families and societies for years on end. They were shorn of their hair and required to dress in the manner of Euro-America, forbidden to speak their languages or practice their religions, and prevented from learning their own histories or being in any other way socialized among their people.[105]

Simultaneously, all students were subjected to a grueling regimen of indoctrination in Christian morality, mainly the "virtues" of private property, sexual repression, and patriarchy; "proper" English and arithmetic; and officially approved versions of history, civics, and natural science, the latter devoted mostly to inculcating prevailing notions of racial hierarchy.[106] To instill the work ethic—that is, to prepare students for the lot assigned their racial group once it had been fully digested by Euro-America—they were also required to spend half of each day during the school year engaged in "industrial vocational training" (i.e., uncompensated manual labor). During the summers, most of the older boys were "jobbed out" at very low wages to work on white-owned farms or local businesses; girls were assigned as domestics and the like.[107]

Individual Native families and often whole societies resisted the process.[108] As a result, in 1891 and again in 1893, Congress authorized the use of police, troops, and other forcible means to compel the transfer of children from reservations to boarding schools and to keep them there once they'd arrived.[109] Hence, despite the best efforts of their elders, and not infrequently of the students themselves, a total of 21,568 indigenous children—about a third of the targeted age group—were confined in the schools in 1900.[110] As of the late 1920s, the system had been diversified and expanded to the point that upwards of 80 percent of each successive generation of Native youth was being comprehensively "acculturated" in a more or less uniform fashion.[111]

By 1924, assimilation had progressed to the point that a "clean-up bill" was passed through which the responsibilities, though not necessarily the rights, of U.S. citizenship were imposed upon all Indians who had not already been naturalized under the allotment act or other federal initiatives.[112] Although it appeared that this might represent the culminating statutory ingredient necessary to bring about a final absorption of Native America, fate intervened in a most unexpected fashion to avert any such outcome (formally, if not in terms of more practical cultural, political, and economic realities). This, rather ironically, took the form of resources: The mostly barren tracts of land left to Indians after allotment, thought to be worthless by nineteenth-century policymakers, had by the late 1920s been revealed as some of the more mineral-rich territory in the world.[113]

Loath to see these newfound assets thrown into the public domain (many had strategic value, real or potential), the more forward-looking federal economic planners quickly perceived the utility of retaining them in trust, where they might be exploited at controlled rates by preferred corporations for designated purposes and in the most profitable fashion imaginable. This resulted, in 1925, in the recommendation by a committee of one hundred officially selected academic experts and business leaders that allotment and the more draconian objectives of assimilation policy be abandoned in favor of preserving the reservations in some permanently subordinated capacity and inaugurating a policy of carefully calibrated economic development therein.[114]

This, in turn, led to passage of the 1934 Indian Reorganization Act (IRA), through which what remained of traditional Native governments were for the most part supplanted by federally designed tribal councils meant to serve as the medium for long-term administration of the freshly conceived internal colonial domain.[115] Although the IRA was imposed behind the democratic facade of reservation-by-reservation referenda, the record reveals that BIA field representatives obtained favorable results by presenting skewed or patently false information to voters in a number of instances, flatly rigging the outcomes in others.[116] And, while democratic appearances were reinforced by the fact that the government of each reorganized reservation functioned on the basis of its own "tribal constitution," the reality is that these "founding" documents were essentially boilerplate contraptions resembling corporate charters hammered out on an assembly line basis by bureau personnel.[117]

Nowhere is this last more obvious than in the language of the IRA constitutions pertaining to criteria of tribal membership. While there are certain variations between instruments, most simply aped the prevailing federal quantum standard of quarter-blood minimum, while all of them, regardless of the degree of blood required, advanced genetics as the linchpin of identity.[118] That there was no noteworthy resistance among Native supporters of the IRA to this conspicuous usurpation of indigenous tradition is unsurprising, given that such persons were all but invariably drawn from the ranks of those indoctrinated in the boarding schools to see themselves in racial rather than national, political, or cultural terms.[119]

With the embrace of the IRA constitutions by what were proclaimed as solid majorities on most reservations, Euro-American definitions of and constraints upon Indian identity were formally as well as psychologically and intellectually internalized by Native America. From there on, the government could increasingly rely upon Indians themselves to enforce its race codes. Consequently, whenever racial formulations of Native identity have been challenged, Washington has been able to lay the onus of responsibility directly at the feet of the IRA councils it not only invented and installed, but which remain utterly and perpetually dependent upon federal patronage for their base funding and whatever limited authority they might wield.[120] In turn, the councils defend Washington's negation of indigenous sovereignty in the name of maintaining it.[121] A more perfect shell game is impossible to imagine.

ENTER THE "PURITY POLICE"

The reconfiguration and structural assimilation of the mechanisms of indigenous governance—by the early 1990s, IRA-style councils were openly referred to as a "third level" of the federal government itself—was facilitated and reinforced, through both the increasingly pervasive indoctrination of Native students via the educational system and by lingering effects of allotment.[122] Foremost in this respect was the "heirship problem" created by the fact that the reserved Native land base had been reduced to a size corresponding to the number of Indians recognized as existing during the 1890s. No provision was made for a population rebound of any sort.[123] As the matter was politely explained in 1994:

> Upon the death of the original allottees the allotments, or portions of them, have descended to heirs or devisees. As these heirs in turn have died, their holdings have been subdivided among their heirs or devisees, and so on through the years. As a result, about half of the allotted Indian lands are in heirship status. The authors of the original legislation failed to anticipate the problems that would be caused by the partitioning of an individual's land following his death. Thousands of the allotments in an heirship status are subject to so many undivided interests that they can be utilized only with great difficulty by their Indian owners. . . . Undivided interests in a single allotment can often be expressed by fractions with a common denominator of 1,000,000 or more [by this point].[124]

In other words, there was no reservation land available to accommodate the 50-percent increase in the number of recognized Indians recorded by the U.S. Census between 1900 and 1950.[125] Rather than correcting the problem by transferring some portion of the territory unlawfully stripped from Native people back to its rightful owners,[126] the government launched a massive and sustained program to relocate the Native "population surplus" from the land altogether, dispersing them for the most part into major urban areas. At the same time, as an incentive for them to leave, funding for on-reservation programming of all sorts was sliced to the bone and sometimes deeper.[127] One result is that, while well over 90 percent of federally recognized Indians lived on the reservations in 1900, fewer than 45 percent do so today.[128]

Another cost-cutting measure, inaugurated in the mid-1950s, was for the Congress to simply "terminate" its recognition of entire nations whose reservations were found to be devoid of minerals, or who were deemed to be too small and insignificant to warrant the expenditures necessary to administer them.[129] A total of 103 peoples, ranging from large groups like the Menominee in Wisconsin and Klamath in Oregon to the tiny "mission bands" of Southern California, were thereby dissolved, their remaining lands absorbed into the U.S. territorial corpus and their population effectively declared to be non-Indians before the process ran its course in the early sixties.[130] Only a handful, including the Menominee but not the Klamath, were ever reinstated.[131]

Predictably, far from seeking to combat such trends, federally installed and supported tribal councils amplified them. In the face of declining federal appropriations to the BIA, the councils by and large set out to reduce the number of Indians eligible to draw upon them. Arguing that the fewer people entitled to receive benefits such as health care and commodity foodstuffs—or to receive per-capita payments against mineral extraction, water diversions, and past land transfers—the larger the share for those who remained, the councils were able to peddle their bill of goods to many of their increasingly impoverished reservation constituents.[132] In short order, the IRA constitutions on many reservations were amended or rewritten to reflect higher blood quantum requirements for tribal enrollment.[133] In a number of instances, reservation residency was required as well, a stipulation that excluded the children of relocatees, regardless of their documentable degree of Indian blood.[134]

The council heads, through a federally funded lobbying organization dubbed the National Tribal Chairmen's Association (NTCA), then launched an aggressive campaign to once again recast the definition of "Indian" in the public consciousness—and, they made it clear, in law—this time as being only those "enrolled in a federally-recognized tribe."[135] Consigned to the status of non-Indians in this perverse scenario were everyone from terminated peoples like the Klamath to the unenrolled traditionals still living on and about many reservations, from nations like the Abnaki of Vermont who had never consented to a treaty with the United States—and who were thus officially unrecognized—to the NTCA members' own nieces and nephews residing in cities.[136] Also sacrificed in the proposed ethnic purge were thousands of hapless children, orphaned and otherwise, whom federal welfare agencies had caused to be adopted by non-Indian families.[137]

The government initially declined to accept the NTCA's simplistic nomenclature of Indianness. Instead, it conjured up a proliferation of what by now amount to at least eighty different and often conflicting definitions of its own, each of them conforming to some particular bureaucratic or policy agenda and sporting a larger or smaller claque of Indian subscribers queued up to defend it under the presumption they will somehow benefit by their endorsement.[138] Under such conditions, it is possible to challenge the legitimacy of virtually anyone identifying as Indian on one or several grounds (often having little or nothing to do with genuine concerns about identity, per se).[139] The result has been a steadily rising tide of infighting, occasioned in most instances by outright race-baiting, between and among Native peoples during the past forty years.[140]

Things did not become truly pathological until 1990, however, when the NTCA's reactionary vision was at least partially realized at the federal level. With passage of the so-called Act for the Protection of American Indian Arts and Crafts in this year, it became a criminal offense punishable by fines of $250,000 to $1 million and imprisonment of up to fifteen years for anyone not enrolled in a federally recognized tribe to identify as an Indian "for purposes of selling artwork."[141] Although Congress did not provide the statute an enabling clause to allow its enforcement until 1996—not least because of concerns that to do so might technically require the arrest and prosecution of individuals deemed to be Indian under other elements of federal law—its very existence unleashed an utter frenzy of witch-hunting among Indians themselves.[142]

Within months, ad hoc patrols of "identity monitors" were prowling selected museums and galleries, demanding to see documentation of the pedigrees of the Native artists exhibited therein, while freelance Indian spokes persons advocated that comparable legislation pertaining to "ethnic fraud" should be enacted with respect to writers, educators, filmmakers, and journalists, among many others.[143] The theme was quickly picked up, tabloid-style, by papers like *Indian Country Today* and *News From Indian Country*, while the Internet came figuratively alive with a swarm of essentially anonymous rumors that dozens of Native America's most distinguished artists, authors, thinkers, and activists weren't "really" Indians after all.[144]

Perhaps most disgustingly, a literal flying squad of self-appointed "purity police" in the San Francisco Bay Area took it upon itself to systematically disrupt the functioning of all manner of community service organizations in 1992 and 1993—their targets ranged from Native programming on radio station KPFA, to an AIDS clinic administered by the Indian Health Service, to the local school district's Indian education project—to ensure that everyone involved fit their particular notion of what an Indian should be (children as young as eight years of age were button holed and ordered to prove they were "genuine" Indians).[145] Meanwhile, back on the "rez," at least some IRA leaders were arguing that the tribal constitutions should be amended yet again, this time to disenroll members who married non-Indians on the premise that such measures had become vital "to protect the purity of our Indian blood."[146]

The Way Ahead

The internalization of Euro-America's conception of race by Native peoples, the virulence with which it is now manifested in all too many sectors of the indigenous community, and the ubiquity of the confusion and divisiveness it has generated among Indians and their potential supporters represents a culmination of federal policy initiatives originating nearly two hundred years ago. To all appearances, Native North America has been rendered effectively self-colonizing and, if present attitudes persist, it stands to become self-liquidating as well. The tale is told in the demographic data pertaining to those who are federally recognized.

> During the twentieth century population recovery of American Indians there has been an increasing mixture between them and non-Indian peoples. Data concerning this may be obtained from the 1910 and 1930 U.S. censuses of American Indians. . . . [In 1910] 56.5 percent of American Indians enumerated in the United States were full-blood—150,053 out of 265,682—with the blood quantum of 8.4 percent (22,207) not reported. . . . In the U.S. census of 1930, however, 46.3 percent—153,933 out of 332,397—were enumerated as full-bloods and 42.4 percent (141,101) were enumerated as mixed-bloods, with the degree of Indian blood of 11.2 percent (37,363) not reported. Thus, whereas the American Indian population size increased by slightly over 66,000 from 1910 to 1930, the number of full-blood American Indians increased by only 4,000; most of the increase was among mixed-blood Indians.[147]

Such trends have not only continued but accelerated. By 1970, approximately two-thirds of the marriages of those on the tribal rolls were to people who were not, with the result that only 59 percent of births reflected a situation in which both parents registered themselves as possessing any Indian blood at all.[148] The number of supposed full-bloods has correspondingly dropped to almost nothing—among populous peoples like the Minnesota-Wisconsin Chippewa, they now represent only 5 percent of the whole—while the proportion and composition of mixed-bloods has climbed dramatically.[149] At present rates of intermarriage, the segment of the federally recognized Native population evidencing less than one-quarter-degree blood quantum, presently about 4 percent, will have climbed to 59 percent or more by 2080.[150] To tighten or even adhere to quantum requirements in the face of such realities is to engage in a sort of autogenocide by definitional and statistical extermination.[151] As historian Patricia Nelson Limerick has observed in this connection:

> Set the blood quantum at one-quarter, hold to it as a rigid definition of Indians, let intermarriage proceed as it [has] for centuries, and eventually Indians will be defined out of existence. When that happens, the federal government will be freed of its persistent "Indian problem."[152]

Cognizant of this, some peoples with smaller numbers, like the Umatilla in Oregon, have already undertaken to preserve racial cant while offsetting the consequent prospect of definitional self-extinguishment by proposing revision of their constitutions to require that future enrollees demonstrate some degree of Umatilla blood, no matter how minute, in addition to "at least one-quarter degree of blood . . . in another federally-recognized tribe or tribes."[153] Left conspicuously unexplained in such convoluted formulations is exactly how being a quarter-blood Lakota or Mohawk supposedly makes a person one whit more Umatilla than does being a full-blood Irishman, Ibo, or Han. Nor is it explained why a person genealogically connected to the group should be less Umatilla in orientation, absent some sort of generic "Indian" genetic structure, than a person who has it.

The implications of such nonsense become most striking when it is considered in juxtaposition to the actual—rather than federally recognized—size of the present indigenous population of the United States, and the potential power deriving from its scale. Jack Forbes, perhaps the closest examiner of the issue, has noted that since 1969,

> The Bureau of the Census, conspiring with the Office of Management and Budget and political special interests, has [deliberately obfuscated] the "racial" character of the U.S. population and, as part of the process, has "lost" some six to eight million persons of Native American ancestry and appearance with a scientifically useless "Hispanic/Spanish" category. In addition, [seven million or more] persons of mixed African and Native American ancestry remain uncounted as such because of the way census questions were asked and the answers tallied.[154]

Forbes estimates that, even using standard blood-quantum criteria, the actual Native population of the "lower 48" in 1980 was well over 15 million rather than the 1.4 million officially admitted by the census bureau.[155] Employing traditional indigenous methods of identifying population rather than racial criteria would have resulted in an even higher number. And, as of 1990, when the official count reached nearly 2 million, inclusion of these most rapidly growing sectors of the Native population results in an aggregate of as many as 30 million persons overall.[156] The ability to wield political and economic clout inherent to the latter tally, as opposed to the former—which comes to less than 0.5 percent of the overall U.S. population—is self-evident.

Fortunately, there is at least one concrete example of how things might be taken in the direction of realizing this potential. The Cherokee Nation of Oklahoma (CNO), in its 1975 constitution, took the unprecedented step, still unparalleled by other twentieth-century indigenous governments, of completely dispensing with blood-quantum requirements in its enrollment procedures. Instead, the CNO placed its reliance upon the more traditional genealogical mode of determining citizenship.[157] This had the effect of increasing the number of persons formally identified as Cherokee from fewer than 10,000 during the late 1950s to slightly over 232,000 by 1980 (and about 300,000 today).[158]

On this basis, the Cherokee, whose reservation was dissolved pursuant to the 1898 Curtis Act, have been able to assert what amounts to a split jurisdiction over their former territory.[159] Moreover, while much has been made by assorted race mongers about how this course of action was "diluting" whatever was left of "real" Cherokee culture and society, the precise opposite result has obtained in practice.

> The Oklahoma Cherokee, without a reservation landbase, have been able to survive tribally by an inclusive definition of what it is to be Cherokee. Their definition allowed relatively large numbers of people with Cherokee lineage but relatively small amounts of Cherokee blood into the tribe. This allowed the tribe to reestablish itself after virtual "dissolution" and to achieve political power in Oklahoma. The tribe, in turn, has protected a smaller group of full-blood, more traditional Cherokee from American non-Indian ways of life.[160]

Plainly, in and of itself, the CNO initiative has neither ended the internecine bickering over identity which has precluded anything resembling unity among Native people, much less established the basis upon which to free even the Cherokee from internal colonial domination by the United States. It does, however, represent a substantial stride in the right direction. If the model it embodies is ultimately seized and acted upon by a broadening spectrum of indigenous nations in the years ahead, the tools required for liberating Native North America may at long last be forged. In the alternative, should the currently predominating racialist perspectives associated with the IRA regimes prevail, the road to extinction can be traversed rather quickly.[161]

Notes

1. On the general concept of the settler-state, see, e.g., J. Sakai, *Settlers: The Myth of the White Proletariat* (Chicago: Morning Star Press, 1983).

2. For discussion, see Andres Rigo Sureda, *The Evolution of the Right to Self-Determination* (Leyden: A. W. Sythoff, 1973).

3. For the most extensive explanation of the concept at issue, see Michael Hector, *Internal Colonialism: The Celtic Fringe in British National Development, 1536–1966* (Berkeley: University of California Press, 1975).

4. An excellent and succinct analysis is presented in Aimé Césaire's *Discourse on Colonialism* (New York: Monthly Review Press, 1972).

5. Burns H. Weston, Richard A. Falk, and Anthony D'Amato, eds., *Basic Documents in International Law and World Order* (St. Paul, MN: West Publishing, 1990), 16–32, 343–4.

6. Albert Memmi, *The Colonizer and the Colonized* (Boston: Beacon Press, 1965), 89.

7. Probably the best examination of this phenomenon will be found in Frantz Fanon, *Black Skin, White Masks: The Experiences of a Black Man in a White World* (New York: Grove Press, 1967).

8. In external rather than internal contexts, the principle is manifested in the form of neocolonialism; see, e.g., Jack Woodis, *Introduction to Neocolonialism* (New York: International Publishers, 1967).

9. A good overview is provided in Richard Falk, *Human Rights and State Sovereignty* (New York: Holmes & Meier, 1981).

10. For useful theoretical discourses on the necessity of "demystification" as a predicate to concrete activity, see J. G. Merquior, *The Veil and the Mask: Essays on Culture and Ideology* (London: Routledge & Kegan Paul, 1979).

11. The three groupings are designated by linguists and geneticists alike as being Amerind, Na-Dene, and Eskimo-Aleut; Joseph H. Greenberg, *Language in the Americas* (Stanford, CA: Stanford University Press, 1988).

12. See generally, Fred Egan, ed., *The Social Anthropology of American Indian Tribes* (Chicago: University of Chicago Press, 1955).

13. See generally, Francis Jennings, *The Ambiguous Iroquois Empire: The Covenant Chain Confederation of Indian Tribes with the New England Colonies* (New York: W.W. Norton, 1984).

14. Probably the most succinct observation on this matter I ever heard was made by the revered Oglala Lakota leader, Frank Fools Crow, then ninety years old, during the 1981 Wounded Knee Memorial conducted in the village of Manderson on the Pine Ridge Reservation. He did not know who might be a "full-blood" Lakota, Fools Crow said, before observing that he doubted there were any. His reasoning? He himself admitted to having a Cheyenne grandmother, a matter which in his opinion made him a "mixed-blood" in terms of his biological "Lakotaness." It should be noted that the Elder's statement was clearly intended to impress the younger members of his audience about the ridiculousness of their preoccupation with blood quantum.

15. Ted Morgan, *Wilderness at Dawn: The Settling of the North American Continent* (New York: Simon and Schuster, 1993) p.82.

16. See, e.g., James Axtell, "The White Indians of Colonial America," in his *The European and the Indian: Essays in the Ethnohistory of North America* (New York: Oxford University Press, 1981), 168–206.

17. Richard Drinnon, *Facing West: The Metaphysics of Indian-Hating and Empire-Building*, 2d. ed. (New York: Schocken, 1990), 3–34.

18. See generally, J. Norman Heard, *White into Red: A Study of the Assimilation of White Persons Captured by the Indians* (Meyuchen, NJ: Scarecrow Press, 1973). Also see Richard Drinnon, *White Savage: The Case of John Dunn Hunter* (New York: Schocken Books, 1972).

19. "The Opinions of George Croughan on the American Indian," *Pennsylvania Magazine of History and Biography* 71 (1947): 157; "Guy Johnson's Opinions on the American Indians," *Pennsylvania Magazine of History and Biography* 77 (1953): 322.

20. Benjamin Franklin, letter to Peter Collinson, May 9, 1753; in Leonard W. Larabee, et al., eds., *The Papers of Benjamin Franklin*, Vol. 4 (New Haven, CT: Yale University Press, 1959), 481–82.

21. Sylvester K. Stevens and Donald H. Kent, eds., *The Papers of Col. Henry Bouquet*, Vol. 17 (Harrisburg: Pennsylvania State Historical Society, 1940–43), 51.

22. Ibid., 38.

23. William Smith, D.D., *Historical Account of Colonel Bouquet's Expedition Against the Ohio Indians, 1764* (Philadelphia, 1765), 80.

24. *A Narrative of the Captivity of John McCullough, Esq.*, in Archibald Loudon, ed., *A Selection, of Some of the Most Interesting Narratives, of Outrages, Committed by the Indians, in Their Wars, with the White People*, Vol. 1 (Carlisle, PA, 1808–11), 326–27.

25. James Sullivan, et al., eds., *The Papers of Sir William Johnson*, Vol. 11 (Albany: State Historical Society of New York, 1921–62), 496–98.

26. Axtell, "White Indians," op. cit., 177.

27. William Walton, *The Captivity and Sufferings of Benjamin Gilbert and His Family, 1780–83* (Philadelphia, 1784), 103, 107.

28. Johnson Papers, op. cit., Vol. 10, 160; Vol. 11, 728.

29. Brewton Berry, *Almost White: A Study of Certain Racial Hybrids in the Eastern United States* (New York: Macmillan, 1963).

30. Robert F. Berkhofer, Jr., *Salvation and the Savage: An Analysis of Protestant Missions and American Indian Response, 1787–1862* (New York: Atheneum, 1972); Clyde A. Milner II and Floyd A. O'Neil, eds., *Churchmen and the Western Indians, 1820–1920* (Norman: University of Oklahoma Press, 1985).

31. See Jack D. Forbes, *Black Africans and Native Americans: Race, Color and Caste in the Making of Red-Black Peoples* (London: Routledge, 1988).

32. Peter H. Wood, "The Changing Population of the Colonial South: An Overview by Race and Region" Peter H. Wood, Gregory A. Waselkov, and M. Thomas Hatley, eds., *Powhatan's Mantle: Indians in the Colonial Southeast* (Lincoln: University of Nebraska Press, 1989).

33. Jack D. Forbes, *Africans and Native Americans: The Language of Race and the Evolution of Red-Black Peoples*, 2d. ed. (Urbana: University of Illinois Press, 1993), 249–64.

34. Edward Lazarus, *Black Hills, White Justice: The Sioux Nation versus the United States, 1775 to the Present* (New York: HarperCollins, 1991).

35. John K. Mahon, *History of the Second Seminole War, 1835–1842* (Gainesville: University of Florida Press, 1967); Alan Axelrod, *Chronicle of the Indian Wars from Colonial Times to Wounded Knee* (New York: Prentice Hall, 1993), 146–47.

36. Rachael E. Eaton, *John Ross and the Cherokee People* (Muskogee, OK: Cherokee National Museum, 1921).

37. Thurman Wilkins, *Cherokee Tragedy: The Ridge Family and the Decimation of a People*, 2d ed. (Norman: University of Oklahoma Press, 1986).

38. Cynthia Schmidt Hacker, *Cynthia Ann Parker: The Life and the Legend* (El Paso: Texas Western Press, 1990).

39. Bill Neeley, *The Last Comanche Chief: The Life and Times of Quanah Parker* (New York: John Wiley, 1995).

40. David Lavender, *Bent's Fort* (Garden City, NY: Doubleday, 1954).

41. George Bird Grinnell, *The Fighting Cheyennes* (Norman: University of Oklahoma Press, 1956).

42. John E. Gray, *The Centennial Campaign: The Sioux War of 1876* (Norman: University of Oklahoma Press, 1988).

43. Mari Sandoz, *Crazy Horse: Strange Man of the Oglalas* (Lincoln: University of Nebraska Press, 1961).

44. See, e.g., James C. Olsen, *Red Cloud and the Sioux Problem* (Lincoln: University of Nebraska Press, 1965).

45. Robert A. Clark, ed., *The Killing of Chief Crazy Horse* (Lincoln: University of Nebraska Press, 1976).

46. John M. Carroll, ed., *The Arrest and Killing of Sitting Bull* (Glendale, CA: Arthur H. Clark, 1986); Thomas Dunlay, *Wolves for the Blue Soldiers: Indian Scouts and Auxiliaries with the U.S. Army, 1860–90* (Lincoln: University of Nebraska Press, 1982); Obie B. Faulk, *The Geronimo Campaign* (New York: Oxford University Press, 1969).

47. Leonard Crow Dog and Richard Erdoes, *Crow Dog: Four Generations of Sioux Medicine Men* (New York: HarperCollins, 1995), 27–39.

48. Jim Beckwourth as told to Thomas D. Bonner, *The Life and Adventures of James P. Beckwourth* (Lincoln: University of Nebraska Press, 1971 reprint of 1866 original).

49. Paul M. Hayes, *Quisling: The Career and Political Ideas of Vikdun Quisling, 1887–1945* (Bloomington: Indiana University Press, 1972).

50. William Stanton, *The Leopard's Spots: Scientific Attitudes Towards Race in America, 1815–1859* (Chicago: University of Chicago Press, 1960).

51. Richard J. Herrstein and Charles Murray *The Bell Curve: Intelligence and Class Structure in American Life* (New York: Free Press, 1994).

52. Samuel George Morton, *Crania Americana, or, A Comparative View of the Skulls of Various Aboriginal Nations of North and South America to Which is Prefixed an Essay on the Varieties of the Human Species* (Philadelphia: John Pennington, 1839).

53. Reginald Horsman, *Race and Manifest Destiny: The Origins of Racial Anglo-Saxonism* (Cambridge: Harvard University Press, 1981).

54. Seymour Drescher, "The Ending of the Slave Trade and the Evolution of European Scientific Racism," in Joseph E. Inikori and Stanley L. Engerman, eds., *The Atlantic Slave Trade: Effects on Economies, Societies, and Peoples in Africa, the Americas, and Europe* (Durham, NC: Duke University Press, 1992).

55. Magnus Mörner, *Race Mixture in the History of Latin America* (Boston: Little, Brown, 1967), 58; Nicolás Sánchez-Alboronoz, *The Population of Latin America: A History* (Berkeley: University of California Press, 1974), 129–30.

56. John Codman Hurd, *The Law of Freedom and Bondage in the United States* (New York: Negro Universities Press, 1968).

57. Robert A. Williams, Jr., *The American Indian in Western Legal Thought: The Discourses of Conquest* (New York: Oxford University Press, 1990).

58. See my *A Little Matter of Genocide: Holocaust and Denial in the Americas* (San Francisco: City Lights, 1997).

59. See, e.g., chapters 7 and 8 in Forbes, *Africans and Native Americans*, op. cit.

60. George M. Frederickson, *White Supremacy: A Comparative Study in American and South African History* (New York: Oxford University Press, 1981); Joel Williamson, *The New People: Miscegenation and Mulattoes in the United States* (New York: Free Press, 1980).

61. Julie Schimmel, "Inventing the Indian" in William H. Truettner, ed., *The West as America: Reinterpreting Images of the Frontier, 1820–1920* (Washington, D.C.: Smithsonian Institution Press, 1991), 174.

62. Stannard, *American Holocaust*, op. cit., 120.

63. Horsman, *Race and Manifest Destiny*, op. cit., 108.

64. Lewis Hanke, *Aristotle and the Indians: A Study in Race Prejudice in the Modern World* (Chicago: Henry Regnery, 1959).

65. Robert F. Berkhofer, Jr., *The White Man's Indian: Images of the American Indian from Columbus to the Present* (New York: Vintage, 1979), 58–59.

66. R. W. Haskins, *History and Progress of Phrenology* (Buffalo, NY: n.p., 1839), 110–11.

67. Robert E. Beider, *Science Encounters the Indian, 1820–1880: The Early Years of American Ethnology* (Norman: University of Oklahoma Press, 1986), 220.

68. Morgan has generally been cast as a "progressive," given that Karl Marx and Friedrich Engels were heavily influenced by his *League of the Ho-de-no-sau-nee or Iroquois* (New York: Dodd Meade, 1851) while preparing their book, *The Origins of the Family, Private Property and the State* (1884), included in Marx and Engels: *Selected Writings*, Vol. 3 (Moscow: Foreign Language Publishers, 1973); William S. Willis, "Divide and Rule: Red, White and Black in the Southeast," *Journal of Negro History* 48 (1963).

69. Francis Paul Prucha, *Americanizing the American Indian: Writings of the "Friends of the Indian," 1800–1900* (Lincoln: University of Nebraska Press, 1973).

70. Edmund Schwarz, *History of the Moravian Missions among the Southern Indian Tribes of the United States* (Bethlehem, PA: Times Publishing, 1923).

71. William G. McLoughlin, *Cherokees and Missionaries, 1789–1839* (New Haven: Yale University Press, 1984), 26.

72. W. G. McLoughlin and Walter H. Conser, Jr., "The Cherokees in Transition," *Journal of American History* 64:3 (1977).

73. See, e.g., Berkhofer, *Salvation and the Savage*, op. cit..

74. Vine Deloria, Jr., "Sovereignty," in Roxanne Dunbar Ortiz and Larry Emerson, eds., *Economic Development in American Indian Reservations* (Albuquerque: Native American Studies Center, University of New Mexico, 1979).

75. 7 Stat. 160; proc. Jan. 4, 1819; text in Kappler, *Indian Treaties*, op. cit., 145–52. The other indigenous peoples were the Seneca, Lenni Lenape (Delaware), Shawnee, Potawatomi, Ottawa, and Chippewa.

76. There are fifty-three such instances in the incomplete compilation of 371 ratified treaty texts assembled by Kappler. There may, of course, be other examples among the dozen or so uncompiled instruments. More than four hundred additional treaties went unratified for one reason or another. The pattern evident in the ratified instruments is doubtless reflected in these as well; conversation with Vine Deloria, Jr., April 1993.

77. 9 Stat. 904, proc. Apr. 3, 1848; Kappler, *Indian Treaties*, op. cit., 567–68. Other examples include 1866 treaties with the Seminole (14 Stat. 755, proclaimed Aug. 16, 1866; ibid., 910–15), Choctaw and Chickasaw (14 Stat. 769, proc. July 10, 1866; ibid., 918–31); Creek (14 Stat. 785, proc. Aug. 11, 1866; ibid., 931–37) and Cherokee (14 Stat. 799, proc. Aug. 11, 1866; ibid. 942–50).

78. 7 Stat. 160.

79. 7 Stat. 189, proc. Jan. 15, 1819; ibid., 171–74.

80. 10 Stat. 1172, proc. Mar. 3, 1855; ibid., 690–93.

81. Under Article 2d, $300,000 was placed in trust as compensation to the people as a whole for a land cession, while an additional $110,000 was allocated for payment to individual mixed-bloods of "one-quarter or more degree"; 7 Stat. 538, proc. June 15, 1838; ibid., 493–94.

82. Article 2 provides that each Indian will be assigned an individual forty-acre plot, while a "P.S.," added by the Senate post hoc, provides that two mixed-bloods, George Bent and Jack Smith, would be allotted 640 acres apiece; 12 Stat. 1163, proc. Dec. 5, 1861; ibid., 807–11.

83. Under Article 9, individually titled parcels are set aside for mixed-bloods wishing to live apart from their people; 11 Stat. 729, proc. Mar. 31, 1858; ibid., 764–67.

84. Article XIII sets aside 640 acres for Joseph Parks, described as being of "one-quarter blood"; 7 Stat. 355, proc. Apr. 6, 1832; ibid., 331–34.

85. See, e.g., the 1863 Treaty with the Red Lake and Pembina Bands of Chippewa (note 78, above).

86. This was accomplished by attachment of a rider to the annual Appropriations Act (ch. 120, 16 Stat. 544, 566, now codified as 25 U.S.C. 71).

87. Elsie M. Rushmore, *The Indian Policy During Grant's Administration* (New York: Marion Press, 1914).

88. Ch. 341, 24 Stat. 362, 385, now codified as 18 U.S.C. 1153; also known as the Seven Major Crimes Act.

89. Ch. 119, 24 Stat. 388, now codified as amended at 25 U.S.C. 331 et seq., also known as the Dawes Act or Dawes Severalty Act, in honor of Massachusetts Senator Henry M. Dawes, its prime sponsor and supposed "Friend of the Indian"; D. S. Otis, *The Dawes Act and the Allotment of Indian Land* (Norman: University of Oklahoma Press, 1973).

90. Kirk Kickingbird and Karen Ducheneaux, *One Hundred Million Acres* (New York: Macmillan, 1973); Janet A. McDonnell, *The Dispossession of the American Indian, 1887–1934* (Bloomington: Indian University Press, 1991).

91. Charles C. Royce, *The Cherokee Nation of Indians, A Narrative of their Official Relations with the Colonial and U.S. Governments* (Washington, DC: Bureau of American Ethnology, Smithsonian Institution, 1887).

92. While blood quantum was seldom mentioned directly in treaty language—"half-breed" being a standard American colloquialism by which to describe persons of obvious Indian-white admixture regardless of actual proportion—U.S. treaty commissioners and Indian agents habitually employed a quarter-blood minimum standard in compiling their lists of mixed-bloods scheduled to receive land titles, monetary awards, etc. Persons of less than one-quarter Indian blood were thus legally construed as being non-Indian by the United States, even though they were often considered full members of Native societies and discriminated against as non-whites by Euro-Americans.

93. Emmett Starr, *A History of the Cherokee Indians* (Oklahoma City: Warden, 1922).

94. Conversation with Jack D. Forbes, April 1993 (notes on file).

95. U.S. Bureau of the Census, "Table 2: Indian Population by Divisions and States, 1890–1930," *Fifteenth Census of the United States, 1930: The Indian Population of the United States and Alaska* (Washington, DC: U.S. Government Printing Office, 1937), 3.

96. Vine Deloria, Jr., and Clifford M. Lytle, *American Indians, American Justice* (Austin: University of Texas Press, 1983), 10.

97. Mixed-bloods also tended to be allotted better properties—e.g., riverfront parcels—than were those enrolled as full-bloods.

98. William E. Unrau, *Mixed Bloods and Tribal Dissolution: Charles Curtis and the Quest for Indian Identity* (Lawrence: University Press of Kansas, 1989).

99. Francis E. Leupp, *The Indian and His Problem* (New York: Scribner's, 1910), 93.

100. Turn-of-the-century literature is replete with such references. See, e.g., "An Interesting Representative of a Vanishing Race," *Arena* (July 1896); Simon Pokagon, "The Future of the Red Man," *Forum* (Aug. 1897).

101. Robert Land, "Henrico and Its College," *William and Mary Quarterly* XXIV (1938).

102. David Wallace Adams, *Education for Extinction: American Indians and the Boarding School Experience, 1875–1928* (Lawrence: University Press of Kansas, 1995), 26–27.

103. Frederick J. Stefon, "Richard Henry Pratt and His Indians," *Journal of Ethnic Studies* 15 (1987).

104. Richard Henry Pratt, "The Advantage of Mingling Indians with Whites," speech delivered to the National Conference on Charities and Corrections, 1892, repeated in Pratt's *Battlefield and Classroom: Four Decades with the American Indian, 1867–1904* (New Haven, CT: Yale University Press, 1964 reprint of 1905 original).

105. Adams, *Education for Extinction*, op. cit.; Sally J. McBride, *Ethnic Identity and the Boarding School Experience of West-Central Oklahoma American Indians* (Washington, DC: University Press of America, 1983).

106. *Annual Report of the Commissioner of Indian Affairs, 1890* (Washington, D.C.: U.S. Government Printing Office, 1890), cxlvi.

107. *Annual Report of the Indian Commissioner* (Washington, DC: U.S. Government Printing Office, 1892), 617.

108. Hamlin Garland, "The Red Man's Present Needs," *North American Review* 174 (1902).

109. *The Statutes at Large of the United States of America*, Vol. 26, 1014.

110. Lawrence F. Schmeickebeir, *The Office of Indian Affairs* (Baltimore: Johns Hopkins University Press, 1927), 216.

111. Evelyn C. Adams, *American Indian Education: Government Schools and Economic Progress* (New York: King's Crown Press, 1946).

112. The Indian Citizenship Act of 1924, ch. 233, 43 Stat. 25.

113. Ronald L. Trosper, "Appendix I: Indian Minerals," in American Indian Policy Review Commission, *Task Force 7 Final Report: Reservation Resource Development and Protection* (Washington, DC: U.S. Government Printing Office, 1977).

114. Lewis Meriam, et al., *The Indian Problem: Resolution of the Committee of One Hundred by the Secretary of the Interior and Review of the Indian Problem* (Washington, DC: U.S. Government Printing Office, 1925); *The Problem of Indian Administration* (Baltimore: Johns Hopkins University Press, 1928).

115. Ch. 576, 48 Stat. 948, now codified at 25 U.S.C. 461–279; also known as the Wheeler-Howard Act after its main congressional sponsors, Senator Burton K. Wheeler and Representative Edgar Howard.

116. Rupert Costo, "Federal Indian Policy, 1933–1945," in Kenneth R. Philp, ed., *Indian Self-Rule: First-Hand Accounts of Indian-White Relations from Roosevelt to Reagan* (Salt Lake City: Howe Bros., 1986).

117. Kenneth R. Philp, "The Indian Reorganization Act Fifty Years Later, " in his *Indian Self-Rule*, op.cit.

118. Thornton, *American Indian Holocaust and Survival*, op. cit., 190-200.

119. Oliver LaFarge, *Running Narrative of the Organization of the Hopi Tribe of Indians*, unpublished manuscript (the LaFarge Collection, University of Texas at Austin).

120. Editors, B.I.A., *I'm Not Your Indian Any More: The Trail of Broken Treaties*, 3rd ed. (Mohawk Nation via Rooseveltown, NY: Akwesasne Notes, 1976), 76.

121. B.I.A., *I'm Not Your Indian Any More*, op. cit., 31–32.

122. U.S. Senate, Select Committee on Indian Affairs, *Final Report and Legislative Recommendations: A Report of the Special Committee on Investigations* (Washington, DC: 101st Cong., 2d Sess., U.S. Government Printing Office, 1989).

123. Ward Shepard, "Land Problems of an Expanding Population," and Allan G. Harper, "Salvaging the Wreckage of Indian Land Allotment," both in Oliver LaFarge, ed., *The Changing Indian* (Norman: University of Oklahoma Press, 1943).

124. Wilcomb Washburn, *Red Man's Land, White Man's Law*, 2d ed. (Norman: University of Oklahoma Press, 1994), 150–51.

125. There were 343,410 "official" Indians in the United States in 1950, up from less than 250,000 fifty years earlier; U.S. Bureau of the Census, "Part 1: United States Summary," *Census of 1950, Vol. 2: Characteristics of the Population* (Washington, DC: U.S. Government Printing Office, 1953).

126. Indian Claims Commission, *Final Report* (Washington, DC: U.S. Government Printing Office, 1978); Russell Barsh, "Indian Land Claims Policy in the United States," *North Dakota Law Review* 58 (1982)

127. Donald L. Fixico, *Termination and Relocation: Federal Indian Policy, 1945–1960* (Albuquerque: University of New Mexico Press, 1986).

128. Thornton, *American Indian Holocaust and Survival*, op. cit., 227; U.S. Bureau of the Census, *1990 Census of the Population, Preliminary Report* (Washington, DC: U.S. Government Printing Office, 1991).

129. The complete text appears in Part II of Edward H. Spicer's *A Short History of the Indians of the United States* (New York: Van Nostrand Rinehold, 1969).

130. Fixico, *Termination and Relocation*, op. cit. Also see Larry W. Burt, *Tribalism in Crisis: Federal Indian Policy, 1953–1961* (Albuquerque: University of New Mexico Press, 1982).

131. Nicholas Peroff, *Menominee DRUMS: Tribal Termination and Restoration, 1954–1974* (Norman: University of Oklahoma Press, 1982).

132. Cheryl McCall, "Life at Pine Ridge Bleak," *Colorado Daily* (May 16, 1975).

133. Thornton, *American Indian Holocaust and Survival*, op. cit., 197–98.

134. C. Matthew Snipp, Appendix 1 of his *American Indians: The First of This Land* (New York: Russell Sage Foundation, 1989).

135. Robert Burnette, *The Tortured Americans* (Englewood Cliffs, NJ: Prentice-Hall, 1971).

136. At a meeting with members of the Abnaki National Council in 1991, it was explained to me that, in their view, the question of federal recognition put things exactly backwards. "The question is not whether we are recognized by the federal government," as one elder put it, "but whether we recognize it. After all, we Abnakis, not the United States or the State of Vermont, were the first people here. Unless they can show us a treaty in which our ancestors recognized their right to land which unquestionably belonged to the Abnaki—which they can't—then it's still our land by law. Our law, their law, international law, it all comes out the same on this point."

137. Tillie Blackbear Walker, "American Indian Children: Foster Care and Adoption," in U.S. Department of Education, Office of Educational Research and Development, National Institute of Education, *Conference on Educational and Occupational Needs of American Indian Women, October 1976* (Washington, DC: U.S. Government Printing Office, 1980).

138. In 1993, I had the misfortune to attend a so-called Workshop on Identity put on by an entity calling itself the American Indian Advocacy Group at my home institution, the University of Colorado at Boulder. At no point was there discussion of such traditional concepts as lineage and genealogy, naturalization, and loyalty to the people.

139. The only reasonable conclusion I can draw from my experience is that the question of my identity was never really at issue. Rather, it was raised quite cynically, for purposes of grinding other axes entirely.

140. Patricia Penn Hilden, *When Nickels Were Indians: An Urban Mixed-Blood Story* (Washington,DC: Smithsonian Institution Press, 1995).

141. Public Law 101-644, enacted Nov. 29, 1990; Herman J. Viola, *Ben Nighthorse Campbell: An American Warrior* (New York: Orion Books, 1993).

142. Gail K. Sheffield, *The Arbitrary Indian: The Indian Arts and Crafts Act of 1990* (Norman: University of Oklahoma Press, 1997).

143. James J. Kilpatrick, "Government Playing the Indian Game," syndicated column ©1992, distributed by the Thomas Jefferson Center, Charlottesville, VA. On Harjo's role as a "prime mover" behind the act, see Jonathan Tilove, "Who's an Indian Artist?" Newhouse News Service (Mar. 25, 1993). On Harjo's stated desire to expand the act, see Sheffield, *The Arbitrary Indian*, op. cit., 52.

144. See, e.g., the 1993 series by Jerry Reynolds in *Indian Country Today* entitled "Indian Writers: The Good, the Bad, and the Could Be."

145. Faith Attaguile, *Why Do You Think We Call It Struggle? The Bellecourt Brothers' Smear Campaign Against Ward Churchill* (Littleton, CO: Aigis, forthcoming).

146. Marc Hillel and Clarissa Henry, *Of Pure Blood: Hitler's Secret Program to Breed the "Master Race"* (New York: McGraw-Hill, 1976).

147. Thornton, *American Indian Holocaust and Survival*, op. cit., 174–75.

148. U.S. Department of Health, Education and Welfare, *A Study of Selected Socio-Economic Characteristics of Ethnic Minorities Based on the 1970 Census, Vol. 3: American Indians* (Washington,DC: U.S. Government Printing Office, 1974), 74, 78.

149. Lenore Stiffarm and Phil Lane, Jr., "The Demography of Native North America: A Question of American Indian Survival," in M. Annette Jaimes, ed., *The State of Native America: Genocide, Colonization and Resistance* (Boston: South End Press, 1992), 45.

150. U.S. Congress, Office of Technology Assessment, *Indian Health Care* (Washington, DC: U.S. Government Printing Office, 1986), 78.

151. Some tribal councils have increased quantum requirements to one-half; Thornton, *American Indian Holocaust and Survival*, op. cit.

152. Patricia Nelson Limerick, *The Legacy of Conquest: The Unbroken Past of the American West* (New York: W. W. Norton, 1987), 338.

153. During the early 1990s, the Umatilla tribal council commissioned University of Colorado anthropologist Deward E. Walker to conduct a study of what would happen if it simply adhered to its present quarter-blood Umatilla requirement for enrollment. The prognosis was that, given the present rate of "outmarriage," there would be virtually no one enrollable as a Umatilla by some point around 2050. It was then that discussion of constitutional revisions began in earnest; conversation with Deward E. Walker, April 1997 (notes on file).

154. Jack D. Forbes, "Undercounting Native Americans: The 1980 Census and Manipulation of Racial Identity in the United States," *Wicazo Sa Review* VI:1 (1980): 23. The census bureau itself inadvertently confirms the thrust of the argument, explaining that it construes the racial category "white" to include "all persons reporting Spanish origin. About 97 percent of persons of Spanish origin, about 99 percent of persons of Mexican origin, and 96 persons of Puerto Rican origin were classified white in the 1970 census; U.S. Bureau of the Census, *Selected Characteristics of Persons and Families of Mexican, Puerto Rican and Other Spanish Origin: March 1971* (Washington, DC: U.S. Government Printing Office, 1971), 15. That only 3,678 Mexican immigrants should have been classified as Indians in 1970—coming as they do from a population deriving overwhelmingly from indigenous gene stocks (Mörner, Race Mixture, op. cit.)—should speak for itself. Similarly, that only 1.9 percent (15,988 people) of the several million strong Mexican-American population should be so categorized is a travesty; U.S. Bureau of the Census, *Current Population Report: Characteristics of the Population by Ethnic Origin, November 1979* (Washington, DC: U.S. Government Printing Office, 1979).

155. Forbes, "Undercounting Native Americans," op. cit.; U.S. Bureau of the Census, *Ancestry of the Population by State, 1980* (Washington, DC: U.S. Government Printing Office, 1983), 3.

156. For the official count, see U.S. Bureau of the Population, *General Characteristics of the Population, 1990* (Washington, DC: U.S. Government Printing Office, 1991), 9. A good in-depth discussion of such demographic trends will be found in Joane Nagel's *American Indian Ethnic Renewal: Red Power and the Resurgence of Identity and Culture* (New York: Oxford University Press, 1996).

157. Even this instrument fails to go the whole distance, making no provision for naturalization by marriage, adoption, or petition. Moreover, since it takes as its point of departure the Dawes Rolls, it explicitly excludes the descendants of Cherokee resisters who refused to move to Oklahoma from Arkansas, Missouri, Kansas, and Texas at the outset of the twentieth century. Still, the present CNO constitution accords much more closely with actual indigenous tradition than any other presently in existence. The constitution of my own Keetoowah Band follows not far behind, providing for enrollment based upon genealogy to anyone who can document it, but restricting voting, the holding of office, and receipt of benefits to those of one-quarter or greater blood quantum. The band also makes provision for "Honorary Members" who demonstrate no genealogical connection, but who provide service or display loyalty to the group; Georgia Rae Leeds, *The United Keetoowah Band of Cherokee Indians in Oklahoma* (New York: Peter Lang, 1996), 215–16.

158. U.S. Bureau of the Census, *1980 Census of the Population, Vol. II, Subject Reports: American Indians, Eskimos and Inuits on Identified Reservations and in Historic Use Areas of Oklahoma (excluding Urbanized Areas)* (Washington, DC: U.S. Government Printing Office, 1985), 99.

159. 30 Stat. 495; named in recognition of Charles Curtis, the mixed-blood Kaw who became vice president of the United States; Unrau, *Mixed Bloods and Tribal Dissolution*, op. cit.

160. Thornton, *American Indian Holocaust and Survival*, op. cit., 200.

161. Indeed, there are already those such as New York attorney Allan van Gestel, who have begun arguing on this basis that American Indians are and have always been "legal fictions" created by the U.S. government for its own purposes. Having outlived its usefulness, he says, the "Indian myth" should now be abolished "in fairness to the country's non-Indian citizens"; see, e.g., his "When Fictions Take Hostages," in James A. Clifton, ed., *The Invented Indian: Cultural Fictions and Government Policies* (New Brunswick, NJ: Transaction, 1990). Van Gestel's cant, which has been widely applauded, finds echoes in many quarters; see, e.g., Fergus M. Bordewich, *Killing the White Man's Indian: Reinventing Native Americans at the End of the Twentieth Century* (New York: Doubleday, 1996).

PART II

GENDER

Through the lenses of Euro-American patriarchy and the modern U. S. feminist movement—each with its own political agenda—understandings of Native gender relations have often been subject to an evolving string of misinterpretations. In many preconquest Native American cultures, women played very important and often powerful social, economic, and political roles. The specific rights of women varied from Nation to Nation and were dependent on the spiritual teachings and laws of the tribe. Since most Native North American communities were matrilineal, descent was reckoned through the mothers' family or clan. Women generally had strong influence over clan relatives, uncles, cousins, and nephews. Many tribes also had three, four, or more gender categories, and individuals who assumed social roles associated with the physical opposite of their gender were frequently considered to have special spiritual tasks. In contemporary language, such people are called not-men, not-women, and Two Spirit people. Since the late 1800s and the rise of Christian values within Indian communities, these kinds of spiritual gender roles have fallen into discredit, except among some traditional people.

Relations with Europeans during the colonial period also led to the devaluation of women as traders and political leaders. Europeans tended to avoid women in trade and government and preferred to work with young men who they presumed to be capable of fighting in wars and providing items for trade. Europeans recognized males as political leaders and pushed women into the background in many formal political encounters with the colonists. In many communities, however, women remained owners of houses, crops, and other property. Since the 1880s, several federal allotment acts divided tribal lands and gave conditions, which further weakened women's economic and political power within Indian communities. Nevertheless, many tribes retain traditions of strong female economic and political leadership. Increasingly, since the 1960s and with the emergence of the Self Determination Policy, women serve not only as family and clan leaders, but also in tribal councils, as tribal chairpersons, and as leaders of national Indian organizations.

Two Spirit people have gathered in urban areas and attempted to form alliances with U.S. gay and lesbian communities. Native Americans, however, were not well received within the gay and lesbian communities because of racism and cultural difference, and many have returned to their home communities to regain the spiritual dimensions that are part of their heritage. Native women have had similarly negative experiences with some feminist organization and communities.

Contemporary Native women are actively participating in their communities as bearers of traditional culture and also as political leaders and supporters of community and family relations. Increasingly, women assume spiritual roles that in recent history were primarily reserved for men. Women participate in sun dances and assume more open roles as healers and spiritual leaders. The chapters in this section examine gender in cultural, spiritual, legal, and political realms. They both outline general conditions and provide specific examples of gender relations and ways in which women assert roles for themselves in contemporary Native communities.

3

Aboriginal Women and Self-Government: Challenging Leviathan

Katherine Beaty Chiste

 CANADA'S LATEST ATTEMPT at constitutional reform, the 1992 Charlottetown Accord process, saw aboriginal peoples involved in a high-profile debate. Representatives of four national aboriginal organizations were invited to participate in the first ministers' conferences as the prime minister, the premiers, and the territorial leaders attempted to thrash out a constitutional package that would satisfy the province of Quebec. In the end, aboriginal leaders and first ministers reached agreement on constitutional amendments that would have, among other things, recognized aboriginal governments as an undefined "third order of government" within the Canadian state. The Canadian electorate, however, rejected the package in an October 1992 referendum. Aboriginal communities that were enumerated separately (Indian reserves) likewise rejected the deal their national leadership had enthusiastically endorsed; moreover, the most prominent organization for aboriginal women was a key player on the "no" side of the debate. One of the important consequences of the Charlottetown process, therefore, became the advertisement to the general public of the numerous divisions within the Canadian aboriginal community. One of the most difficult questions for outside policymakers, partners, and other interested parties is how to respond to this factionalism.

THE CHARLOTTETOWN ACCORD

Among the notable provisions of the Charlottetown Accord was its series of proposals on aboriginal self-government. The accord would have amended the constitution to recognize aboriginal peoples' "inherent right to self-government within Canada." After vigorous debate about the trustworthiness of leaders, the accord also provided that aboriginal governments would be bound by the Charter of Rights and Freedoms, albeit with access to the "notwithstanding" clause.[1] The former proposition—recognition of inherence—represented a major policy

Katherine Beaty Chiste is a faculty member with the Aboriginal Management Program at the University of Lethbridge, Alberta, Canada.

shift by provincial and federal governments. The latter proposition—access to the "notwithstanding" clause—was a concession to the argument that the liberal, individualistic values of the charter are inappropriate for aboriginal governments. The recognition that these and other clauses of the accord would have given to aboriginal peoples and governments might have been expected to receive a warm welcome in aboriginal communities. But when it came to a vote, two-thirds of Indians voting on reserve (the only aboriginal group tallied separately) rejected the Charlottetown Accord.[2] Moreover, during the debate over the accord, various segments of the aboriginal community publicly dissented from their leadership's endorsement of the deal.

The leaders of all the aboriginal groups involved in negotiation of the accord—the Assembly of First Nations (AFN), the Native Council of Canada (NCC),[3] the Métis National Council (MNC), and the Inuit Tapirisat of Canada (ITC)[4]—supported the final text. Yet their grassroots constituencies by and large rejected the leaders' position, albeit for varying reasons. The points of contention were many. Some argued that treaty rights would be undermined by the new constitutional arrangement. Some felt that the proposals on self-government did not go far enough toward recognition of aboriginal governmental authority. Other critics took the opposite tack and questioned whether aboriginal communities are "ready" for self-government. Poignant testimony in front of the AFN's "Constitutional Circle" hearings expressed the fears of unfettered leadership. Aboriginal women were particularly vocal in this regard, to the extent of initiating a court challenge to the Charlottetown process itself.

The Native Women's Association of Canada (NWAC) spearheaded the challenge. First, they publicly opposed the AFN's position that aboriginal governments should be shielded from the charter and claimed that the accord did not contain enough protection for the rights of aboriginal women. NWAC argued that the gender equality guarantee of section 15 is a universal human right that must be respected by aboriginal governments. Without that guarantee, aboriginal women could continue to face gender discrimination from male-dominated band councils and would have little protection against violence and oppression in their communities.

Second, NWAC challenged the AFN's legitimacy as a representative of aboriginal women. Claiming that the AFN does not speak for their constituency, NWAC launched a suit in the Federal Court of Canada to achieve participant status in the constitutional negotiations. Their argument was that by funding the four "male-dominated" organizations but not the women's group, the federal government was acting in a discriminatory manner. Although the court agreed with the NWAC position, the case has been appealed to the Supreme Court.

The roots of the confrontation between the NWAC and the AFN lie in the past and what the NWAC leaders conceive to be the AFN's opposition to their efforts to end sexual discrimination against Indian women via Bill C-31, enacted in Parliament in 1985. Bill C-31, mandated by the equality provision of the charter, provided, among other things, for the restoration of Indian status and band membership to persons who had lost them because of provisions in the Indian Act; these persons quite often were women who had lost Indian status by marrying non-Indians. The AFN opposed the bill as an unwarranted intrusion on band government authority, and many communities were less than eager to share scant resources with returning women and their children. The AFN leadership's opposition at that time to Bill C-31 has left a legacy of mistrust on the part of many aboriginal women.

The Native women's association does not, however, speak for all aboriginal women, and some aboriginal women's groups made an effort to distance themselves from NWAC's dispute with the AFN. Métis and Inuit organizations, in particular, portrayed the battle as a problem for Indian women, not Inuit or Métis, and northern groups saw it as a problem for southern women. The divisions that became apparent between different aboriginal women's groups raise a question: Was the opposition of the NWAC to the Charlottetown Accord a gender-based critique, typical of mainstream feminism, about political exclusion, or was it something else?

THE SOURCES OF DISSENT

There are multiple causes of factionalism at any level of aboriginal organization: differences in ideology, religion, and education; varying blood quantum and kinship factors; nonindigenous barriers created by Canadian political history; and disparate commands of economic resources. The factor of gender has been presented as yet another potential fault line for aboriginal communities. But is it a genuine one? Among the divisions that cross-cut aboriginal communities, there is historically a common ground where factors such as gender, poverty, and loss of Indian status coincide and protective kinship networks have broken down. I believe it is this marginalized faction of aboriginal society that is challenging its own entrenched leadership through the voice of aboriginal women, using mainstream institutions and mainstream rhetoric in the process.

In political science, a *faction* is understood as "any group organized for political ends, which defines itself at least partly by its opposition to some rival group."[5] Factions exist within an organization (such as a community) rather than outside of it and are held together by commonality of purpose rather than rules of membership. Recognition of the destabilizing effect of warring factions in a community was one of the intellectual motivators for theorists such as Hobbes, who prescribed the absolute sovereign Leviathan as an antidote to the human state of nature: "solitary, poor, nasty, brutish, and short."[6]

Leviathan is an appropriate metaphor in the context of Canadian aboriginal politics in two senses. First of all, it is well documented that for more than a century the Department of Indian Affairs acted as an "absolute sovereign" in the lives of aboriginal peoples, failing, however, to alleviate the poverty and brutishness of life with which many were afflicted under its regime. Second, in the discussions over the Charlottetown Accord's provisions for self-government, fears were expressed about the possibility of indigenous "absolute sovereigns" in aboriginal communities, i.e., petty Leviathans unchecked by the Charter of Rights and Freedoms or any other code of ethics, customary or imposed.[7] One way of viewing the quest for aboriginal self-government is as a challenge to overthrow Leviathan, in either an aboriginal or nonaboriginal form.

The political factions for which Leviathan was prescribed as an antidote have been observed in contemporary aboriginal communities, and the "commonality of purpose" that defines a faction in the aboriginal community context has often been observed as the tie of kinship. Despite the diversity of traditional Indian societies, in contemporary times kinship-linked factionalism is a commonly observed political phenomenon linked to the disruption of traditional political systems and the selective poverty within aboriginal communities.[8]

Many traditional tribal societies have dealt with their environment and ensured their survival by organizing themselves along clan and kinship lines. As Huff describes it,

> Tribal societies are vulnerable to the exigency of nature, but this is minimized by utilizing the clan system. A clan is a group of families that usually is responsible for some aspect of tribal life. Each clan has allegiance to the tribe and is responsible for some economic, social, or religious function. This diffused responsibility was a kind of broad-based insurance policy that provided for tribal survival.[9]

But where overall commitment to the well-being of the tribe is lacking, this form of social organization may degenerate into factionalism as tribal members are forced to compete against each other for scarce resources. A recent study of tribal political cultures in the American context has found two outstanding characteristics: a politics of scarcity and a politics of interference, "found in differing degrees on reservations throughout the country."[10] As these authors observe, "economic scarcity, coupled with pronounced loyalty on reservations to the social group, influences the political behavior of tribal leaders."[11] The attempt by tribal leaders to pursue overall community goals faces interference from both external interests and internal factions seeking to affect the outcome of their decisions.

The current decision-making structures of most aboriginal communities in Canada are antithetical to most of their political traditions, as Boldt and Long have pointed out at length.[12] Representative governments and the bureaucratic norms of political neutrality do not mesh well with the values of a small kinship-linked community. The suggestion has been made that, rather than try to suppress the natural tendencies of clans to look after their own, aboriginal governments could incorporate kinship networks into their formal political structures,[13] and there are communities that are actively considering this possibility. But traditional tribal structures of clan responsibility rested on a roughly egalitarian division of resources among community members.[14] The question, then, is whether a rough egalitarianism prevails today in Canadian aboriginal communities.

Several recent studies suggest that it does not. In many cases, socioeconomic classes have developed to replace formerly egalitarian structures in aboriginal communities. This process has taken place under the aegis of the Department of Indian Affairs (DIAND), the aging Leviathan in aboriginal life. Boldt, for example, describes contemporary Indian societies as consisting of a "two-class social order":

> A small, virtually closed, élite class comprising influential landowners, politicians, bureaucrats, and a few entrepreneurs, and a large lower class comprising destitute, dependent, and powerless people.[15]

Boldt attributes this development to DIAND's historical policy of recruiting cooperative Indian families to manage its bureaucracy and conferring special privileges on them; this ruling class has now evolved into a socioeconomic elite.[16]

In another recent book, Wotherspoon and Satzewich also make the point that aboriginal peoples in Canada do not constitute a single socioeconomic class. Writing from the standpoint of political economy, these authors reject the stereotypical view that all aboriginal people fall into an underclass of "permanently unemployed and decrepit" people; rather, they are distributed "across the range of class sites within Canada."[17] The factors of gender and sociolegal status of aboriginal individuals further complicate the picture. The labor market experience of aboriginal women, for example, was found to be closer to the experience of nonaboriginal women than to the experience of aboriginal men.[18] Further distinctions can be made between Indian, Inuit, and Métis in the work force. Wotherspoon and Satzewich also identify an aboriginal elite. They describe the aboriginal bourgeoisie as being in its embryonic stage, very small,[19] but "one of the most dynamic sectors of the aboriginal population" and "one that is able to wield a considerable amount of power and influence."[20] The authors also note the hostility towards this new class from other community members:

> Animosities directed to the bourgeoisie and the new and old petite bourgeoisie are reflective of antagonistic class relations; they are not solely an "Indian" phenomenon. Such conflicts within minority communities are not uncommon and reflect a complex intersection of racism, sexism, and class in the shaping of people's lives.[21]

Another way to analyze socioeconomic relationships in contemporary aboriginal communities is described by Elias as "Marcosian" economics, in which political power is exploited by the unscrupulous for their own private gain.[22] Elias's study of northern Canadian aboriginal communities suggests that cultural change has made their economies "ripe for the emergence of 'Marcosian' economies."[23] He observes that "kinship is still a basic organizing principle in Northern economies" and that members of larger households have a number of economic advantages.[24] Traditionally, a community would have contained primarily close relations among whom gifting and sharing was standard.[25] Today, northern communities are not necessarily interrelated but may consist of several kin groups competing for the same employment and education opportunities, and, as Elias observes, "in the setting of large villages, kinship serves to bind families, but divide communities."[26]

Largely uninvestigated, at least in the scholarly sense, is the extent to which the economic elite of a community is itself kinship linked. The results of studies such as the one by Lopach, Brown, and Clow suggest that, under conditions of scarcity, the predominant economic players will indeed look after their own first. Also largely unexplored are the interconnections in aboriginal communities between political and economic power: Is Leviathan rich? And if development of socioeconomic class structures—and the opportunity for Marcosian dominion over resources—is indeed becoming a feature of contemporary aboriginal cultures, where, then, do aboriginal women fit in?

GENDER AND STATUS IN ABORIGINAL COMMUNITIES

Testimony before the current Royal Commission on Aboriginal Peoples[27] and before several provincial inquiries into aboriginal justice issues provide clear evidence of the plight of many aboriginal women. The socioeconomic changes that have served to marginalize many aboriginal men have also wreaked havoc in the lives of aboriginal women, and a couple of generations of the residential school experience have further distorted relationships between the sexes. The voices of aboriginal women are increasingly being heard in Canada, but they carry a message different from that of most other Canadian women. Two features distinguish the politics of many aboriginal women from the politics of mainstream Canadian feminists. First, far from rejecting traditional gender roles in their societies, aboriginal women have repeatedly called for a return to traditional ways and the respect with which they once were held in their communities. Testimony before the ongoing Royal Commission has been particularly eloquent in this regard. Second, the substantive changes sought by aboriginal spokeswomen do not focus on the same areas of life as do mainstream feminist aspirations.

Monture-Okanee has discussed the limitations of feminist analysis in its application to aboriginal peoples, concluding that "many Aboriginal women are aware of [the] basic contradiction between their experience and the constructs of feminist thought."[28] The feminist discourse, albeit a varied one, has directed its energies towards social changes that would enable women to participate fully in economics and politics outside of their homes. Aboriginal women, however, typically are seeking a reconstruction of family ties and obligations rather than their deconstruction. As LaFramboise, Heyle, and Ozer observe, "[N]on-Indian feminists emphasize middle-class themes of independence and androgyny whereas Indian women often see their work in the context of their families, their nations, and Sacred Mother Earth."[29] Moreover, the arguments of aboriginal women's groups lack an adversarial approach to the male gender in general, regardless of socioeconomic class; rather, they focus on the currently empowered aboriginal male elite.

It is common in recent testimonials to hear that the current inequities faced by aboriginal women are due to the distorting effect of European colonialism and its introduction of patriarchal structures—in particular, patriarchal political structures that created an aboriginal male elite.[30] For example, the Manitoba Justice Inquiry (focusing on societies in that province) concluded that "Aboriginal men and women were equal in power and each had autonomy within their personal lives . . . . [W]omen were never considered inferior in Aboriginal society until Europeans arrived."[31] Likewise, the Royal Commission summarized the testimony they had heard:

> Aboriginal women appearing before the Commission noted that, in Aboriginal society, women had historically been treated as equals. Many societies were matriarchal, and women were respected and revered as first educators and life carriers. Although women played a domestic role in gathering food and raising children, they were also warriors and sat at the bargaining table—until these roles were destroyed by outside forces coming from European society.[32]

According to this line of argument, European colonialism brought to North America the tradition of inferior status and diminished legal rights for women; the European insistence on dealing "man-to-man" with aboriginal societies served to lessen the importance of their women. Further, Christian missionaries' promotion of female submissiveness within the nuclear family diminished the ability of extended family networks to protect individual women and their status in the community.

Two recent papers caution about generalizing across North America about traditional gender roles in aboriginal societies or about the effects contact with Europeans had on the status of aboriginal women. Bonvillain looked at gender differences in five traditional aboriginal societies—the Naskapi, the Iroquois, the Plains, the Navajo, and the Inuit—and found egalitarian gender relations in three of the five.[33] Bonvillain defines gender as a social construct underlain and structured by sexual division of labor.[34] She identifies the factors that determine gender role allocation as primary subsistence modes, individual roles within kinship groups, postmarital residence patterns, behavior within households, participation in communitywide activities, and religious belief and practice.[35] Furthermore, Bonvillain observes, all aboriginal societies in North America were affected by colonization:

> These societies experienced differences in the time and circumstances of contact, but colonial policies everywhere affected subsistence, sociopolitical organizations and belief systems. Gender relations were concomitantly disrupted, both through directed attacks upon existing sex role plans and through change in other intra-cultural patterns.[36]

Cooper's analysis of Nishga and Tsimshian women in the nineteenth century focused on changes brought by European fur traders along the coast of British Columbia.[37] She found that the European presence opened up economic opportunities for aboriginal women. While Cooper accepts the argument that in egalitarian aboriginal societies the regime of European traders and missionaries led to a reduction in the status of women, she disputes that this was the case for hierarchically differentiated aboriginal societies such as those in the Pacific Northwest. These women already exerted control over production and distribution of economic resources, and the development of a capitalist economy offered them further opportunities to create and control wealth—through engagement in the fur trading and, eventually, the salmon-canning industries.[38] Moreover, the doctrines of Christianity failed to inculcate submissive behavior in high-ranked women, nor did the nuclear family become the norm.[39] Cooper concludes that women in these societies were able to retain their status "to a large degree because of their continuing economic importance in their communities."[40]

A number of similar studies present varying scenarios for changing gender roles in aboriginal societies upon first and subsequent contact with Europeans.[41] In most cases, a crucial point is the degree to which women's economic contribution to their household and community became marginalized as traditional economies were disrupted and changed. The economic contributions of some men, of course, were likewise decreased, and they also suffered the consequences of powerlessness and marginalization. A call for a return to traditional gender relations is, then, to some extent a call for a return to traditional economic relations in a community and the sociopolitical structures that overlay them. However, as described in the previous section, egalitarian economies do not appear to be typical of most Canadian aboriginal communities today, and the potential is clear for "warring factions" to be forced to squabble over the few economic opportunities available.

CONTEMPORARY GENDER ISSUES

There is little scholarship on contemporary gender relationships in aboriginal communities. Exceptions are LaFramboise, Heyle, and Ozer, and Miller.[42] Miller analyzed the role of women in sixty-two Coast Salish communities of Washington State and British Columbia, as measured by their election to band and tribal councils. He found that in recent years there has been a dramatic increase in the participation of women in the formal structures of Coast Salish politics and that women "do better in smaller tribes, in tribes where there is no disproportionate male income available, and in tribes with a relatively high degree of institutional completeness."[43] But outside of Miller, as LaFramboise, Heyle, and Ozer point out, "there has been scant research on contemporary Indian women outside of a clinical or pathological perspective."[44]

There is, however, quite a lot of public domain testimony beyond mere collection of socioeconomic indicators, much of it brought to light during the various public hearings mentioned earlier. There is a pattern to the public comments of aboriginal women, and what I am interested in is expressions of the "common interest" of women, if they are to be considered a political faction within their community. A few of the concerns intersect the discourse of mainstream feminism; many of them, as I suggested earlier, do not.[45]

The Royal Commission hearings identified family violence and its consequences as the number one concern for aboriginal women who testified before them.[46] Like many mainstream feminists, these women spoke of family violence as a political matter and as one that is of greater urgency than any other political issue for aboriginal communities:

> Our attempts to convince our elected Aboriginal leadership of the need
> to treat the issue of violence against Aboriginal women and children as a
> political concern equal in importance to achieving recognition of our
> inherent rights and govern ourselves was unsuccessful. In fact, we
> believe that self-government is not possible without the resolution of vio-
> lence within Aboriginal communities.[47]

A concern that is parallel to the need to address issues of violence within families is the way in which domestic violence will be addressed. Here, most aboriginal women express different sentiments of justice from those of mainstream or radical feminists; the concern is not punishing but rather healing the abuser in conjunction with the abused. Some also question whether "justice" rather than "harmony" or "healing" is even an appropriate goal.[48] For example, one woman testified before the Royal Commission, "We have to concentrate on the healing of the whole family, not just one individual. In the area of abuse, the victim and the offender, and all of the family members affected by this situation of abuse must be healed."[49] This testimony generally lacks the kind of gender-based antagonism that is occasionally apparent in radical, if not mainstream, feminism.

The family issues addressed by aboriginal women in various public hearings are a different set from those presented by mainstream feminist groups. In the area of reproductive services, for example, little, if any, mention is made of abortion rights. Rather, women express concern about fetal alcohol syndrome, holistic health care, and traditional birthing practices.[50] In the area of child care, rather than pressing for a national day-care program, aboriginal women called for a return to customary adoptions and customary child care, and a rethinking of the practice of placing aboriginal children in nonaboriginal homes.[51]

In the area of economic development, aboriginal women focused on employment opportunities in their communities, which, in many instances, present *sui generis* problems. One concern is the situation of women who were banished from their communities upon marrying non-Indians and who face discrimination and disadvantage in the mainstream work force. Statistics were quoted at one hearing:

Unemployment among off-reserve women was 28 percent, almost triple the national average; the earnings of aboriginal women off reserve were three-quarters of the national average for women; and their families were larger than average.[52]

Another *sui generis* concern is equal access to treaty entitlements and benefits such as education for all aboriginal women in a community; again, the situation is even worse for urban aboriginal women.[53] Overall, this constellation of concerns revolves at a much more modest economic level than do mainstream feminist demands; providing day-care deductions for self-employed lawyers, policing employment equity schemes, or shattering glass ceilings in the corporate world are not part of this dialogue.

Issues of equality likewise have a unique flavor for the primary aboriginal spokeswomen, some of whom have been victims of the inequities wrought upon aboriginal women and children for years by the Indian Act, which denied status and its benefits to women who married non-Indian men. Equality in this context has little to do with gender parity in the dominant society but rather with a more balanced relationship between aboriginal women and men in their own communities. As two Saskatchewan women testifying before the Royal Commission expressed it, "Women as keepers of the culture want to walk beside men in the healing and decision making process, rather than behind or ahead of them."[54]

Mainstream feminism typically approaches politics by calling for gender parity in the electoral processes of municipal, provincial, and federal governments and equal representation in their institutions.[55] The arena of politics in which aboriginal women express a desire for greater involvement is, by and large, not the mainstream one but rather the local governing structures of their communities. Some have been highly critical of the male-dominated chief and council system, expressing the opinion that now is the time to speak out:

> Aboriginal women have been reluctant in the past to challenge the positions taken by the leadership out of the perceived need to present a united front to the outside society that oppresses us equally as Aboriginal peoples. However, it must be understood that Aboriginal women suffer the additional oppression of sexism within our community. Not only are we the victims of violence at the hands of Aboriginal men, our voice as women is not valued in the male-dominated political structures.[56]

In one of the discussion papers prepared for the Royal Commission, Monture-Okanee observes

> The goal that we set for ourselves should be to eliminate the disadvantage that women face because it is more profound. It is the greatest of the challenges that face Aboriginal people. By confronting the disadvantage that women face as both women and as Aboriginal, we will also be confronting the discrimination, disadvantage, oppression and dependency faced by our fathers, uncles, brothers, sons, and husbands. We must also accept that in some circumstances it is no longer the descendants of the

European settlers that oppress us, but it is Aboriginal men in our communities who now fulfill this role.[57]

The political problem is to ensure accountability of the current political leadership, trapped as it is in processes and structures of governance foreign to many Canadian aboriginal cultures. The liberal, individualistic ideals and underlying norms of behavior that are a feature of representative government find little resonance in the aboriginal communities on which they have been imposed. As Long has pointed out, the resulting political culture is marked by frustration, dissatisfaction, and a lack of leadership accountability.[58] The aberrations that have resulted from the absence of effective mechanisms to ensure leadership accountability are increasingly being brought to the attention of the general public, through public hearings and the media. In *Canadian Dimension*, Fontaine-Brightstar writes,

> All too often oppressed people refuse to address conflicts of abuse of power within their ranks in the interest of maintaining solidarity . . . [but] overcoming internal problems is an essential component of the power struggle for justice and equality.[59]

The lawsuit brought by the Native Women's Association of Canada (NWAC) against the federal government is best viewed as an attempt to redress abuses of power within aboriginal communities against both oppressed females and males.

NATIVE WOMEN'S ASSOCIATION OF CANADA v. CANADA

The suit was launched in the Federal Court of Canada during the 1992 debate over the Charlottetown Accord. Of particular concern to the NWAC were the accord's provisions on aboriginal self-government and the application of the Charter of Rights and Freedoms to existing and emerging aboriginal governments. The Assembly of First Nations, representing status Indians on reserve, argued that the charter's liberal, individualistic values conflict with aboriginal political traditions and that aboriginal governments should not be bound by the charter; the Native women's association took exception to this position.[60]

During the Charlottetown negotiations, aboriginal organizations were given an unprecedented opportunity to articulate their demands in both the public and constitutional forums. The four national political organizations—the Assembly of First Nations, the Native Council of Canada, the Métis National Council, and the Inuit Tapirisat of Canada—participated in the public consultation process; in the end, all four became an active part of the "yes" side in the referendum campaign. The split between the NWAC and the other four groups became apparent in January 1992. At a special assembly of the AFN on women's issues, aboriginal women expressed mistrust of their leadership and of male-dominated aboriginal governments, pointing out, in particular, their leaders' unwillingness to accept women and children back into their communities under Bill C-31. In February and March, fears continued to be raised, not only by aboriginal women but also by some aboriginal men who had come into conflict with the chief and council system, about the possibility of unlimited autonomy of aboriginal governments.

As constitutional consultations continued, the debate between the NWAC and the AFN began to focus around the charter. Aboriginal women demonstrated outside of constitutional conferences and called for charter application. "We will not accept a regime of self-government without guarantees of basic human rights," declared Gail Stacey-Moore, then leader of the NWAC.[61] Her organization went to the Federal Court of Canada, claiming that the federal government was discriminating against them by funding the four other organizations for constitutional participation but not the NWAC. Their counsel also argued that aboriginal women's freedom of speech was being infringed on by existing arrangements. The NWAC asked that further disbursement of federal funds be prohibited until the NWAC received equal funding and was provided equal rights to participate in constitutional negotiations over the next two years. The Native Council of Canada, the Métis National Council, and the Inuit Tapirisat all intervened in the case, saying that they represented both men and women;[62] the Assembly of First Nations stayed out of the court battle.

The applicants contended that the proposed distribution of funding enabled some of the other organizations to propagate their position that the charter should not apply to aboriginal governments; the NWAC sought funding to argue that it should. The NWAC argued moreover that the federal government's "exhibited historical preference for the views of male-dominated Aboriginal groups" contravened their freedom of expression rights under the charter s.2(b); violated the guarantee in s.35(4) that aboriginal rights are guaranteed equally to men and women; and violated the charter's sex discrimination provision s.15.[63]

The first decision, handed down 30 March 1992, was unsympathetic to the NWAC. Justice Walsh of the federal court identified the issue before the court as follows:

> The constitutionality of the said unequal distribution of funds as between male dominated Aboriginal groups and groups representing Aboriginal women, and whether this constituted a breach of the Charter of Rights and Freedoms.[64]

Walsh made it clear that "the issue of alleged unequal and unfair treatment of Aboriginal women by Aboriginal men is not a matter to be considered in the present proceedings."[65] Justice Walsh noted, "[I]t is primarily the position of the Assembly of First Nations that they fear" that, while the MNC supported retention of the charter, the ITC was willing to consider it, and the NCC's position was "somewhat more equivocal."[66] Walsh further noted that the ITC contended that the NWAC did not represent Inuit women and that "in their society women are not disadvantaged and do not contend that they are."[67] Walsh rejected the

NWAC argument that, without equal funding and participation, they were being denied their freedom of speech:

> On the facts it is evident that the Native Women's Association of Canada has had and will continue to have many opportunities to express its views . . . . Undoubtedly the more money placed at their disposal the louder their voice could be heard, but it certainly cannot be said that they are being deprived of the right of freedom of speech in contravention of the Charter.[68]

Walsh denied the NWAC application, and the NWAC appealed his decision to the Federal Court of Appeal.

As the Charlottetown consultation process continued, the distance between the NWAC and the AFN widened. In July, the debate again erupted publicly when the women's group sent letters to the premiers and to Constitutional Affairs Minister Joe Clark, repeating their demand for participant status and criticizing the Charlottetown deal for failing to protect aboriginal women. Specifically, they were critical of the proposition to give aboriginal governments access to s.33 of the charter, which would allow them to operate "notwithstanding" a violation of charter rights and freedoms. The Native Council of Canada reported that it had tried to gain support for the NWAC position but lacked the support of the other organizations, and NCC leadership agreed to defer sexual equality issues until later.

The main feminist group in Canada—the National Action Committee on the Status of Women—entered the fray in support of the NWAC, and the NCC and AFN were moved to defend themselves. The Native council was reported to be "stung" by the NWAC attack and denied making any attempt to intimidate NWAC members over their lawsuit. The AFN, for its part, maintained that it had attempted to involve the NWAC in constitutional discussions and accused the organization of reneging on an agreement over the wording of the Charlottetown provisions. Chief Wendy Grant of British Columbia defended the AFN's position and argued that all community members would be protected under the proposed arrangement.

In August, the Federal Court of Appeal ruled in partial favor of the Native women's association on the same day that the first ministers reached agreement on the self-government provisions, thereby rendering the decision—in the short term—moot. Justice Mahoney found that the federal government's actions had "restricted the freedom of expression of Aboriginal women in a manner offensive to ss.2(b) and 28 of the charter."[69] The court found the argument based on s.35 "without merit" and the s.15 guarantee of equality before the law to apply to "individuals and not collectives."[70] However, the appeal court reached the conclusion that the Assembly of First Nations "proved to be adverse in interest to Aboriginal Women."[71] The court found that, by funding the AFN, NCC, MNC, and ITC but excluding the NWAC, the federal government "accorded the advocates of male dominated Aboriginal self-governments a preferred position in the exercise of an expressive activity."[72] In the absence of NWAC participation, aboriginal women's interests were not properly represented:

> Using the norms of Canadian society as a measure, it is in the interests of Aboriginal women that, if and when they become the subjects of Aboriginal self-governments, they continue to enjoy the protections of the Charter, especially the rights and freedoms guaranteed by ss.15 and 28, or by equivalent provisions entrenched in Aboriginal charters. The interests of Aboriginal women were not represented by the Assembly of First Nations which is strongly of the opinion that the Charter should not apply to Aboriginal self-government, nor by the ambivalence of the Native Council of Canada and the Inuit Tapirisat of Canada on this issue.[73]

This decision, in turn, has been appealed to the Supreme Court of Canada.

As Canada moved closer to a decision on the Charlottetown Accord, the various fault lines in the aboriginal community were still on display. Leadership of all the national political associations, including Inuit and Métis women leaders, continued to press for the accord's acceptance. Meanwhile, a host of legal, linguistic, and bureaucratic experts tinkered away in private with draft amendments. A final legal text emerged in early October, with revisions designed specifically to address the concerns of the NWAC. An AFN constitutional adviser, Mary Ellen Turpel, defended the final text:

> It makes it clear that gender equality prevails, and it applies to aboriginal women. They have an extra gender-equality guarantee, beyond what non-aboriginal women have. And it makes it clear that aboriginal and treaty rights will be protected, but certainly not in a way that would undermine the rights of women.[74]

Some aboriginal women's groups came on board in support of the final version, including the Ontario Native Women's Association and the Inuit Women's Association of Canada. The NWAC continued to object, however, not just to the text but also to the process. The group had also initiated a lawsuit in the federal court asking for an injunction to block the 26 October referendum. The argument was that, since the NWAC had been excluded from the Charlottetown negotiations, the referendum would be invalid. The federal court, however, ruled the group's suit a matter of politics rather than law and decided that the referendum would not be a violation of NWAC rights.

The NWAC got the result it wanted when the Canadian electorate rejected the Charlottetown Accord. Status Indians on reserve (the AFN's constituency and the only aboriginal group tallied separately) voted against the Charlottetown Accord by close to a two-thirds margin. But it is open to debate how much the aboriginal rejection of Charlottetown related to the merits of the agreement and how much it resulted from generalized mistrust of the national aboriginal leadership that had supported it or of the local leaders of aboriginal communities. Southern Alberta chiefs, for example, banned polling stations on their reserves, and residents who chose to vote (a small minority) had to vote in nearby nonaboriginal communities. A majority voted no, but many said their vote was a protest against band leadership; local headlines read, "Native Voters Aim at Chiefs" and "Indians Use Accord to Lash Leadership."[75]

THE NWAC AS A "FACTION"

A number of observations can be made about this episode in Canadian aboriginal political history. First, the Native Women's Association of Canada has succeeded in establishing itself as one of the national aboriginal political players, given further legitimacy by the Federal Court of Appeal decision. For example, the group was invited to the annual premiers' meeting in August 1993 along with the AFN, NCC, MNC, and ITC. In the kaleidoscope of aboriginal political representation, there are now five, not four, national organizations. However, these groups all emerged to prominence through the process of constitutional negotiations, and constitutional negotiations appear to be at an indefinite standstill in Canada in the wake of the Charlottetown defeat, while various levels of government concentrate on their fiscal problems. Whether these organizations can maintain their national prominence in the changed political environment remains to be seen.

Second, the NWAC's use of mainstream Canadian institutions, its employment of mainstream feminist rhetoric, and its alliance with mainstream feminists are quite interesting. Nahanee has explored at length NWAC's employment of the "individualistic feminist perspective" in its argument for charter application to aboriginal governments. She rejects as a false dichotomy the notion that the NWAC's struggle represents a fight between individual and collective rights and points out that aboriginal communities themselves are made up of individuals;[76] Monture-Okanee makes a similar argument.[77] Nahanee points to the Universal Declaration of Human Rights and the Canadian Charter of Rights and Freedoms as seminal documents for aboriginal women activists:

> Stripped of equality by patriarchal laws that created "male privilege" as the norm on reserve lands, Indian women have had a tremendous struggle to regain their social position. It was the *Canadian Charter of Rights and Freedoms* that turned around our hopeless struggle.[78]

As to the rights of aboriginal women, Nahanee presents a dichotomy of her own: "What Aboriginal women have shown over the past 18 months is their preparedness to mount a full-scale assault against anyone wishing to deny individual rights and establish totalitarian regimes."[79] She identifies male-dominated aboriginal governments as the potential totalitarians.

It is clear from the evidence that a significant number of Canadian aboriginal communities are not happy with their leadership. If the NWAC is to be considered one representative of this segment, certain questions have to be answered. As defined earlier, a faction is "any group organized for political ends, which defines itself at least partly by its opposition to some rival group."[80] What, then, is the "end" for which this faction of aboriginal society is organized? What is their "commonality of purpose"? Who is the "rival" whose power they seek to displace? Authors such as Nahanee and Monture-Okanee, and testimony at Royal Commission and aboriginal justice hearings, suggest some answers. The "rival" is easy to identify: the currently entrenched elite of aboriginal communities; in the case of Indian communities, the Leviathans of the chief and council system. As Nahanee points out, reorganization of this entrenched power structure will not be universally welcomed: "[T]here will be those—likely many—who will resist . . . because it means some Chiefs will be out of a job, or will have a new and less powerful job."[81]

The "commonality of purpose" is suggested by testimony summarized earlier in this paper: a reconstruction of aboriginal family and community life, which clearly involves both women and men. This reconstruction would include a holistic healing approach to widespread domestic abuse and equitable distribution of community resources and power among community members, including women and their children affected by Bill C-31. To this end, "retraditionalization" and a return to some sort of traditional values has been suggested as one path by which aboriginal communities can reconstruct themselves:

> The extension of traditional care-taking and cultural transmission roles
> to include activities vital to the continuity of Indian communities within
> a predominantly non-Indian society . . . represents a major current
> attempt on the part of Indian women to integrate traditional and con-
> temporary demands.[82]

These authors also observe that retraditionalization efforts by aboriginal women "are often inconsistent with some goals of the current majority-culture women's movement."[83]

As was suggested earlier, a return to traditional domestic and community relations may depend on a return to traditional economic practices—if not in the material sense, at least in the distributional sense. Studies have found that aboriginal women traditionally received the most respect and autonomy in societies that were roughly egalitarian in nature.[84] However, evidence suggests that "rough egalitarianism" is not common in contemporary aboriginal communities,[85] and the material basis that underlay formerly egalitarian structures is missing.

A key indicator of how aboriginal elites will handle calls for a return to traditional values may prove to be the way in which they respond to one of the most disadvantaged segments of Canadian society: those aboriginal persons marginalized by the unfortunate processes that Bill C-31 was intended to redress. A recent survey by *Native Issues Monthly* of "1993 in Review" identifies the issues surrounding Bill C-31 as being of the most importance to aboriginal women. These issues include reacceptance—political, social, and economic—into their communities. It is the aboriginal political elite that influences, if not controls, band membership and the distribution of resources; aboriginal women affected by the bill have testified that the elite has not always been welcoming to them and their families.

In many cases, already impoverished communities are being asked to share their resources even further and are understandably reluctant. But the most prominent case revolving around Bill C-31 involves some relatively wealthy Indian bands in Alberta—including Senator Walter Twinn's Sawridge band—

who have gone to federal court to block the return of reinstated aboriginal people to their reserves on the grounds that only bands themselves can determine band membership. The case has been proceeding amidst controversy about intimidation of witnesses and accusations that the plaintiffs' motivations are base ones.[86] As a summary article in *Native Issues Monthly* observed,

> Instead of dividing native communities and turning their reserves into privileged fortresses, Twinn and others with such enormous resources would do much better if they focused their effort on pressuring the government to properly resource the influx of C-31 natives.[87]

The famous simile of Felix Cohen comparing American Indians to the miner's canary, signaling shifts from fresh air to poison gas in the political atmosphere, might also be applied to aboriginal women and their families now seeking a return to their communities.[88] The testimony of aboriginal women suggests that neither the massive Leviathan of Indian Affairs nor the petty Leviathans of the chief and council system have ameliorated the brutishness and poverty of many of their lives. How the aboriginal elite will respond in the future to this marginalized sector of its society will not only reflect on the health of the aboriginal political atmosphere and its leaders; it is also likely to have a strong impact on outside policymakers, partners, and other interested parties.

Acknowledgments

I would like to thank Professors Menno Boldt and J. Anthony Long of the University of Lethbridge for their constructive readings of this paper, as well as the anonymous referees of this journal. I would also like to thank students in the Aboriginal Management Program at the university for their vigorous participation in classroom discussions of gender issues.

Notes

1. Section 33, which permits Parliament or provincial legislatures to enact laws "notwithstanding" a conflict with charter rights or freedoms.

2. *Toronto Star*, 28 October 1992.

3. Now the Council of Aboriginal Peoples.

4. Respectively representing status Indians on reserve, nonstatus and urban Indians, prairie Métis, and the Inuit.

5. Roger Scruton, *A Dictionary of Political Thought* (London: Pan Books, 1983), 164.

6. Thomas Hobbes, *Leviathan: Or the Matter, Forme and Power of a Commonwealth Ecclesiasticall and Civil* (1651; New York: Collier Books, 1962), 100.

7. See, for example, "Women Fear Their Communities Will Be Dictatorships," *Vancouver Sun*, 21 January 1992.

8. See, for example, J. Anthony Long, "Political Revitalization in Canadian Native Indian Societies," *Canadian Journal of Political Science* 23: 4 (1990): 751–73; James J. Lopach, Margery Hunter Brown, and Richmond L. Clow, *Tribal Government Today: Politics on Montana Indian Reservations* (Boulder, CO: Westview Press, 1990); and Robert L. Bee, "The Predicament of the Native American Leader: A Second Look," *Human Organization* 49:1 (1990): 56–63.

9. Delores J. Huff, "The Tribal Ethic, the Protestant Ethic, and American Indian Economic Development," in *American Indian Policy and Cultural Values: Conflict and Accommodation*, ed. J. R. Joe (Los Angeles: UCLA American Indian Studies Center, 1986), 77.

10. Lopach, Brown, and Clow, *Tribal Government Today*, 181.

11. Ibid.

12. Menno Boldt and J. Anthony Long, "Tribal Traditions and European-Western Political Ideologies: The Dilemma of Canada's Native Indians," *Canadian Journal of Political Science* 17:3 (1984): 537–53.

13. Long, "Political Revitalization," 772–73.

14. Huff, "The Tribal Ethic," 77.

15. Menno Boldt, *Surviving as Indians: The Challenge of Self-Government* (Toronto: University of Toronto Press, 1993), 124.

16. Ibid., 120–27.

17. Vic Satzewich and Terry Wotherspoon, *First Nations: Race, Class, and Gender Relations* (Scarborough, ON: Nelson Canada, 1993), 51.

18. Ibid., 60–61.

19. The authors quote a study suggesting that the aboriginal bourgeoisie comprises less than 1 percent of the total aboriginal population.

20. Satzewich and Wotherspoon, *First Nations*, 65.

21. Ibid., 71–72.

22. As in Ferdinand Marcos.

23. Peter Douglas Elias, "A Framework for Understanding Northern Economies" (Unpublished paper, 1993), 8.

24. Ibid., 15–16.

25. Ibid., 16.

26. Ibid., 18.

27. A generously funded national panel conducting a broad inquiry into the economic, social, and political issues affecting the lives of aboriginal peoples. The Royal Commission is scheduled to report and make recommendations to the federal government in the mid-1990s.

28. Patricia A. Monture-Okanee, "Reclaiming Justice: Aboriginal Women and Justice Initiatives in the 1990s," in *Aboriginal Peoples and the Justice System: Report of the National Round Table on Aboriginal Justice Issues* (Ottawa: Ministry of Supply and Services, 1993), 117.

29. Teresa D. LaFramboise, Anneliese M. Heyle, and Emily J. Ozer, "Changing and Diverse Roles of Women in American Indian Cultures," *Sex Roles* 22:7; 8:471.

30. I am indebted to Menno Boldt for emphasizing this point to me.

31. A. C. Hamilton and C. M. Sinclair, *Report of the Aboriginal Justice Inquiry of Manitoba*, vol. 1 (Winnipeg: Queen's Printer, 1991), 476.

32. Royal Commission of Aboriginal Peoples (RCAP), *Overview of the First Round* (Ottawa: Minister of Supply and Services, 1992), 27.

33. Nancy Bonvillain, "Gender Relations in Native North America," *American Indian Culture and Research Journal* 13:2 (1989): 1–28.

34. Ibid., 2.

35. Ibid., 3–4.

36. Ibid., 4.

37. Carol Cooper, "Native Women of the Northern Pacific Coast: An Historical Perspective, 1830–1900," *Journal of Canadian Studies* 27:4 (1992–93): 44–75.

38. Ibid., 45.

39. Ibid., 61–67.

40. Ibid., 70.

41. For example, see Patricia C. Albers, "Autonomy and Dependency in the Lives of Dakota Women: A Study in Historical Change," *Review of Radical Political Economics* 17:3 (1985): 109–34; Paula Gunn Allen, *The Sacred Hoop* (Boston: Beacon Press, 1986); Marlene Brant Castellano, "Women in Huron and Ojibwa Societies," *Canadian Woman Studies* 10:2&3 (1989): 45–48; Mona Etienne and Eleanor Leacock, eds., *Women and Colonization: Anthropological Perspectives* (New York: Praeger, 1980); Kathryn E. Holland, "Guardians of Tradition and Handmaidens to Change: Women's Roles in Creek Economic and Social Life during the Eighteenth Century," *American Indian Quarterly* 14:3 (1990): 239–58; Jennifer S.H. Brown, *Strangers in Blood: Fur Trade Families in Indian Country* (Vancouver, BC: University of British Columbia Press, 1980); Lisa E. Emmerich, "Right in the Midst of My Own Peoples: Native American Women and the Field Matron Program," *American Indian Quarterly* 15:2 (1991): 201–16; Martha Harroun Foster, "Of Baggage and Bondage," *American Indian Culture and Research Journal* 17:2 (1993): 121–52; Clara Sue Kidwell, "Indian Women as Cultural Mediators," *Ethnohistory* 39:2 (1992): 97–107; Verna Kirkness, "Emerging Native Women," *Canadian Journal of Women and the Law* 2:2 (1988–89): 408–15; and Sylvia Van Kirk, *Many Tender Ties: Women in Fur Trade Society, 1670–1870* (Winnipeg, MB: Watson and Dwyer, 1980).

42. La Framboise, Heyle, and Ozer, "Changing and Diverse Roles of Women"; and Bruce G. Miller, "Women and Politics: Comparative Evidence from the Northwest Coast," *Ethnology* 32 (1992): 367–83.

43. Miller, "Women and Politics," 380.

44. LaFramboise, Heyle, and Ozer, "Changing and Diverse Roles of Women," 456.

45. I am necessarily generalizing about feminist thought. For a standard text outlining the different schools, see Rosemarie Tong, *Feminist Thought* (Boulder, CO: Westview Press, 1989).

46. Royal Commission on Aboriginal Peoples, *Discussion Paper 1: Framing the Issues* (Ottawa: Ministry of Supply and Services, 1992), 12.

47. Marilyn Fontaine-Brightstar, "Breaking the Silence," *Canadian Dimension*, (1992), 5–6.

48. Monture-Okanee, "Reclaiming Justice," 121.

49. Royal Commission on Aboriginal Peoples, *Framing the Issues*, 13.

50. Idem, *Overview of the Second Round* (Ottawa: Ministry of Supply and Services,1993), 39.

51. Ibid., 39–40.

52. Royal Commission on Aboriginal Peoples, *Overview of the First Round*, 28.

53. Idem, *Overview of the Second Round*, 38.

54. Idem, *Overview of the First Round*, 28.

55. Janine Brodie with Celia Chandler, "Women and the Electoral Process in Canada," in *Women in Canadian Politics: Toward Equity in Representation*, ed. Kathy Megyerg (Toronto: Dundurn Press, 1991), 3–79.

56. Fontaine-Brightstar, "Breaking the Silence," 6.

57. Monture-Okanee, "Reclaiming Justice," 115.

58. Long, "Political Revitalization in Canadian Native Indian Societies," *Canadian Journal of Political Science* 23:4: 751–73.

59. Fontaine-Brightstar, "Breaking the Silence," 5.

60. The following discussion covers events well-documented in the mainstream Canadian media.

61. *Globe and Mail*, 14 March 1992.

62. They were granted intervener status on the grounds that they "had a real interest, offered a different point of view from the parties involved and because they had a financial interest to protect" (*Native Women's Association of Canada* v. *Canada* [1992], 4 C.N.L.R., 60).

63. *Native Women's Association of Canada* v. *Canada*, 59.

64. Ibid., 60.

65. Ibid., 62.

66. Ibid., 66.

67. Ibid., 63.

68. Ibid., 67.

69. Ibid., 73.

70. Ibid., 72.

71. Ibid., 73.

72. Ibid., 72.

73. Ibid., 72.

74. *Globe and Mail*, 7 October 1992.

75. *Lethbridge Herald*, 27 October 1992.

76. Teressa Nahanee, "Dancing with a Gorilla: Aboriginal Women, Justice and the Charter," in *Aboriginal Peoples and the Justice System: Report of the National Round Table on Aboriginal Justice Issues* (Ottawa: Minister of Supply and Services, 1993), 370.

77. Monture-Okanee, "Reclaiming Justice," 119.

78. Nahanee, "Dancing with a Gorilla," 372.

79. Ibid., 377.

80. Scruton, *Dictionary of Political Thought*, 164.

81. Nahanee, "Dancing with a Gorilla," 374.

82. LaFramboise, Heyle, and Ozer, "Changing and Diverse Roles of Women," 469.

83. Ibid., 471.

84. Bonvillain, "Gender Relations."

85. Boldt, *Surviving as Indians*; Satzewich and Wotherspoon, *First Nations*.

86. *Windspeaker*, 20 December 1993–2 January 1994.

87. *Native Issues Monthly*, December 1993, 10.

88. Felix Cohen, "The Erosion of Indian Rights, 1950–53: A Case Study in Bureaucracy," *Yale Law Journal* 62: 390.

4

The Good Red Road: Journeys of Homecoming in Native Women's Writing

Beth Brant

There are those who think they pay me a compliment in saying that I am just like a white woman. My aim, my joy, my pride is to sing the glories of my own people. Ours is the race that taught the world that avarice veiled by any name is crime. Ours are the people of the blue air and the green woods, and ours the faith that taught men and women to live without greed and die without fear.[1]

 THESE ARE THE WORDS of Emily Pauline Johnson, Mohawk writer and actor. Born of an English mother and Mohawk father, Pauline Johnson began a movement that has proved unstoppable in its momentum—the movement of First Nations women to write down our stories of history, of revolution, of sorrow, of love.

THE SONG MY PADDLE SINGS

August is laughing across the sky
Laughing while paddle, canoe and I
Drift, drift
Where the hills uplift
On either side of the current swift.[2]

This is the familiar poem of Pauline Johnson, the one that school children, white school children were taught. Her love of land made her the poet she was. Yet, in reading Johnson, a non-Native might come away with the impression that she only wrote idyllic sonnets to the glory of nature, the "noble savage," or "vanishing redman" themes that were popular at the turn of the century. It is time to take another look at Pauline Johnson.

Beth Brant is a Bay of Quinte Mohawk from Tyedinaga Mohawk Territory in Ontario, Canada.

The Cattle Thief
How have you paid us for our game?
How paid us for
our land?
By a *book*, to save our souls from the sins *you* brought
in your other hand.
Go back with your new religion, we never have
understood
Your robbing an Indian's *body,* and mocking his *soul*
with food.
Go back with your new religion, and find—if find
you can -
The *honest* man you have ever made from out of a *starving*
man.
You say your cattle are not ours, your meat is not our meat;
When you pay for the land you live in, we'll pay for the meat we eat.[3]

It is also time to recognize Johnson for the revolutionary she was. Publicized as the "Mohawk Princess" on her many tours as a recitalist, she despised the misconceptions non-Natives had about her people. Her anger and the courage to express that anger also made her the poet she was. She was determined to destroy stereotypes that categorized and diminished her people. Breaking out of the Victorian strictures of her day, she drew a map for all women to follow. She had political integrity and spiritual honesty, the true hallmarks of a revolutionary.

The key to understanding Native women's poetry and prose is that we love, unashamedly, our own. Pauline Johnson wrote down that love. Her short stories are filled with Native women who have dignity, pride, anger, strength, and spiritual empowerment.[4]

Pauline Johnson was a nationalist. Canada may attempt to claim her as theirs, but Johnson belonged to only one nation, the Mohawk Nation. She wrote at great length in her poems, stories and articles about this kind of nationalism. She had a great love for Canada, the Canada of oceans, mountains, pine trees, lakes, animals and birds, not the Canada of politicians and racism that attempted to regulate her people's lives.

In 1892, she was writing articles on cultural appropriation, especially critiquing the portrayal of Native women in the fiction of the day. She tore apart popular white writers such as Charles Mair and Helen Hunt Jackson for their depictions of Native women as subservient, foolish in love, suicidal "squaws." Her anger is tempered with humor as she castigates these authors for their unimaginative use of language and for their insistence on naming the Native heroines Winona or a derivative thereof.[5]

Pauline Johnson is a spiritual grandmother to those of us who are women writers of the First Nations. She has been ignored and dismissed by present-day critics and feminists, but this is just another chapter in the long novel of dismissal of Native women's writing.

Pauline Johnson's physical body died in 1913, but her spirit still communicates to us who are Native women writers. She walked the writing path clearing the brush for us to follow. And the road gets wider and clearer each time a Native woman picks up her pen and puts her mark on paper.

I look on Native women's writing as a gift, a give-away of the truest meaning. Our spirit, our sweat, our tears, our laughter, our love, our anger, our bodies are distilled into words that we bead together to make power. Not power *over* anything. Power. Power that speaks to hearts as well as to minds.

Land. Spirit. History, present, future. These are expressed in sensual language. We labor with the English language, so unlike our own. The result of that labor has produced a new kind of writing. I sometimes think that one of the reasons our work is not reviewed or incorporated into literature courses, (besides the obvious racism) is that we go against what has been considered "literature." Our work is considered "too political" and we do not stay in our place—the place that white North America deems acceptable. It is no coincidence that most Native women's work that gets published is done so by the small presses: feminist, leftist, or alternative. These presses are moving outside the mainstream and dominant prescriptions of what constitutes good writing. The key word here is "moving." There is a movement going on that is challenging formerly held beliefs of writing and who does that writing. And it is no coincidence that when our work is taught, it is being done so by women's studies instructors and/or those teachers who are movers and hold beliefs that challenge those of the dominant culture. This is not to say that *all* women's studies are as forward thinking as we would like. At women's studies conferences, the topics of discussion usually center around white, European precepts of theory and literature. I am tired of hearing Virginia Wolfe and Emily Dickinson held up as the matriarchs of feminist and/or women's literature. Wolfe was a racist, Dickinson was a woman of privilege who never left her house, nor had to deal with issues beyond which white dress to wear on a given day. Race and class have yet to be addressed; or if they are discussed, it is on *their* terms, not *ours*.

We are told by the mainstream presses that our work doesn't sell. To quote Chief Sealth: "Who can sell the sky or the wind? Who can sell the land or the Creator?" The few women of color who have broken through this racist system are held up as the spokes people for our races. It is implied that these women are the only ones *good* enough to "make it." These women are marketed as exotic oddities. (After all, we all know that women of color can't write or read, eh?)

Pauline Johnson faced this racism constantly. The Mohawk Princess was considered an anomaly, and I can't say that things have changed all that much. I think of Pauline a lot, especially when I rise to read my stories. For like her, "My aim, my joy, my pride is to sing the glories of my own people."

Because of our long history of oral tradition and our short history of literacy (in the European time frame) the amount of books and written material by Native people is relatively small. Yet, to us, these are precious treasures carefully nurtured by our communities. And the number of Native women who are writing and publishing is growing. Like all growing things, there is a need and desire to ensure the flowering of this growth. You see, these fruits feed our communities. These flowers give us survival tools. I would say that Native women's writing is the Good Medicine that can heal us as a human people. When we hold up the mirror to our lives, we are also reflecting what has been done to us by the culture that lives outside that mirror. It is possible for all of us to learn the way to healing and self-love.

It is so obvious to me that Native women's writing is a generous sharing of our history and our dreams for the future. That generosity is a collective experience. And perhaps this is the major difference between aboriginal writing and that of European-based "literature." We do not write as individuals communing with a muse. We write as members of an ancient, cultural consciousness. Our muse is *us*. Our muse is our ancestors. Our muse is our children, our grandchildren, our partners, our lovers. Our muse is Earth and the stories She holds in the rocks, the trees, the birds, the fish, the animals, the waters. Our words come from the very place of all life, the spirits who swirl around us, teaching us, cajoling us, chastising us, loving us.

The first known novel written by a Native woman was *Cogewea—The Half-Blood*.[6] Written by Hum-Ishu-Ma, Okanagan Nation, in 1927, this novel depicts the difficulties of being called half-breed. Hum-Ishu-Ma concentrates on the relationship the female protagonist has with her Indian grandmother, and how Cogewea does not turn her back on her people, although she is courted and temporarily seduced by the white world. Hum-Ishu-Ma worked as a migrant laborer, carrying her typewriter everywhere with her, snatching moments to write. Again, I am reminded of Pauline Johnson and her Indian women who remain steadfast in their aboriginal beliefs and spiritual connections to their land and people and the desire to make this truth known.

Fifty years later, Maria Campbell wrote her ground-breaking *Half-Breed*,[7] taking up the theme of despair that comes as a result of the imbalance that racism and poverty create in a people. Maria has a grandmother whose words and strength give her nurturance and hope and a way back to the Good Red Road. The Good Red Road is a way of life among Native peoples that is one of balance and continuity. Again, this seems to be the overwhelming message that Native women bring to writing. Creating a balance in their protagonists' worlds, remembering what the Elders taught, recovering from the effects of colonialism. This is not to say that Native women's writings contain "happy" endings or resolutions. In fact, to wrap things up in a tidy package is not following the Good Red Road—it's a falsehood. Perhaps this is what irritates white critics: our work is said to have no plots! If we won't conform, how can these conformist reviewers write reviews? Perhaps the questions should be: why are critics so unimaginative in *their* writing? Why are they so ignorant of what is being written by my sisters? Why is a white, European standard still being held up as the criteria for all writing? Why is racism still so rampant in the arts?

Leslie Marmon Silko published her novel, *Ceremony*,[8] in 1976. In 1992, *Almanac of the Dead*,[9] by the same author, was published. Between those years and after, Paula Gunn Allen, Louise Erdrich, Jeannette Armstrong, Anna Lee Walters, Ella Deloria, Beatrice Culleton, Ruby Slipperjack, Cindy Baskin, Betty Bell, and Linda Hogan also published novels.[10]

In the field of autobiographical works, the number of Native women's books is outstanding. Minnie Freeman, Maria Campbell, Ruby Slipperjack, Alice French, Ignatia Broker, Lee Maracle, Madeline Katt, Florence Davidson, Mary John, Gertrude Bonnin, Verna Johnson, and others[11] tell their stories for all to hear, and we become witness to the truth of Native lives. Throughout these writings, strong female images and personas are evident. The Cheyenne saying "A Nation is not conquered until its women's hearts are on the ground," becomes a prophecy about Native women's writings. First Nations women's hearts are not on the ground. We soar with the birds, and our writing soars with us because it contains the essence of our hearts.

Deep connections with our female Elders and ancestors is another truth that we witness. Grandmothers, mothers, aunties, all abound in our writings. This respect for a female wisdom is manifested in our lives, therefore, in our writings.

Poetry seems to be the choice of telling for many Native women. In our capable hands, poetry is torn from the elitist enclave of intellectuals and white male posturing and returned to the lyrical singing of the drum, the turtle rattle, the continuation of the Good Red Road and the balance of Earth. We write poems of pain and power, of ancient beliefs, of sexual love, of broken treaties, of despoiled beauty. We write with our human souls and voices. We write songs that honor those who came before us and those in our present lives, and those who will carry on the work of our Nations. We write songs that honor the every-day, we write songs to food; we even incorporate recipes into our work. Chrystos, Mary TallMountain, Nora Danhauer, and Mary Moran,[12] are just a few who have written about the joys of fry bread, salmon, corn soup, and whale blubber, then turn around and give instruction for preparing these treats! To me, this is so ineffably Indian. Mouths salivating with the descriptions of our basic foods, readers are then generously offered the gift of how to do this themselves. No wonder the critics have so much trouble with us! How could food possibly be art?! How can art remain for the elite if these Native women are going to be writing recipes in poems? What will the world come to, when food is glorified in the same way as Titian glorified red hair?

There are numerous books of poetry written by Native women.[13] Our poems are being published in forward-thinking journals and magazines, although there are still the literary journals that wish to ghettoize our work into "special" issues, which, if you will notice, happen about every ten years or so. And their editors are usually white and educated in the mainstream constructs of European sensibility.

When I was asked in 1983 to edit a Native women's issue of the feminist journal, *Sinister Wisdom*, I did not expect the earthquake *A Gathering of Spirit* would cause. Eventually, this work became a book, published in 1984, then re-issued by Firebrand Books and by Women's Press in 1989.[14] Perhaps there is a lesson here. When Natives have the opportunities to do *our own* editing and writing, a remarkable thing can happen. This thing is called *telling the truth for ourselves*—a novel idea to be sure and one that is essential to the nurturance of new voices in our communities. I conduct writing workshops with Native women throughout North America, and the overriding desire present in these workshops is to heal. Not just the individual, but the broken circles occurring in our Nations. So, writing does become the Good Medicine that is necessary to our continuation into wholeness. And when we are whole our voices sail into the lake of all human experience. The ripple effect is inevitable, vast and transcendent.

There are women who are writing bilingually. Salli Benedict, Lenore Keeshig-Tobias, Rita Joe, Beatrice Medicine, Anna Lee Walters, Luci Tapahonso, Mary TallMountain, Nia Francisco, Ofelia Zepeda, and Donna Goodleaf[15] are just some of the Native women who are choosing to use their own Nations' languages when English won't suffice or convey the integrity of the meaning. I find this an exciting movement within our movement. And an exciting consequence would be the development of our *own* critics and publishing houses that do bilingual work. Our languages are rich, full of metaphor, nuance, and life. Our languages are not dead or conquered—like women's hearts, they are soaring and spreading the culture to our youth and our unborn.

Pauline Johnson must be smiling. She was fluent in Mohawk, but unable to publish those poems that contained her language. There is a story that on one of her tours, she attempted to do a reading in Mohawk. She was booed off the stage. Keeping her dignity, she reminded members of the audience that she had to learn their language, wouldn't it be polite to hear hers? Needless to say, impoliteness won the day.

From Pauline Johnson to Margaret Sam-Cromarty,[16] Native women write about the land, the land, the land. This land that brought us into existence, this land that houses the bones of our ancestors, this land that was stolen, this land that withers without our love and care. This land that calls us in our dreams and visions, this land that bleeds and cries, this land that runs through our bodies.

From Pauline Johnson to Marie Baker, Native women write with humor. Even in our grief, we find laughter. Laughter at our human failings, laughter with our Tricksters, laughter at the stereotypes presented about us. In her play, *Princess Pocahontas and the Blue Spots*,[17] Monique Mojica, Kuna/Rappahannock, lays bare the lies perpetrated against Native women. And she does it with laughter and anger—a potent combination in the hands of a Native woman. Marie Baker, Anishanabe, has written a play that takes place on the set of an Indian soap opera, "As the Bannock Burns." Baker's characters are few—the Native star of the soap, and the new co-star, a Native woman who gives shaman lessons to wannabes. In the course of the one-act play, the star shows the would-be shaman the error of her ways under the watchful eyes and chorus of a group of women of color. Not only does Baker poke fun at the Greek chorus concept in theater, she turns this European device to her own and our amusement in a caustic but loving way, to bring the would-be shaman to a solid understanding of herself and her own tradition.

Sarah Winnemucca, Suzette La Flesch,[18] and Pauline Johnson also left them laughing as they took their work on the road. To tell a good story, one has to be good actor. I remember my grandad telling me stories when I was little, punctuating the sentences with movement and grand gestures, changing his facial expressions and voice. I think we are likely to witness more Native women writing for the theater. Margo Kane has ventured into that place with her play *Moon Lodge*. Vera Manuel has written *The Spirit in the Circle*, addressing the painful past of residential schools and the painful present of alcoholism and family dysfunction. But she also posits a vision for the future out of these violent truths. Spider Woman's Theater has been writing, producing, and acting in their plays for a number of years. And Muriel Miguel, one of the Spiders, has done a one-woman show incorporating lesbian humor, Native tricksters, and female history. Native women are writing the scripts for their videos and directing and producing these films. How Pauline Johnson would have loved video!

As Native women writers, we have formed our own circles of support. At least once a week, I receive poems and stories in the mail, sent to me by First Nations women I know and some I have never met. It thrills me to read the words brought forth by my sisters. This is another form our writing takes—being responsible and supportive to our sisters who are struggling to begin the journey of writing truth. The WordCraft Circle, a mentoring program that matches up more experienced writers with our younger brothers and sisters, was born out of a Native writers' gathering held in 1992 in Oklahoma. I am currently working with a young, Native lesbian, and it moves my heart that it is now possible for lesbian Natives to give voice to *all* of who we are. Keeping ourselves secret, separating parts of ourselves in order to get heard and/or published has been detrimental to our communities and to our younger sisters and brothers who long for gay and lesbian role models. I am proud of the burgeoning Native lesbian writing that is expanding the idea of what constitutes Native women's writing.

There are my sisters who have internalized the homophobia so rampant in the dominant culture and that has found its way into our own territories and homes. These sisters are afraid, and I understand that fear. Yet, I ask for a greater courage to overcome the fear. The courage to be who we are for the sake of our young and to honor those who have come before us. Courage of the kind that Connie Fife, Chrystos, Barbara Cameron, Sharon Day, Susan Beaver, Nicole Tanguay, Two Feathers, Donna Goodleaf, Janice Gould, Vickie Sears, Donna Marchand, Mary Moran, Elaine Hall, Victoria Lena ManyArrows, Shirley Brozzo, and many others have displayed.[19] Writing with our whole selves is an act that can revision our world.

The use of erotic imaging in Native lesbian work becomes a tool by which we heal ourselves. This tool is powerfully and deftly evident in the hands of these writers, especially the poems of Janice Gould and Chrystos. In my own work, I have explored such themes as self-lovemaking and the act of love between two women[20] as a way to mend the broken circles of my own life, and hopefully to give sustenance to other women who are searching for new maps for their lives. But Native lesbian writing is not only about sex and/or sexuality. There is a broader cultural definition of sexuality that is at work here. Strong bonds to Earth and Her inhabitants serve as a pivotal edge to our most sensual writing. Like our heterosexual sisters, Native lesbians who write are swift to call out the oppressions that are at work in our lives. Homophobia is the eldest son of racism—they work in concert with each other—whether externally or internally. Native lesbian writing *names* those twin evils that would cause destruction to us.

A major theme in the work of Vickie Sears, Cherokee Nation, is the power over children's bodies by the state.[21] Sexual abuse, physical abuse, emotional abuse are "normal" occurrences to the girl children in Vickie's short stories. Herself a survivor of the foster-care system, Sears finds her solace and empowerment through the things of Earth and the love between women. Her short stories emphasize these possibilities of self-recovery. Indeed, one could say that much of Native lesbian writing celebrates Earth as woman, as lover, as companion. Woman, lover, companion celebrated as Earth. Two-spirit writers are merging the selves that colonialism splits apart.

Recovery writing is another component in the movement of Native women writers: recovery from substance abuse, as well as racism, sexism and homophobia. Two Feathers, Cayuga Nation, is a wonderful example of this kind of recovery writing, as is Sharon Day of the Ojibwa Nation.[22] Again, Chrystos, Menominee poet, excels in the naming of what it feels like to be hooked and in thrall to the substances that deaden the pain of being Native in the twentieth century. Highly charged with anger, this recovery writing is, at the same time, gentle with the knowing of how difficult the path is toward the Good Red Road. There is empathy and compassion in the telling of our people's struggle to stay clean and sober; there is rage against the state that employed *and* employs addiction to attempt our cultural annihilation. Many of my short stories focus on that moment between staying sober and taking "just one" drink. The characters are caught in that timescape of traditional Native "seeing," and the unnatural landscape of colonization through addiction. In my stories, as in my life, Creator brings gifts of the natural to "speak" to these characters. It then becomes a choice to live on the Good Red Road, or to die the death of being out of balance—a kind of "virtual reality," as opposed to the real, the natural.

Pauline Johnson knew firsthand the effects of these attempts at annihilation. Her father, a chief of the Mohawk Nation, was a political activist against the rum runners who would have weakened his people. Severely beaten many times by these smugglers and murderers, his life was considerably shortened. Many of Pauline's stories are filled with righteous anger against the whiteman who wished to rape our land, using alcohol as a weapon to confuse and subjugate us. I think she would applaud the recovery writing and name it for what it is—an Indian war cry—against the assassination of our culture.

Oral tradition requires a telling and a listening that is intense, and intentional. Giving, receiving, giving—it makes a complete circle of indigenous truth. First Nations writing utilizes the power and gift of story, like oral tradition, to convey history, lessons, culture, and spirit. And perhaps the overwhelming instinct in our spirit is to love. I would say that Native writing gives the gift of love. And love is a word that is abused and made empty by the dominant culture. In fact, the letters l-o-v-e have become just that, blank cyphers used frivolously to cover up deep places of the spirit.

I began writing when I turned forty. I imagine the spirits knew I wasn't ready to receive that gift until I was mature enough and open enough to understand the natural meaning of love. I believe that the writing being created by First Nations women is writing done with a community consciousness. Individuality is a concept and philosophy that has little meaning for us. Even while being torn from our spiritual places of home; having our ancestors' names stolen and used to sell sports teams, automobiles, and articles of clothing; having our languages beaten out of us through residential school systems even while having our spirits defiled and blasphemed, our families torn apart by institutionalized violence and genocide—even after this long war, we still remain connected to our own.

Our connections take many forms. I, as a Mohawk, feel deep spiritual bonds towards many who do not come from my Nation. These people—Carrier, Menominee, Cree, Cherokee, Lakota, Inuit, Abnaki, and many others—are like the threads of a weaving. This Mohawk and the people of many Nations are warp and woof to each other. While the color and beauty of each thread is unique and important, together they make a communal material of strength and durability. Such is our writing, because such is our belief system. Writing is an act that can take place in physical isolation, but the memory of history, of culture, of land, of Nation, is always present, like another being. That is how we create. Writing with all our senses, and with the ones that have not been named or colonized, we create.

Janice Gould, Maidu Nation, has written, "I would like to believe there are vast reserves of silences that can never be *forced* to speak, that remain sacred and safe from violation."[23] I feel that these sacred silences are the places *from* which we write. That place that has not been touched or stained by imperialism and hatred. That sacred place. That place.

Like Pauline Johnson, mixed-blood writers find those sacred places in the blood that courses through our bodies, whispering, "come home, come home." Although we have never left that home, in a sense we have been pulled and pushed into accepting the lies told about our Indian selves. For those of us who do not conform to a stereotype of what Native people "look like," claiming our identities as Native people becomes an exercise in racism. "Gee, you don't look like an Indian." "Gee, I didn't know Indians had blue eyes." "My great-great-grandmother was a Cherokee princess, does that make me an Indian too?" After a while it almost becomes humorous, even while it's tiresome. Perhaps the feeling is that we're getting away with something, that we are tapping into unknown strengths, for which we are not entitled. And how the dominant culture loves to quantify suffering and pain! And how well it has worked to divide us from each other and from ourself. Colorism is another face of racism. And we write about that—exposing our fears of abandonment by the people we love, the people whose opinion matters, the very people who, in our dreams, whisper, "Come home, come home." Yet, mixed-blood writing is also what I have been examining; for most of us are bloods of many mixes and Nations. Linda Hogan, Chickasaw Nation, calls us "New People." New People are the survivors of five hundred years of colonial rule. Our grandmothers bodies were appropriated by the conquerors, but the New People have not forgotten this grandmother, nor the legacy she carried in her womb.

In Mexico, a story is told of La Llorona. It is told that she wanders throughout the land, looking for her lost children. Her voice is the wind. She weeps and moans and calls to the children of her blood. She is the Indian, the mother of our blood, the grandmother of our hearts. She calls to us. "Come home, come home," she whispers, she cries, she calls to us. She comes into that sacred place we hold inviolate. She is birthing us in that sacred place. "Come home, come home," the voice of the umbilical, the whisper of the placenta. "Come home, come home." We listen. And we write.

Notes

1. E. Pauline Johnson as quoted in Betty Keller, *Pauline: A Biography of Pauline Johnson* (Vancouver: Douglas & McIntyre, 1981).

2. E. Pauline Johnson, "The Song My Paddle Sings" in *Flint & Feather* (Toronto: Hodder & Stoughton, 1931).

3. E. Pauline Johnson, "The Cattle Thief" in *Flint & Feather*.

4. E. Pauline Johnson, *The Moccasin Maker* (Tucson: University of Arizona, 1987).

5. E. Pauline Johnson. "A Strong Race Opinion on the Indian Girl in Modern Fiction" originally published in the *Toronto Sunday Globe*, 22 May 1982.

6. Hum-Ishu-Ma (Mourning Dove) *Cogewea, The Half-Blood* (Lincoln: University of Nebraska, 1981). Hum-Ishu-Ma's mentor was a white man. My reading of *Cogewea* is that much of it was influenced by his perceptions, not Hum-Ishu-Ma's.

7. Maria Campbell, *Half-Breed* (Toronto: McClelland & Stewart, 1973).

8. Leslie Marmon Silko, *Ceremony* (New York: Viking Press, 1977).

9. Leslie Marmon Silko, *Almanac of the Dead* (New York, Toronto: Simon & Schuster, 1991).

10. Paula Gunn Allen, *The Woman Who Owned the Shadows* (San Francisco: Spinsters/Aunt Lute, 1983); Louise Erdrich, *Love Medicine* (Toronto, New York: Bantam, 1989); Jeanette Armstrong, *Slash* (Penticton: Theytus, 1986); Anna Lee Walters, *Ghost-Singer* (Flagstaff: Northland, 1988); Beatrice Culleton, *In Search of April Raintree* (Winnipeg: Pemmican, 1983); Ella Deloria, *Waterlily* (Lincoln: University of Nebraska, 1988); Ruby Slipperjack, *Honour the Sun* (Winnipeg: Pemmican, 1987); Ruby Slipperjack, *Silent Words* (Saskatoon: Fifth House,1992); Cyndy Baskin, *The Invitation* (Toronto: Sister Vision, 1993); Linda Hogan, *Mean Spirit* (New York: Atheneum, 1990); Lee Maracle, *Ravensong* (Vancouver: Press Gang, 1993); Velma Wallis, *Two Old Women* (New York: Harper Perennial, 1993); Betty Louise Bell, *Face in the Moon* (Norman: University of Oklahoma Press, 1994).

11. Minnie Freeman, *Life Among the Oallunaat* (Edmonton: Hurtig, 1978); Ignatia

Broker, *Night Flying Woman: An Ojibway Narrative* (St. Paul: Minnesota Historical Society, 1983); Verna Patronella Johnson, *I Am Nokomis, Too* (Don Mills: General Publishing Ltd., 1977); Madline Katt Theriault, *Moose to Moccasins* (Toronto: Natural Heritage/Natural History Inc., 1992); Janet Campbell Hale, *Bloodlines* (New York: Harper Perennial, 1993); Wilma Mankiller, *Mankiller: A Chief and Her People* (New York: St. Martin's Press, 1993); Bonita Wa Wa Calachaw Nunez, *Spirit Woman* (New York: Harper & Row, 1980); Helen Pease Wolf, *Reaching Both Ways* (Laramie: Jelm Mountain Publications, 1989); Zitkala-Sa, *American Indian Stories* (Washington: Hayworth, 1921); Ida Patterson, *Montana Memories* (Pablo: Salish Kootenai Community College, 1981).

12. Chrystos, "I Am Not Your Princess" in *Not Vanishing* (Vancouver: Press Gang, 1988); Mary Tall Mountain, "Good Grease" in *The Light On the Tent* (Los Angeles: University of California, 1990); Nora Marks Dauenhaur, "How to Make a Good Baked Salmon" in *The Droning Shaman* (Haines: Black Currant, 1985); Mary Moran, *Metisse Patchwork,* unpublished manuscript.

13. Poets include Beth Cuthand, Joy Harjo, Marie Baker (Annharte), Janice Gould, Wendy Rose, Diane Glancy, Awiakta, Elizabeth Woody, Joanne Arnott, Carol Lee Sanchez, Paula Gunn Allen, and Doris Seale.

14. Beth Brant, ed. *A Gathering of Spirit* (Sinister Wisdom Books, 1984; Ithaca: Firebrand, 1988; Toronto: Women's Press, 1989).

15. Lenore Keeshig-Tobias, *Bird Talk* (Toronto: Sister Vision, 1992); Rita Joe, *Poems of Rita Joe* (Halifax: Abnaki, 1978); Beatrice (Bea) Medicine, "Ina" in *A Gathering of Spirit;* Anna Lee Walters, *Talking Indian* (Ithaca: Firebrand, 1992); Nia Francisco, *Blue Horses For Navajo Women* (Greenfield Center: Greenfield Review, 1988); Ofelia Zepeda, unpublished manuscript; Donna Goodlead, unpublished manuscript.

16. Margaret Sam-Cromarty, *James Bay Memoirs* (Lakefield: Waapoone Publishing, 1992).

17. Monique Mojica, *Princess Pocahontas and the Blue Spots* (Toronto: Women's Press, 1991).

18. Sarah Winnemucca and Suzette La Flesch (Bright Eyes) travelled and performed in the United States, talking about their people in poetry and story, within the same time frame as Pauline Johnson's career.

19. Makeda Silvera, ed. *Piece of May Heart* (Toronto: Sister Vision, 1991); Will Roscoe, ed. *Living the Spirit* (New York: St. Martin's, 1988); Connie Fife, ed. *The Colour of Resistance* (Toronto: Sister Vision, 1993); Gloria Anzaldua, ed. *This Bridge Called My Back* (Albany: Kitchen Table Press) are just four of the collections containing Native lesbian work. See also Connie Fife, *Beneath the Naked Sun* (Toronto: Sister Vision, 1992); Chrystos, *Not Vanishing, Dream On, In Her I Am* (Vancouver, Press Gang); Janice Gould, *Beneath My Heart,* (Ithaca, Firebrand, 1990); Victoria Lena ManyArrows. *Songs From the Native Lands,* (San Francisco, Nopal Press, 1995).

20. Beth Brant, *Mohawk Trail* (Ithaca: Firebrand, 1985; Toronto: Women's Press, 1990); Beth Brant, *Food & Spirits* (Vancouver, Press Gang, 1991).

21. Vickie Sears, *Simple Songs* (Ithaca: Firebrand, 1990).

22. Sharon Day and Two Feathers, unpublished manuscripts.

23. Janice Gould, "Disobedience in Language: Texts by Lesbian Natives" unpublished speech to the Modern Language Association, New York, 1990.

5

Contemporary Tribal Codes and Gender Issues

Bruce G. Miller

 THIS PAPER MAKES THREE related points: first, that many of the present-day legal codes of U.S. Indian tribes are unexpectedly innovative and representative of contemporary indigenous viewpoints, especially in the ways in which individual rights are conceived; second, that the variability in the way the codes treat issues of special concern to women demonstrates the extent of the imprint of local tribal people on their own codes; and third, that analysis of the implications of tribal codes for Indian women is a valuable and hitherto undeveloped avenue in clarifying women's circumstances. I address these points by comparing the categories of code that eight western Washington tribes have created and by looking at a set of legal issues that particularly influence women's lives. This essay is intended as a preliminary effort to make use of legal materials in the analysis of contemporary Coast Salish life.[1] The codes of these eight tribes vary in their overall emphases, in their legal treatment of family networks, in the rights of parents, and in attention given to women's issues generally.

In 1985, William Rodman commented that legal innovation in small-scale societies "is a topic so few anthropologists have studied that a summary of relevant sources takes only a few paragraphs"; he noted further that "[l]egal scholars use 'innovation' exclusively to denote changes that the state introduces, never changes that local people make of their own accord. . . ."[2] Rodman correctly argued that the trend towards "legal centralism" (a state-centered view of the law) and an emphasis on the coercive nature of the state have made it difficult to perceive indigenous legal innovation. Further, Vincent[3] wrote that the anthropology of law has turned to the study of historical legal change "in the guise of legal pluralism," thereby resurrecting diffusionist theory and diverting attention from local developments.

The study of tribal law and legal innovation among native North Americans appears to be similarly burdened. What little is written about Indian legal systems suggests co-option by the mainstream political system of tribal governments (under whose authority tribal legal systems are developed) and a disproportionate influence of the non-native legal system through the importation of legal language (or "boilerplate").[4] Barsh and Henderson,[5] for example, argued that the procedural codes of tribal courts are forced for financial reasons into conformity with model

Bruce G. Miller is an assistant professor of anthropology at the University of British Columbia.

codes derived from those followed in federally administered Bureau of Indian Affairs (BIA) courts. These model codes, they reason, are built on a "police idea" of law and order, with little civil code. Through this process, Barsh and Henderson conclude, the state works to limit the scope of Indian law and sets Indians against their own government. O'Brien's view of contemporary Indian law exemplifies this approach:

> When tribes started replacing the Code of Federal Regulations with their own codes, few had the expertise or the resources to do a professional job of establishing new tribal laws. As a result the codes in operation on many reservations today look much like the federal code they replaced: they are outdated, Anglo-oriented, and poorly reflective of tribal philosophy and culture.[6]

One analyst recently addressed the issue of how women are faring in tribal courts but started from the unstated assumption that women are unable to exercise political power in tribal communities and that, consequently, women's only remedy for a male bias in tribal codes and courts was through the intervention of a reworked Indian Civil Rights Act. This work includes virtually no analysis of tribal codes themselves.[7]

Although there are sizable literatures on the topics of federal, state, and provincial laws concerning Indian people, and on customary law, little literature exists concerning the law that applies in Indian courts. The analysis of a 1978 publication of the American Bar Foundation still holds true:

> There is a wealth of literature, including "legal" literature, on Indian matters, but it rarely deals with contemporary issues. Apart from a few short pieces dealing mainly with the theory rather than practices, there is no legal literature on the present-day tribal court system. Instead the bulk of it concerns jurisdictional issues and treaty rights or land or water use. . . . In addition, there are studies with an anthropological focus— typically, historical quests to uncover the traditional "law-ways" of selected tribes. . . . Practically the only works that deal specifically with the contemporary tribal court system are the reports of the Senate Hearings on the Constitutional Rights of the American Indian (Hearings before the Subcomm. on Constitutional Rights of the Senate Comm. on the Judiciary, 87th Cong., 1st sess., 89th Cong., 1st sess [1961–65]).[8]

The emphasis on understanding Indian codes from the perspective of Indian-white power relations, while necessary, places the analytic frame outside the Indian communities and has the unfortunate result of causing the contents of the codes to be overlooked. Although analysis of tribal law is now overdue, there is still the chance to examine the contemporary tribal code while it is in its infancy, to understand the forces internally acting on its creation and development, and to gain an understanding of the direction the law is headed.[9]

Tribal codes are best understood as innovative and responsive to highly localized circumstances, variable from tribe to tribe. If nothing else, tribal codes are not simply boilerplate, although on cursory examination they may appear to be so. Even in those cases where code is imported from the mainstream system, it is often quickly adapted to local circumstances. In part because these codes are so recent (as described below), they are still relatively uncluttered and the discernible products of individuals and can be thought of, with due caution, as road maps for the visions of political and other leaders for the future of their communities.[10] Perhaps most significantly, many contemporary tribal leaders and tribal councils have found their own balance points between collective and individual rights, a balance that varies considerably between tribes.[11]

More specifically, for several reasons, analysis of the legal codes provides new leverage that is helpful in understanding multiple dimensions of the gender systems operant in reservation communities. First, the new codes crystallize, for the moment, issues that communities have heretofore struggled over and have often left unresolved. Second, the laws themselves have a direct, immediate impact on the behavior and lives of women and men. Third, as is true of legal systems elsewhere, embedded in these new systems are notions of what it means to be male and female. The laws create male and female "legal statuses"—statuses that themselves come to influence how community members construct gender and organize gender relations.[12] Finally, the codes regulate issues thought to be generally of concern to women, including violence towards women and children, divorce, spousal support, inheritance and ownership of real property, responsibility for children and elders, custody, access to positions of public authority, access to tribal membership, the availability of social and other services, and so on.

THE STUDY

This study is built around interviews with tribal code writers and tribal councillors and a reading of the published codes of eight small Coast Salish tribes in northern Washington State, which range in size from about three hundred to three thousand enrolled members.[13] In 1979, the tribes participated in creating the Northwest Intertribal Court System (NICS), which provides judicial services for the member tribes, including supplying the judge, but each tribe maintains its own laws. One of the eight tribes, Lummi, is no longer a member of the NICS. The NICS is described in more detail below.

The eight Coast Salish tribes (Nisqually, Lummi, Skokomish, Sauk-Suiattle, Upper Skagit, Tulalip, Muckleshoot, Nooksack) are situated in close proximity to metropolitan centers, and members live both on the small reservations and in the nearby cities and towns. Many members of the eight tribes live traditional religious and ceremonial lives, engage in subsistence harvests of shellfish, plants, and other materials, and participate in the regional system of social relations. Although tribal members participate in the local economy, all eight tribes place a heavy emphasis on the commercial salmon harvest. Perhaps most germane to this study is that the tribal communities are themselves organized into competing, temporal family networks. Family leaders, both men and women, help coordinate family economic activities, including fishing, provide for the sharing of resources and labor, and help in the arrangement of the ceremonial and spiritual life of the members of the family network. Family networks typically create voting blocs in tribal elections, and the legal regulation of these units is a critical issue.[14]

HISTORICAL BACKGROUND

Customary Law and the Tribal Court System

Customary law in the Coast Salish region employed a range of sanctions to control behavior and restore communities in the event of a breach. These sanctions included restitution, ostracism, social pressures, and even violent recrimination.[15] Public ceremonies were (and continue to be) carried out in the process of the public debate and resolution of conflicts. The region has been characterized by a cultural emphasis on the avoidance of conflict through proper training in the absence of coercive authority (see the NICS report for a fuller treatment of the topic).[16] After several decades of contact with Europeans and Americans in the nineteenth century, new concepts of political organization, leadership, and law developed. For example, a mid-nineteenth-century Skagit innovator, Slabebtkud, organized loosely affiliated villages and imposed rule based on coercion. He established a system of subchiefs who enforced new, Christian-influenced concepts through the threat of incarceration in stocks.[17]

In 1883, the U.S. Bureau of Indian Affairs (BIA) authorized the creation of Courts of Indian Offenses (CFR courts) for reservation people in order to fill a perceived leadership void following an apparent decline in traditional authority, and to diminish the residual authority of traditional chiefs.[18] The BIA exercised great authority over this court system, selecting the police and judges and promulgating the rules and procedures. BIA authority over this court system was diminished with the Indian Reorganization Act of 1934. Tribes were encouraged to establish governments and court systems modeled on those of the dominant society, although the BIA is said to have simply imposed its own bylaws on "tribes . . . ill-prepared for self-government."[19] Later, particularly during the termination period of the 1950s when federal policy aimed at ending the trust relationship between tribes and the federal government, little money was available for tribal legal systems.[20]

In the 1970s, federal policy again produced contradictory effects on Indian courts. The new federal policy of encouraging tribal self-determination was accompanied by the efforts of tribes with independent courts and those with CFR courts to rewrite their codes for their own ends. However, the Indian Civil Rights Act of 1968 imposed most of the federal Bill of Rights on tribes, thereby reducing self-governance and imposing new requirements on tribal courts. For example, it became unlawful for a tribal government, without a jury trial, to enact a law that imposes punishment.[21]The passage of the Self-Determination Act of 1976 required that further regulations be adopted. In some cases, specific provisions must be contained in tribal law so that jurisdiction can be obtained (i.e., provisions for the detention of criminals, specific provisions for recourse under the law) or so that funding requirements can be fulfilled. Today tribal courts, CFR courts, and traditional dispute settlement institutions all still exist in Indian Country.

THE NORTHWEST INTERTRIBAL COURT SYSTEM

The Northwest Intertribal Court System, a judicial services consortium, was established in 1979 following the fishing litigation (*U.S.* v. *Washington*, 384 F. Supp. 312, 1974) that held that the treaties of the mid-nineteenth century gave Indians of Washington State half the salmon catch in state waters. The ruling created a need for fish and game codes and a venue to adjudicate violations. The NICS courts exercise general jurisdiction over tribal members, as limited by the tribal code and constitution and by federal law. In the case of Upper Skagit, for example, NICS courts hold jurisdiction over civil, traffic, fisheries, and some elements of criminal domains for both Indians and non-Indians. The tribal council is responsible for passing tribal code and is assisted in its work by hired code writers and by suggestions from the community itself. In some cases, tribal councils have created formal advisory boards to advise the code writers. There is, as yet, limited development of case law.

Court is convened on the Upper Skagit reservation once a month, or more often if needed, at the community center on the reservation near Sedro Woolley, Washington. The court staff includes one part-time clerk and one part-time deputy prosecutor. NICS provides the other personnel, most notably the judge. In this case, the source of the law is the tribal constitution, approved in 1974 and amended in 1977, and customary law. The tribal code may "codify or refer to customary practices. The sitting judge may also have discretion to consider and apply custom in individual cases."[22] In fiscal year 1990, the Upper Skagit court, which serves 540 tribal members, heard 43 criminal cases and 15 civil cases. NICS data (which does not include Lummi, the largest of the tribes) give some measure of court activity. The data show that, in 1990, the court heard 147 criminal cases (ranging from 8 to 43 per tribe, with a mean of 21) and 21 civil cases (with a range from 0 to 15; six of the seven tribes had no civil litigation).[23]

The formal court system is thought to be used as a last resort after a variety of informal mechanisms have been exhausted, especially in the case of intrafamily disputes.[24] In one case, for example, the NICS judge ordered a young married couple to "work out their problems" after a restraining order was brought against the husband at the suggestion of tribal social service staff. Interfamily disputes, public disorder, fishing violations, and vandalism are more likely to end up in court than intrafamily problems. For these reasons, court hears more criminal cases than civil. There is, so far, a limited infrastructure of lawyers versed in tribal law to help bring civil action in the NICS court, and the formal court system is not easily accessible to ordinary people. In addition, the NICS prosecutors are frequently non-Indian and nonresident and must work with police reports, thereby making the application of nonjudicial remedies more difficult. Also, the presence of non-Indian tribal police, who are largely unaware of community processes, produces a formal treatment of cases and increases use of the courts.[25] These features of the legal system, by their very nature, exacerbate the alienation that some people feel from their own community institutions and make protection of the rights of the relatively powerless, including some women, difficult, especially in establishing civil litigation.

Underlying the tribal system of laws is the system of law enforcement. According to Upper Skagit records, in 1991 officers were on active duty patrol 16.9 percent of hours, a total of 1,478 hours, compared to the 2,551 in 1990.[26] However, 155 cases involving violations of tribal laws and ordinances were logged in 1991 compared to 87 in 1990. Of the 155 offenses, 86 involved adults, and 52 of these were alcohol related. Forty-six incidents involved juveniles; 22 of these were alcohol related. Subsequently, 13 adult males, 5 adult females, and 4 each of juvenile boys and girls were referred to the NICS prosecutor. The offenses can be categorized as follows:

Table 1
Offenses, Upper Skagit 1990–1991

Category	Year	
	1990	1991
	(n=87)	(n=155)
Mixed	5.7%	5.8%
Property	12.6	8.4
Public order	35.6	37.4
Offenses against persons	19.5	13.5
Other offenses	26.4	34.8

Source: 1991 Upper Skagit Tribal Police FY91 Activities Report, 25 January 1992.

The NICS and Upper Skagit data conform to the generalization that a high volume of cases of alcohol-related crimes against persons are brought in tribal court.[27] Crimes against persons are often offenses against family and children, and these data point to the importance of tribal code for women.

Legal Statuses

The eight sets of tribal codes and constitutions create complex, overlapping systems of legal statuses, about which some generalizations can be made. Men and women are treated by the codes as undifferentiated individuals with entitlements (interests in community-held resources of various sorts). These legally distinct individuals are restrained in their interests by two other sets of interests, those of the tribe and also, in limited ways, the rights of family networks. Secondly, men and women are legally members (citizens) of the tribe (and, separately, of the community) and, as such, are entitled to residence in Indian Country and to shares in community assets (such as fisheries resources, education programs, Indian Health Service care, and reservation housing). Community membership alone does not confer these entitlements. Thirdly, in most codes, men and women have legal standing as extended family (or family network) members. As such, in some tribes people are entitled to make claims to fishing locations (under customary provisions of use-rights) and hold rights to oversight of the children of the family network. In addition, the law places restrictions on citizens on the basis of kinship affiliations, which overlap in various ways with membership in corporate, temporal family networks. For example, several of the codes restrict individuals from running for office in the event a relative is a council incumbent. Finally, people are legally parents, with an array of parental rights and obligations.

The various legal statuses an individual may occupy are not fully compatible (in part because of the long history of federal policy and court rulings that have imposed and reconstructed concepts of membership), a circumstance that leads to significant disagreement in the communities. Some people residing on the reservations are legally members of the community but not members of the tribe. (Some are legally members of other tribes; others are non-Indians.) A further complication is that some nontribal members who are resident on the reservation are family network members and hold legal rights as such. They may, for example, have priority in adoption or in provisions for the care of family network children, or may have legal rights to attend family-sponsored ceremonial events while incarcerated. (The jurisdictional complexities of Indians who are not members of the tribe in whose territory they reside are not yet resolved and have been complicated by *Duro v. Reina*, 495 U.S. 676, 1990, and subsequent legislation.)[28]

These incompatible statuses give rise to role conflict. A debate arose recently on one reservation, for example, over whether community members who were not tribal members were entitled to treaty fishing rights, a vital resource. Tribal council members split over this issue by sex, with three women arguing to allow these community men to keep fishing (and thereby provisioning Indian family members) and three council men arguing against granting permission. In this case, women's status as tribal members was in conflict with their role in provisioning family members. Table 2 summarizes the primary generalizable legal statuses that individuals occupy, and the associated legal entitlements.

Table 2
Legal Statuses

Legal Status	Key Legal Entitlements
1. minor	some rights to participate in customary practice
2. adult (as defined by activity) / emancipated minor	fishing, hunting, voting rights
3. kinfolk	limitations imposed (nepotism rules)
4. parent	limited rights to control of offspring
5. household head	emancipation, rights to resources (if tribal member)
6. community member	residence, some services
7. family network member	some rights regarding children some customary resource use-rights
8. tribal member	vote, office-holding, rights to collective resources, jobs

The legal codes differentiate on the basis of age and other criteria. Legal minors are distinguished from adults in a variety of ways: Voting for public office is a privilege available to tribal members over 18; children are restricted from fishing and hunting (with some exceptions when supervised); and, in some cases, children's movements are restricted by curfews. But some of the codes (Skokomish, Tulalip, Upper Skagit, Nooksack, Muckleshoot) allow for the formal age requirements of adulthood to be set aside under certain circumstances. In two of the codes (Skokomish, Tulalip), children can be emancipated when acting as a household head—a circumstance of special importance to females, who frequently begin families while in their early teens and who assume responsibility for the provisioning of their offspring.[29] Emancipation releases minors from restrictions on fishing or hunting by virtue of age.

Adult men and women also assume secondary legal statuses as owners of real property, as heirs to the property of others within the community, as members of a regulated community that provides rights to safety and comfort, as voters and potential tribal councillors, as official tribal committee members, and as jury members or witnesses. The implications of each of these legal status are somewhat different for men than for women, as indicated below.

REGIONAL GENERALIZATION

Analysis of the Subject Index of Tribal Codes

The codes of the eight tribes vary in their inclusiveness, due in part to the variation in institutional completeness of tribal governments and in the range of services provided. But the raw fact that tribal governments have enacted codes in some areas and not others reflects the interests and specializations of these governments. Table 3 displays the content of the tribal codes by heading.

Table 3
Subject Index of Tribal Codes

Subject	Tribe							
	Lummi	Muckleshoot	Nisqually	Nooksack	Sauk–Suiattle	Skokomish	Tulalip	Upper Skagit
Administration	X							
Building	X						X	
Business		X		X		X	X	
Domestic Relations	X				X			
Elections					X			X
Enroll/Member					X	X		X
Exclusion	X	X	X		X			X
Fish/Hunt	X			X		X		X
Gaming	X			X				
Housing	X	X		X		X		X
Juvenile/children	X	X		X		X		X
Labor/employ	X							
Tenant	X			X				
Liquor/tobacco	X	X		X				
Natural resources					X	X		
Probate	X							
Sentence			X					
Tax		X		X		X		X
Traffic		X				X		X
Tribal enterprise								X
Utilities					X			X
Water								
Zoning		X					X	

These data can be comprehended by grouping the codes, thereby allowing for a very rough measure of the interests and intentions of particular tribes. The codes are grouped as follows:

Table 4
Categories of Legal Codes

Category	Type of Code
A. Economic Development	business, fish, gaming, natural resources, enterprise, tax
B. Regulation	building, housing, landlord/tenant, probate, sentencing, utilities, water, zoning, liquor
C. Peace and Safety	domestic relations, juvenile, exclusion, traffic
D. Governance/Politics	administration, elections, enrollment, labor

---

Laws concerning exclusion from the reservation are included in category C because they have most to do with public safety, ordinarily the only grounds on which nonmembers may be excluded.

Once categorized, raw counts in each of the four categories for each tribe can be computed, giving a picture of the emphases of the tribal councils, under whose authority codes are created. Table 5 presents these results.

Briefly, these data show the divergence among the codes. Lummi has the most comprehensive code (sixteen areas), with code in all four areas categorized as "Peace and Safety." The Upper Skagit and Muckleshoot codes are second and third most complete, respectively (ten and nine areas), and well-developed in the areas of peace and safety. On the other extreme, the Tulalip and Nooksack codes focus on economic development and regulation. The Tulalip code is silent on issues of peace and safety, and Nooksack nearly so (one area). The Nisqually code is by far the least developed of the eight (code in two areas) and contains little concerning peace and safety. The Sauk-Suiattle code is also relatively unelaborated (six areas) but has code in two of the peace and safety areas.

Table 5
Emphases of Tribal Codes—Raw Scores

Tribe	Type				
	A Econ. Dev.	**B** Regulation	**C** Safety	**D** Govern.	Totals
Lummi	3	7	4	2	16
Muckleshoot	3	3	3	0	9
Nisqually	0	1	1	0	2
Nooksack	4	3	1	0	8
Sauk-Suiattle	1	1	2	2	6
Skokomish	4	1	2	0	7
Tulalip	2	2	0	1	5
Upper Skagit	3	2	3	2	10
Totals	20	20	16	7	63

The analysis thus far shows somewhat roughly the differing emphases between the tribes' codes. The next step is to look more closely at how the codes treat issues particularly relevant to women's lives.

LEGAL CODES AND GENDER ISSUES

Inheritance

Here the focus is on a subset of particular legal issues important to understanding women's circumstances. The first such issue is inheritance. Generally, tribal codes follow state law in matters of property inheritance, but there are some important exceptions, especially in areas that state law does not cover. One such exception is the issue of the inheritance of traditional resource procurement stations, particularly along waterways. The eight tribes vary significantly in how this issue is treated. At Skokomish and Upper Skagit, these rights are directly embedded in the code, along with provisions for the reallocation of fishing stations in the event of abandonment of the site. Since traditional fisheries resource use-rights are primarily inherited patrilineally (with the exception of female-set net sites), the pattern of inheritance favors men who can control the disposition of the grounds. With the loss of tribal land to white settlers in the nineteenth century, women have lost control of gathering grounds, the primary female-controlled resource. The Lummi, Sauk-Suiattle, Muckleshoot, and

Tulalip codes are silent on this issue, and traditional use-rights are not protected legally.

A second exception to the institution of the mainstream society's patterns of inheritance is the section of the Lummi code that concerns spousal relations. Title II of the Domestic Relations Act, 11.3.01, specifies,

> Property and pecuniary rights of the husband before marriage and that acquired by him afterwards by gift, bequest, devise or descent, with the rents, issues, and profits thereof, shall not be subject to the debts or contracts of his wife, and he may manage, lease, sell, convey, encumber as fully to the same effect as though he were unmarried. . . .

Section 11.3.02 provides the same terms for the wife.[30] In the case of the other tribes, state law obtains concerning spousal legal obligations. The Lummi code, however, conforms to the aboriginal practice of the separation of the property of spouses at the time of divorce or death and appears to have the effect of making divorce easy and protecting the critical connections between sibling sets and family networks. The code may have the additional effects of protecting the interests of Indians from non-Indian spouses and of preventing the alienation of extremely valuable property—purse seine boats—from male owners at the time of divorce.[31]

Although inheritance of material objects at the time of death had not been an important practice among Puget Sound Salish, with many items distributed to people beyond the immediate family and household, valuable incorporeal objects were traditionally inherited.[32] Indian names and control of resource procurement sites are among the most important.[33] The effect of the new pattern of inheritance, with the exception of Lummi, is to narrow the claims women may make as sisters and senior members within family networks (with important influence over the disposition of family possessions and the labor of kin) and to reinforce their position as wives and mothers, with primary inheritance coming from a spouse rather than a brother, sister, or parent. In practice, this may be an advantage or a disadvantage for individual women (some women have benefited through amassing large land holdings through consecutive marriages to short-lived men). But, on balance, these inheritance patterns, although gender neutral in appearance, have differential impact. Modern inheritance practices reinforce the subordination of women to male cohouseholders (affinal relatives) and deemphasizes women's potential for superordination as senior members of a corporate family group.

Regulation of Work

A second important domain of the law concerns the regulation of work. Four of the tribal codes (Upper Skagit, Tulalip, Nisqually, Muckleshoot) contain specific provisions under the tribal bill of rights for equal access by individuals to economic resources and programs of the tribe. Of the eight, the Upper Skagit code is the most focused on the issue of safeguarding the rights of workers to gain access to tribal jobs and protecting them from harassment while working. Both provisions are crucial for women because, at Upper Skagit, as at the majority of Coast Salish tribal and band offices, the bulk of tribal employees are female.[34] The Upper Skagit bill of rights provides economic rights to individuals that are not accorded to family networks. The code protects individuals from criticism by community members in the conduct of their work. Chapter 6 of the Law and Order Code (6.530–Verbal Threat to Public Officials) specifies, "Any person, who shall, when speaking to a public official, including a council member, employee, judge, prosecutor or other public official threaten such person with an act of violence or otherwise try to influence an official act by means of a verbal threat shall be guilty of an offense. . . ." Similar language is used in two other places to prohibit threats to officials and employees. These provisions were created with the expressed purpose of providing a work place free of disruption by factionalized conflict and to ensure a productive community.[35] The effect is to provide for safety in a work place occupied largely by women. Several tribal codes contain references to threats against officials (judges, police, or elected officials) but, significantly, not rank-and-file tribal employees. These include Lummi, Muckleshoot, and Nooksack. There is no such language in the Skokomish, Tulalip, and Nisqually codes, leaving employees without special legal protection from harassment.

Finally, the Tulalip code contains provisions aimed at increasing employment on the reservation. Ordinance 61 charters a "Tulalip Construction Company" and provides for educational activities designed to furnish training in jobs related to the construction industry. These provisions appear to favor male employment as an issue of tribal policy, since the Coast Salish construction work force is overwhelmingly male.[36]

Political Enfranchisement

Political enfranchisement of women and replacement of postcontact male quasijudicial bodies by the system of tribal courts and codes are areas of the law with significant impact on women's lives. For example, the all-male Elder's Council that adjudicated community issues and established sanctions for transgressors among the Sauk-Suiattle of the postcontact period is now replaced by the court system.[37] Sauk-Suiattle women now may influence the direction of the legal community through election to the council or participation on advisory committees.

Similarly, prior to the creation of a constitution in 1974, Upper Skagit women were disenfranchised from the formal political system, although individual women maintained significant influence in the community.[38] The system of selection of tribal councillors left women out: Sitting councillors, under the direction of the chair, nominated candidates who were then ratified by the general membership of the tribe through a process of acclamation. Women served as nonvoting secretaries and treasurers on the council.[39] Immediately after enfranchisement, women ran for public office and, by the 1980s, regularly won the majority of seats. No legal barriers have been posed for women in voting, and, in fact, women control the process of establishing eligibility to vote through tribal membership. Strong evidence suggests that many community members now associate femininity with political life, a rapid transformation of gender ideology.[40] The changes in the constitution altered the nature of women's citizenship and their access to politically important institutions. Women are now full participants as voters and councillors, as well as jury members and members of tribal committees.

Child Care Responsibilities

Another significant area of legal activity has been the creation of laws regulating the behavior of children on the reservation and the associated definition of parental obligations. Ordinarily, children are most closely associated with women, who perform the bulk of child care. For many women, child-care responsibilities begin as a preteen looking after younger siblings. Many, although not all, women continue to carry out child care through young adulthood and into grandmotherhood. Laws affecting the behavior of children, then, differentially affect women and the organization of their daily lives. The creation of penalties for parental negligence, including fines and possible loss of custody, has been a hotly contested issue, with different resolutions on different reservations. Some men on the Upper Skagit reservation have employed a discourse of traditionality, arguing that strict guidelines for the behavior of children violate traditional cultural values by failing to recognize the autonomy of children and by rejecting cultural patterns of reliance on a network of relatives to ensure that children come to no harm. This argument holds that requiring parents alone to oversee the behavior of children releases other men and women from their duties toward related children. Despite these claims, Upper Skagit code has moved toward defining parental obligations to include both parents and to exclude extended family members, and towards requiring that children be protected from their own actions and the actions of other people. Code therefore may redefine the concept of childhood by moving away from emphasis on children's personal autonomy and on oversight by the extended family.[41]

Chapter 3 of the Upper Skagit Children's Code provides for termination of parental rights in the event of abandonment; willful, repeated physical abuse that creates a substantial risk of death; sexual abuse; or consent of both parents. Chapter 5 of the same code provides for guardians to be appointed for minors, with no rights for family network members. Upper Skagit has also enacted a series of codes designed to protect children's rights, each of which imposes burdens on parents. Chapter 5.110 of the law and order code forbids leaving children under ten years of age unattended in a car; 6.160 forbids desertion and nonsupport of a child; and, significantly, 6.130 specifies that "[a]ny person who, lacking the legal right to do so, interferes with another's custody of a child shall be guilty of an offense. . . ." This last is the clause that most effectively removes children from the oversight of extended family members (that is, extended family involvement without the consent of the parent). Finally, the fishing ordinance forbids those under eighteen from fishing during school hours unless holding a GED (high school equivalency) certificate.

Other tribes' codes regulate the behavior of children but do not specify the legal obligations of both parents, even in those cases where the obligations are spelled out. Since women are more likely to have custody of children, this appears to create a burden for women but not men. Sauk-Suiattle and Skokomish, in particular, have created legal structures concerning children and care responsibilities that are quite different from those of Upper Skagit. Section 1.4.060 of the Sauk-Suiattle Family Code contains the broadest possible definition of extended family membership in the context of provisions for responsibility for youth. This definition reads as follows:

> Extended Family Member: a person who has reached the age of eighteen years, or who is of sufficient maturity to care for a child, and who is the Indian youth's grandparent, aunt or uncle, brother or sister, brother-in-law or sister-in-law, niece or nephew, first or second cousin, or step-parent, and any other person who is considered a family member under tribal law or custom; a non-Indian relative who is an accepted member of the Sauk-Suiattle Indian community and would be considered a family member by tribal custom shall also be considered part of the youth's extended family. . . .

Elsewhere (Family Code 3.1.010), the Sauk-Suiattle code specifies that termination of parental rights is not permissible under any circumstances and that the "supportive network of extended family . . . ," as defined above, is to provide care. Family Code 2.1.010 mentions "raising another person's child" as a customary alternative that does not terminate parental rights and as not necessarily indicating a need for legal "care action." Family Code 3.2.110 specifies that extended family members are preferred in the appointment of guardians for youth. The Law and Order Code, section 5.035, establishes a curfew forbidding children under fourteen from appearing "on the streets, highways, roads, or other public places without responsible adult supervision between the hours of 10 PM and 6 AM," placing the burden on the parent or guardian. In addition, Sauk-Suiattle has ordinances (Law and Order Code 5.110), identical to those of Upper Skagit, forbidding leaving children under the age of ten unattended in a car and concerning desertion and nonsupport (6.160).

For both Upper Skagit and Sauk-Suiattle, the new codes place heavy responsibilities on adults for the protection and support of children. In the former case, the responsibility rests strictly with the parents, and ordinarily this means the mother. Other family members are not only not legally responsible but are explicitly excluded from entitlement. In the latter case, a wider range of kinfolk are entitled to intervene in the lives of children.

Parental Rights and the Establishment of Paternity

A closely related and critical domain for understanding women's and men's legal status is that of parental rights. Once again there is tremendous variation in how these issues are handled. The codes range from not incorporating this category of law at all (Tulalip), or including few specifics (Nooksack recognizes termination of parental rights and calls for the placement of children with extended family members, where possible), to complex efforts to define paternity and to create legal obligations to testify in court about paternity (Muckleshoot).

A few generalizations may be made. Most of the codes either state explicitly or imply that parental rights are considered individually; that is, either a father or a mother may have such rights terminated (Lummi, Upper Skagit, Muckleshoot, and Nooksack specifically allow for termination), although in Sauk-Suiattle termination is explicitly rejected. Mothers are thereby able to assume sole custody in the event of the unsuitability of the father. Most of the codes specify that children must be supported, leaving open the prosecution of delinquent parents, ordinarily fathers. These circumstances, although gender-neutral on the surface, provide some legal protection for women's relationships with their minor offspring.

A related issue is where provisions for child support are placed within the code. Particular problems arise where child support is handled under criminal law. In these cases, the police must decide whether to pursue the issue (a serious problem in light of police understaffing); criminal convictions depend on a higher burden of proof than civil cases, thereby increasing the difficulty of obtaining legal relief and getting child support; and a criminal conviction carries a stigma and may actually make it difficult for a man to obtain a job and carry out his legal and financial obligations. Beyond these points, the codes diverge.

The Muckleshoot code is unique in its remarkable emphasis on the question of establishing paternity. Parenthood is defined through biology or adoption, except that the legal status of parenthood is not extended to a father whose paternity is not established by the court, through public records, or acknowledged by him. This places an obligation on the mother to take the father to court to prove his fatherhood and establish his legal responsibilities to his child. However, a legal mechanism exists to establish paternity, regardless of the marital status of the mother and alleged father. A second clause creates additional problems for women: Any person who has sexual intercourse on the reservation thereby places himself or herself under the jurisdiction of the tribal court with respect to any resulting children. This potentially places a very difficult, almost unmanageable, burden on women to establish jurisdiction and resolve issues of child support. Evidence regarding paternity can be taken from statistical probabilities, medical or anthropological evidence, or, simply, reputation in the community concerning paternity. Furthermore, a presumption of paternity is made if the mother and the purported father are married and the child is born within three hundred days of termination of the relationship; if they cohabited or attempted to marry by state or tribal custom and the child is born within three hundred days; or, finally, if the child is under eighteen and the purported father receives the child in his home and "openly holds the child as his to the community." The last provision appears to allow for establishment of paternity under conditions adverse to the interests of the mother, while simultaneously making it difficult to establish paternity when the man wishes to avoid it. In addition, no provisions are included to compel a father (or mother) to make child support payments. Despite the problems, the focus of the Muckleshoot code is not to enfranchise extended family members—provisions useful for men who wish to place the burden for child care elsewhere—but rather to create a mechanism, albeit a difficult one, to place legal obligations on fathers. Furthermore, the Muckleshoot law deals with nonsupport in the civil, not criminal, sections of the code.

The Sauk-Suiattle code provides no rights for the unmarried father whose paternity is not established or acknowledged. This code does not clarify who must make the acknowledgment, and the implications vary considerably if the testimony of the mother, father, either, or some third party is sufficient to establish paternity. Nonsupport, neglect, or desertion of children is handled within the criminal code.

The Nisqually code adds another, quite significant, twist (and burden to women) by limiting tribal membership to the children of women who are resident in the community at the time of birth. Women who are mobile for employment or other reasons thus jeopardize their offsprings' tribal membership, a hardship that does not apply to men, who may live elsewhere for employment and have offspring born to mothers resident on the reservation.

The Upper Skagit code provides for the termination of parental rights under specific circumstances (including sexual and repeated physical abuse) and makes desertion of children a criminal offense.

The Lummi code's domestic relations approach to the issues of parental rights and marriage explicitly creates what appears to be the most advantageous circumstances for women of all of the eight codes, although there is no paternity section as such. Civil procedures are established to order payments from delinquent parties—a clause that is not directed to domestic relations issues but that potentially creates a way for women to seek child support payments from fathers. The code provides for arrangements to be made for custody, visitation, maintenance of a spouse (gender is not specified), and child support. Further, the code creates a legal obligation to support one's child, even those born out of wedlock (under common law, tribal custom, or as established by intent to live together). Additionally, parental rights may be terminated for either the mother or father. The Lummi code also restricts categories of marriage partners: People of the same sex are excluded, as are a range of other people who, in earlier times, would have been included in the pool of potential spouses through the Coast Salish institutions of the sororate and levirate.[42] This code eliminates obligations of women to affinal relatives through these earlier marriage proscriptions. Finally, the code separates the property and legal obligations of wives and husbands to each other during marriage and at divorce.

There are several difficulties in the Lummi code for women with children. One problem with Title 5, Code of Offenses (5.6.01 Offenses Involving Children), is determining whether the father is financially responsible for his offspring if the parental couple has split up and the father is not residing with the child. Secondly, criminal rather than civil proceedings are required if a man, "because of habitual intemperance or gambling, or for any other reason, refuse or neglect to furnish food, shelter, or care, to those dependent upon him. . . ." These features of the code potentially make obtaining child support difficult.

The Tulalip code creates no youth court, has no provisions against nonsupport or for establishing paternity, nor regulations against child abuse. Issues concerning women and children are not the focus of this code. However, as is the case with the Nisqually code, a clause in Article II, section 2 of the membership code specifies that membership is contingent on being born to a member of the

Tulalip tribes who is a resident of the reservation at the time of birth. This creates difficulties for women, but not men, who wish to move for employment.

The issue of emancipation is related to the topic of parental rights. Minors may sever the parent-child bond through actions of their own, just as parents may seek to avoid parental responsibilities or the tribal court may end parental rights. In most of the tribes, marriage creates the status of adulthood, independent of age (this is explicitly rejected in the Upper Skagit code). In addition, children who are self-supporting or who live apart (these are regarded as simultaneous conditions) or are heads of households may be emancipated (Muckleshoot, Nooksack, Skokomish, Tulalip). This raises three points: First, emancipation is an advantage for minor females seeking to care for themselves and their children, in that it removes them from a whole series of restrictions that could obstruct their working careers (such as attendance at job training programs and age-linked restrictions from treaty fishing and hunting). Emancipation also removes restrictions as to the types of contracts that minor women can be bound or can enter into. Thus an emancipated woman could execute legal obligations necessary for self-sufficiency, such as buying a car or renting an apartment. Second, the code also creates the grounds under which parental obligations can be overturned. Negligent parents, who are most likely to be the ones whose children establish separate residence, are, in effect, rewarded for their negligence by the diminution of their obligations. Third, emancipation creates a mechanism for older children to get out of abusive situations without being placed in foster care.

Peace and Safety

As with the other issues, there is significant variability in how conditions of peace and safety are achieved on the reservation and in the meaning of these provisions for men and women. A wide range of regulations have been created to ensure peaceful communities. One significant passage for women is contained in the Lummi code (Upper Skagit has a similar code; the others do not), Title 5.1.08, which specifies,

> In the practice of the culture, traditions, or religions of the Lummi people, no person shall be subjected to any of the following: (1) brutal treatment, including . . . hitting, clubbing . . . biting . . . (3) deprivation of medical treatment . . . (4) forcing any person to take part in any activity relative to traditional culture or religious practices against their will.

These provisions refer to the involuntary seizure and initiation of tribal members into Winter Spirit Dancing societies, occurrences that have produced death and injury in the recent past (precipitating legal action) and that are believed by some women to be differentially abusive to women.[43] Physical contact is used in order to bring a spirit power to the initiate. In addition, the Lummi code (Juvenile Code 8.6.07) establishes legal requirements to report abuse or neglect of children and permits termination of parental rights for cause (8.7.01). Other Lummi code serves to regulate the community, including the following: Chapter 20.6, Illegal Activities, expressively forbids furnishing liquor to minors; the Code of Offenses 5.4.03

requires advance notice and approval for holding public dances, games, or gatherings; and the Housing Authority Declaration of Need 32.2.01 declares the need for "decent, safe and sanitary dwellings," which cannot be relieved through the operation of private enterprise.

Nooksack code (Title 53, Gambling Ordinance, 53.01.010) includes the statement that "in order to safeguard the public health and morals on tribal lands it is necessary to prohibit certain undesirable forms of gambling and to regulate the incidence of those acceptable forms of gambling. . . ." (Nooksack has since opened a public gambling casino.) The code also regulates liquor sales and bans the sale of alcohol, marijuana, and drugs to children (Title 20, Crimes, 20.02.040). These passages are commonly incorporated into the legal codes of the eight tribes, except Nisqually and Tulalip.

Finally, the codes deal with rape in several ways. These provisions must be understood in light of the federal Major Crimes Act, which gives federal courts jurisdiction over seven areas of violent crime committed on reservations. However, in an effort to assert autonomy and in the event the federal court fails to prosecute, tribes have created their own code, and criminal provisions are created for rape in most of the codes. The Lummi code forbids attempted rape or rape or assisting another. Muckleshoot (Title 5 of the criminal code [5.1.50]) forbids "any person who willfully and knowingly by force or violence, rapes, attempts to rape another, or assists. . . ." Sauk-Suiattle and Upper Skagit forbid forcible sexual intercourse. Tulalip, Nooksack, Nisqually, and Skokomish have no relevant code. The Muckleshoot code adds the burden of demonstrating a mental element and allows for the defense of a "reasonable and honest mistake." It is remarkable that such code has developed at all in the absence of clear jurisdiction.

CONCLUSION

To date, no developed literature exists concerning the legal codes of U.S. tribes, and attention concerning legal issues affecting Indians has been focused elsewhere. The variability of the present-day Puget Sound tribal codes considered here puts to rest the notion that the codes merely reflect imposed legal concepts of the mainstream society, a view that implies uniformity. The fact that the communities considered in this study—with similar traditional cultures and engaged in regular social interaction—have chosen differing routes in establishing their own legal codes argues against such a position. It is true that the use of formalized court systems and the employment of non-Indian code writers does not reflect aboriginal practice, but these facts are not sufficient to allow generalizations about the nature of the codes. This paper suggests three methods to begin the process of understanding the nature of the codes and the implications for women: analysis of legal statuses, comparative examination of the domains of code, and consideration of code.

The eight codes vary significantly in how they balance the rights of individuals and the rights of extended family networks. One aspect that the codes have in common is that they do not rely solely on traditional family networks to provide safety and peace in the community. However, while some codes, such as that of Sauk-Suiattle, broadly incorporate the rights of family networks, the emphasis of other codes, particularly the Upper Skagit, is to regard entrenched family networks as potentially the locus of women's difficulties and to restrain the exercise of influence and authority of kin groups in order to enhance women's lives.[44] Under the Upper Skagit code, women are affirmed as heads of households through their eligibility for tribal housing, jobs, and services, independent of male relatives. Women are given explicit protection as wage earners on the reservation, thereby facilitating their contributions to the reservation's families and to the economy. Such restraints on family networks have contradictory implications for women, however: Although restraints provide protections for women, they also limit the powerful roles women have played as influential sisters of significant men and as senior members of family networks.[45]

Among the eight codes included in this study, significant differences exist in overall emphasis and elaboration.[46] Some tribal codes focus on economic development and community regulation, with little attention given to women's issues. Other codes are more directed to peace and safety issues. The differentiation in approach has implications for women, particularly regarding such issues as the rights of parents, legal protections accorded women in the workplace, and procedures for establishing paternity and obtaining child support. Among the codes, the Lummi code is notable for its attention to women's issues, even though women have achieved limited success in tribal elections.[47] The code provides for women's control of their own productivity, for the protection of children, and for child and spousal support. The Upper Skagit code is similarly notable for the protection provided for women in the workplace.

Generally, tribal codes reinforce women's double burden of responsibility to home and work, particularly through the provisions regarding child care. But the codes simultaneously allow a full expression of women's activities: Under the current codes, women are legally full citizens, with the rights to vote and run for office. Older, postcontact feminine ideals of passivity and lesser involvement in spiritual life are not the basis of present legal constructions. In fact, legal avenues have developed that recognize the differing life courses of young men and women.[48] In earlier generations, young women were secluded from public life at adolescence; today provisions allow for women's early careers as mothers and wage earners through procedures for emancipation.

This examination of eight tribal codes shows the relevance of further study of codes in understanding contemporary women's lives. Subsequent research should give attention to the relationship between the rights of individuals and of the collective, noting carefully how the extended family (or other collective body) is defined in various passages of the code. In the Puget Sound case, the extended family is defined as many as seven ways in single codes, thereby allowing restraints on the networks in some areas and facilitating the networks in others. Future work might employ a comparative perspective in order to provide useful material for band councils developing legal structures in Canada and elsewhere. In addition, the development of legal histories can clarify the issue of the interaction between political actors and legal systems in order to provide insights into the factors influencing code construction. Examination of the relationship between the gender composition of tribal councils and tribal code, and of the community economic structures and the code would be particularly valuable.

Acknowledgments

I would like to thank Ted Maloney, Upper Skagit tribal attorney and code writer, and Doreen Maloney, Upper Skagit councillor, for their observations concerning the Upper Skagit legal system; also, Talus Woodward, a bridal code writer; Emily Mansfield, NICS attorney and tribal code writer; and Catriona Elliott, my research assistant for this project. Any errors of fact and interpretation are my own. I also wish to thank the tribal council women from several tribes, anonymous here, who have discussed tribal political life.

Notes

1. This study does not include analysis of the workings of the court and is not directed to explain why tribal codes differ. Although both are useful topics, the focus here is on the codes themselves. See Chief Justice Tom Tso, "Process of Decision Making in Tribal Courts," *Arizona Law Review* 31 (1989): 225–35, for details of the workings of the Navajo court; and Bruce G. Miller, "The Northwest Intertribal Court System and Indian Law," a paper presented at the 46th Annual Northwest Anthropological Conference, Bellingham, Washington, 1993. Analysis of actual trials would supplement the work presented here, a point made by Peter Just in "History, Power, Ideology, and Culture: Current Directions in the Anthropology of Law," *Law and Society Review* 26 (1992): 373–411.

2. William L. Rodman, "A Law Unto Themselves": Legal Innovation in Ambae, Vanuatu," *American Ethnologist* 12 (1985): 602–24.

3. Joan Vincent, *Anthropology and Politics: Visions, Traditions, and Trends* (Tucson: University of Arizona Press, 1990), 429.

4. Augie Fleras and Jean Leonard Elliott, *The Nations Within: Aboriginal-State Relations in Canada, the United States and New Zealand* (Toronto: Oxford University Press, 1992); Sandra Robinson Weber, "Native-Americans Before the Bench: The Nature of Contrast and Conflict in Native-American Law Ways and Western Legal Systems," *The Social Science Journal* 19 (1982): 47–57; Mari J. Matsuda, "Native Custom and Official Law in Hawaii," *Law and Anthropology* 3 (1988): 135–46; Sharon O'Brien, *American Indian Tribal Government* (Norman: University of Oklahoma Press, 1989).

5. Russell Lawrence Barsh and J. Youngblood Henderson, "Tribal Courts, The Model Code, and the Police Idea in American Indian Policy," *Law and Contemporary Problems* 40 (1976): 25–60.

6. Sharon O'Brien, *American Indian Tribal Government*.

7. Carla Christofferson, "Tribal Court's Failure to Protect Native American Women: A Reevaluation of the Indian Civil Rights Act," *The Yale Law Journal* 101 (1991): 169–85.

8. Samuel J. Brakel, *American Indian Tribal Courts: The Costs of Separate Justice* (Chicago: American Bar Association, 1979). See also Susan Lupton, "American Indian Tribal Codes," *Legal Reference Services Quarterly* 1 (1981): 25–41.

9. Miller, "The Northwest Intertribal Court System."

10. In *Law as Process: An Anthropological Approach* (London: Routledge and Keegan Paul, 1978), Sally Falk Moore observed that it is misleading to seek out core ideas in the law that express important social values because of the slow construction of the law through aggregation. Nonetheless, I argue that despite the fact that much of the law does not result from a rational, considered process, the newly emerging codes clearly reflect the values and aims of influential community leaders. For example, one Upper Skagit tribal councillor held specific concerns that protections be provided tribal employees in order that the community be productive. Her concerns were addressed in specific code. Sometimes the interests of the councillors are more personal. I was told of a case in one of the tribes in which a councillor pushed for code that would accommodate the interests of her underaged son. This is not ordinarily the case, however. These leaders and their values are more fully addressed elsewhere (Miller, "A Sociocultural Explanation of the Election of Women to Tribal Council: The Upper Skagit Case" [Ph.D. dissertation, Arizona State University, 1989]; idem, "Women and Politics: Comparative Evidence from the Northwest Coast," *Ethnology* 31 (1992): 367–83.

11. Harry Chesnin, a Seattle lawyer involved in the process of code writing in Puget Sound since the 1970s, has pointed out that variation in tribal codes may reflect the period in which code was written and the personal outlook and interests of particular code writers hired by the tribes. Code writers, however, clearly assign priority to the interests of the councils and advisory committees. The writers are given guidelines and frequently asked by the tribal councils to revise code, particularly in the last decade.

12. Carrie Menkel-Meadow and Shari Seidman Diamond, "The Content, Method, and Epistemology of Gender in Sociolegal Studies," *Law and Society Review* 25 (1991): 221–38.

13. Ralph W. Johnson, "Introduction," in *Indian Tribal Codes: A Microfiche Collection of Indian Tribal Codes*, ed. Ralph W. Johnson (Seattle: Marian Gould Law Library, University of Washington School of Law, 1981).

14. Miller, "Women and Politics."

15. Northwest Intertribal Court System (NICS), "Traditional and Informal Dispute Resolution Processes in Tribes of the Puget Sound and Olympic Peninsula Region" (unpublished ms.); Miller, "The Northwest Intertribal Court System."

16. NICS, "Traditional and Informal Dispute Resolution."

17. June Collins, *Valley of the Spirits* (Seattle: University of Washington Press, 1974); Chief Martin J. Sampson, *Indians of Skagit County* (Mount Vernon, WA: Skagit County Historical Series no. 2, 1972).

18. Ralph W. Johnson and Rachael Paschal, eds., *Tribal Court Handbook for the 26 Federally Recognized Tribes in Washington State* (Olympia, WA: Office of the Administrator for the Courts, State of Washington, 1991); Donald L. Burnett, Jr., "An Historical Analysis of the 1968 'Indian Civil Rights' Act," *Harvard Journal on Legislation* 9 (1972): 556–626.

19. Burnett, "An Historical Analysis," 565.

20. Johnson and Pascal, "Tribal Court Handbook," 3; Burnett, "An Historical Analysis," 590.

21. Johnson and Pascal, "Tribal Court Handbook," 3.

22. Ibid., 37.

23. Data compiled from Johnson and Pascal, "Tribal Court Handbook."

24. Ted Maloney, Upper Skagit tribal attorney and sometime code writer, personal communication.

25. Public Law 83-280 (1953) empowered states to impose jurisdiction over Indian reservations in several legal domains. Subsequently, Washington State enacted RCW 37.12.010, requiring tribal consent to do so. The Muckleshoot, Nisqually, and Tulalip

tribes, among those under consideration here, came under these terms. The Upper Skagit, Nooksack, and Sauk-Suiattle reservations were created later, and it is unclear if P.L. 280 applies. Tribal and state jurisdiction are concurrent under P.L. 280, creating the possibilities for a "race to the courthouse, and a race to final judgment" (Johnson and Pascal 199:9).

26. Upper Skagit Tribal Police Report, 1992 (unpublished ms.).

27. Brakel, "American Indian Tribal Courts," 36.

28. William Quinn "Intertribal Integration: The Ethnological Argument in *Duro v. Reina*," *Ethnology* 40 (1993): 34–69.

29. Miller, "A Sociocultural Explanation."

30. The Lummi code differs from Washington State code concerning common property in that the Lummi code provides for separability of property acquired during marriage. The more important issue is that the present Lummi code is in accordance with traditional practice.

31. These male boat owners have composed the majority in the tribal councils, a fact noted by Daniel L. Boxberger, *To Fish in Common: The Ethnohistory of Lummi Indian Salmon Fishing* (Lincoln: University of Nebraska Press, 1989).

32. June McC. Collins, *Valley of the Spirits.*

33. Marian W. Smith, "The Coast Salish of Puget Sound," *American Anthropologist* 43 (1941): 197–211.

34. Miller, "A Sociocultural Explanation"; idem, "Women and Politics."

35. Personal communication, Ted Maloney.

36. Miller, "Women and Politics."

37. NICS, "Traditional and Informal Dispute Resolution."

38. Miller, "Women and Politics"; Collins, *Valley of the Spirits.*

39. Miller, "A Sociocultural Explanation."

40. Ibid.

41. See Sally Snyder, "Skagit Society and Its Existential Basis: An Ethnofolkloristic Reconstruction" (Ph.D. dissertation, University of Washington, 1964); Collins, *Valley of the Spirits*; Miller, "A Sociocultural Explanation"; and Pamela Amoss, *Coast Salish Spirit Dancing: the Survival of an Ancestral Religion* (Seattle: University of Washington Press, 1978), for details of male and female life course.

42. Collins, *Valley of the Spirits.*

43. Coast Salish men who were involuntarily "grabbed" have also recently complained of assault in winter ceremonials. A recent case involved Rocky Thomas of the Lyackson band in British Columbia. He was awarded $12,000 in damages by the British Columbia Supreme Court (*Vancouver Sun*, August 1992). It is important to note that not all community members have a negative view of winter ceremonials. There are many participants and supporters.

44. This strategy does not appear to be accounted for in the literature. One analyst argued, for example, that principles of legal and political individualism have been "extended" into tribal governance as a result of the Indian Bill of Rights of 1968 and at the expense of group-based rights (Frances Svensson, "Liberal Democracy and Group Rights: The Legacy of Individualism and Its Impact on American Indian Tribes," *Political Studies* 27 (1979): 421–39). This approach fails to entertain the possibility that innovators within communities may see advantage in reconstructing the relationship between group and individual entitlements.

An interesting comparison may be made with Coast Salish communities of southern Vancouver Island, immediately adjacent to those in Washington State, who lack the jurisdiction to establish their own court systems. Experiments in alternative justice systems that divert charges from the mainstream societies' court system to a band's male-dominated council of elders have foundered on charges of abuse of the system by powerful family networks. Women have criticized the system for covering up sexual abuse of women and perpetuating the influence of the family system. A reporter noted that one woman "says she knows of several cases where powerful families pressured women to use the alternative system, which involves the band's council of elders, rather than bringing sexual assault charges to court. Mavis Henry, a member of the Pauquachin band of southern Vancouver Island, stated, 'It can happen in subtle ways. . . . A family will offer to buy a car or do repairs on your house in return'" (*Vancouver Sun*, 31 July 1992). The article points out that other women were forced to move from their reserve. The implication of the article is that large, politically powerful families attempt to coerce assault victims into using traditional systems of restitution or to completely bury their charges of abuse.

In a related debate, Jo-anne Fiske, in "Child of the State, Mother of the Nation: Aboriginal Women and the Ideology of Motherhood" (a paper presented to the Joint Meetings of the Atlantic Canada Studies and B.C. Studies Association, 21–24 May 1992), has shown how Carrier and Micmac women have relied on metaphors of motherhood in making claims to a present-day political position for women based on "sexual equality [of] folk laws instead of . . . state law" (p. 5). In this discourse, motherhood is represented as traditionally the dominant social identity in the community, the font of cultural knowledge, and the source of band identity. Further, these claims are said to be made "not as women seeking individual rights as against their male peers" (p. 24) but in the struggle against the intrusion of the state. "It is because of their [women's] *collective* responsibility for future generations that they seek sexual equality . . ." (ibid.). In this case, traditional kinship structures are viewed as the source of women's protection, and new systems of justice are seen as creating difficulties. See also Teressa Nahanee, "Do Native Women Need Charter Rights? *Priorities: A Feminist Voice in a Socialist Movement* 20 (1992): 5–7; Karlene Faith, Mary Gottfriedson, Cherry Joe, Wendy Leonard, and Sharon McIvor, "Native Women in Canada: A Quest for Justice," *Social Justice* 17 (1991): 167–88; Wendy Moss, "Indigenous Self-Government in Canada and Sexual Equality under the Indian Act: Resolving Conflicts Between Collective and Individual Rights," *Queens Law Journal* 15 (1990): 279–305.

45. Such family networks persist as underlying political structures, but women as individuals are free to amass resources outside of this system of resource ownership and control. Many women have responded by directing their resources back within the family network through regular patterns of generalized reciprocity, and others have emphasized development of careers as cultural mediators and technical experts.

46. There are other background similarities between codes. None of the eight legal systems is based on an explicit notion of differences between the sexes. None relies on special theories of femininity or masculinity. Women are not excluded from voting because of theories of differential intellect or moral development, although some codes recognize differing circumstances for men and women in limited ways. Women are not partitioned into legal categories with separate rights. (For example, married and unmarried women are not treated separately except as this applies to the emancipation of youth.)

47. Miller, "Women and Politics."

48. Snyder, "Skagit Society and its Existential Basis"; Collins, *Valley of the Spirits*.

PART III

CONTEMPORARY POWWOW

The contemporary powwow is a culturally innovative and diverse phenomenon in contemporary Native life. It is not only intertribal but also a mixture of sacred and social dances, and may contain spiritual, cultural, political, and economic dimensions. Often traditional tribal dances are performed as special presentations at powwows, and in the southern drum style, members of the Kiowa Gourd Society frequently purify the event with special dances and ceremonies. Contemporary powwows also have many social dances and competitive dances, and dancers may travel from one powwow to the next throughout the entire powwow season. Many communities offer a place to set up a tent and provide food, and dancers who win the contests receive cash prizes. The offering of prizes helps support native dancers by providing economic rewards for their efforts, for the dances take time to perfect and the costumes are costly and must be maintained.

Powwows are now practiced in a variety of settings throughout much of the nation. Some large urban areas such as Los Angeles have active rounds of powwows, and on many weekends one or more powwows draw crowds. The powwow organizers invite local dancers, and often drum groups from reservation communities are invited to participate. Reservation communities continue to hold powwows where dancers from local and other reservations attend. While most powwows are intertribal, some tribal communities do not have strong cultural ties to the powwow tradition, which emphasizes plains style dancing and drum music. Thus many tribal communities, such as the pueblo, Navajo, and Apache, do not participate directly in the powwow tradition and their dances and ceremonies are very different from the powwow style. Even among plains tribes, the Northern Cheyenne have dances and ceremonies that are very unique, and few members of other tribes attend. The Crow, however, have a very large intertribal gathering called Crow Fair, which takes place near the site of the Little Bighorn Battlefield, where George Custer and his men were defeated in 1876.

There are two major powwow styles: northern and southern. The powwows are distinguished by their musical beats and their symbolic arrangement. In the northern style, the drums are located on the outside of the dance circle. In the southern style, the drums are located in the middle of the dance circle and symbolize the sacred center or fire. Although the dance rhythms and songs vary between the northern and southern powwow styles, many dancers learn to dance both styles.

Contemporary powwows are also ways in which urban Indian and tribal people can participate in pan-Indian cultural and community events. Powwows have grown into a style and tradition of their own with new dances and songs. Drum groups record their songs on compact disks, and there is considerable borrowing of dance style and dress, as well as songs and dances among the drum groups and dancers. The powwow represents a creative mixture of tradition, the sacred, social community, identity, and change.

6

The Powwow as a Public Arena for Negotiating Unity and Diversity in American Indian Life

Mark Mattern

INTRODUCTION

THE POWWOW[1] IS OFTEN CITED for its importance in contemporary Indian life as a constituent of tribal and Indian identity, and as a unifying force in Indian life.[2] Although each of these testimonies may be true, each tells an incomplete story. Each downplays or ignores entirely the disagreements and conflicts that occur within the powwow grounds and that swirl around powwow practices. Each erases the multiple differences among Indians and implies that Indian identity and commitments are simply reinforced and reproduced through powwow practices, rather than debated, negotiated, and changed. Each also erases the constitutive presence of power and politics within the powwow arena. Powwows are constituents of identity and a unifying force in contemporary Indian life, but they are also arenas of conflict and disagreement in which power plays an important role and in which Indians implicitly and explicitly debate their identity and mutual commitments.

In this article I will argue that the powwow can best be understood in these dual, paradoxical terms: It plays a unifying role in Indian life while providing a public arena for negotiation of differences and disagreements. The unifying role played by powwows is especially significant in light of the diversity within and among tribes. Although others have argued that the powwow plays a unifying role in this context of diversity, much can nevertheless still be added to our understanding of the specific practices that foster this unifying role. In the first part of this article, I will examine specific powwow practices in light of their unifying role. I will interpret the powwow as a communicative arena in which common experiences help create and sustain a common ground of memory, experience, identity, and commitment out of disparate experiences and identities.

On the other hand, the powwow is also a public arena where Indians explicitly and implicitly negotiate their differences and their disagreements over

Mark Mattern is an assistant professor of political science at Chapman University, Orange, California.

their identifying traits and mutual commitments. This role of enabling the negotiation of differences and disagreements helps manage the tension between unity and diversity, making Indian communities more resilient and adaptable. As in other public arenas, the role of power at a powwow is central in helping determine both the nature and the outcome of disagreement and negotiation.

Throughout this article I will be using the terms Indian, American Indian, and indigenous people to refer to indigenous people of Minnesota and western Wisconsin and, unless I say otherwise, only those people. The powwow practices that I describe should be viewed as specific to the region and not necessarily generalizable beyond the region. Whenever possible, I will refer to specific tribes. Although this paper focuses primarily on the powwow experiences of Ojibwa, Dakota, Winnebago, and Menominee tribes of Minnesota and western Wisconsin, it is often difficult to speak only in terms of select tribes. Members of many different tribes and bands live in Minnesota and western Wisconsin, especially in urban areas such as the Twin Cities. Many of these people attend powwows in the area, most of which are now intertribal.

THE POWWOW AS A UNIFYING FORCE IN INDIAN LIFE[3]

Indian tribes differ widely in tradition, custom, commitment, and interests. Multiple differences also exist within each tribe. According to one Ojibwa expression, "If you put five Ojibwa in a room together, there will be at least ten different opinions on any subject."[4] With the exception of powwows hosted by supratribal and intertribal organizations such as the American Indian Movement (AIM) or university-based American Indian centers, powwows are usually hosted by a single tribe. However, most modern powwows are attended by members of several or more tribes. As many as sixty or more tribes from the United States and Canada may be represented at a large powwow. Although there are significant differences between tribes, powwow practices among tribes of Minnesota and western Wisconsin remain largely the same, enabling me to write at a certain level of generalization. The practices that I emphasize are generic to powwow experience in the region. Some of the specific powwow elements and practices that play a unifying role in this context of diversity include the philosophy and spirituality that underlie powwow practices; the emcee; music and dance; and explicit community-affirming practices such as feasts, honoring, giveaways, and rituals of inclusion.

PHILOSOPHY AND SPIRITUALITY

Although contemporary powwows include many secular dimensions, they are supported by philosophical and spiritual traditions that emphasize unity and inclusiveness.[5] For example, the physical space in which communicative interactions occur, a circle, is itself rich with significance for this discussion of American Indian unity and diversity. Among Indians of Minnesota and western Wisconsin, the circle carries spiritual significance as an embodiment of all living creatures, and relations within this circle are characterized by unity, harmony, and inclusiveness. This imagery of the circle permeates powwow experience. The dance arena is always set up as a circle, or an oval if the physical space will not accommodate a circle. This includes powwows held indoors in gymnasiums, auditoriums, church basements, and other square or rectangular physical spaces. Musical performance is organized into drum groups—groups of approximately four to ten drummer-singers who encircle the drum in performance. These drum groups set up either in the center of the dance arena or around its perimeter. Dancers move in a circle around the arena. Around the dance arena are seats for the audience, and around these seats are various food and craft vendors. Each powwow is thus a material embodiment of the underlying philosophy represented by the circle, and participation in a powwow signifies membership in the circle.

At the core of powwow experience in Minnesota and western Wisconsin is the drum, which, in American Indian philosophy in this region, symbolizes the heart of all living creatures and of indigenous people. As some see it, without the drum there would be no powwow and no indigenous people. In secular terms, the powwow relies on the drum for its central activities of singing and dancing. Since the drum is "the heartbeat of our sacred circle," and since the "sacred circle" refers to an inclusive wholeness of humans and all living creatures, the drum also has a deep spiritual significance in American Indian philosophy. It is considered the heartbeat of all living creatures and, "if ever that heartbeat should discontinue, we are gone, everyone is gone."[6]

Of course, not everyone brings philosophical or spiritual interests to a powwow. Although many, perhaps most, Indians can recite the philosophical and spiritual meaning underlying powwow practices, it is unclear how many take it seriously. As we will see later, some Indians are concerned with a trend that they perceive of an increasing secularization of the powwow. Regardless of the philosophical and spiritual orientation of participants, the powwow represents for most people a place where differences can be set aside, at least temporarily, in favor of fellowship and unity. Adding a philosophical and spiritual dimension intensifies this commitment to, and experience of, fellowship and unity for some participants.

THE EMCEE

In addition to his (the vast majority of emcees are men) role of announcing the order of events and keeping the powwow moving, the emcee plays a central role in informing participants and observers of the significance of the events and practices as they unfold, and in (selectively) enforcing tribal and Indian customs. The emcee frequently explains what is happening and the reason for it. Much of this is directed at non-Indians and members of other tribes, but it is also intended to remind tribal members of the meaning of their practices. Some emcees accomplish this through appeals to collective memory, exhorting listeners to "remember." Collective memory is also reinforced in the powwow program guide with articles on tribal history, dedications to prominent tribal members, and central events in indigenous peoples' history such as Wounded Knee. At other times the emcee enforces tribal customs and traditions with statements such as "children should not be carried in the dance arena" and "dogs are not allowed in the powwow arena unless they arrive in a cooking pot," and exhorts participants to "watch the leaders and do what they do."[7]

In making public and explicit some of the assumptions and beliefs that underlie powwow practices, the emcee recalls to participants' minds the significance of their actions, including, sometimes, their philosophical and spiritual dimensions, and reinforces collective memories. The articulation of shared memories reminds tribal members and others of common histories. Overall, the emcee contributes to a common awareness among powwow participants of the significance of their actions, of their similarities and differences, of partially common histories and traditions, and of partially common interests and commitments. Of course, different emcees handle their role differently. Some emcees limit their role to moving things along and entertainment, while others are more likely to offer explanations and commentary. The emcee and other featured speakers also sometimes endorse particular stands on key political issues such as American Indian self-determination, sovereignty, tribal treaty rights, and the environment. This is especially true of the powwows organized by AIM but often is true for other powwows as well. The articulation and rearticulation of these issues contribute to a common awareness among participants of political issues facing them at tribal and supratribal levels.

MUSIC AND DANCE

Beliefs and commitments that foster unity are embedded in the music and dancing. The aesthetics of the music and dancing, which emphasize repetition and unison, reinforce the commitment to unity represented by the circle in which they take place. The most common rhythms are straightforward duple, with occasional "honor" beats struck on the offbeat to honor Mother Earth or a specific person, event, or idea. The musicians drum and sing entirely in unison except for the leader's brief solo introductions. One measure of the quality of performance is the extent to which the musicians achieve a tight, cohesive sound. Although songs vary widely in intent, meaning, style, and sound, the song structure remains standard within each type of song. The so-called incomplete repetition form, or AA/BCD/BCD, is the most common and, like the other song forms, is quite short.[8] Thus, in order to play for a dance, the song is repeated in "pushups" a designated or requested number of times, normally four or five times but usually longer during a grand entry and sometimes longer for popular dances.

The drumming is associated with both aesthetic and spiritual power. Whatever the drumming might lack in complexity it makes up for in intensity and forcefulness of expression and reception. In his study of Menominee powwow music, J. S. Slotkin refers to "the tremendous dominating drumbeat which makes everything vibrate to it. . . . I never had such a sense of rhythm penetrating me."[9] The unison singing, when done with skill and conviction, adds power and forcefulness to this shared affective experience. The net effect is a potent physical and, for some, emotional experience shared by musicians, dancers, and listeners. Everyone in the powwow grounds shares the physical experience of hearing and physically feeling the drum. It focuses attention and experience, contributing to a sharing of experience. Powwow participants share this experience in qualitatively different ways and to varying degrees of intensity, but most find it hard to ignore. For people who bring spiritual interests to the powwow, the drum is also "the most important material embodiment of [spiritual] power."[10] Since the drum is considered the heartbeat of Mother Earth, beating on the drum puts people in touch with spiritual powers. It is a form of communication between humans and spiritual powers, a means of summoning strength from the spiritual world.

The "intertribal" dance is the most common social, noncontest dance. Anyone can dance, including non-Indians and people wearing street clothes. The step is a basic one-two, touch-step requiring only minimal expertise, but experienced dancers sometimes display their more advanced steps during an intertribal. There are several dancer categories on the Northern Plains powwow circuit, each characterized by a distinct set of stylistic norms and movements. These include, for men, traditional, grass, and fancy dancing and, for women, traditional, jingle dress, and fancy shawl dancing. Individual expression occurs, but within the parameters of each type of dance. Despite the variations in style, each dance builds on multiple repetitions of the simple one-two, touch-step that characterizes the grand entries and the intertribal dancing. Variations are woven around the basic step according to the artistic fancy of the dancer. For most dances, the dancers must pay close attention to the singers in order to stop dancing at the same time that the singers stop. This is especially true for contest dancing, where points are deducted or the dancer is disqualified for not stopping on cue. Attention is thus necessarily focused intently on the singing and the drumming in order to follow the song and know where the singers are in the song. This is made easier by the fact that most songs have a similar structure and that the musicians provide various cues such as slight changes in drumming patterns.

These aesthetic qualities of repetition and unison found in powwow music and dancing complement and reinforce in sound and motion the philosophy underlying the powwow experience of unity and inclusiveness. They add impetus and reinforce them by making them material. They encourage a concentration and focusing of attention, and intensify the experience of sharing during the powwow, as different participants engage simultaneously, if temporarily and at varying levels of engagement, in the central practices that define the powwow.

The net effect is at least a partial unifying and integrating of experience within the powwow grounds.[11]

EXPLICIT COMMUNITY-AFFIRMING PRACTICES

Several powwow practices explicitly affirm and reinforce unity among Indians. One practice that occurs frequently at a powwow and that reinforces the implied and explicit commitments to respect and fellowship within powwow experience is the custom of "honoring." Implicit forms of honoring include the grand entries—the inaugural events occurring several times during a powwow in which the dancers "enter the circle" to the sound of singing and drumming—which are led by honored military veterans. Many instances of honoring occur explicitly. Participants generally funnel their requests through the emcee to honor a relative, friend, or member of another tribe, so it is usually done publicly and often is accompanied by a giveaway. The giveaways themselves are explicit expressions of honor and appreciation for one or more individuals. This custom of honoring plays the role of affirming and cementing social relationships among various tribal members. It is a formal means of publicly acknowledging an important social relationship, and of expressing an enduring commitment to other members of the tribe and, sometimes, to members of other tribes.

Various formal and informal mechanisms are used to invite inclusion and participation in the powwow circle. For example, the emcee typically issues an explicit invitation to join the circle, welcoming tribal members, members of visiting tribes, non-Indians, and other prominent visitors and encouraging everyone to participate. Other powwow practices such as the communal feasts to which everyone is invited reinforce this invitation to join and participate. Other mechanisms for inviting or signaling inclusion involve ritualized use of singing and dancing. For example, grand entries are led by military veterans, signaling to powwow participants their integration into the circle and their place of honor within it. This holds special significance to Vietnam veterans, for whom reintegration into U.S. life has sometimes proven difficult. Other ritualized welcomes can occur at the request of powwow participants who wish to "return to the circle" themselves or to invite or signal another's return or entrance into the circle. One such event occurred at the 1993 Prairie Island Dakota powwow. A young man who had been "out of the circle" for six years wished to return. Working through the emcee, he announced a special song and dance, accompanied by a giveaway and a public honoring of his grandfather, to mark his return. Accompanied by two special friends and followed by tribal elders and family members, he began dancing slowly around the arena. People from the audience entered the arena to greet the young man and welcome him back, then joined the dancers at the rear. As they danced around the arena, slowly increasing in number, family members strewed blankets, shawls, and money around the arena, which members of the audience were free to pick up. The arena gradually filled up with tribal members dancing the young man back into the circle and with others participating in the giveaway. During this event, the emcee told the young man's story of falling away from the circle and his reasons for wishing to return, articulated the importance of this public affirmation of his return, and encouraged everyone to "come down and welcome him back."[12]

The invitation to participate is not unlimited. While an effort is made to make the powwow experience inclusive, participation requires at least partial respect for and adoption of the norms of the host tribe or organization. The host tribe expects visitors to respect its customs and behave more or less in accordance with them. Also, financial considerations partially underlie the commitment to welcoming and inclusion. The powwow committee often needs the gate receipts of members of other tribes and of non-Indians to pay the bills, which include the honorariums for dancers and singers, the feasts, and prize money if it is a contest powwow.

In daily and weekly powwow experience, these practices reinforce and recreate existing beliefs and commitments and foster their common possession. This process of "making common" occurs at both tribal and supratribal levels. Specifically, tribal identity is re-created and reinforced at a powwow through the articulation of distinctively tribal commitments, as well as through the frequent references to tribal memory, history, and tradition, and through the reinforcement of tribal customs and styles of singing and dancing. A similar process of identification occurs for many across tribal boundaries at a powwow through the articulation of commitments that span tribes, through the development and reinforcement of common memories and histories, and through the occasional references to political, social, cultural, and economic issues that span several tribes. The partial consolidation of musical and dance styles that characterizes contemporary Northern Plains powwow practice[13] both reflects this growth of a supratribal identity and helps create it. Identification at a supratribal level does not replace tribal identification. Some powwow participants identify only with their particular tribe. For others, a supratribal identification, representing points of commonality spanning tribal differences, complements their tribal identification without replacing it.

In sum, the powwow is a unifying force in American Indian life at both tribal and supratribal levels. It gathers diverse Indians together where communicative interactions can take place that, taken together, define a partly common ground of identity, belief, and commitment. The practices that define the powwow experience—the singing and dancing, the feasts and giveaways, the fry bread and Indian tacos—together help define a sense of "who we are," of what it means to be both a member of a particular tribe and an American Indian. In affirming and re-creating tribal and supratribal identity and commitment, powwow practices contribute to social cohesion and the survival of Indians as Indians. Participants leave a powwow with a reinforced sense of what it means to be a tribal Indian and an American Indian.

POWER AND POLITICS IN POWWOWS: NEGOTIATING AMERICAN INDIAN IDENTITY AND COMMITMENT

Thus far I have treated the powwow as an arena in which unity and social cohesion among American Indians is fostered. While acknowledging differences between individuals and tribes, I have posed this discussion in terms that downplay the role of power and that are free of disagreement and conflict. Indeed, most powwow practice concerns the routine reinforcement of existing beliefs and practices. However, the powwow arena is constituted partly by differences and disagreements that provoke conflict and challenges to existing beliefs and practices. These disagreements sometimes fuel explicit debate over powwow practice as Indians discuss among themselves the relative merits of different practices. The debate occurs within the powwow arena and on its sidelines, among members of powwow organizing committees, in informal interactions among powwow participants, and in discussions and arguments entirely outside of powwow grounds. Sometimes these disagreements are worked out directly within powwow practice, while others are not. Also, sometimes the debate occurs in wordless challenges to existing practices and the responses by others. Since these various powwow practices embody communal identity and commitments, challenges to them and debates over them are, by extension, challenges to and debates over communal identity and commitment. In other words, Indians do not simply reaffirm and reinforce their mutual identity and commitments through powwow practices; they negotiate them.

In this light, the powwow can be viewed as a public arena of negotiation and deliberation over American Indian identity and commitment. The outcome of these disagreements and deliberations depends at least partly on power, understood to mean both domination (control of others) and capacity (possession of the abilities and resources necessary to formulate goals and bring them to fruition).[14] In the following pages, I will discuss disagreements and conflicts generated around gender differences, the tension between secular and spiritual interests, and the relations between Indians and non-Indians.

GENDER DIFFERENCES

Powwow practices are gendered in many ways, and these gendered practices both reveal and reinforce relations of power between genders. This is apparent in music and dance performance. Music performance is organized into drum groups, or groups of approximately four to ten male singers who sit around the drum and beat on it with a drumstick as they sing. In Canadian tribes and tribes of the western and northwestern United States, women sometimes join or form drum groups, but in Minnesota and western Wisconsin women rarely participate in drum groups. Women's roles are generally limited to occasionally "helping the men" musically by singing along an octave above the men's voices.

Day-to-day musical performance implicitly reinforces the commitment to this form of gender exclusion. Some women have attempted to challenge this practice of exclusion by forming all women drum groups. However, their efforts have met with limited acceptance, and today women are not active participants in drum groups in the Minnesota and western Wisconsin powwow circuit.[15]

A more successful attempt by women to challenge gender roles occurred in powwow dancing. Traditionally, male dancing is athletic and vigorous, while female dancing is relatively demure and restrained. However, one of the most popular contemporary forms of dancing for girls and young women, fancy shawl dancing, involves spirited and athletic movements. Fancy shawl dancing is a relative newcomer to the powwow scene, introduced within the last thirty-five years by girls and young women who persisted in its practice in the face of opposition by many who believed that its spirited athleticism was inconsistent with traditional expectations of women. Now it is an accepted form of dance on the Northern Plains powwow circuit.[16]

The outcome of challenges to gendered practices depends on relative power. The attempts by some women to redefine their status within powwow practices depend partly on the support or nonsupport of the emcee, who is responsible for articulating and enforcing tribal customs—a role that most emcees play selectively. The emcee represents a dominant voice, chosen by a dominant powwow organizing committee, and may or may not fairly represent the interests and views of the entire tribe. The attempts by some women to redefine gender relations also depends on their ability to enlist the support of other women and men, and to challenge other related commitments such as the commitment to unity that pervades powwow experience and discourages participants from raising public challenges to prevailing norms and practices.

SECULAR VERSUS SPIRITUAL INTERESTS

Another point of disagreement that sometimes surfaces in contemporary powwow experience is over the relative weight in powwow experience of secular versus spiritual concerns. Some Indians fear that the powwow is being increasingly secularized, denuded of its spiritual content. One expression of this disagreement concerns the use of the eagle bone whistle or similar carved whistles. These whistles are carried by select military veterans and, in traditional usage, are blown during the start of spiritual ceremonies in order to call in the power of the spirits. However, some of these whistle carriers now also use it for secular purposes during powwow music and dance performance. In contemporary powwow practice, a dancer with a whistle will sometimes blow it in order to signal to the members of the performing drum group that they should play another pass through the song. Given that twenty or more drums may show up to play at a powwow, the time allotted to each drum can be very small. One way for dancers who have been honored as whistle carriers to prolong the play of favorites is to blow their whistles. Some powwow participants object to this secular use of the whistle, arguing that it dilutes its spiritual significance. Sometimes, the emcee or a spiritual elder will interrupt the dancing to publicly admonish the whistle carriers for using their whistles in this secular way.[17]

Another example of this disagreement over the relative weight of secular versus spiritual matters concerns the growing prominence of financial concerns in powwow experience. As the number of powwows multiplies, there is more and more competition among powwow organizing committees to attract dancers and singers. One way to lure them is to offer more prize money and honorariums. The development of a casino economy among some Indian populations has made considerably more money available to devote to powwows. Some Indians fear that these developments encourage greater emphasis on financial incentives and less emphasis on spiritual, cultural, and political incentives for participating in powwows. Some Indians also believe that the increasing emphasis on contest dancing and singing introduces unhealthy competition into the dance arena, which disrupts the Good Medicine of friendship and fellowship. Contest powwows are observably disruptive of at least some traditional practices such as the giveaways, which are likely to be shunted aside to early morning hours, and the social dancing, which must be deemphasized in order to free enough time for the contest dancing.

A related disagreement concerns the practice associated with some contest powwows of making the powwow a "closed drum" event. Traditionally, the powwow organizing committee simply issues a general invitation to drum groups to show up and register to play on a first-come-first-served basis, sometimes up to an advertised limit of twenty to thirty drum groups. Some of the drum groups that show up to play are composed of seasoned and accomplished veteran musicians, while others are composed of amateurs whose musical performance may be well short of accomplished. In traditional practice, no attempt is made to favor drum groups, and musical performance simply occurs on a rotating basis. In hopes of assuring better quality musical performance and attracting more and better dancers, some organizing committees now hire one or sometimes two or three exceptional drum groups to play the role of host drum(s). Some powwow organizing committees further limit musical participation by designating their powwow as a "closed drum" powwow, meaning that only invited drums whose musical performance is assured can play. This is a controversial practice, since many believe that it contradicts the powwow ethics of welcoming and inclusiveness.

Indians also disagree over whether it is appropriate to politicize the powwow. Some Indians distance themselves from any political uses whatsoever of the powwow or powwow practices such as drumming. These Indians argue against political uses of powwow practices on the grounds that politics is divisive and this contradicts the ethic of unity and the spiritual dimensions (which emphasize wholeness and unity) that they believe should pervade powwow experience. They also object to the introduction of political themes by the emcee or by others. In contrast to these Indians who disavow any political significance or use of the powwow and powwow practices, others explicitly and pointedly introduce political themes and issues into the powwow arena and carry the powwow drum into other explicitly political arenas such as demonstrations. This is especially true of the powwows organized by members of AIM.

In this ongoing disagreement over secular versus spiritual concerns in powwow experience, the secular power of factors such as casino money plays an increasingly influential role in determining the nature of powwows. Especially when viewed in the context of economic marginalization experienced by many Indians, it is not surprising that this secular power often overwhelms the power wielded by spiritual elders and others who are determined to maintain the spiritual character of powwows. Similarly, the spiritual authority of elders is sometimes overwhelmed by the wholly secular interest held by many, especially youth, in having a good time dancing to the best drum groups, whose play is prolonged by blowing an eagle bone whistle. Finally, members of AIM sometimes enlist the power of the media in publicizing their political goals through powwows or powwow practices. For example, members of AIM garnered national television attention during the 1991 baseball World Series and the 1992 football Superbowl, both held at the Humphrey Metrodome in Minneapolis, by organizing political demonstrations to protest the use of American Indian names and symbols as mascots: Braves and Redskins, respectively. Demonstrators at both events were led by American Indian drummers who were present to summon spiritual and aesthetic power, to focus attention, and to encourage solidarity. These events inevitably encouraged national audiences to associate American Indian drumming with political protest, whether or not the majority of Indians view the association as appropriate.

RELATIONS BETWEEN INDIANS AND NON-INDIANS

Disagreements over the appropriate relation between Indians and non-Indians are sometimes negotiated in and around powwow practices. While the invitation issued by the emcee to non-Indians to participate in powwow practices appears genuine, it is sometimes uncertain how to handle situations that arise such as inappropriate dancing or photography of dancers. Although the majority of non-Indians who attend powwows may behave respectfully and appropriately, some do not. A common sight at a powwow is a non-Indian snapping photographs of dancers. This strikes some Indians, especially those for whom the powwow carries spiritual significance, as inappropriate, especially when the photographer actually gets in the way. Some Indian dancers, on the other hand, are apparently happy to oblige requests for posed photographs. Another common sight at some powwows is the attempt by some non-Indians to participate in the social dancing. While some fit well into the dancing, others stand out by attempting to improvise. Sometimes inappropriate behavior is studiously ignored, sometimes it is guardedly ridiculed, and sometimes the emcee or others may intervene.

It is also uncertain if the invitation issued to non-Indians should extend to participation in drum groups. Participation by non-Indians in drum groups is rare in Minnesota and western Wisconsin. My research turned up only one non-Indian who regularly participates in a drum group on the powwow circuit in Minnesota and western Wisconsin, and his presence occasionally provoked controversy as some Indians questioned his presence and his right to join in the practice of "drum-hopping" in which drummers circulate among various drum groups.

Indian relations with non-Indians are also partly negotiated at powwows in discussions and debates over the best response to the appropriation of Indian culture by non-Indians. One example, already noted, is the use of Indian symbols and names by sports teams. At some powwows, one can observe simultaneously a representative from AIM decrying such uses and several Indian youth wearing sports caps and jackets imprinted with the offending logos. It may be tempting, on the one hand, to discount the wearing of these sports logos as the ignorance of youth or, on the other hand, to romanticize it as a defiant gesture of reappropriation. These may both be true. However, another plausible interpretation would simply emphasize that some Indians do not object to the use of these names by sports teams. The powwow is apparently open and flexible enough to accommodate these competing views on this issue, even when AIM is the powwow organizer. Another example of disagreement over the best response to the appropriation of Indian culture by non-Indians concerns the use by New Age spiritualists of American Indian practices such as drumming and sweat lodges. Some Indians cooperate in these appropriations for various reasons, including to make a profit and to help non-Indians gain spiritual guidance and understanding. On the other hand, other Indians criticize these practices on grounds of cultural appropriation and theft of key identifying symbols and practices which, many believe, degrade and dilute their significance.

SUMMARY AND CONCLUSION

Focusing on specific powwow practices enables us to see more clearly how the powwow fosters at least some unity and social cohesion among American Indians. However, it is important to move beyond this focus on unity and social cohesion to a recognition of the multiple differences that are present at a powwow, and the disagreements that arise from them. For most of these disagreements, there are no formal guidelines that could serve as decision rules. Each disagreement is typically subject to debate and negotiation. The disagreements are worked out in various ways ranging from mutual tolerance to wordless acts of rebellion to explicit forms of conflict and negotiation. Actual outcomes of disagreements and conflict depend on multiple factors such as the emcee and his mood or inclination on a particular issue, the powwow organizing committee with its incomplete control over powwow events, the tribe and its customs, the mix of participants, and the relative power of different participants. The outcome of these disagreements also changes from powwow to powwow, even within a given tribe.

The powwow arena itself provides a communicative forum where these challenges and debates can occur in various implicit and explicit forms and processes. At other times, the powwow stimulates debate on the sidelines of powwow experience. This debate over powwow practices is, by extension, a debate over the character of indigenous communities. Out of the implicit and explicit negotiation surrounding powwow practices emerges a set of beliefs, commitments, and practices that partially determine the identity of Indian communities. This set of beliefs, commitments, and practices remains subject to future challenges, suggesting a shifting, dynamic tribal and Indian identity and a shifting border between Indian and non-Indian.

While the dual roles of the powwow—fostering unity while enabling disagreement and debate—may seem mutually incompatible, in fact they are complementary. The latter role of enabling disagreement and debate contributes to the resiliency and flexibility of Indian communities by helping manage the tension between unity and diversity. Disagreement and conflict are inevitable among diverse peoples. The significance of the powwow is partly understood in the terms that I have suggested of providing a public, communicative forum where differences can be expressed and potentially negotiated. This marks, on balance, a sign of healthy, vital communities that have available some communicative arenas for working out at least some differences without squelching them or ignoring them. Powwow practices provide a means of finding sufficient unity for survival and partial prosperity in part because they enable and even foster healthy disagreement and discussion over differences that divide Indians.

Notes

1. The term *powwow* derives from a Narragansett Algonquian word *pauau* initially meaning a gathering of medicine men for a curing ceremony but gradually coming to mean a gathering of people to celebrate an important event.

2. For example, R. D. Theisz argued that Lakota powwow songs and the powwow practices in which they are set are the "centerpiece" of contemporary Lakota identity formation. See Theisz, "Song Texts and Their Performers: The Centerpiece of Contemporary Lakota Identity Formulation," *Great Plains Quarterly* 7 (Spring 1987): 116–24. According to Lynn Huenemann, music and dance "are among the strongest overt expressions and measures of the perpetuation of Indian life and culture." See Huenemann, "Northern Plains Dance," in *Native American Dance: Ceremonies and Social Traditions,* ed. Charlotte Heth (Washington, DC: National Museum of the American Indian, Smithsonian Institution with Starwood Publishing, Inc., 1992), 125. Chris Roberts argues that the powwow is the "heartbeat of Indian country" and exemplifies the "greatest renaissance [in Indian culture] since the late 1800s." See Roberts, *Powwow Country* (Helena, MT: American and World Geographic Publishing, 1992), 8. Thomas Kavanagh sees powwow music and dance as establishing an "emotional connection with the values of 'Indianness.'" See Kavanagh, "Southern Plains Dance: Tradition and Dynamics," in *Native American Dance: Ceremonies and Social Traditions,* 112. Paul Robert Parthun argues that "the powwow is central to the feeling of Indianess [sic]." See Parthun, "Ojibwa Music in Minnesota" (Ph.D. dissertation, University of Minnesota, 1976), 68. At least some powwow

participants claim to experience a "unity," a "unity of spirit," a "unified mix of people," and a "feeling of belonging." See David Hopkins, "Truly an Explosion of Culture," *The Circle* (October 1991), 19; testimonies in Roberts, *Powwow Country*, 25, 72, 112. According to the editor of a Canadian Indian magazine, *Windspeaker*, "[p]owwows break down the barriers and unify all who take part. Whether you're from the southernmost regions of the United States or far northern Canada—common ground is found at a powwow." (Quoted in Roberts, *Powwow Country*, 9.)

3. The following portrait of powwow experience is based on the literature on powwows and on my empirical study of powwows in Minnesota and western Wisconsin during the period of approximately 1988–93. My interpretation adopts the methodological approach of researchers such as Theodor W. Adorno, *Introduction to the Sociology of Music* (New York: Seabury Press, 1976); John Chernoff, *African Rhythm and African Sensibility* (Chicago: University of Chicago Press, 1979); Helen Kivnick, *Where Is the Way: Song and Struggle in South Africa* (New York: Penguin Books, 1990); and Susan McClary, *Feminine Endings: Music, Gender, and Sexuality* (Minneapolis: University of Minnesota Press, 1991). These researchers interpret musical practices in terms of how they model social relationships and embody ethical and political commitments.

4. For one use of this expression, see Joseph Geshick, "Letter to the Editor," *The Native American Press* 2:10 (17 July 1992), 4.

5. For one discussion of the philosophy and spiritualism that underlie powwow practices in Minnesota and western Minnesota, see, for example, Edward Benton-Benai', *The Mishomis Book: The Voice of the Ojibway* (St. Paul, MN: Red School House, 1988). Although Benton-Benai's discussion is tied to the Ojibwa, the main themes that are pertinent to this article remain the same among tribes in Minnesota and western Wisconsin.

6. "Sixth Annual Heart of the Earth Contest Powwow Program" (Minneapolis, 1991), 2; emcee, Lac Courte Oreilles 20th Annual Honor the Earth Homecoming Powwow, recorded on tape by author, 16 July 1993, Lac Courte Oreilles, Wisconsin.

7. Emcee, Lac Courte Oreilles 20th Annual Honor the Earth Homecoming Powwow. Children are not allowed to be carried in the dance arena because doing so represents an invitation to Mother Earth to take the child into the spirit world. Dogs used to "arrive in a cooking pot" for ceremonial dinners. Although the use of dogs in ceremonial dinners is rare today, the custom of excluding live dogs from the dance arena is sometimes still enforced. The third reference to "watching the leaders and do what they do" appeared to be an attempt to discourage inappropriate improvisation by non-Indians participating in a two-step social dance.

8. For a discussion of this "incomplete repetition" form, see, for example, Thomas Vennum, Jr., *Ojibway Music from Minnesota: Continuity and Change* (St. Paul, MN: Minnesota Historical Society Press and the Minnesota State Arts Board, 1989), 8.

9. J. S. Slotkin, *The Menomini Powwow* (Milwaukee: Milwaukee Public Museum, 1957), 14, 15. See also Gladys and Reginald Laubins, who argue that in powwow music "there is strength and power. . . . With several men around the drum all striking it together, all singing at the top of their lungs, the stirring, throbbing pulse of the music vibrates right through you." Reginald Laubin and Gladys Laubin, *Indian Dances of North America* (Norman: University of Oklahoma Press, 1977), 94.

10. Slotkin, *The Menomini Powwow*, 35.

11. Slotkin argues that powwow drumming and singing "welds" participants "into a collective unity." See Slotkin, *The Menominee Powwow*, 14. My argument that powwow music and dance both reveal and reinforce ethical and philosophical beliefs is consistent

with the research that I cited earlier in endnote 3 above.

12. Recorded on tape by author, 9 July 1993, Prairie Island, Minnesota.

13. For an extended discussion of this partial consolidation of styles, see, especially, William K. Powers, *War Dance: Plains Indian Musical Performance* (Tucson: University of Arizona Press, 1990).

14. The literature on power is extensive. A common, although by no means simple or uncontested, distinction made about power is between "power over" and "power to," referring to a sense of power as domination and constraint on the one hand and power as a positive capacity on the other hand. See, for example, Thomas Wartenberg, *The Forms of Power: From Domination to Transformation* (Philadelphia: Temple University Press, 1990) for both a summary of this basic distinction between power as domination and power as capacity and a challenge to it. For summaries and applications of contemporary literatures on power, see John Gaventa, *Power and Powerlessness: Quiescence and Rebellion in an Appalachian Valley* (Urbana: University of Illinois Press, 1980), and Peter Digeser, "The Fourth Face of Power," *The Journal of Politics* 54:4 (November 1992): 977–1007.

15. See Thomas Vennum, Jr., "The Changing Role of Women in Ojibway Music History," in *Women in North American Indian Music,* ed. Richard Keeling (The Society for Ethnomusicology, Inc., Special Series No. 6, 1989), 20. The two most common explanations for women's exclusion from drum groups are that it is traditional and, as one scholar put it, "it is strictly taboo" for a menstruating woman to participate in certain ceremonial and cultural practices (Judith Vander, "From the Musical Experience of Five Shoshone Women," In *Women in North American Indian Music,* 5). This form of gender inequality is not necessarily indicative of gender relations in all aspects of American Indian life. For one brief discussion of an attempt to form an all-women drum group, see Vennum, "The Changing Role of Women in Ojibway Music History," 13. Vennum refers to a women's drum group at Minnesota's Red Lake Ojibwa Reservation, briefly active during 1973, which was "ridiculed during their first public performance" but later met with limited, grudging acceptance. Vennum does not say how long this women's drum circle remained active. Finally, it should be noted that American Indian women disagree over the significance of their exclusion from drum groups. While some are critical of this exclusion, others defend the practice.

16. Other examples of how powwows are gendered include the fact that most emcees are male, that military veterans—the vast majority of whom are male—often are honored, and that the related overall commitment is to warriorism.

17. This occurred, for example, at the 1993 Lac du Flambeau, Wisconsin, Ojibwa powwow (John Sanford [pseud.], interview by author, tape recording, 11 June 1993, Minneapolis, MN), the 1993 Prairie Island Dakota powwow (recorded on tape by author, 9 July 1993, Prairie Island, Minnesota), and the 1991 Black River Falls Winnebago powwow (Sanford, interview, 1993).

7

Southwestern Oklahoma, the Gourd Dance, and "Charlie Brown"

Luke E. Lassiter

 ONE EVENING IN SEPTEMBER, 1994, I walked down the street to have dinner with Theresa Carter, Danieala Vickers, and Richard and Diana Kauahquo.[1] We finished eating about 8:30, settled back for coffee, and began discussing a Gourd Dance song called "Charlie Brown." After several minutes, Theresa began talking about the way of life that revolves around going to Gourd Dances. I asked her to elaborate.

"I can't imagine being without it and not going," said Theresa. "It's, I don't know, it's just part of us."

"It's just like a *disease*," added Richard, slightly chuckling under his breath. "Yeah, we have to go," said Theresa.

"It gets in you and you can't get rid of it," continued Richard. "Anywhere you see it, wherever you go, to Gourd Dancing—I'll get out there and I'll dance with them."

"You could start a Gourd Dancing Anonymous," I said jokingly. We all laughed.

After a short while, Theresa continued, "Even if I moved away, I would have to come back for the dances, for the feeling that I get from them."

"So when you're away from it, do you feel absent from that feeling?" I asked.

"Oh yeah," said Theresa. "You *miss* it. It's part of our everyday life that we've developed in the last years. If we didn't have it. . . ." Theresa paused. "I get *tired* sometimes, and I *gripe*. Then I might stay away for a little bit. But then after a while you go back for the music, for the *songs*. It's just like some of our War Mothers songs."

Richard nodded his head and whistled slightly under his breath, "Boy!"

"Ah!" Theresa clutched at her heart. "You know," she continued, "they just get you, because they tell a story. And you feel that story. It's like the Desert Storm song. *That*, I'll *always* get this feeling, this choked up feeling, because it affected me; because my son was there then. But, I need that music, and those songs—whether I dance or not."

Luke E. Lassiter is an assistant professor of anthropology at Ball State University.

Later, Theresa began talking about "Charlie Brown" again: "['Charlie Brown'] is one of the songs that really brings everything out in us. *All* the feelings we have, *all* the good feelings we have. It comes through with that song."[2]

THE GOURD DANCE: ON THE NEED TO ENGAGE IN COMMUNITY-WIDE CONVERSATIONS

Theresa, Danieala, Richard, and Diana live in southwestern Oklahoma. In what many here call "our Indian world," Kiowa, Comanche, Kiowa-Apache, Wichita, Caddo, Delaware, and Chirichaua Apache peoples and their traditions converge, creating a dynamic and diverse community. Traditions such as language, world view, religion, and community narrative help to demarcate this Indian world. Several dance and song traditions are among the most heralded. The conversation above is about one of these: the Gourd Dance.

Ethnographers and other scholars have recently written much about this dance. They have discussed its form and choreography, history, and significance to Oklahoma communities, especially the Kiowas.[3] This scholarly interest is not surprising, especially since the dance's popularity has become so widespread after its revival in the 1950s. Since then, it has nearly replaced the War Dance's prominence in some Oklahoma communities. In southwestern Oklahoma, while many weekends pass without a War Dance, no weekend passes without one or more community organizations hosting an eight- to ten-hour Gourd Dance. Indeed, the dance is now one of southwestern Oklahoma's most visible aesthetic forms.

The Gourd Dance is a simple dance. Its attire is simple. Men most often wear jeans or slacks, a nice shirt, moccasins or cowboy boots or sneakers, and silver and bead bandoliers. They wear cloth sashes (many made of velvet) wrapped around their waists and knotted on the right; the ends—which hang past the knees—are beaded and fringed with polyester chainette. In their hands they carry feather fans and rattles made, for the most part, of tin. Sometimes they wear a Gourd Dance blanket—half red, half blue—draped over the shoulders and hanging to the knees or draped across the chest. Women dancers often wear fringed shawls over street clothes. Sometimes they wear more formal dance attire.

The movement of the dance is simple as well—restrained and understated. For about eight to ten hours per dance, with breaks, men and women bob up and down in place in accord with the rhythm of Gourd Dance songs. The men, separate from the women, shake their rattles in time with the song, and at certain breaks in the song, they slowly move clockwise around a group of singers. Compared to the War Dance's visibility in many other Plains communities, this is not what many expect to see when it comes to Native American dance. Many outsiders express disappointment that the Gourd Dance doesn't look "Indian." But this illustrates a very important point: The Gourd Dance experience is not entirely visual—it's not something altogether to *see*.

For community members, the dance's overriding meaning resides with what can be heard, not seen. "Gourd dancing is a big part of Indian life right now," says

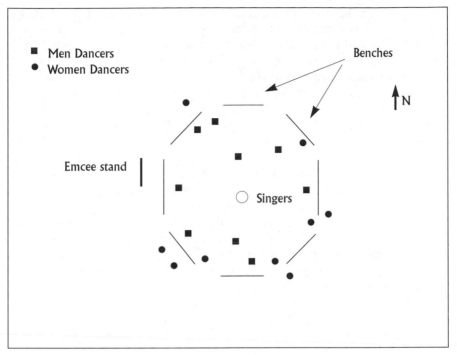

Fig. 1. General Choreography

Frankie Ware, speaking about the popularity of the Gourd Dance in her community. "You go to the powwows and that's all you *hear* is gourd dancing" [emphasis added].[4]

The Gourd Dance event revolves around song. Singers and their songs are both the literal and metaphorical center of the Gourd Dance. Each and every dance cannot begin until the singers arrive; it can happen neither without them nor without the songs they sing. As the Gourd Dance is a label that refers to both a dance and song tradition, the latter tradition is that which community members most often emphasize when they talk about this dance.

The song tradition about which they talk is Kiowa. Although community members regularly dispute this detail among themselves and with other communities (for instance, the Cheyenne and Arapaho), they generally concur that the Gourd Dance is a Kiowa dance. Considering the Gourd Dance's popularity in the community, the Kiowa song tradition now enjoys immense popularity and dominance in the community. Kiowa people enjoy equal prominence in defining the dance's purpose at their annual July Fourth Gourd Dance celebrations, where they also assert their distinctive connection to the dance.[5] (Some Kiowa organizations, for example, emphasize a more formal and distinct Kiowa dress code during these annuals.) But even at these annual celebrations, participation in the dance is by no means limited to Kiowas alone: Comanche, Kiowa-Apache, Wichita, Caddo, Delaware, and Chirichaua Apache peoples all go to Gourd

Dances. What unites these Gourd Dance practitioners is a common experience, established not in a singular history, but in a collective encounter with song.

The community discussions about the Gourd Dance, like community discussions about peyote meetings or church services, almost always push towards this encounter with song and what it means to hear and understand it. But most especially, for many community members the point of hearing song goes beyond symbolic association. To know song on its deepest levels is to *feel it*: "The whole essence of this thing is to feel good," says Billy Evans Horse, who first pointed this out to me.[6] On some levels, felt encounter with song transcends obvious differences between Kiowa or Apache or Comanche song in the community. As in my conversation with Theresa and Richard above, when many community members talk about the Gourd Dance, they often refer to several other song traditions as a way to talk about the power of song in general.

Talk about the power of Gourd Dance songs, then, is only part of a larger community-wide conversation about song. Community members regularly talk about all of their song traditions—from dance songs to peyote songs to church hymns. Song surfaces again and again in community-wide conversations. From this talk, it quickly becomes apparent that song is one of this Indian world's more defining characteristics. For many community members, all so-called Indian song enjoys equal footing with language as the most vital tradition for maintaining a distinctive way of life. As Native language is being spoken less and less, however, song is looming as a dominant cultural symbol. Song cannot go unrecognized for anyone who lives in the community and engages in its community-wide conversations. Yet scholars who have studied here have done little in the way of articulating this exchange.

Although previous treatises of the Gourd Dance have indeed mentioned song, most of these have situated song within the narrow confines of simple functional relationships.[7] To put it another way, because scholars have not fully explored how community members talk about song, they have not yet sufficiently elaborated and interpreted what song *means* to community members. Much of the previous literature on the Gourd Dance has been instead largely historical, focused on models of change and continuity, with much space given to questionable applications of theory—which have led, I believe, to poor understandings of the Gourd Dance. James H. Howard's application of Anthony F. C. Wallace's revitalization and Benjamin R. Kracht's application of Victor Turner's *communitas* are notable examples.[8] When applied resourcefully, the theoretical models presented by scholars of the Gourd Dance are indeed important to larger ethnological discussions. These same models, however, often forego one of the more provoking components of the Gourd Dance—individual experience. By their very nature, such models systematically gloss individual experience to pose experience as pattern cross-culturally. For community members, however, the Gourd Dance experience rests not on behavior that can be seen and observed and patterned, but on what can be heard, understood, and felt on an individual level. Such experience is then negotiated, not patterned, by community-wide conversations about the dance. Engaging in this dialogue is absolutely necessary to understanding the Gourd Dance's deepest experiential meanings. "Societies, like lives, contain their own interpretations," writes Clifford Geertz. "One has only to learn how to gain access to them."[9]

This is a methodological point to which I shall return below. But suffice it to say that scholars and community members tell two different kinds of stories about southwestern Oklahoma's Gourd Dance. Community members discuss the Gourd Dance in ways that scholars conventionally ignore, and scholars discuss the Gourd Dance in ways that community members conventionally ignore. As such, they each relate two different sets of meaningful relationships: Academic stories are meaningful to academics and community stories are meaningful to Gourd Dance practitioners. For example, Benjamin R. Kracht's article, "Kiowa Powwows: Continuity in Ritual Practice," chronicles the Gourd Dance's emergence within the powwow culture of southwestern Oklahoma, which, to reiterate, is now dominated by the Gourd Dance.[10] Kracht offers an intriguing narrative of change and continuity, yet this narrative is set within an ethnohistorical frame, especially as based on archival documents. Several community members read Kracht's article after its publication. They found it interesting and pointed out some discrepancies (which have been cited elsewhere).[11] This academically positioned history, however, has little relevance to their own conversations about the dance. Simply put, they do not include archival documents in their conversations. They employ another set of diverse narratives about individual experience centered on an encounter with song, which the above conversation so clearly illustrates.

In this essay, I address the disparity that these two story types represent. I offer what follows as a supplement to earlier discussions of the Gourd Dance. But the central problem discussed here, and a broader anthropological and ethnomusicological problem, is how academic conversations about experience and song differ from the community's conversations about experience and song. This problem presents serious obstacles for understanding what the Gourd Dance experience *means to its practitioners* and, in turn, what the Gourd Dance means to larger discussions of cultural change and revival. This essay is about these obstacles and the need to incorporate community conversations into academic discussions about these topics of study. Indeed, community conversations about song are central to understanding the Gourd Dance's unique community meanings. This is the stuff of human diversity and why we do ethnography. Ethnographers have long regarded a community's interpretation of their own aesthetic forms as a valid and important ethnographic endeavor. To understand what Theresa Carter means when she says "[Charlie Brown] is one of the songs that really brings everything out in us," one has only to listen.[12]

"Charlie Brown": On Song and Experience

In the conversation above, Theresa and Richard are talking about encounter with song. "Charlie Brown" represents only one song in the Gourd Dance repertoire, which is part of a larger Kiowa song tradition, which is in turn part of a larger community song repertoire.[13] Several dozen songs are sung at each Gourd Dance event, but these represent only a small sample of the total Gourd Dance song repertoire;

singers assert that these songs are innumerable.[14] Although talk about "Charlie Brown" provides only one window into the world of song in this community, it does offer a way to understand the uniqueness of the Gourd Dance experience.

"Charlie Brown" is perhaps one of the most widely known songs among Gourd Dance practitioners. If one goes to any Gourd Dance in the country, whether in southwestern Oklahoma or in Navajo country—and many Navajo are now enthusiastic Gourd Dance adherents—one will always hear two songs: the "Starting Song" and "Charlie Brown." All other Gourd Dance songs fall somewhere in between. The "Starting Song," as its name implies, must be sung at all Gourd Dances to initiate the dance. Singers conventionally, but by no means always, sing three other songs after the "Starting Song." After these four songs, singers sing songs at random from memory. They sing them one after the other, take a break—which may be quite long during "specials," (i.e., "giveaways")—and sing another session of songs, take another break, and so on until the dance's close. "Charlie Brown" is usually sung as the last song.

Throughout a Gourd Dance, singers ideally build up the dance from slow to fast. Near the dance's close, singers begin to sing what they call the fast songs, rhythm songs, or in Kiowa, *bhawl dawgeah*. "Charlie Brown" is a *bhawl dawgeah*, and it is the culmination of the dance's gradual buildup. Singers and dancers negotiate this buildup throughout to engage a heightened feeling, a feeling based in hearing and understanding song. "You have to be careful with the singing portion of it," says Billy Evans Horse about singing Gourd Dance songs, "so you can make sure that if you've got the feeling, the dancers get the feeling. And transmit it back and forth. Then your audience will get the vibes, so to speak."[15]

This sentiment, as emergent in sound, demarcates the most powerfully defined cultural boundaries. When one watches a Gourd Dance, one observes something vastly different from what Gourd Dance practitioners experience. Indeed, observation alone can be misleading. For example, at first glance the Gourd Dance event appears to be almost entirely a men's event. The men dominate the dancing and singing, while women singers sit behind the men seated at the drum. All community members stress that the Gourd Dance is a time-honored men's dance. When women dance, they must, ideally, dance behind the men—although in practice they don't always do this. Participation, however, is by no means limited to the men dancers and men singers. At any Gourd Dance event in southwestern Oklahoma, community spectators almost always outnumber the ten or fifteen or fifty dancers and ten or fifteen or fifty singers. These spectators include men and women, but women are often in the majority. Both spectators and dancers, both men and women, all participate as listeners. Although they may or may not seem to participate equally, they do share a common denominator that observation alone cannot elicit: they go to Gourd Dances to hear the songs. As Theresa says above, "I need that music, and those songs—whether I dance or not."[16]

Thus, when an outside observer listens to a Gourd Dance, or more precisely, "Charlie Brown," what he or she is hearing is not the same as what community members are hearing. For community members, "Charlie Brown," like all songs, invokes a host of referents lost on outside observers.[17] A central problem arises, however, when one seeks to cross these "sound barriers" to translate and interpret through the written text what a song like "Charlie Brown" means.

ACADEMICALLY POSITIONED CONVERSATIONS ABOUT SONG AND EXPERIENCE: TWO EXAMPLES

Many Native American studies scholars often look to two conventional models to translate song in the written text. The first is to transcribe oral song traditions in what is generally called Western notation; figure 2 illustrates "Charlie Brown" written in Western notation. The immediate question here is what does this communicate in the written text? What does this tell the reader about "Charlie Brown"? Obviously, Western notation communicates little about how "Charlie Brown" is performed. It does communicate to the reader that if, for example, you played this on the piano at home, you may get, at the very best, the gist of this song's sound. To be truthful, playing "Charlie Brown" on the piano is a bit irrelevant to Gourd Dance practitioners—especially when compared to an intimate listening of the song. What is equally irrelevant is for Kiowa singers to open books about their own song traditions and see them written as in figure 2. Simply put, this is not the way *they* communicate their song traditions.

To be sure, Western notation has its place in certain kinds of ethnography, but that place is not part of the sound world that includes "Charlie Brown." Western

Fig. 2. "Charlie Brown?"

notation, which focuses solely on representing and translating *sound*, overlooks communicative context. Charlie Brown's fullest meanings materialize when the song comes to life at a dance among those people for whom it has its deepest meanings. Writing "Charlie Brown" in Western notation disregards the experience of hearing "Charlie Brown," which, for many Gourd Dance practitioners, is the reason why such songs are so powerful.[18]

Perhaps the main problem with using Western notation to transcribe "Charlie Brown" is that it breaks down song into smaller units of sound. Community members do not explicitly do this, except when identifying the so-called breaks, cuts, and curves in a song; they talk about song in holistic terms. When, for example, new songs "come" to individuals, or when someone makes, composes, or receives a new song, it comes as a whole. This whole is "straightened out"— meaning worked through to make the breaks, cuts, and curves acceptable to a particular song tradition—and then presented as an individual song. For community members, a song is the basic unit of sound. To understand each song is to understand a special kind of language. Like the messages imparted by a single word in spoken language, each song generally operates as a whole rather than as a collection of discrete parts; the total assemblage of sounds makes a complete and unique, yet multidimensional, symbolic statement.[19] One key to understanding the meanings of these statements is eliciting the many diverse referents, narratives, and knowledge that surround each song.

The musicological problem presented by Western notation actually reflects a larger ethnographic problem. How do we represent song in text? How do we translate one form of expression into another? Many scholars also look to song lyrics to address these questions, especially because a song's lyrics can be easily written.[20] This represents a second conventional model that many Native American studies scholars often employ to translate song in the written text.

Song lyrics are extremely effective for purposes of illustration. Much too often, however, ethnographers seem to assume that song lyrics alone circumscribe a song's meaning, that a song's text encompasses all that song communicates. In so doing, authors are essentially assuming that song and the written word belong to the same genre, and we know that they do not. Much more serious is the assumption that songs without lyrics—and several Native song repertoires fall into this category—do not communicate meaning. Consider, for example, this excerpt from John Beatty's treatise of Kiowa-Apache songs, a song tradition closely related to the Kiowa song tradition:

> A large number of songs in Kiowa-Apache have no words at all, but employ vocables or nonsense syllables. These are specifically ordered sounds carrying semantic meaning. The final song of the Blackfeet Society has in it the phrase "yo he yo he yo yo he yo he o we" which is completely without meaning.[21]

Surely, any serious musicologist would not say that the grand finale of Tchaikovsky's "1812 Overture" is "completely without meaning" because it lacks a linguistic component. But Beatty is essentially saying as much for the crescendo of a song that is as moving for Kiowa-Apache Blackfeet Society practitioners as Tchaikovsky's grand finale is for some classical listeners.[22] As with Western notation, this song's meaning cannot be found in its discrete parts, but in its expressive whole.

Beatty is not alone in his treatise of song. Many students of Native song routinely select against songs that they cannot easily write down on paper. In so doing, they completely dismiss an entire world of meaning, especially experiential meaning. The few Gourd Dance scholars, in glossing the role that song has in the Gourd Dance experience, have done just this. Like the Kiowa-Apache Blackfeet Society ceremonials, Gourd Dances often take place without a single song containing lyrics. Out of hundreds of Gourd Dance songs, only a few have lyrics. "Charlie Brown" is representative of most Gourd Dance songs. It has no lyrics. Does one then assume that no meaning has transpired? Is *nothing* going on? Considering Theresa's comment about "Charlie Brown" above, one can only conclude the contrary.

Ethnomusicologists have labeled such songs vocable songs.[23] But Gourd Dance practitioners do not use the label, calling these songs, in English, "songs without words," in contrast to "songs with words." According to these singers, both kinds of songs carry a kind of meaning that spoken language only begins to express.[24] These so-called nonsense syllables or vocables, along with spoken language, make powerful statements about experience. In the crescendo of a Kiowa-Apache Blackfeet ceremonial or when "Charlie Brown" closes the Gourd Dance, a host of symbolic statements are made through a communicative channel as meaningful and as significant as spoken language; but these are often completely inaccessible to those who do not understand this world of sound on the same levels as do Gourd Dance practitioners. Thus, when scholars ignore songs without words, or delete them from the text because they cannot easily write them, they dismiss an entire world of meaning. To be sure, because we know that spoken language is only one component of a larger system of communication grounded in the context of any communicative event, a song's text is only one small part of what song communicates in any particular social setting.[25]

These preceding examples—the use of Western notation and the sole reliance on song lyrics—seem to suggest that because many available treatises of the Gourd Dance in particular and Native American music in general are mostly crafted for academically positioned discussions, the use of these textual devices is somewhat counterproductive to understanding the experience with song about which the people in this community talk.[26] For Gourd Dance practitioners, each Gourd Dance song has a distinct sound, purpose, use, and story or stories, all of which invoke complex meanings within the context of the community. This is the vernacular model to which I shall now turn to interpret what "Charlie Brown" means for community members.

COMMUNITY CONVERSATIONS ABOUT SONG AND EXPERIENCE: ON HEARING AND UNDERSTANDING "CHARLIE BROWN"

How do I, then, translate through written text the meaning that "Charlie Brown," and other songs like it, hold for this community? The first step is to decipher what this song communicates within its community context. I noted above that in order to understand a song like "Charlie Brown," we need to understand a special kind of language; one key to understanding the meanings of these statements is eliciting the referents, stories, and knowledge that surround each song.

Richard Kauahquo, whom I cited in the conversation above, says about "Charlie Brown":

> When I hear "Charlie Brown," it makes me go crazy. It makes me want to get out there and just dance as hard as I can and just holler. That song right there and when daddy's comes up. . . . You know it belongs to your family. . . . You just want to get out there and just dance your heart out.[27]

Here, Richard is talking about how "Charlie Brown" references a relationship to his mother's family (and how another song references a relationship to his father's family—but that is another song). His mother's family, the Komalty family, and many other Gourd Dance practitioners—especially Kiowas—often refer to this song as the "Komalty family song" because family members have rights to the song. That is, the Komalty family essentially "owns" the song, which for them invokes a host of particular family relationships.

One of these relationships is a narrative specific to Komalty family history. The Komaltys are Kiowa, and because they are Kiowa, the Komalty family song also embraces another history specific to Kiowa people—around whom the Gourd Dance revolves in this community. Richard tells a history of this song told to him by his mother. He relates that the Komalty family song originated soon after 1910, when, near present-day Hobart, Oklahoma, Kiowa people gathered for a Taimpego encampment. The Taimpego was one of the Kiowa's seven military societies, prominent throughout the prereservation era. The Gourd Dance, or Ton-goon-get in Kiowa, which literally translates as "Rattle Dance," was the dance of the Taimpego society.[28] As the reservation era began to define the end of the Plains lifestyle, Kiowa military societies like the Taimpego began to lose their significance. But surviving members of Taimpego and their families held their dances sporadically until after the turn of the century. At the Taimpego encampment near present-day Hobart, Oklahoma, two brothers, Kiowa Bill and Komalty, composed four new songs, one of which is the song now belonging to the Komalty family and often called "Charlie Brown." Since then, the song has belonged to the families descended from Kiowa Bill and Komalty.[29]

For Kiowa people like Richard, the Komalty family song represents an important component of an enduring tradition that has survived many changes since Kiowa Bill and Komalty received the song. The Kiowa held Taimpego encampments less and less often after the turn of the century and by the early 1940s they had all but ceased.[30] Yet during the inactivity of the dance, the song tradition remained active.[31] This Komalty family song, and countless Taimpego songs like it, lived on in the memory of singers. Singers sang Taimpego and other Kiowa songs at "singings" (gatherings of singers), which they hosted at their homes on a regular basis, as they continue to do today.[32]

In 1957, a group of Kiowa men publicly revived the Taimpego Rattle Dance, calling it, in English, the Gourd Dance. They called their new organization the Kiowa Gourd Clan and held their first celebration on July Fourth of that same year. Because any dance is inconceivable without songs, the men approached singers to sing the songs for the revival. Billy Evans Horse says,

> "It began when the songs were brought back, or sung. And then the old people that were here at that time, like my grandpa, [the men who revived the dance] were asking them questions: 'What is that? What song is that?' And they [the old people] give a little history about it."
>
> "'Well that sounds good. How did they dance?'"
>
> "And so they [the old people] said, 'They dance this way.'"
>
> "'And how did they dress?'"
>
> "'Well, [they said], you could dress this way since it's modern times,' and so forth."
>
> "And they began to meet at homes around here, and then they were singing the songs, and grandpa would sing it to them, and they would listen and pick them up, and help him sing. . . . They had singing sessions at so and so's home once a week and then it began to go [the revival of the Gourd Dance]."[33]

Among the revived songs that Billy Evans refers to here was the Komalty family song.

The Kiowa men who revived the Taimpego's dance essentially established their revival on meaningful sound. Although they did emphasize particulars like dress and ritual codes, songs such as the Komalty family song were stressed above and beyond such particulars in the revival ("Well, you could dress this way since it's modern times"). In so doing, although Taimpego was originally a warrior's society, the Gourd Clan did not revive the Gourd Dance as a veterans organization. They opened the dance to all Kiowa men and their families.

Beginning in the 1960s and 1970s, as the dance increased in popularity, several Kiowa families formed their own Gourd Dance organizations—including the Kiowa Tai-Piah Society of Oklahoma, Tai-Piah Society of Carnegie (now known as Kiowa Tai-Piah Society), and the Kiowa Warrior Descendants. By the late 1970s and early 1980s, many in southwestern Oklahoma's Indian community had become enthusiastic adherents as the dance spread throughout Indian country (especially Oklahoma). Today, several dozen Gourd Dance organizations—for instance, the Comanche Gourd Clan and the Dirty Shame Gourd Club—host their own Gourd Dances several times a year. And because they do, it is now possible to go to a Gourd Dance every single weekend of the year.[34]

Just as the songs defined the revival, song now seems to provide the most forceful boundaries by which Kiowa people assert their unique connection to the dance among many other groups who also cite specific connections to the dance. Many Cheyenne people, for example, also claim the Gourd Dance as their own. Kiowa people regularly contest these assertions, pointing out that Kiowa songs—and not those of other groups—were the impetus for the revival. One Kiowa Gourd Dance organization, the Kiowa Tai-Piah Society, puts it thus:

> Cheyennes say this is their dance, but all of the old Gourd Dance songs are Kiowa. Of course, a lot of songs were recently composed and some by different tribes beside the Kiowas, but even today most of the Gourd Dance songs are Kiowa. The older Kiowa say that this is a Kiowa Dance.[35]

To be sure, the origin of the Gourd Dance is an ongoing dialogue within and among Indian communities throughout Oklahoma. But who "owns" the Gourd Dance is not really the issue here. What is significant is that song has emerged as the most meaningful component of this dialogue. For many Kiowa people, a larger Kiowa continuity story of change, revival, and continuity hinges on songs, songs like the Komalty family's. While some scholars have attributed the Gourd Dance's popularity to its simple attire and choreography or to its pan-Indian style, community members attribute its popularity to what is heard and understood in song; and most especially, they attribute its popularity to what is *felt* in song.[36]

The story behind the Komalty family song's nickname, "Charlie Brown," is a case in point. During the 1960s, a U.S. Army General named Charles Brown visited a Gourd Dance on the Fort Sill Army Base. Hearing this song, he was apparently so moved that he danced. Some Kiowa singers thus nicknamed the song "Charlie Brown." This name has stuck to this day, and it is now more widely known than is the Komalty family label.[37]

Now, I presume that General Charles Brown had little to no knowledge of this song; he was where most outsiders stand when they hear this song for the first time. But if the general had no knowledge of the song, how could he be moved at all? How could he feel it if he didn't know its referents or stories? After all, doesn't Theresa, in the conversation above, imply that to feel a song is to feel its story? Actually, Charles Brown's behavior is not that odd to many Gourd Dance practitioners. Although this song invokes several layers of knowledge from the general—a Kiowa continuity story as told by many Kiowa people—to the specific—the Komalty family history as told by Richard—it also engages very personal narratives of experience similar to that of General Charles Brown. Gourd Dance practitioners frequently talk about how song touches and moves them. Although song knowledge is often at the heart of how it moves them, many Gourd Dance practitioners assert that one need not necessarily hear and know the stories surrounding "Charlie Brown" to appreciate the power of song. Indeed, community members attribute the Gourd Dance's popularity within the community and among other enthusiastic adherents, like the Navajo people, to what is *felt in song* rather than what is translated by song.

> "When I was down on the floor," says a KTNN radio announcer, broadcasting from the 1991 Navajo Nation Inaugural Ceremony Powwow, "the

dancers were all around. And when I was sitting next to the singers, and the dancers were around, it was like they were transmitting an energy that could make a person feel good. . . . For me, this is my first Gourd Dance I've been to. I've spent my whole life on the reservation, and this is the first one I've been to."[38]

Understanding what it means to feel song is central to appreciating the unique quality of the Gourd Dance experience. This is not to suggest that song knowledge is unimportant; for it is very important in this community. To be sure, song knowledge is precious knowledge for many. Community members debate song knowledge regularly; they often have conversations before, during, and after Gourd Dances about the songs. Deciphering this community dialogue is a difficult task, because this one song, like all of its counterparts, communicates meaning on several different levels for several different people, meanings that I have only begun to explicate here. Kiowa people regularly and heatedly debate the interpretation of songs such as this; even the song's nickname is a point of contention. I have heard one person say that "Charlie Brown" refers to an old Kiowa man who lived around the turn of the century named Kiowa Charlie. Another reports that a Comanche man jokingly labeled the song after the cartoon character, Charlie Brown, and it stuck.[39] Still another argues that this song should be called neither "Charlie Brown" nor "the Komalty family song" because it belongs to another family.

Engaging the talk about this song thus means engaging a polyphonic community discourse, a discourse that often has many conflicting components that resist the glossing effects of patterning. In addition, many have access to knowledge that others do not, and as the saying goes, knowledge is power—singers possibly hold the highest status in the community. I am convinced, however, that the power of the Gourd Dance in this community rests in the many diverse voices and opinions about the dance's practice. At each and every dance, and in their conversations about the dance, Kiowa people and other Gourd Dance practitioners negotiate the dance's meaning.

This is the community context in which song is felt. Consequently, recurrent and common experience with songs like "Charlie Brown" establishes the base on which people talk about their personal experience with song. In most all conversations about the dance, as in the conversation that initiated this essay, talk about song often moves to how one feels it. Here we leave symbolism and song knowledge behind and enter a deeper level of experiential encounter.[40]

COMMUNITY CONVERSATIONS ABOUT SONG AND EXPERIENCE: ON FEELING "CHARLIE BROWN"

Theresa says that "['Charlie Brown'] is one of the songs that really brings everything out in us. *All* the feelings we have, *all* the good feelings we have. It comes through with that song."[41] "Charlie Brown" is today the crescendo of the Gourd Dance. As the last song, it concludes the dance. When Theresa says that "Charlie

Brown" "really brings everything out in us," she is referring to all of the feelings felt in song at the end of an eight- to ten-hour dance. Truly, to experience the culmination of the Gourd Dance is to sense the intersection of coexisting lives charged with feeling, sentiment, and force in the context of event.[42] "All, *everybody*, coming together," says Ralph Kotay. "It's just like if another tribe of Indians will be at the dance, you know, we *all* know one another. That's the one thing that I really like about it, because we all get together, we enjoy that one thing, our Indian music, our Indian dancing" [Kotay's emphasis].[43] And Napoleon "Nipper" Tiddark says, "*That's* the Gourd Dance. That's the music. That's the drum. . . . If they *didn't* feel good, if the Gourd Dance wasn't good, [and] the music wasn't *good*, they wouldn't do it" [Tiddark's emphasis].[44]

Outside observers can easily know what it is to hear a Gourd Dance song. Gourd Dance practitioners, however, distinguish between hearing, understanding, and feeling a song. For community members, to understand a song, one can know its story, who made it, where it came from, who it belongs to, what it says, and what it means. For singers, especially, this includes knowing all the varied versions and interpretations of a song. But this is very different from sensing and feeling a song, which for many community members is knowing song on a much deeper and more intimate level of experiential encounter. This may be extremely difficult for many outside observers to appreciate and understand. Yet *feeling song* should not be underestimated. Universally, encounter and perception are central to every human experience; we perceive encounter with our world through that which we feel as imparted by our senses.[45]

Ethnographers have always been interested in the similarities and differences of cultural experience. But because they more often than not look to the patterned expressions of experience (e.g., behavior), they have conventionally steered clear of the unwieldy world of emotion and feeling. As a result, little is known about the phenomenological meanings of experience cross-culturally.

Like the negotiation of knowledge, community members regularly negotiate feeling song on several different levels—both in conversation and in the communicative exchanges at Gourd Dances. Theresa makes a symbolic identification with song when she says: "[the songs] just get you, because they tell a story. And you *feel* that story."[46] This is an emotional connection. But she and others explain that what is felt in song is built upon a deeper relationship with endowed power, a power that is not entirely built upon symbolic association. These community members say that to sense and feel song is to catch and touch something that exists both inside and outside of song simultaneously.

Community members offer several different perspectives on this feeling. Billy Evans Horse and I have spent several years discussing what Gourd Dance practitioners say is felt in song. He explains that "each feeling is different, contingent on the individual. And it's just that unseen spirit that's there, when the song is let out."[47] For him, the "something" that exists inside and outside of song simultaneously is what is called in the Kiowa language *daw*, or what Billy Evans and many others simply call in English, "spirit." *Daw* is the root of the Kiowa word for song: daw-geah. *Daw* roughly translates into English as "power." *Geah* means "to catch" or "to gather," hence, the literal translation of song as "catching power." Everything that is instilled with power has as its root *daw*. The Kiowa word for God, for example, is *Daw-K'ee*, which literally translates as "throwing power." To sing, Billy Evans explains, is to catch or gather the power thrown by *Daw-K'ee*. Because Billy Evans, and many other singers, sees himself as a vehicle for *Daw-K'ee*, the power invoked by song is an actual extension of *Daw-K'ee*. The *daw*, or power felt in song is spirit (see figure 3).[48]

Many others in this community talk about song in these same terms, using spirit to describe the sense that song embodies a godly reality and communicates an awareness. Native American Church practitioners talk about peyote songs manifesting spirit in peyote meetings; Christians talk about Indian hymns (and other church songs) manifesting the Holy Spirit in churches. Although the expressions of these godly realities are obviously different in their respective contexts, Billy Evans seems to suggest that the way song embraces God's power in peyote meetings, churches, and dances ultimately makes them comparable. "[Song] is a gathering of medicine words," says Billy Evans. "'Medicine words' means 'God's word.' And it gives you that power."[49]

For Billy Evans and many other community members, what is being caught in song is much more than merely a concept as it may appear here. It is encounter with something that is very real and tangible, something that is felt in sound as imparted by the senses, something that most everyone refers to as the spirit of the song. Richard Kauahquo says, for example, "It's just like Holiness [churches]. You catch the spirit when you hear these songs, these Gourd Dance songs. The spirit hits you, and man, you just get out there and dance. And especially when that 'Charlie Brown' comes up."[50] When community members talk about spirit like this, they don't talk about it as a concept. They talk about it as a reality.

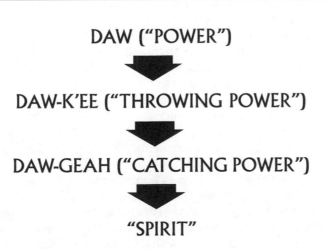

Fig. 3. Spirit

This idea first began to sink in for me in 1992 when I wrote a paper on the Gourd Dance as a graduate student at the University of North Carolina at Chapel Hill. The essay focused on conversations that began in 1988 between Billy Evans Horse and me. It was supposed to revolve around the encounter with spirit. Yet it lacked a real feel for the experience about which Billy Evans spoke in our recorded conversations. After Billy Evans read the paper, we talked at length about the text. "This sounds too beautiful," he began.[51] For over an hour, Billy Evans struggled to help me understand just what he meant by spirit and what it meant to experience it. After seeing that I was not fully understanding his point, he went to his room and came back with his peyote rattle. He sang a peyote song. When he finished singing, he said, "Now *this, this* is spirit." He began singing again, stopped again, and said, "Now *this, this* is spirit." From our talk, a newer and deeper collaborative understanding began to take shape, an understanding that focused on the experience of hearing, understanding, and feeling song in its very performance—not merely as concept, but, to reiterate, as a real, tangible entity.

When one compares such testimony with the ethnographic literature, one finds that scholars more often than not approach such subjects in very different ways. Despite compelling arguments, ethnographers continue to explain such entities as spirit through metaphoric or psychological models, dismissing that they really exist as they do for their consultants.[52] For those like Billy Evans Horse, spirit is not a metaphor; it is. Scholars may suggest, for example, that *Daw, Daw-K'ee*, and spirit don't really exist as empirical realities; they exist because community members believe they exist. It is a part of their cultural world. And because culture is very real, spirit is very real. But, again, for those like Billy Evans Horse, encountering and touching spirit in sound is as real as picking up a rock. Encounter with spirit through song informs belief, not the other way around.

In distinguishing between the long-established traditions of disbelief within the academy and its incongruence with traditions of belief in the communities in which academics study, critical theorists initiated the discussion of these problems several years ago.[53] I don't mean to suggest that metaphoric or psychological models are unimportant to ethnography. But in order to understand the complexities of song in this community, one must elaborate spirit as the reality that community members say it is. Academically positioned models like revitalization or *communitas* do more to obscure this reality than explain what it means to community members.[54] Community models for explaining spirit are absolutely valid to the academic production of knowledge—especially in terms of belief and experiential encounter. Indeed, our very job as ethnographers, as Bronislaw Malinowski put it, is "to grasp the native's point of view, his relation to life, to realise *his* vision of *his* world" [Malinowski's emphasis].[55]

This may sound perfectly in line with the traditions of ethnographic inquiry. "We are in no place to assume that spirit exists or doesn't exist," as the argument may go. Yet, as several ethnographers have pointed out, there continues to be a clear ethnographic separation between the dialogues that define understandings in the field and those understandings we present our readers in the ethnographic text.[56] In the course of moving from ethnographic practice in the field to ethnographic writing in the academy, an academically created tension develops. The frame for ethnographic fieldwork is close, intimate relationships, where dialogue between ethnographers and their consultants moves to common understanding. Yet in the ethnographic text, ethnographers more often than not distances themselves from these very relationships and dialogues to shape the final text.[57]

As is well known, this tension often sets up a clear separation between the ethnographer and his or her "subjects," between Self and Other, and between the academy and the ethnographic site. Although they begin as dialogues, many ethnographies become monologues written about the "native point of view" for a non-Native audience. Control of this conversation about culture rests solely with the ethnographer.[58]

Certainly not always but often enough to be problematic in this process of distancing themselves from field dialogues, ethnographers often gloss cultural realities like spirit, failing to recognize how the expressions of these tangible realities play into peoples' everyday lives everywhere. Much too often, because we may not accept these realities like our consultants do, we mute a critically important facet of their experience. Whether we realize it or not, anthropologists may end up explaining away these realities, rather than elaborating on them, and in essence may help to explain away some of the more provoking aspects of human diversity. "It is time," writes Edith Turner, "that we recognize the ability to experience different levels of reality as one of the normal human abilities and place it where it belongs, central to the study of ritual."[59]

With this understood, it may be tempting to place the encounter with song on a sacred/secular continuum, equating spirit with sacred or religious experience.[60] Indeed, Gourd Dances often open and end with prayer, and many community members compare what is felt in song with religion. "Those [Gourd Dance] songs, they feel good about it. It's just like our religion," says Ralph Kotay.[61] Billy Evans Horse further cements this analogy: "I feel good about worshiping God in these songs."[62]

Placing the Gourd Dance on an academic pole opposite the secular, however, quickly becomes problematic for my consultants as a mode of explanation in the written text. "Sacred has a different meaning to me," said Billy Evans Horse when we first discussed it.[63] He and others emphatically pointed out that although community members use terms like *sacred* or *religious*, these terms have very different meanings to them than they do for academics. "When *we* say it's 'sacred,' it means we respect it," says one individual.[64] "We have to take care of it, to pass it on to our children. It's our way of life, and it goes with us all the time, every day." I found that many community members resent outsiders overemphasizing the so-called sacred aspects of their dances, including the Gourd Dance. "I think this spiritualism stuff is taken too far," says one individual when we talked about it, "I don't like it." Another individual responded to this problem by citing a professor who talked about the sacred dance arena in class: "It's not sacred! It's social! We go to have a good time."

Through our conversations about spirit, it is obviously apparent that the *sacred* label undermines the experiential complexity of the Gourd Dance and denies the shared and negotiated experiences that surround the dance and its songs. While academics may decide to use *sacred* to distinguish ritual from that which is secular, they may ignore the fact that the meanings of terms such as *sacred* and *religious* are contested, situational, and multifaceted within their community contexts. Sentiments about the Gourd Dance range from public assertions that the Gourd Dance is religion to personal testimonies like this one: "A religious dance? It may have been years ago. To me, today, it isn't. It's just a social dance."

The tendency of outsiders to ignore such community complexity often leads them to talk about such deep experience in traditional Judeo-Christian terms, in which so-called religious feelings should emerge only within a delimited realm of dogma or belief. Experiencing song does indeed turn the mind towards the sacred on many levels. Yet Gourd Dance practitioners in southwestern Oklahoma do not situate this experience within a distinct religious system. Although feeling song can be as deep as religious experience—thus perhaps prompting many to compare it with established religion—it exists unto itself without the trappings of a set system of dogma. Instead, it occurs within what Gourd Dance practitioners call a good dance, a realm which also turns the mind towards pure fun and recreation as do other "Indian doings"—like handgames or family reunions. As community members often point out, the call for such godly expressions as song surfaces in every aspect of their lives—from church to eating to softball games to everyday hardships. This in itself suggests that Gourd Dances, while being diversions from the everyday, the secular, are at the same time much more than weekend rituals with distinct boundaries; rather, they are intrinsic to peoples' everyday lives.[65]

So where does all of this leave us? Where do we place spirit in our understandings of the Gourd Dance experience in southwestern Oklahoma among Kiowas and other Gourd Dance practitioners? Academically positioned models that explain the Gourd Dance and its songs have been useful for understanding what the Gourd Dance experience means in southwestern Oklahoma, but they have not gone far enough. I believe it is time to include the significance of song in our discussions, especially in terms of how community members talk about it. To do so necessarily means defining felt encounter with song as ethnographic fact. Ultimately, understanding spirit in these phenomenological terms may point us towards understanding something about the nature of experience itself. To be sure, experience is that fundamental human medium through which we all encounter life. Narratives about experience, in turn, reveal the realities that distinguish us from one another. Talking about the encounter with song in a collaborative framework thus opens a window into human diversity. At the same time, it may even open a window into those similarities of experience that may transcend difference. Indeed, the general felt it.

Notes

1. Portions of this essay and some of its figures also appear in Luke E. Lassiter, "Towards Understanding the Power of Kiowa Song: A Collaborative Exercise in Meaning" (Ph.D. diss., University of North Carolina at Chapel Hill, 1995) and shall appear in a forthcoming manuscript published by the University of Arizona Press. Portions of the research that appear in this essay were carried out under the auspices of the University of North Carolina Graduate School's Off-Campus Dissertation Fellowship (Chapel Hill), the American Indian Inter Tribal Cultural Organization's Graydon Frick Memorial Scholarship (Rockville, Maryland), and the Whatcom Museum Society's Jacobs Research Funds (Bellingham, Washington).

2. Theresa Carter, Danieala Vickers, Richard and Diana Kauahquo, recorded conversation with author, Anadarko, Oklahoma, 6 September 1994.

3. See, e.g., Maurice Boyd, *Kiowa Voices: Ceremonial Dance, Ritual, and Song* (Fort Worth: Texas Christian University Press, 1981), 112–22; Clyde Ellis, "Truly Dancing Their Own Way: Modern Revival and Diffusion of the Gourd Dance," *American Indian Quarterly* 14:1(1990): 19–33; and "A Gathering of Life Itself: The Kiowa Gourd Dance," in *Native American Values: Survival and Renewal*, ed. Thomas E. Schirer and Susan B. Branstner (Sault Ste. Marie, MI: Lake Superior State University Press, 1993), 365–74; James H. Howard, "The Plains Gourd Dance as a Revitalization Movement," *American Ethnologist* 3:2 (1976): 243–59; Thomas W. Kavanagh, "Southern Plains Dance: Tradition and Dynamism," in *Native American Dance: Ceremonies and Social Traditions* (Washington, DC: Smithsonian Institution, 1992), 107; Benjamin R. Kracht, "Kiowa Powwows: Continuity in Ritual Practice," *American Indian Quarterly* 18:3 (1994): 321–48; Eric Lassiter, "Towards Understanding the Power of Kiowa Song," 165ff.; and William C. Meadows, "Remaining Veterans: A Symbolic and Comparative Ethnohistory of Southern Plains Indian Military Societies" (Ph.D. diss., University of Oklahoma, 1995), 177–80, 184–201.

4. Frankie Ware, recorded conversation with author, Apache, Oklahoma, 8 July 1992.

5. Cf. Ellis, "Truly Dancing Their Own Way."

6. Billy Evans Horse, recorded conversation with author, Carnegie, Oklahoma, 11 July 1991.

7. See, e.g., Boyd, *Kiowa Voices*, 123–29. I also admit complicity to situating song within the narrow confines of simple functional relationships. See Eric Lassiter, "'They Left Us These Songs . . . That's All We Got Now': The Significance of Music in the Kiowa Gourd Dance and Its Relation to Native American Cultural Continuity," in *Native American Values: Survival and Renewal*, ed. Thomas E. Schirer and Susan M. Branstner (Sault Ste. Marie, MI: Lake Superior State University Press, 1993), 375–84.

8. James H. Howard's "The Plains Gourd Dance as a Revitalization Movement" was among the first articles written about the Gourd Dance and is cited widely. Howard essentially argued that the Gourd Dance shared observable patterns with revitalization movements; thus, he argued, the Gourd Dance was a revitalization movement. In the same article, due to lack of "identifiable leadership," Howard recast the Gourd Dance's "revitalization" as an "articulatory movement" after Nancy O. Lurie, "The Contemporary Indian Scene," in *North American Indians in Historical Perspective*, ed. Eleanor B. Leacock and Nancy O. Lurie (New York: Random House, 1971), 418-80. But these shared attributes alone do not make the Gourd Dance a revitalization movement. See Anthony F. C. Wallace, "Revitalization Movements," American Anthropologist 58 (1956): 264-81. Wal-

lace's theory of revitalization focused primarily on how groups consciously create a more satisfying culture through a process of "mazeway reformulation," the response to "mazeway disintegration" created by increased social stress on a social system. Revitalization is necessary, as Wallace put it, for "effective stress reduction." The revived Gourd Dance did not fulfill such a role in any way. During the most dramatic social changes on the Plains, the dance ceased at the same time that another dance thrived: the Ghost Dance. And that movement was clearly a revitalization movement. For the Kiowa, the Gourd Dances' revival revolved around public performances of the dance in the 1940s and 1950s. This performance and the community memory it evoked was the impetus for imparting the revival, not the social instability of the 1940s and 1950s—a time when "cultural stress" was apparently reduced by the economic and cultural rehabilitation characteristic of the period. I have discussed this problem more extensively elsewhere. For a fuller discussion of the Kiowa revival and the problems with Howard's application of the model, see Eric Lassiter, "Towards Understanding the Power of Kiowa Song," 188–209. For a discussion of Benjamin R. Kracht's application of *communitas* to the Gourd Dance, see Luke E. Lassiter and R. Clyde Ellis, "Applying Communitas to Kiowa Powwows: Some Methodological and Theoretical Problems," *American Indian Quarterly* (forthcoming).

9. Clifford Geertz, *The Interpretation of Cultures* (New York: Basic Books, 1973), 453.

10. Kracht, "Kiowa Powwows."

11. See Lassiter and Ellis, "Applying Communitas to Kiowa Powwows."

12. Carter, et al., 6 September 1994.

13. To hear "Charlie Brown," you can download a 22 second excerpt of the song from http://bsuvc.bus.edu/~lelassiter/. For a rendition of the entire song, several commercial recordings are available. See, e.g., side 2, selection 3, on "Gourd Dance Songs of the Kiowa," CR-6148-C, Canyon Records, 4143 North 16th Street, Phoenix, Arizona, 85016.

14. Ernest Doyebi, recorded conversation with author, Anadarko, Oklahoma, 6 August 1991; and Billy Evans Horse, recorded conversation with author, Anadarko, Oklahoma, 11 June 1991.

15. Billy Evans Horse, taped conversation with author, Carnegie, Oklahoma, 28 June 1990.

16. Carter, et al., 6 September 1994.

17. It is interesting to note that the first major article on the Gourd Dance, Howard's "The Plains Gourd Dance as a Revitalization Movement," gave much attention to form and choreography and little to music.

18. Several ethnomusicologists have discussed this issue before. For a fuller treatise of Western notation, including its potentials and problems, see, e.g., Bruno Nettl, *The Study of Ethnomusicology: Twenty-nine Issues and Concepts* (Urbana: University of Illinois Press, 1983), 65–81.

19. Admittedly, I am simplifying the linguistic process here to make a point. How song communicates meaning is actually a little more complex than this. Many songs, for example, have semantic components that operate much like phonemes, discrete sounds that distinguish one song from another.

20. See, e.g., Boyd , *Kiowa Voices*, 123–9.

21. John Joseph Beatty, *Kiowa-Apache Music and Dance*, University of Northern Colorado, Museum of Anthropology, Ethnology Series, no. 31 (Greeley, 1974), 12.

22. Although Beatty begins this quotation by suggesting some level of non-referential meaning, he then effectively undercuts this assertion, declaring the sounds "completely without meaning." To discuss song diffusion, he chooses to reduce the symbolic relation-

ships evoked by these songs to sound analysis, and ultimately ignores how Kiowa-Apache people experience their songs.

23. See, e.g., Charlotte Frisbie, "Vocables in Navajo Ceremonial Music," *Ethnomusicology* 24:3) (1980): 347–92.

24. Doyebi, 6 August 1991; Billy Evans Horse, taped conversation with author, Carnegie, Oklahoma, 10 July 1990; and Ralph Kotay, taped conversation with author, Apache, Oklahoma, 15 July 1992.

25. Several authors have addressed the relationship between language and non-linguistic components of communication. See, e.g., Dell Hymes, *Foundations in Sociolinguistics: An Ethnographic Approach* (Philadelphia: University of Pennsylvania Press, 1974). Hymes argues that in any given communicative event, language is only one component of a larger system of communication grounded in the context of community and event. "Songs without words" force us to consider this larger system of communication. Hymes identifies the participants, channels, codes, context, forms, attitudes, and the event itself as communicative components simultaneously present at any given event. Understanding their relationships, their capacity and state, and their activity within the entire system, Hymes argues, brings one closer to understanding how communication achieves meaning.

26. An exception may be Boyd's *Kiowa Voices*.

27. Carter, et al., 6 September 1994.

28. Horse, 11 June 1991.

29. Carter, et al., 6 September 1994; and Horse, 11 June 1991. Cf. Meadows, "Remaining Veterans," 58–223.

30. Cf. Meadows, "Remaining Veterans,"151–53.

31. Cf. Kenneth Goldstein, "On the Application of the Concepts of Active and Inactive Traditions to the Study of Repertory," *Journal of American Folklore* 84:62–7 (1971).

32. Horse, 11 July 1991.

33. Horse, 11 July 1991. See also Ellis, "A Gathering of Life Itself"; and Lassiter, "'They Left Us These Songs'" for a fuller treatise of this revival as founded on song.

34. See Lassiter, "Towards Understanding the Power of Kiowa Song," 188–224, for a much more extensive discussion of the Gourd Dance's organizational development in the 1970s, 1980s, and 1990s.

35. Kiowa Tai-Piah Society, "Annual Celebration: July 1, 2, 3, 4, 1990." Photocopy in author's possession.

36. See Howard, "The Plains Gourd Dance as a Revitalization Movement," 255ff.; and Ellis, "Truly Dancing Their Own Way," 25ff.

37. Carter, et al., 6 September 1994; and Ralph Kotay, personal communication with author, Apache, Oklahoma, 22 February 1995.

38. KTNN, taped copy of live coverage of "Navajo Nation Inaugural Ceremony Pow-wow" radio broadcast, AM 660, Window Rock, Arizona, 15 January 1991.

39. M. A. Anquoe, "Now You Know," *Kiowa Indian News*, vol. 25, no. 1, 3.

40. For a fuller discussion of the knowledge surrounding Gourd Dance songs, including "Charlie Brown," see Lassiter, "Towards Understanding the Power of Kiowa Song," 210ff.

41. Carter, et al., 6 September 1994.

42. I borrow the view of ritual as "the intersection of multiple coexisting social processes" from Renato Rosaldo, *Culture and Truth: The Remaking of Social Analysis* (Boston: Beacon Press, 1989), 11ff.

43. Kotay, 15 July 1992.

44. Napoleon "Nipper" and Cora Tiddark, taped conversation with author, Apache, Oklahoma, 14 July 1992.

45. Cf. Edward M. Bruner, "Experience and Its Expressions," in *The Anthropology of Experience*, ed. Victor W. Turner and Edward M. Bruner (Chicago: University of Illinois Press, 1986), 3–30.

46. Carter, et al., 6 September 1994.

47. Horse, 20 June 1991.

48. Horse, 11 June 1991; idem, 11 July 1991; idem, taped conversation with author, Carnegie, Oklahoma, 6 September 1994.

49. Horse, 6 September 1994.

50. Carter, et al., 6 September 1994.

51. Billy Evans Horse, taped conversation with author, Carnegie, Oklahoma, 30 June 1992.

52. Cf. David E. Young and Jean-Guy Goulet, eds., *Being Changed by Cross-Cultural Encounter: The Anthropology of Extraordinary Experience* (Ontario: Broadview Press, 1994).

53. See, e.g., David Hufford, "Traditions of Disbelief," *New York Folklore Quarterly* 8 (1982): 47–55.

54. See Howard, "The Plains Gourd Dance as a Revitalization Movement"; and Kracht, "Kiowa Powwows."

55. Bronislaw Malinowski, *Argonauts of the Western Pacific* (New York: Dutton, 1922), 25.

56. See, e.g., Rosaldo, *Culture and Truth*; Paul Stoller, *The Taste of Ethnographic Things: The Senses in Anthropology* (Philadelphia: University of Pennsylvania Press, 1989); and Barbara Tedlock, "From Participant Observation to the Observation of Participation: The Emergence of Narrative Ethnography," *Journal of Anthropological Research* 47 (1991): 69–94.

57. Tedlock, "From Participant Observation to the Observation of Participation."

58. James Clifford, "On Ethnographic Authority," *Representations* 1 (1983): 118–46.

59. Edith Turner, "A Visible Spirit Form in Zambia," in *Being Changed by Cross-Cultural Encounter: The Anthropology of Extraordinary Experience*, ed. David E. Young and Jean-Guy Goulet (Ontario: Broadview Press, 1994), 94.

60. See Kracht, "Kiowa Powwows."

61. Ralph Kotay, taped conversation with author, Apache, Oklahoma, 6 September 1994.

62. Horse, 11 July 1991.

63. Horse, 11 June 1991.

64. Quotations that do not appear with a name denote an anonymous contribution.

65. Horse, 11 June 1991; Carter, et al., 6 September 1994; idem, taped conversation with author, Anadarko, Oklahoma, 19 July 1994; Kotay, 15 July 1992; and Tiddark and Tiddark, 14 July 1992.

PART IV

FILM AND OTHER MEDIA

As advances have been made during the 1990s in a variety of media, Native Americans are developing creative interpretations of Native life and culture in an increasing number of formats. These media represent the vitality and dynamism of Native cultural life as an extension of old forms combined with an appropriation of new ones that configure innovative and empowering expressions of Native experience.

The novel is one such medium. Since the 1960s, but more recently during the 1990s, a proliferation of Native novels and poetry has occurred, many of which investigate contemporary and historical dilemmas and contradictions of Native life and colonial life situations. A very western form of cultural expression, the novel has increasingly become a powerful tool for many Native authors who explore cultural and colonial themes and present them to broad, largely non-Indian audiences, that would otherwise not have access to such transcultural and Native perspectives.

The cinema is another medium increasingly used by Native people, and it is an realm in which economic and cultural issues are closely linked as Native filmmakers struggle with mainstream studios for access to resources and audiences. Since the great commercial success of Dances with Wolves, *many movies have been produced with Native themes, and the opportunities for Native actors, producers, support staff, and screen writers has greatly increased. Until the late 1990s, most films with Native American content were produced and directed by non-Indians, but today, new projects are emerging with increasingly greater control and participation from Native people. Still, while Native people may help direct and provide cultural expertise to the film-making process, non-Indians typically front the money and therefore make the final decisions. Many older movies tended to stereotype Native*

167

Americans in the worst light, such as the classic image of an Indian falling off a horse while circling a wagon train of pioneers. More recently, cinematic representation has been more sensitive, but nevertheless, the films have followed classical American hero formats and have not told stories from an Indian perspective.

Native producers long for the financial wherewithal to produce independent Native film and theater. Stories, plays, and films written and produced from Indian cultural perspectives are yet to emerge in numbers. Financial backing is very difficult to gather, and stories or plots that do not appeal to broad American audiences do not attract the support of major studios. Nevertheless, Native film and theater are ways in which communities can develop stories and plays based on their own traditional teachings and colonial experiences.

Native theater, dance, film, and literature provide Native artists with ways to reclaim Native culture, history, and tradition within new, nontraditional formats. Such formats have already extended the range of Native experience and promise to provide ways to not only preserve Native teachings and lifeways, but also the means for new interpretations and creative preservation of Native cultures.

8

Cultural Imperialism and the Marketing of Native America

Laurie Anne Whitt

INTRODUCTION

 IN 1992, MAINSTREAM EURO-AMERICA demonstrated the short, selective, and sanitized character of both the national memory and the official history that sustains it by celebrating an anniversary: the Columbus Quincentenary, the "discovery" of the "New World." The vast majority of activities generated by this event were festive and culturally self-congratulatory. Yet there were powerful subcurrents of protest, indigenous and otherwise, in wide evidence, contesting the sharply edited, profoundly revisionist nature of the commemoration. They drove home the moral and methodological implications of the fact that history is not only written from a particular standpoint, but that that standpoint has been of the colonizers, not the colonized.[1] The response of Native America was also a determined assertion of presence and continuity, pointedly captured by the defiant counter spilling over with t-shirts, posters, and bumper stickers: "Still Here! Celebrating 49,500 years . . . before Columbus."

Partly as a result of these cultural dynamics, the writing of history has become more problematic within the general public's awareness. Some began openly to question longstanding practices, notably the racist dimensions of the continued stereotyping of Indian people by Hollywood, the media, and the sporting world.[2] Yet many deeply disturbing aspects of contemporary Western/indigenous cultural relations were left largely unexamined and unquestioned. One of these is a particularly virulent form of cultural imperialism—the marketing of Native America and, most tellingly, of Native spirituality.

Consider, for example, that a leading figure of the New Age recently announced he intended to patent the sweat lodge ceremony since Native people were no longer performing it correctly.[3] Could he receive intellectual property protection from the U.S. government for the sweat lodge ceremony, acquiring the right to prohibit Native people from performing it? To sue them if they do so? Astoundingly, it is at least legally arguable that he could,[4] thereby

---

Laurie Anne Whitt is an associate professor of philosophy at Michigan Technological University, Houghton, Michigan. She is of Choctaw descent.

placing himself in a position to limit the access of Native peoples to their own cultural expressions.[5] Yet, were such to occur, it would be only an escalation (albeit a particularly egregious one) of a phenomenon already deeply entrenched in Western culture, the commodification of indigenous spirituality. The transformation of indigenous spiritual knowledge, objects, and rituals into commodities, and their commercial exploitation, constitute a concrete manifestation of the more general, and chronic, marketing of Native America.[6]

Cultural imperialism is one of a number of oppressive relations that may hold between dominant and subordinated cultures.[7] Whether or not it is conscious and intentional, it serves to extend the political power, secure the social control, and further the economic profit of the dominant culture. The commodification of indigenous spirituality is a paradigmatic instance of cultural imperialism. As such, it plays a politically vital diversionary role, serving to colonize and assimilate the knowledge and belief systems of indigenous cultures. Ultimately, it facilitates a type of cultural acquisition via conceptual assimilation: Euro-American culture seeks to establish itself in indigenous cultures by appropriating, mining, and redefining what is distinctive, constitutive of them. The mechanism for this is an oft-repeated pattern of cultural subordination that turns vitally on legal and popular views of ownership and property, as formulated within the dominant culture.

MARKETING NATIVE AMERICA

Whether peddled by white shamans, plastic medicine men and women, opportunistic academics, entrepreneurs, or enterprising New Agers, Indian spirituality—like Indian lands before it—is rapidly being reduced to the status of a commodity, seized, and sold. Sacred ceremonies and ceremonial objects can be purchased at weekend medicine conferences or via mail order catalogs.[8] How-to books with veritable recipes for conducting traditional rituals are written and dispensed by trade publishers.[9] A succession of born-again medicine people[10] have—with greater or lesser subtlety—set themselves and their services up for hire, ready to sell their spiritual knowledge and power to anyone willing and able to meet their price.[11] And a literary cult of Indian identity appropriation known as white shamanism continues to be practiced.[12] Instead of contributing to the many Native-run organizations devoted to enhancing the lives and prospects of Indian people, New Agers are regularly enticed into contributing to the continued expropriation and exploitation of Native culture by purchasing an array of items marketed as means for enhancing their knowledge of Indian spirituality.

Recently, the National Congress of American Indians (an organization not exactly known for radicalism) issued a "declaration of war" against "non-Indian wannabes, hucksters, cultists, commercial profiteers and self-styled New Age shamans" who have been exploiting sacred knowledge and rituals.[13] Throughout Indian Country, eloquent, forceful critiques of these cultural developments have been mounted. Writers, intellectuals, activists, and spiritual leaders[14] have joined in identifying and resisting what has been described as "a new growth industry . . . known as 'American Indian Spiritualism'"[15] (henceforth AIS). The phenomena being protested are diverse and include literary, artistic, scholarly, and commercial products intended for consumption in the markets of popular culture as well as in those of the cultural elite.[16]

When the spiritual knowledge, rituals, and objects of historically subordinated cultures are transformed into commodities, economic and political power merge to produce cultural imperialism. A form of oppression exerted by a dominant society upon other cultures, and typically a source of economic profit, cultural imperialism secures and deepens the subordinated status of those cultures. In the case of indigenous cultures, it undermines their integrity and distinctiveness, assimilating them to the dominant culture by seizing and processing vital cultural resources, then remaking them in the image and marketplaces of the dominant culture. Such "taking of the essentials of cultural lifeways," Geary Hobson observes, "is as imperialistic as those simpler forms of theft, such as the theft of homeland by treaty."[17]

It is a phenomenon that spans Native North America, sparking the fierce resistance of indigenous people in Canada as well as the United States. Lenore Keeshig-Tobias, a Toronto-based Ojibwa poet and storyteller, is a founding member of the Committee to Re-establish the Trickster, an organization devoted to reclaiming the Native voice in literature. The Canadian cultural industry, she protests,

> is stealing—unconsciously, perhaps, but with the same devastating results—native stories as surely as the missionaries stole our religion and the politicians stole our land and the residential schools stole our language. . . . (It) amount(s) to cultural theft, theft of voice.[18]

Wendy Rose makes it plain that the issue here is not that "only Indians can make valid observations on themselves" and their cultures; rather, it is "one of integrity and intent":

> We accept as given that whites have as much prerogative to write and speak about us and our cultures as we have to write and speak about them and theirs. The question is how this is done and . . . why it is done.[19]

Some forms of cultural imperialism are the product of academic privilege and opportunism. The "name of Truth or Scholarship"[20] may be invoked, the cause of scholarly progress, of advancing knowledge.[21] Ojibwa author Gerald Vizenor reproaches the "culture cultists (who) have hatched and possessed distorted images of tribal cultures."[22] Their obsession with the tribal past, he contends, "is not an innocent collection of arrowheads, not a crude map of public camp sites in sacred places, but rather a statement of academic power and control over tribal images."[23] Sometimes the "cause" is one of ethical progress, of moral duty:

> Given the state of the world today, we all have not only the right but the obligation to pursue all forms of spiritual insight. . . . [I]t seems to me that I have as much right to pursue and articulate the belief systems of Native Americans as they do.[24]

On this reading, the colonization of indigenous knowledge and belief systems (and the attendant economic profit that their repackaging brings in the marketplaces of the dominant culture) is not only morally permissible, it is morally mandated.

Whatever its form, cultural imperialism often plays a diversionary role that is politically advantageous, for it serves to extend—while effectively diverting attention from—the continued oppression of indigenous peoples. Acoma Pueblo writer Simon Ortiz underscores this aspect of the phenomenon. Condemning white shamanism as a "process of colonialism" and a "usurping (of) the indigenous power of the people," he charges that

> symbols are taken and are popularized, diverting attention from real issues about land and resources and Indian peoples' working hours. The real struggle is really what should be prominent, but no, it's much easier to talk about drums and feathers and ceremonies and those sorts of things. "Real Indians," but "real Indians" only in quotes, stereotypes, and "interesting exotica. . . ." So it's a rip-off.[25]

Keeshig-Tobias refers to it as "escapist" and a "form of exorcism," enabling Canadians "to look to an ideal Native living in never-never land" rather than confront "the horrible reality of native-Canadian relations."[26] The extent to which cultural imperialism turns on conceptual colonization, and what is ultimately at stake in this, has been succinctly captured by Oneida scholar Pam Colorado. She contends that the commodification of indigenous spirituality enables the dominant culture to supplant Indian people even in the area of their own spirituality. This moves beyond ensuring their physical subordination to securing absolute ideological/conceptual subordination. If this continues,

> non-Indians will have complete power to define what is and is not Indian, even for Indians. . . . When this happens, the last vestiges of real Indian society and Indian rights will disappear. Non-Indians will then "own" our heritage and ideas as thoroughly as they now claim to own our land and resources.[27]

Some practitioners of AIS are genuinely surprised when they are charged with arrogance, theft, hucksterism. They see themselves as respectfully "sharing" indigenous spirituality, even as they make a living on its commercialization, charging hefty fees to "share" their version of the pipe ceremony and the sweat lodge, and to sponsor New Agers through vision quests. Moreover, they see nothing problematic in this behavior, castigating their critics as "advocates of censorship . . . trying to shackle artistic imagination"[28] or as "Indian fundamentalists" guilty of "reverse racism"[29] and of a selfish refusal to share traditional knowledge.[30] This last is to distort massively what is at issue and the source of indigenous concern. The Traditional Elders Circle, meeting at the Northern Cheyenne Nation, is very clear on the point:

> [T]he authority to carry . . . sacred objects is given by the people, and the purpose and procedure is specific to time and the needs of the people. . . . [P]rofit is not the motivation. . . . We concern ourselves only with those

who use spiritual ceremonies with non-Indian people for profit. There are many things to be shared with the Four Colors of humanity in our common destiny as one with the Mother Earth. It is this sharing that must be considered with great care by the Elders and the medicine people who carry the Sacred Trusts.[31]

That those engaged in the buying and selling of products generated by the AIS industry fail to recognize their behavior as reprehensible suggests that the diversionary function of cultural imperialism is operative at the individual level as well, where it deflects critical self-reflection.[32] Hobson speaks of this as an "assumption . . . that one's 'interest' in an Indian culture makes it okay . . . to collect 'data' from Indian people."[33] Ward Churchill describes a comparable development. New Age practitioners of AIS, he maintains,

have proven themselves willing to disregard the rights of American Indians to any modicum of cultural sanctity or psychological sanctuary. They . . . willingly and consistently disregard the protests and objections of their victims, speaking only of their own "right to know."[34]

He characterizes the process as one of self-deception. Their task is simultaneously to hang on to what has been stolen while

separating themselves from the way in which it was stolen. It is a somewhat tricky psychological project of being able to "feel good about themselves". . . through legitimizing the maintenance of their own colonial privilege.[35]

Such posturing effectively hides or diverts individuals' attention from the nature and consequences of their behavior. It is, in Renato Rosaldo's terms, grounded on a courting of nostalgia, wherein the agents of colonialism yearn for what they themselves have altered or transformed. "Imperialist nostalgia" has a paradoxical element to it:

[S]omeone deliberately alters a form of life, and then regrets that things have not remained as they were prior to the intervention. At one remove, people destroy their environment, and then they worship nature. In any of its versions, imperialist nostalgia uses a pose of "innocent yearning" both to capture people's imaginations and to conceal its complicity with often brutal domination.[36]

This nostalgia is integral to the cultivation of self-deception. It is a "particularly appropriate emotion to invoke in attempting to establish one's innocence and at the same time talk about what one has destroyed."[37]

THE CULTURAL POLITICS OF OWNERSHIP

When confronted by their critics, those engaged in the marketing of Native America frequently do attempt to justify their behavior. From their reasoning and rhetoric we can elicit some distinctive features of this variant of cultural imperialism. What we will find is a rationale that has reverberated throughout the history of dominant/indigenous relations, one that starkly reveals how the cultural politics of ownership are played out in the context of oppression.

Consider Gary Snyder's response to indigenous protests. "Spirituality is not something that can be 'owned' like a car or a house," he asserts. It "belongs to all humanity equally."[38] Or Alberto Manguel's response to Keeshig-Tobias: "No one," he contends, "can 'steal' a story because stories don't belong to anyone. Stories belong to everyone. . . . No one . . . has the right to instruct a writer as to what stories to tell."[39] Yet those who write and copyright "native" stories, those white shamans who sell poetry that "romanticize(s) their 'power' as writers to inhabit (Indian) souls and consciousness"[40] and those culture capitalists who traffic in "Indian" rituals and sacred objects are all clearly making individual profit on what "no one" (allegedly) owns. Such responses are both diversionary and delusionary. They attempt to dictate the terms of the debate by focusing attention on issues of freedom of speech and thought and deflecting it from the active commercial exploitation and the historical realities of power that condition current dominant/indigenous relations. In the words of Margo Thunderbird,

> They came for our land, for what grew or could be grown on it, for the resources in it, and for our clean air and pure water. They stole these things from us . . . and now . . . they've come for the very last of our possessions; now they want our pride, our history, our spiritual traditions. They want to rewrite and remake these things, to claim them for themselves.[41]

The colonists indeed displayed an array of motivations regarding their presence and conduct in America, and it is similar to that of the AIS practitioners currently vending Native Americana. The prospect of profits from speculation lured some to seize Native lands; others, wanting to escape poverty and enhance their lives, regarded themselves as merely "sharing" underused lands; most found it convenient to believe that the indigenous inhabitants of this continent could have no legitimate claims to land.[42]

Analogous reasoning and rhetoric accompany numerous parallel tales of acquisition in contemporary Western/indigenous relations. By examining some of these, we can better elicit the specious justificatory appeals on which cultural imperialism relies to extend and legitimize such practice. Their cumulative weight suggests that cultural imperialism, in its late capitalist mode, requires a legitimating rationale, one that enables the dominant culture to mask the fundamentally oppressive nature of its treatment of subordinated cultures. This rationale is fashioned by invoking legal and popular views of ownership and property prevalent in Euro-American culture and conceptually imposing these on indigenous cultures. It may take one, and usually both, of two forms—an appeal to common property and an appeal to private property. In the first, the dominant culture enhances its political power, social control, and economic profit by declaring the (material, cultural, genetic) resources of indigenous cultures to be common property, freely available to everyone. Thus, whatever the dominant culture finds desirable in indigenous cultures is declared to be part of the "public domain." The second appeal accomplishes the same ends through opposing means, facilitating privatization and the transformation of valued indigenous resources into commodity form. These appeals lie at the heart of cultural imperialism. As we will see, they commonly function in tandem, with the former preparing and paving the way for the latter. Three examples will be examined: (1) the copyrighting of traditional indigenous music; (2) the patenting of indigenous genetic resources; and (3) the patenting of human cell lines of indigenous people themselves. We will see how, through the development of the notion of intellectual property and the articulation of intellectual property laws, the established legal system extends and enforces the practice of cultural imperialism. First, however, to facilitate appreciation of where these examples fall on the continuum of expropriative strategies invoked by Euro-American culture, I offer a few remarks about some of their historical antecedents.

In an earlier day, imperial powers could appeal to three competing legal theories of territorial acquisition to justify their claims to sovereignty over new lands: occupation, conquest, and cession. The first of these, unlike the other two, required that the land be *terra nullius*, devoid of people. According to Blackstone,

> if an uninhabited country be discovered and planted by English subjects,
> all the English laws then in being . . . are immediately there in force.[43]

Declaring that the land belonged to no one set the stage for its conversion into private or individual property—a legally protected possession. But other legitimating rationales for the privatizing of property were needed, particularly to accommodate other types of property in addition to land. By declaring the intellectual and cultural properties of indigenous peoples to be in the public domain—that is, to belong to everyone—the stage is equally well set for their conversion into private property. These two rationales (terra nullius and public domain) clearly resemble each other. The notion of property belonging to no one is the functional equivalent of the notion of property belonging to everyone; they both serve as the terms of a conversion process that results in the privatization of property. However, while the concept of terra nullius enabled the privatizing only of lands, the notion that property in the public domain could come to be owned by individuals applies to other types of property as well, such as intellectual and cultural property. The latter conversion process is addressed below; it might thus be regarded as a legal theory of cultural acquisition, whereby Western intellectual property rights are invoked in the interests of cultural imperialism in order to appropriate valued intangible indigenous resources.

The politics of property is the central historical dynamic mediating Euro-American/indigenous relations. Certainly one of the more obvious examples of this is the General Allotment Act of 1887, which served to privatize communally owned tribal lands. A more recent case is that of the struggle to protect Newe Segobia (Western Shoshone homelands) from further encroachment by the U.S. government. It is a struggle at least as old as the 1863 Treaty of Ruby Valley, in which the United States first acknowledged native title to the land. The Western Shoshone have steadfastly refused payment for the subsequent theft of a large portion of their land, rejecting the government's offer of $26 million in damages for land taken by "gradual encroachment." The eight-hundred-acre cattle ranch of Mary and Carrie Dann has been a focal point in this controversy.

In the early 1970s, the Dann sisters were told that their cattle were trespassing on "public range land" and that they must purchase federal grazing permits to run livestock on "public land." (The terms public lands and public domain lands designate lands that are subject to sale or other disposal under the general laws of the United States or the states.)[44] They have been locked in lawsuits ever since. Their home has been raided by federal agents, their livestock impounded, and their brother imprisoned. They were also recently awarded the "alternative Nobel Peace Prize" by the Stockholm-based Right Livelihood Foundation.[45] Says Carrie Dann, "The real issue is that the United States is attempting to claim control over sovereign Western Shoshone land and people. Our land has never been ceded or deeded to the U.S., so it's not possible for them just to take it and determine that our title to the land has been extinguished."[46]

But the politics of property has never been confined to land. Consider the struggle between Euro-American and indigenous cultures over the ownership of human remains. Since the United States claims title to all "cultural property" found on federal public lands, material items of indigenous cultures discovered on these lands belong to the U.S. government, provided that they are at least one hundred years of age.[47] This includes human skeletal materials, which find themselves—together with these other items—thereby transformed into the "archaeological resources" of the dominant culture.[48] Ultimate authority to regulate the disposition of such "resources" rests with the secretary of the interior, according to the Archaeological Resources Protection Act of 1979.[49] Moreover, since the majority of states do not strictly regulate the excavation of Native graves and sacred sites on state or private lands, private landowners have historically been at liberty to sell, destroy, or otherwise dispose of any material remains of indigenous cultures as they saw fit or profitable.[50]

Thus, whether it is legally permissible to dig up a grave, to display or sell the contents of it, will turn in part on whether that grave is in an Indian or non-Indian cemetery. This discriminatory treatment of skeletal remains has been noted by various critics. C. Dean Higginbotham has observed that "only the burial and religious sites of Native Americans are regularly subjected to archaeological excavation and study in the United States."[51] Walter Echo-Hawk concurs:

> If human remains and burial offerings of Native people are so easily desecrated and removed, wherever located, while the sanctity of the final resting place of other races is strictly protected, it is obvious that Native burial practices and associated beliefs were never considered during the development of American property law.[52]

Cultural imperialism, then, embraces a spectrum of expropriative strategies. At one end of this spectrum we find legal theories of acquisition that facilitate the dominant culture's ownership of indigenous land and of the material remains of indigenous peoples within the land. At the other end, we find theories of acquisition that rely on laws of intellectual property to legitimate the privatization of less tangible indigenous resources. We can turn now to three examples in which the legitimating rationale of public domain is invoked to provide moral and legal cover for the theft of indigenous cultural and genetic resources.

MUSICAL PIRACY AND LETTERS OF MARQUE

Like the rest of U.S. property law, music copyright is based on an individualized conception of ownership. Existing copyright law fails to acknowledge any rights of indigenous communities to their traditional music. Indeed, the United States is among the most reluctant of nations to "consider changes in the copyright law which would give broad rights to intellectual property for 'traditional' rather than individually created culture."[53] Traditional indigenous music is considered to be in the "public domain" and so not subject to copyright.[54] Anyone may borrow extensively from materials in the public domain. Moreover, entire works may be "borrowed" from the public domain and receive copyright protection provided the author or composer has contributed some "modicum of creative work"[55] and is able to meet the "originality" requirement. Originality has been interpreted minimally: A work has originality if it is "one man's alone."[56] Any "distinguishable variation" of a prior work "will constitute sufficient originality to support a copyright if such variation is the product of the author's independent efforts, and is more than merely trivial."[57] The threshold for originality is particularly low in music: "[A] musical composition is original if it is 'the spontaneous, unsuggested result of the author's imagination.'"[58] It may be achieved by slight variations in the use of rhythm, harmony, accent, or tempo.

Thus, as Anthony Seeger protests, "the real issue is . . . the economic and cultural exploitation of one group by another group or individual." Under existing copyright law,

> there is nothing illegal about taking a piece of "traditional" music, modifying it slightly, performing it, and copyrighting it. When music is owned by indigenous people it is seen as "public domain." If it becomes popular in its "mainstream" form, though, it suddenly becomes "individual property." The song brings a steady income to the person who individualized it, not to the people from whose culture it is derived.[59]

While others are free to copy the original indigenous song with impunity, were someone to attempt to copy the "original" copy (now transformed into the legally protected individual property of a composer who has "borrowed" it from the indigenous "public domain"), he or she would be subject to prosecution for copyright infringement.[60] This includes any members of the indigenous community of the song's origin who cannot meet the requirements of "fair use."[61]

According to the Universal Declaration of Human Rights, "Everyone has the right to the protection of the moral and material interests resulting from any scientific, literary or artistic production of which he is the author."[62] Copyright, then, is recognized as a human right but only as an individual human right. Since copyright laws turn on identifying specific individuals who have produced the work to be copyrighted, they afford no protection to the traditional music of indigenous communities. In response to this, a United Nations agency—the World Intellectual Property Rights Organization (WIPO)—proposed in 1984 a set of "Model Provisions for National Laws on the Protection of Expressions of Folklore against Illicit Exploitation and Other Prejudicial Actions." (In this context, the term folklore refers to traditions that transcend the lifespan of individuals. To receive protection, moreover, they need not be "reduced to material form.")[63] Recognizing that "no share of the returns from . . . exploitation is conceded to the communities who have developed and maintained" their traditions, the model provisions would treat as a punishable offense any unauthorized use or willful distortion of folkloric traditions that is "prejudicial to the cultural interests of the community concerned."[64] A review of the model provisions by a U.N. group of experts concluded that, despite a desperate need for protections of this nature, an international treaty would be premature, since there were no (1) workable mechanisms for resolving disputes or (2) appropriate sources for identifying the folkloric expressions to be protected. Accordingly, to date, no country has adopted these provisions; they remain proposals for member states. As Darrell Posey notes, acquiescence to such arguments is "akin to allowing people to steal property whenever the owner has failed to announce his or her possession."[65]

Current copyright laws not only fail to protect the intellectual property of indigenous communities but directly facilitate cultural imperialism by consigning traditional music to the public domain, then providing for its facile "conversion" to private property. In such circumstances, copyrights offer legal and intellectual cover for cultural theft. They give an aura of legitimacy to the privateering activities of individuals who, like Blackbeard and Henry Morgan, have been granted letters of marque and reprisal by the government "so that they could do whatever they wanted."[66] Two critics of the music copyright system have recently demonstrated an emerging pattern in this regard:

> [S]ongs from small countries are often picked up and exploited internationally, with the original collector or publisher claiming the copyright on the "first there, first claim" principle, and with the original local composers or "collectors" getting left out.[67]

Their evidence includes various examples of the appropriation by American artists and record companies of the traditional music of the Caribbean, where profits on a single calypso song can easily run in the millions without any of this flowing back to the peoples or countries of its origin. They document in detail the confusion and exploitation that results when "international copyright systems . . . come into conflict with traditional thinking":[68]

> [T]he identity of the actual composer becomes irrelevant in the traditional [calypsonian] system. This "positive" public domain attitude can of

course be totally exploited by the legally wise when exposed to a system where the first registered copyright claimant is accepted as the legal owner. . . . It's not easy to merge the cultural norms of a society where music is regarded as a gift to the public with the legal norms of a society where individual ownership is the holiest pinnacle![69]

GENETIC IMPERIALISM AND THE "COMMON HERITAGE"

In what has been described as "the last great resource rush,"[70] commercial seed and drug industries are extracting, transforming, and commodifying the valuable genetic resources of indigenous peoples. This time around, it is not land or natural resources that imperialism has targeted but indigenous genetic wealth and pharmaceutical knowledge. Indigenous peoples inhabit the most genetically diverse areas of the world, and, once again,

> their areas, and their knowledge, are . . . being mined—for information. Unless indigenous rights to this material and knowledge are respected, this gene rush will leave indigenous people in the same hole as the other resource rushes.[71]

Corporate and academic scientists engaged in "gene-hunting" and "chemical prospecting" first mine indigenous medicinal and agricultural knowledge. They then identify and extract selected plant materials, process these in laboratories and finally through the legal system—ultimately transforming them into commodities and legally protected private property, for whose use indigenous people must pay. The key first step is to declare that these indigenous genetic resources belong to everyone. As the "common heritage of humankind . . . to be traded as a 'free good' among the community of nations,"[72] they are "not owned by any one people and are quite literally a part of our human heritage from the past."[73] Thus, they are "looked upon as a public good for which no payment is necessary or appropriate."[74] One may then convert these free "public" goods into private property and a source of enormous economic profit.

A current example is the use by the Uru-eu-wau-wau Indians of Brazil of the bark of the Tike-Uba tree in a preparation that acts as an anticoagulant.[75] Reportedly, a large U.S.-based chemical company is attempting to patent these properties of the plant,[76] following a study by corporate scientists of sap and bark specimens provided to them by members of the Goiana Institute for Prehistory and Anthropology.[77] The Uru-eu-wau-wau, protesting this commercialization of their knowledge, are challenging that company's right to patent their traditional medicines.[78] However, as Janet McGowan notes,

> much like Columbus' voyage, when it comes to U.S. patent law, it isn't always a question of getting there first, but having the resources to control and protect your discovery. . . . U.S. patent law really protect(s) (and financially reward[s]) the discovery of the known.[79]

Despite the fact that some 80 percent of the world's population relies on traditional health care based on medicinal plants and that 74 percent of contemporary drugs have the same or related uses in Western medicine as they do in traditional medical systems, the pharmaceutical knowledge and medicinal skills of indigenous peoples are neither acknowledged nor rewarded. As one commentator observes,

> Traditional remedies . . . are products of human knowledge. To transform a plant into medicine, one has to know the correct species, its location, the proper time of collection . . . , the part to be used, how to prepare it . . . , the solvent to be used . . . , the way to prepare it . . . , and, finally, posolog . . . curers have to diagnose and select the right medicine for the right patients.[80]

Yet, while indigenous pharmaceutical knowledge, like industrial knowledge, has been accumulated by trial-and-error, "it has been made public with no patent rights attached. . . . What are the ethics behind recording customary knowledge and making it publicly available without adequate compensation?"[81] Such questions are all the more pressing because, often, this knowledge is obtained from specialists in the indigenous community only after the scientist "has established credibility within that society and a position of trust with the specialist."[82] Research in ethnopharmacology[83] cannot ignore the omnipresence of pharmaceutical corporations eager "to analyze, develop, and market plant products," to secure "exclusive rights to pertinent information" collected.[84] While some ethnopharmacologists have worked to develop products managed by indigenous communities, others have been accused of "stealing valuable plant materials and appropriating esoteric plant knowledge for financial profit and professional advancement."[85] Witting or not, this collusion of Western science, business, and legal systems is a potent extractive device:

> [C]ontemporary patent systems tend to disregard the creative intelligence of peoples and communities around the world. Thus the Western scientific and industrial establishment freely benefits from a steady flow of people nurtured genetic material and associated knowledge, and, at times, after only a superficial tinkering, reaps enormous economic profits through patents, without even token recognition, and much less economic reward to the rightful owners of such resources.[86]

Rural sociologist Jack Kloppenburg describes this phenomenon as "the commodification of the seed."[87] He notes that scientists from the advanced industrial nations have, for more than two centuries, appropriated plant genetic resources, yet,

> [d]espite their tremendous utility, such materials have been obtained free of charge as the "common heritage," and therefore common good, of humanity. On the other hand, the elite cultivars developed by the commercial seed industries . . . are accorded the status of private property. They are commodities obtainable by purchase.[88]

The process wholly discounts the tremendous investment of generations of indigenous labor that is involved in the cultivation of specific plant varieties for their medicinal and nutrient value.[89] It credits solely the "chop-shop" laboratory labor of corporate and academic scientists who "modify" what they have taken. Victoria Tauli-Corpus, representing indigenous peoples at a meeting of the U.N. Commission on Sustainable Development (CSD), underscores the exploitation and skewed reasoning that is at work:

> Without our knowing these seeds and medicinal plants were altered in laboratories and now we have to buy these because companies had them patented. . . . We are told that the companies have intellectual property rights over these genetic plant materials because they improved on them. This logic is beyond us. Why is it that we, indigenous peoples who have developed and preserved these plants over thousands of years, do not have the rights to them anymore because the laboratories altered them?[90]

THE "VAMPIRE PROJECT": PATENTING INDIGENOUS PEOPLE

There seems to be little that is indigenous that is not potentially intellectual property.[91] This includes indigenous people themselves or, more exactly, indigenous cell lines. The Human Genome Organization (HUGO) is currently engaged in an NIH-sponsored effort to map and sequence the human genome. This $3-billion project is supposed to be completed in fifteen years. Since the project does not consider population-level variation, a collateral study has been proposed—a "genetic survey of vanishing peoples"[92] known as the Human Genome Diversity Project (HGDP). It proposes to create thousands of cell lines from DNA collected from "rapidly disappearing indigenous populations."[93] Some 722 indigenous communities have been targeted for "collection."[94]

A recent article in *Science* presents the following rationale for such a study:

> Indigenous peoples are disappearing across the globe. . . . As they vanish, they are taking with them a wealth of information buried in their genes about human origins, evolution, and diversity. . . . [E]ach (population) offers "a window into the past". . . a unique glimpse into the gene pool of our ancestors. . . . Already, there are indications of the wealth of information harbored in the DNA of aboriginal peoples.[95]

Sir Walter Bodmer, HUGO's president, refers to the proposed survey (dubbed the "vampire project" by indigenous delegates to the United Nations) as "a cultural obligation of the genome project."[96] At an HGDP workshop on "Ethical and Human Rights Implications," it was suggested that sampling begin "with the least politically risky groups. . . . If the Project does not proceed carefully and properly, it could spoil the last good opportunity to obtain some of this data."[97] What are "proper procedures?" Dr. Paul Weiss, an anthropologist, proposed the following strategy, according to the summary report:

"Immortalization" can be a very sensitive term and should be avoided when talking about the intended creation of cell lines. (Someone suggested using "transformation," the standard European practice.) Whether to tell people what you intend to do, as a technical matter, is a difficult question.[98]

Not surprisingly, native rights activists such as Jeanette Armstrong of Canada's En'owkin Center describe the ethics committee as "a P.R. operation for the project."[99]

Indigenous opposition has been extensive and emphatic. After heated debate with Stanford law professor Henry Greely, chair of the HGDP ethics sub-committee, the 1993 Annual Assembly of the World Council of Indigenous Peoples unanimously resolved to "categorically reject and condemn the HGDP as it applies to our rights, lives, and dignity."[100] In January 1994, John Liddle, director of the Central Australian Aboriginal Congress, protested,

If the Vampire Project goes ahead and patents are put on genetic material from Aboriginal people, this would be legalized theft. Over the last 200 years, non-Aboriginal people have taken our land, language, culture and health—even our children. Now they want to take the genetic material which makes us Aboriginal people as well.[101]

And at the June 1993 session of the CSD, indigenous representatives described the HGDP as "very alarming": "[W]e are calling for a stop to the Human Genome Diversity Project which is basically an appropriation of our lives and being as indigenous peoples."[102] Project opponents

believe we are endangered. . . . After being subjected to ethnocide and genocide for 500 years (which is why we are endangered), the alternative is for our DNA to be collected and stored. This is just a more sophisticated version of how the remains of our ancestors are collected and stored in museums and scientific institutions.

Why don't they address the causes of our being endangered instead of spending $20 million for five years to collect and store us in cold laboratories. If this money will be used instead to provide us with basic social services and promote our rights as indigenous peoples, then our biodiversity will be protected.[103]

They also raised concerns about patenting and commercial exploitation: "How soon will it be before they apply for IPRs to these genes and sell them for a profit?"[104]

The legitimacy of these concerns is without question. Indeed, the U.S. Centers for Disease Control and Prevention (CDC) had already, in November 1991, applied for a patent to a cell line created from a Guaymi woman. They did so because of its commercial promise and since "the government encourages scientists to patent anything of interest."[105] However, lack of commercial interest, together with pressure from indigenous organizations and their supporters, prompted the CDC to abandon its application in 1993.[106] The Canadian-based

Rural Advancement Foundation International (RAFI) was responsible for discovering the patent application and sounding the alarm regarding it, noting that it "represented the sort of profiteering from the biological inheritance of indigenous people that could become commonplace as a result of the proposed Human Genome Diversity Project."[107]

CONCLUSION

The justificatory rhetoric embedded in these examples is essentially the same as that invoked by those we encountered at the outset of this essay who are actively engaged in the marketing of indigenous spirituality. In all of these cases, appeals to common property, private property, and usually both in succession constitute the legitimating rationale of cultural imperialism. It enables the dominant culture to secure political and social control as well as to profit economically from the cultural and genetic resources of indigenous cultures. Just as the concept of terra nullius once provided legal and moral cover for the imperial powers' treatment of indigenous peoples, the concept of public domain plays a comparable role in late capitalism.

As we have seen, far from being mutually exclusive, these appeals function together to facilitate a conversion, or privatization, process. When intellectual property laws of the dominant culture are imposed on indigenous peoples, the first appeal to common property or the public domain lays the legal groundwork for the private ownership secured by the second. What "flows out . . . as the 'common heritage of mankind' . . . returns as a commodity."[108] This is a particularly effective strategy for acquiring desired but intangible indigenous resources—medicinal and spiritual knowledge, ceremonies, artistic expressions. Ownership of such intangibles may in turn (as in the case of genetic information) lead to control of, and denial of indigenous access to, tangible resources. This is not only "legal theft" of indigenous resources; it is legally sanctioned and facilitated theft. As Vandana Shiva comments, "[C]ommunities have invested . . . centuries of care, respect, and knowledge" in developing these resources, yet

> today, this material and knowledge heritage is being stolen under the garb of IPRs (intellectual property rights). IPRs are a sophisticated name for modern piracy.[109]

The payoff of imperialistic cultural practice is substantial. There is considerable economic profit to be reaped from the commodification and marketing of indigenous cultural resources. It is also politically invaluable. As the established legal system extends and enforces the practice of cultural imperialism, it brings with it its own legitimating rationale. This, simply put, is a way of speaking about and thinking about what is going on—a rhetoric and a reasoning that plays a politically diversionary role as, at the individual level, it nurtures self-deception.[110] Ultimately, the two appeals explored here constitute a logic of domination—a structure of fallacious reasoning that seeks to justify subordination. The dominant conceptual framework is held to have certain features that indigenous frameworks lack and that render it superior. Such alleged superiority, it is assumed, justifies the assimilation of those frameworks and cultures to it.[111]

This logic of domination figures vitally in the marketing of Native America. If strategies of resistance to it are to be effective, they must be situated within the broader social context that informs it. The extension of the commodity form to new areas is one of the principal historical processes associated with the political economy of capitalism. It provides a way of reproducing the social relations needed if capital is to survive and grow in a particular sector.[112] The development of the notion of intellectual property and the articulation of intellectual property laws is a significant moment in the self-expansion of capital, another instance of "the relentless extension of market assumptions into areas where the market has not ruled."[113] We are, as Christopher Lind protests, "forced to genuflect before the great god market in yet one more area of . . . life."[114] It is also a significant move in the dynamics of power that structure dominant/indigenous relations, in the growth of cultural imperialism. It wrests away from indigenous peoples the power to control their cultural, spiritual, and genetic resources. As Kloppenburg notes, "business interests in the developed nations have worked very hard over the past ten years to put in place a legal framework that ensures that genetically engineered materials . . . can be owned."[115]

Let us be clear about what is being critiqued. It is not the concepts of public domain or common heritage, nor even that of private property per se. It is a particular set of social and power relations—specifically, the dynamic of oppression and domination mediating Western and indigenous cultures that sustains the practice of cultural imperialism. As outlined here, that practice is one wherein elements of the dominant culture's conceptual framework—notably, its concepts of ownership and property—are thrust upon indigenous cultures and enforced by the power of the state. These concepts tend to dictate the terms of the struggle, to reinforce current relations of power, and to sustain existing inequities between dominant and indigenous cultures. Resistance to this is pronounced, adamant, and growing. While indigenous representatives to the Commission on Sustainable Development acknowledged that many of the cultural and genetic resources of indigenous cultures can be shared with the rest of the world, they were resolute that

> we will be the ones who will determine how these will be shared based on our own conditions and our own terms. We cannot buy the arguments that we have to play within the field of existing patent and copyright laws to be able to protect our resources and knowledge. . . . Is there a way of preserving and promoting biodiversity and indigenous peoples' knowledge and technology without necessarily being pushed into the field of intellectual property rights? We are still seeking for the answers to this.[116]

The task is as daunting as it is vital. Morton Horwitz has documented how, during the post-Revolutionary War period, merchant and entrepreneurial groups rose to political and economic power, forging an alliance with the legal profession to advance their own interests through a transformation of the legal system. By the mid-nineteenth century, they had succeeded in reshaping the legal system to their own advantage and at the expense of other less powerful groups in society.[117] A comparable phenomenon appears to be currently in process at the international level. Through coercive instruments such as the GATT, the United States and other leading industrial nations have succeeded in furthering their interests at the expense of indigenous peoples and developing nations by strengthening Western intellectual property systems worldwide. All of this demonstrates the degree to which law, as various critical legal theorists have insisted,[118] is a form of politics. The politics of property and ownership that we have seen played out in the various examples above is ample testimony to the fact that, when it comes to dominant/indigenous relations, law has never been separate from politics. Whether as appeals to terra nullius or to the public domain, legal theories of acquisition have, since contact, provided the legitimating rationale for territorial and cultural imperialism and for the privatization of indigenous land and resources. A first step in undermining this process (although it is no more than that) may be to set to rest the fractured fairy tale of a neutral, apolitical legal system.

Acknowledgments

I am grateful to Alan W. Clarke for extended discussions on the issues raised in this essay and to Jack Kloppenburg and M. Annette Jaimes Guerrero for sharing research materials with me.

Notes

1. This was nicely demonstrated by the quietly reflective and rhetorically effective query that the Mennonite community employed to raise the popular conscience: "500 Years Ago the Americans Discovered Columbus on Their Shores. How Do You Think They Felt about It?"

2. The work of the American Indian Anti-defamation Council and of activist scholars such as Ward Churchill in *Fantasies of the Master Race,* ed. M. Annette Jaimes (Monroe, ME: Common Courage Press, 1992) and *Indians Are Us?* (Monroe, ME: Common Courage Press, 1994) has been instrumental in this regard.

3. This was related by Robert Antone in "Education as a Vehicle for Values and Sovereignty," an address given at the Third International Native American Studies conference at Lake Superior State University in October 1991.

4. However, the more probable route would be a copyright, not a patent. See 17 U.S.C. 106 (Exclusive Rights in Copyrighted Works). This would involve reducing the ceremony to some tangible expression, then claiming authorship of it. The broad construal of the salient legal terms, especially *writings* (*Goldstein* v. *California,* 412 U.S. 546 [1973]), suggests this is feasible. However, given constitutionally protected religious freedom, any suit for copyright infringement would likely be dismissed out of hand.

5. See 17 U.S.C. 110 (Exemptions of Certain Performances and Displays); see also *Robert Stigwood Group Ltd.* v. *O'Reilly,* 530 F.2d 1096 (2d. Cir. 1976).

6. The sale of "authentic" Indian images and "genuine handmade" trinkets reaches far into the history of Euro-American/indigenous relations.

7. Various radical theorists and social critics have alluded to cultural imperialism, although few characterize it at length. My discussion differs somewhat from that of Iris Young (in "Five Faces of Oppression," *Rethinking Power,* ed. Thomas Wartenberg [Albany, NY: SUNY Press, 1992]). I agree with her that it is one of several forms of oppression, but I emphasize its impact on the cultures rather than the individuals subjected to it. I move freely in this paper between references to indigenous cultures generally and native North American cultures more specifically, since the practice of cultural imperialism under consideration is similarly imposed upon them. However, closer analyses of how specific historical, political, cultural, and socioeconomic circumstances condition and modify such practice are needed.

8. The crassness of this commodification is stunning, as a perusal of the Berkeley, California–based Gaia Bookstore and Catalog Company readily reveals. Their 1991 catalog, for example, offers a series of oracular Medicine Cards and Sacred Path Cards (with titles such as "Medicine Bowl," "Give-Away Ceremony," and "Dreamtime") that promise "the Discovery of Self Through Native Teachings." Such spirituality, noted Osage scholar George Tinker observes, is "centered on the self, a sort of Western individualism run amok" (in David Johnston, "Spiritual Seekers Borrow Indian Ways," *New York Times,* 27 December 1993, section A), whereas Indian spirituality focuses on the larger community, the tribe, and never on the individual.

9. Two illustrative examples are John Redtail Freesoul's *Breath of the Invisible: The Way of the Pipe* (Wheaton, IL: Theosophical Pub. House, 1986) and Ed McGaa's *Mother Earth Spirituality* (San Francisco: Harper Books, 1990).

10. Among these are Sun Bear, Wallace Black Elk, Grace Spotted Eagle, Brook Medicine Eagle, Osheana Fast Wolf, Cyfus McDonald, Dyhani Ywahoo, Rolling Thunder, and "Beautiful Painted Arrow." See Churchill's *Indians Are Us?* for a powerful critique of these and other spiritual hucksters.

11. Consider, for example, a recent flyer advertising the 1994 Rochester workshops of Brook Medicine Eagle, who is pictured in feathers, bone, leather, and braids. The text describes her as an "American native Earthkeeper" whose book *Buffalo Woman Comes Singing* (New York: Ballantine, 1991) offers "ancient truths concerning how to live . . . in harmony with All Our Relations." She is currently offering a $150 workshop on "shamanic empowerment" to "awaken the higher level of functioning possible for two-leggeds."

12. For more extensive discussion, see Leslie Silko, "An Old-Time Indian Attack Conducted in Two Parts: Part One: Imitation 'Indian' Poems; Part Two: Gary Snyder's *Turtle Island,*" in *The Remembered Earth: An Anthology of Contemporary Native American Literature,* ed. Geary Hobson (Albuquerque: University of New Mexico Press, 1979); Wendy Rose, "Just What's All This Fuss about White Shamanism Anyway?" in *Coyote Was Here,* ed. Bo Scholer (Aarhus, Denmark: University of Aarhus Press, 1984); and Churchill's *Fantasies of the Master Race.*

13. Johnston, "Spiritual Seekers Borrow Indian Ways," 1.

14. These include Leslie Silko, Vine Deloria, Wendy Rose, Oren Lyons, Geary Hobson, Joy Harjo, Gerald Vizenor, Ward Churchill, Russell Means, AIM, the Circle of Elders of the Indigenous Nations of North America, and many others.

15. Churchill, *Fantasies of the Master Race,* 215.

16. Christopher Lind, "The Idea of Capitalism or the Capitalism of Ideas? A Moral Critique of the Copyright Act," *Intellectual Property Journal* 7 (December 1991). Lind

misunderstands the nature of this protest and of the "claim being made by aboriginal artists and writers of colour . . . that whites are 'stealing' their stories"(p. 69). He insists that "(w)hat is being stolen is not the story itself but the market for the story . . . or the possibility of being able to exploit the commercial potential" (ibid.) of the story. Indigenous critiques are directed against the very fact of commercialization, against the extension of the market mechanism to these cultural materials by the dominant society. The claim being made is that this continues and extends a long history of oppression, that it constitutes theft of culture, of voice, of power.

17. Hobson, *The Remembered Earth,* 101.

18. Laura Keeshig-Tobias, "Stop Stealing Native Stories," *Toronto Globe and Mail,* 26 January 1990, section A.

19. Wendy Rose, "The Great Pretenders," in *The State of Native America,* ed. M. Annette Jaimes (Boston, MA: South End Press, 1992), 415–16.

20. Hobson, *The Remembered Earth,* 101.

21. Cultural imperialism is often at its apex in the academy. As a result of the stubborn influence of positivism, knowledge claims within the dominant (academic) culture continue to be regarded as value-free. An instructive example of this is Wilcomb Washburn's "Distinguishing History from Moral Philosophy and Public Advocacy" (in *The American Indian and the Problem of History,* ed. Calvin Martin [New York: Oxford University Press, 1987]). A past president of the American Society for Ethnohistory, Washburn is particularly upset about "the process of using history to promote nonhistorical causes." He reacts with consternation to the recent call for historians to "form alliances with non-scholarly groups organized for action to solve specified societal problems," which he associates with "leftist academics" and "Indian activists" (p. 95).

Washburn offers himself as an example of a historian committed to what one is tempted to call a Great White Truth, a Truth properly cleansed of all values:

[M]y efforts are guided by, and subject to, the limitations of historical truth. . . . There is no place in the scholarly profession of history for such distorting lenses. History to me means a commitment to truth . . . however contradictory it may be to our . . . acquired convictions about how the world should be. (p. 97)

He assumes that his work, like his conception of truth, is unburdened by such distorting lenses and remains both value-free and politically neutral. Yet note that this work includes his "recent experiences in writing Indian history, which involve combat with radical theorists on the ideological front"; his letters to the *Dartmouth Review* in support of the use of the Indian as a symbol; his efforts abroad to "justify United States policy . . . to spike assertions of genocide . . . to disprove the assertion that . . . multinational corporations control the United States Government and seek to exploit the resources of all native peoples against their will" (p. 94). All this, we are to suppose, is "value-free." And he goes on to claim that some will recognize his "lifelong and quixotic pursuit of the reality of the Indian as 'noble'" (p. 97).

22. Gerald Vizenor, "Socioacupuncture: Mythic Reversals and the Striptease in Four Scenes," in Martin, *The American Indian and the Problem of History,* 183.

23. Ibid.

24. Gary Snyder, as cited in Churchill, *Fantasies of the Master Race,* 192.

25. Simon Ortiz in an interview in *Winged Words: American Indian Writers Speak,* Laura Coltelli (Lincoln, NE: University of Nebraska Press, 1990), 111–12.

26. Keeshig-Tobias, "Stop Stealing Native Stories," 7.

27. Pam Colorado, as cited in Churchill, *Fantasies of the Master Race*, 101.

28. Keeshig-Tobias, "Stop Stealing Native Stories," 7.

29. Johnston, "Spiritual Seekers Borrow Indian Ways," 15.

30. See, for example, Ed McGaa's comments in Johnston, "Spiritual Seekers Borrow Indian Ways," 15. Wendy Rose also addresses herself to rebutting this point, noting that white shamanism has touched upon something very real and that its critics are not set on hoarding or on purposively withholding spiritual knowledge:

> An entire population is crying out for help, for alternatives to the spiritual barrenness they experience. . . . They know . . . that . . . part of the answers to the questions producing their agony may be found within the codes of knowledge belonging to the native peoples of this land. Despite what they have done . . . it would be far less than Indian of us were we not to endeavor to help them. Such are our Ways, and have always been our Ways. (Rose, p. 418)

31. Cited in Churchill, *Fantasies of the Master Race,* 223–24.

32. I refer to this facet of cultural imperialism elsewhere as a "no-fault" assumption—the belief that the literary, artistic, scholarly, and commercial products of AIS are neither epistemologically nor ethically suspect or at fault, that they are legitimate and morally unproblematic vehicles of spiritual knowledge and power. (See Laurie Anne Whitt, "Indigenous Peoples and the Cultural Politics of Knowledge," in *Issues in American Indian Cultural Identity,* ed. Michael Green [New York: Peter Lang Press, 1995]). There I also address the commodification of indigenous spirituality and develop some of the epistemological issues raised by it at greater length. In particular, I focus on some central features of the dominant knowledge system that facilitate the "no-fault" assumption, features that permit and facilitate the marketing of Native America more generally.)

33. Hobson, *The Remembered Earth,* 101.

34. Churchill, *Fantasies of the Master Race,* 210.

35. Ibid.

36. Renato Rosaldo, *Culture and Truth* (Boston: Beacon Press, 1993), 70.

37. Ibid.

38. Gary Snyder, as cited in Churchill, *Fantasies of the Master Race,* 192.

39. Alberto Manguel, "Equal Rights to Stories," *Toronto Globe and Mail,* 3 February 1990, Section D.

40. Leslie Silko, as cited in Michael Castro, *Interpreting the Indian* (Albuquerque: University of New Mexico Press, 1983), 161.

41. Churchill, *Indians Are Us?* 216.

42. David Lyons, "The Balance of Injustice and the War for Independence," *Monthly Review* 45 (1945): 20.

43. Gerry Simpson, "*Maybo,* International Law, *Terra Nullius* and the Stories of Settlement: An Unresolved Jurisprudence," *Melbourne University Law Review* 19 (1993): 199.

44. *Northern Pac. Ry. Co. v. Hirzel,* 161 P. 854, 859 (Idaho 1916).

45. The Dann sisters were honored for "their courage and perseverance in asserting the right of Indigenous peoples to their land" (Valerie Taliman, "Dann Sisters Win International Award for Commitment to Native Rights," *News from Indian Country* 7:20 (1993): 1.

46. Taliman, "Dann Sisters Win International Award," 5. More detailed consideration of this case can be found in Glenn Morris, "The Battle for Newe Segobia: The Western

Shoshone Land Rights Struggle," in *Critical Issues in Native North America,* vol. 2, ed. Ward Churchill (Copenhagen: International Working Group for Indigenous Affairs [IWGIA], 1990).

47. Speaking of the Antiquities Act of 1906, Walter Echo-Hawk notes that "the underlying assumption . . . is that all 'cultural resources' located on federal land 'belong' to the United States, and can be excavated only for the benefit of public museums. There are no provisions for Native ownership or disposition." (Walter Echo-Hawk, "Museum Rights vs. Indian Rights: Guidelines for Assessing Competing Legal Interests in Native Cultural Resources," *Review of Law and Social Change* 14 [1986]: 449. See this article for a discussion of the American Indian Religious Freedom Act and its implications for ownership of Native resources.) The Antiquities Act has never been formally repealed, although it has been superseded by the Archaeological Resources Protection Act of 1979.

48. The term *cultural property* is generally considered to include "objects of artistic, archaeological, ethnological, or historical interest" (John Merryman, "Two Ways of Thinking about Cultural Property," *The American Journal of International Law* 80:4 [1986]: 831). An "archaeological resource" refers to any material remains of past human life and activities that have been determined to be of "archaeological interest." See 16 *United States Code,* section 470bb(1).

49. 16 *United States Code,* section 470(dd). However, this act, unlike the earlier Antiquities Act, does require that Indian tribes be notified of any excavation permit that might cause harm to the cultural sites. See 16 *United States Code,* section 470cc(c).

50. Indeed, according to a recent article on a Colorado development known as "Indian Camp Ranch," prospective homeowners

> can now purchase land where more than 200 Anasazi sites have been identified. . . .
> Those who buy property . . . will also be allowed to excavate sites on their land. . . .
> Artifacts recovered will become the property of a museum to be built in the area.
> Homeowners will be allowed to display recovered artifacts in their residences, provided they are turned over to the museum upon their death. (*Archaeology,*
> [March/April 1995], 14)

According to the state archaeologist of Colorado, such land-use plans are legal.

51. C. Dean Higginbotham, "Native Americans versus Archaeologists: The Legal Issues," *American Indian Law Review* 10 (1982): 99–100.

52. Echo-Hawk, "Museum Rights vs. Indian Rights," 448.

53. Anthony Seeger, "Singing Other Peoples' Songs," *Cultural Survival Quarterly* 15:3 (Summer 1991): 39.

54. Moreover, since the 1976 Copyright Act extends copyright protection for the lifetime of the author plus fifty years, only "recent" compositions qualify for copyright protection. See 17 *United States Code,* section 302 (a).

55. *Amsterdam v. Triangle Publications, Inc.,* 189 F.2d. 104, 294 (3d Cir. 1951).

56. *Bleistein v. Donaldson Lithographing Co.,* 188 U.S. 239 (1903).

57. M. B. Nimmer, as cited in Maureen Baker, "La(w)—A Note to Follow So: Have We Forgotten the Federal Rules of Evidence in Music Plagiarism Cases?" *Southern California Law Review* 65 (1992): 1590.

58. *Hirsch v. Paramount Pictures,* 17 F. Supp. 816, 817 (S.D. Cal. 1937).

59. Seeger, "Singing Other Peoples' Songs," 38.

60. See *Bleistein v. Donaldson Lithographing Co.,* 188 U.S. 239 (1903).

61. 17 *United States Code,* section 107 (amended 1992).

62. U.S. Constitution, Article 27 (2).

63. Darrell Posey, "Effecting International Change," *Cultural Survival Quarterly* 15:3 (Summer 1991): 31.

64. Ibid.

65. Ibid.

66. Jack Kloppenburg, "Conservationists or Corsairs?" *Seedling* (June/July 1992): 14.

67. Roger Wallis and Krister Malm, *Big Sounds from Small People* (New York: Pendragon Press, 1984), 190–91.

68. Ibid., 199.

69. Ibid., 199, 188.

70. Jason Clay, "Editorial: Genes, Genius, and Genocide," *Cultural Survival Quarterly* 14:4 (1990): 1.

71. Ibid.

72. Norman Myers, *A Wealth of Wild Species* (Boulder, CO: Westview Press, 1983), 24.

73. Garrison Wilkes, "Current Status of Crop Germplasm," *Critical Reviews in Plant Sciences* 1:2 (1983): 156.

74. Jack Kloppenburg and Daniel Kleinman, "Seed Wars: Common Heritage, Private Property, and Political Strategy," *Socialist Review* 95 (September/October 1987): 8.

75. Kloppenburg, "No Hunting!" *Z Magazine* (September 1990): 106.

76. Clay, "Editorial: Genes, Genius, and Genocide," 1.

77. John Jacobs et al., "Characterization of the Anticoagulant Activities from a Brazilian Arrow Poison," *Journal of Thrombosis and Haemostasis* 63:1 (1991): 34.

78. Andrew Gray, "The Impact of Biodiversity Conservation on Indigenous Peoples," in *Biodiversity: Social and Ecological Perspectives,* ed. Vandana Shiva (Atlantic Highlands, NJ: Zed Books, 1991), 67.

79. Janet McGowan, "Who Is the Inventor?" *Cultural Survival Quarterly* 15:1 (Summer 1991): 20.

80. Elaine Elisabetsky, "Folklore, Tradition, or Know-How?" *Cultural Survival Quarterly* 15:1 (Summer 1991): 10.

81. A. B. Cunningham, "Indigenous Knowledge and Biodiversity," *Cultural Survival Quarterly* 15:1 (Summer 1991): 4.

82. Brian Boom, "Ethics in Ethnopharmacology," in *Ethnobiology: Implications and Applications,* ed. Darrell A. Posey et al. (Belém, Brazil: Proceedings of the First International Congress of Ethnobiology, 1990), 150–51.

83. Defined from the perspective of the dominant science, ethnopharmacology is the "scientific study of the medicinal uses of plants and animals by human groups other than the dominant Western society" (Boom, "Ethics in Ethnopharmacology," 148).

84. Boom, "Ethics in Ethnopharmacology," 149.

85. Ibid.

86. GRAIN (Genetic Resources Action International), "GATT, the Convention and IPRS," *Econet,* in the conference "Biodiversity" (28 June 1994).

87. Kloppenburg, *First the Seed: The Political Economy of Plant Biotechnology, 1492–2000* (Cambridge, England: Cambridge University Press, 1988), 11.

88. Kloppenburg and Kleinman, "Seed Wars," 24.

89. This was acknowledged by Illinois congressman John Porter who, in 1990, introduced a resolution to discontinue the ongoing GATT negotiations regarding the extension of intellectual property rights to genetic and biological resources. The difficulty with the U.S. proposal on trade-related aspects of intellectual property rights, Porter charged, is that

it fails to consider the value of biological and genetic material and processes in developing nations, as well as the invaluable and historic contributions of local people in the use of that material.

Since these people typically do not have access to representation to ensure that their interests are protected in the GATT process, we have an obligation to recognize their rights. (John Porter, "A Resolution Affecting the GATT Negotiations on Intellectual Property Rights for Genetic and Biological Resources," Congressional Record, 101st Cong., 2d sess., vol. 136, no. 94 [20 July 1990], E 2425)

90. Victoria Tauli-Corpus, "We Are Part of Biodiversity, Respect Our Rights," *Third World Resurgence* 36 (1993): 25.

91. Or, for that matter, little at all. U.S. patents protect "anything under the sun made by man." New life forms have been patented (*Diamond* v. *Chakrabarty,* 447 U.S. 303 [1980]). And the right to patent and commercially exploit human cells, even over the protests of that individual, has been recognized (*Moore* v. *Regents of the University of California,* 793 P.2d 479 [Cal.1990], cert. denied 111 S.Ct. 1388 [1991]).

92. Leslie Roberts, "A Genetic Survey of Vanishing Peoples," *Science* 252 (1991): 1614.

93. Ibid.

94. A valuable overview of these and related developments can be found in the following RAFI (Rural Advancement Foundation International) *Communiqués:* "Patents, Indigenous Peoples, and Human Genetic Diversity," May 1993; "The Patenting of Human Genetic Material," January/February 1994; and "'Gene Boutiques' Stake Claim to Human Genome," May/June 1994.

95. Roberts, "A Genetic Survey of Vanishing Peoples," 1614, 1617.

96. Ibid., 1615. Perhaps he refers to it thus for reasons of expediency, since, "for reasons of expediency, the human genome being mapped and sequenced (by HUGO) is essentially a Caucasian one" (Roberts, "A Genetic Survey of Vanishing Peoples," 1614).

97. Henry Greely, "Summary of Planning Workshop 3(B): Ethical and Human Rights Implications" (Bethesda, MD: Human Genome Diversity Project Organizing Committee, 1993), 22–23.

98. Paul Weiss, as cited in Greely, "Summary of Planning Workshop 3(B)," 6.

99. Beth Burrows, "Life, Liberty and the Pursuit of Patents," *The Boycott Quarterly* 2:1 (1994): 33.

100. Ibid. HGDP was unanimously denounced at the December 1993 meeting of the World Council of Indigenous Peoples:

The assumption that indigenous people will disappear and their cells will continue helping science for decades is very abhorrent to us. . . . We're not opposed to progress. For centuries indigenous people have contributed to science and medicine, contributions that are not recognized. What upsets us is the behavior of colonization. (Rodrigo Contreras, as cited in Patricia Kahn, "Genetic Diversity Project Tries Again," Science 266 [November 1994]: 721).

101. John Liddle, as cited in Burrows, "Life, Liberty and the Pursuit of Patents," 33–34.

102. Tauli-Corpus, "We Are Part of Biodiversity," 26.

103. Ibid., 25–26.

104. Ibid., 26. For a copy of the "Declaration of Indigenous Peoples of the Western Hemisphere Regarding the Human Genome Diversity Project," signed on 19 February 1995 by numerous indigenous organizations, see *Indigenous Woman* 2:2: 32–33.

105. Christopher Anderson, ". . . While CDC Drops Indian Tissue Claim," *Science* 262 (1993): 831.

106. There are other reported cases as well. According to Miges Baumann, of Swissaid, two more patent applications by the U.S. government of indigenous cell lines (from Papua New Guinea and the Solomon Islands) exist. See Burrows, "Life, Liberty and the Pursuit of Patents," 33.

107. Anderson, ". . . While CDC Drops Indian Tissue Claim," 831.

108. Kloppenburg and Kleinman, "Seed Wars," 25.

109. Vandana Shiva, as cited in Beth Burrows, "How Do You Spell Patent? P-I-R-A-C-Y," *The Boycott Quarterly* 1:3 (1994): 6, 5.

110. Intellectual property policies are justified in the Constitution on utilitarian grounds as a means "to promote the progress of science and useful arts" (U.S. Constitution, art. 1, sec. 8, cl. 8). Yet the lack of evidential support for the claim that patents and copyrights have indeed effectively promoted these ends has been noted (see Gerald Dworkin, "Commentary: Legal and Ethical Issues," *Science, Technology, & Human Values* 12:1 [1987]). In its place, one is generally offered appeals to "faith" that they are doing so; for example, "Faith in the private sector's ability to produce beneficial innovations is strong at the moment" (Pamela Samuelson, "Innovation and Competition: Conflicts over Intellectual Property Rights in New Technologies," *Science, Technology & Human Values* 12:1 [1987]).

111. For a characterization of oppressive conceptual frameworks and discussion of the logic of domination, see Karen Warren, "A Philosophical Perspective on the Ethics and Resolution of Cultural Properties Issues," in *The Ethics of Collecting Cultural Property,* ed. Phyllis Messenger (Albuquerque: University of New Mexico Press, 1989).

112. See Kloppenburg, *First the Seed,* and Kloppenburg and Kleinman, "Seed Wars."

113. Lind, "The Idea of Capitalism or the Capitalism of Ideas?" 70.

114. Ibid.

115. Kloppenburg, "No Hunting!" 106.

116. Tauli-Corpus, "We Are Part of Biodiversity," 26.

117. Morton Horwitz, *The Transformation of American Law, 1780–1860* (Cambridge, MA: Harvard University Press, 1977).

118. See Joseph William Singer, "Legal Realism," *California Law Review* 76 (1988).

9

Native Media's Communities

Steven Leuthold

As VIDEO TECHNOLOGY becomes more accessible to individuals and communities, people are exploiting its communication potential. Native Americans, for instance, are pursuing the cultural, informational, political, economic, and entertainment potentials of video and film through a new subgenre of documentary: indigenous documentary. An indigenous documentary is one made by members of an indigenous community or in close interaction with the community; it is a video produced or coproduced by members of the group that it is about.[1] Communities can document, preserve, or even revitalize local practices through media. Showing the programs outside of the local area communicates cultural beliefs seen as important by community members; practices shown in the videos identify the group for the wider public. But indigenous films and videos also communicate within a group and increase group affiliation. They both preserve knowledge for future generations and communicate the group's identity to the wider public.

Native Americans explain that their own awareness of the power of visual imagery lies deep in the past. Pueblo petroglyphs of spiritual significance that date from eighteen thousand years ago reveal this deep belief in the power, even sacredness, of visual imagery.[2] Since the early twentieth century, many Indian people, including those in the most traditional and conservative households, have used photographs to evoke memories and narratives of the past.[3] Visual imagery has played and continues to play a central role in many Native American communities.

The stereotypical idea that Indians object to photographs for their own sake is misleading. Writing of early attempts by whites to photograph Indian religious ceremonies, the noted Native author Leslie Marmon Silko states that the actual source of Indians' distrust was—and remains—the photographer, not the tool.

> At first, white men and their cameras were not barred from the sacred
> *Katsina* dances and *Kiva* rites. But soon the Hopis and other Pueblo people
> learned from experience that most white photographers attending sacred

Steven Leuthold is an assistant professor in the School of Art and Design at Syracuse University, New York. This chapter relates to issues discussed in *Indigenous Aesthetics: Native Art, Media and Identity* (University of Texas Press, 1998).

dances were cheap voyeurs who had no reverence for the spiritual. Worse, the Pueblo leaders feared the photographs would be used to prosecute the *Cusiques* and other *Kiva* members, because the U.S. government had outlawed the practice of the Pueblo religion in favor of Christianity exclusively.[4]

This same distrust extends to the present for some tribes such as the Hopi. Though religious leaders will allow outsiders to observe traditional ceremonies, they disallow photographic recording of the events. A recent instance, the attempt by Robert Redford to film a production of *The Dark Wind*, a Tony Hillerman novel set on the Hopi and Navajo reservations, led to a rift in the tribe between the tribal council and religious leaders. Tribal council members, while committed to preserving traditional Hopi culture, approved the project in the belief that "stepping into the future is an economic necessity."[5] The religious leaders, who view all Hopi land and ceremonies as sacred, took a harder line toward outside intrusion into the inner Hopi world and the project.[6] Given previous Hollywood depictions of Native Americans,[7] it seems inevitable that many Indians will object to the way outsiders portray them and will desire more control over the visual depiction of their culture.

DOCUMENTARY AS COMMUNAL CONTROL AND HEALING

A central desire of indigenous peoples, then, is to maintain *community* control over the depiction of tribal life, a desire implicit in the indigenous production of documentaries. Not only do most commercial films misrepresent Native ways of life and reinforce dominant culture stereotypes, but many documentaries produced by outsiders provide few benefits to the communities in which they were filmed. Native American media spans about twenty years—from the mid-seventies to the mid-nineties—which is a short time period. But what does the emergence of these new indigenous communication forms tell us about the changing nature of contemporary Native communities? What is the relationship between Native media and their varied communities of reception? New media not only serve to document communal lives, but also instantiate communities. Communication technologies affect our relationship to each other, and therefore our sense of community as an idea changes. Because of the newness of Native media, I feel it is useful to discuss these communal changes and ways that the relationship between medium and community may lead to challenges for Native media producers. What are possible directions for positive change in Native media? Since some of these questions are oriented toward the future, many of the responses in this paper reflect my personal views and are obviously open to disagreement. But through these comments I hope to contribute positively to the conversation about Native media's future.

Whether film and video are important media for understanding Native communities is an open question and an issue that needs to be acknowledged early in this paper. An opposite thesis, that film and video—as mass media—

undermine local communities, has more often been assumed: "the content and hegemonic control of mass media irreversibly erode traditional languages and cultures, replacing them with alien social values and an attraction to western consumer goods."[8] In this sense, TV and film are more like a cultural invasion than a new medium of localized expression. Not only the technologies, but the form of Western visual narratives may undermine traditional storytelling and visual modes.

The increasing use of video technology by indigenous and ideologically divergent groups points to alternative scenarios for media production and use: "for example, a networked cooperative of autonomous community stations resisting hegemony and homogenization."[9] This scenario may run counter to dominant culture assumptions about the inevitable demise of Native cultures in the face of Euro-American progress, assumptions that have been ingrained by centuries of imagery portraying Indians as enemies, then vanquished foes, and subsequently relegating Indians in the popular imagination to movies, curio shops, museum exhibits, and the shelves of New Age bookstores. And it also counters assumptions found in mass media research about the centralizing nature of media technologies.

With its emphasis on *local* aspects of video production, this paper differs significantly from studies that have focused on video/television in the context of mass distribution. Eric Michaels, in his study of the emergence of indigenous media at an aboriginal village in Central Australia, made this distinction very clear. "The bias of mass broadcasting is concentration and unification; the bias of Aboriginal culture is diversity and autonomy. Electronic media are everywhere; Aboriginal culture is local and land-based."[10] Though mass-mediated television contributes to cultural homogenization, I explore a potential counter-tendency: that video technology may foster cultural and political autonomy. The potential for cultural standardization is apparent in media that transcend spatial and temporal boundaries, but the alternate possibility, that film and video can be used for purposes of cultural self-determination, has been less frequently explored. Can the localized aspects of indigenous video production and reception counter some of the negative effects of mass reproduction? One goal of this paper, then, is to discover how Native-produced film and video challenge mass media's centralizing, homogenizing tendencies by constructing a multi-dimensional understanding of community.

There have been many historical challenges to Native communities. These are reflected by but also a result of Native people's consistent misrepresentation in popular media. The representation of the vanishing Indian in novels, films, photographs, and art legitimized the assimilationist policies of colonialist governments: boarding schools, political reorganization along Euro-American models, white expansionism into remaining Indian territories, and forced religious conversion. The idea of Natives as "uncivilized" legitimizes the need for a non-Native education system; the idea of Indian communities and economies as unsustainable on their own terms leads to white paternalism—the dole, casinos, touristic exploitation, and so on. The effects of paternalism—cycles of rebelliousness and dependency that manifest themselves in drug and alcohol abuse, criminal behavior, violence, and broken families—result, in part, from the stereotyping of Natives in mainstream representation. In an attempt to break these cycles, Phil Lucas's *Honor of All* (1985) videos reenact the struggle of the Alkali Lake (dubbed "alcohol lake" by local whites), British Columbia, band with alcohol and its effect upon the community, from its introduction by white traders in the 1940s to the successful effort of the community to go 95 percent dry in the late 1970s. Between 1960 and 1972 adult alcoholism in this community had approached 100 percent. Lucas focuses on the efforts of one family, with the help of a local priest and the Alcoholics Anonymous philosophy, to release the grip of alcohol on the tribe. Lucas directs from the heart, notably through his casting of tribal members in the lead roles; they play their own former, alcoholic selves in a convincing, moving way. At the end of part one, Lucas shows a community gathering where lead characters in the video talk about the experience of acting out their former selves. The self-revealing group therapy style of this epilogue ties the docu-drama to the present, further underscoring the reality of the emotional trauma and healing depicted in this drama. Lucas's docu-drama of the Alkali Lake community's dramatic turnaround from near total alcoholism to a rejection of alcohol demonstrates an awareness of the serious challenges that have faced and continue to face Native communities, rooted both in their misrepresentation and mistreatment by outsiders and in the negative self-perception of some Natives themselves. The video invites a reevaluation of the relationship between media and Native communities by demonstrating how media can have positive, even cathartic, effects.

MODELS OF COMMUNITY

Though documentary can help increase communal control of representation and foster healing, this does not imply that only one model of community is put forth as "acceptable" in Native media. What are the different models of community represented in and through Native film and video? That Native media address heterogeneous audiences is without question. Within Native communities, there are generational, racial, political, and religious differences. The broad, pan-Indian community varies widely, and the existence of multiple non-Native communities, often in conflictual relationships with each other, adds layers of complexity to the relationship between Native media and its varied audiences. A primary challenge for Indian producers seems to be to define their goals relative to the needs of divergent communities: their home communities, Native tribes across North America, indigenous peoples worldwide, and the broader non-Native population of North America and the world. Diverse communities exist within the professional circles that Native media people encounter: organizations of Native producers, public and commercial television organizations, the Hollywood and New York entertainment industries, academic institutions, and varied sponsors.

In a pluralistic cultural and political context, as exists in contemporary North America, the needs and interests of these varied communities might well be in conflict. For instance, Natives may disagree inter- or intratribally over issues of taxation, gambling, natural resource use, economic development, and religion, to name just a few issues. Native media's representation of varied interests is complex and potentially conflictual. However, a pluralistic model that assumes potential conflict between members of competing communities seems to be inconsistent with the understanding of community that many natives have traditionally envisioned.

In their videos, Indian directors implicitly put forth a model of community different than that found in middle-class America. Native Americans base their model of community on assumptions of togetherness, interdependence, and mutual accountability. By contrast, American cultural traditions, with their emphasis on self-reliance, may leave individuals isolated. Even the most central American value, freedom, is largely understood as freedom from external constraints and obligations (being left alone) rather than the freedom to be involved in community governance and participation. Clear evidence of this contrast is found in the two cultures' attitudes toward ancestors and elders. Many of the indigenous documentaries that I watched demonstrated a great respect for Elders as holders of wisdom and sources of collective memory in Indian cultures. (This respect is so profound that *Elder* is often capitalized in print form, as it is throughout this volume.) However, as de Tocqueville wrote as early as the 1830s, many non-Native Americans' individualistic outlooks lead them to view themselves in isolation from others, an outlook that eventually leads to their estrangement from both their ancestors and their descendants. Robert Bellah paraphrases and quotes de Tocqueville's insightful analysis of the American character:

> "They form the habit of thinking of themselves in isolation and imagine that their whole destiny is in their hands"… such people come to "forget their ancestors," but also their descendants, as well as isolating themselves from their contemporaries. "Each man is forever thrown back on himself alone, and there is danger that he may be shut up in the solitude of his own heart."[11]

An individualist stance eventually results in severance from the past or, at the very least, a loss of the collective memory traditionally preserved by elders in collectivist societies. Individual and expressive autonomy extracts a cost: the loss of a larger context provided by an encompassing belief system.

A challenge for Native media producers, then, is communicating their visions of community to the broad communities with diverse world views that are reached through broadcasting, which is inherently an intercultural enterprise. How might pressures on Native producers to succeed, or just survive, affect the particular quality of Native visions? Viewing one's expression as a product that must survive in a marketplace may be tempting in a commercial, media-saturated environment. The view that media encompass commercial products in itself is a departure from earlier Native traditions which emphasized the personal or collective, not the commercial, function of images and narratives. During the last few years, we have seen the continued commodification of the image of "Indianness" in the broader culture, from slick calendars to blockbuster films to "Indian" earrings (often made in Taiwan). It can be argued that in the interest of survival Natives should have the option to think of their expressive traditions in a commercial sense; judging from the extensive Native arts and crafts market geared toward non-Native buyers, many already do. But this option also may entail a cost: the loss of communal ideals. How Native producers balance commercial pressures with their own goals and visions of their communities will continue to be a key ingredient of the future of Native media production. Yet intercultural and commercial factors are not the only elements that help define community in indigenous media. What are some of the other formative elements?

INTERGENERATIONAL CONTINUITY AS COMMUNAL CONSCIOUSNESS

One communal element that popular, mainstream media are assumed to undermine, and therefore an element that has greatly concerned Native producers, is intergenerational continuity. The intergenerational aspect of Native song pervades both parts of the two-part *Circle of Song* documentary from the *Real People* series (produced by Spokane School District under a grant from the U.S. Department of Health, Education, and Welfare and aired by KSPS-TV, Spokane). In part two, grandma sings a song for a young child, rocking him in her arms to a gentle lullaby. Cliff Sijohn, the subject of the film, explains that the song is "our first orientation into Indian life, [our] Indian heartbeat. . . . Before he learns how to speak he shall already have heard the words of the Indian heart. Before he learns to walk, he will learn the feelings of the Indian heart. This is where his education begins." The intergenerational theme is also well developed in some non-Native productions such as *Seasons of the Navajo* (1984). As Elizabeth Weatherford, the bibliographer of Native film and video, writes, "Possibly no image conveys this sense of continuity better than a scene in which Chauncey Neboyia sings, holding close a baby who is thus literally encircled by the rhythm of his people's tradition."[12]

Intergenerational continuity is achieved through symbolic participation in powwows, naming ceremonies, feasts, and so on that form the glue which holds communities together. Quite possibly, symbolic participation that affirms relations to family and clan is more primary than tribal political involvement in creating Native collective identities. This is due in part to the social organization of precontact Native cultures. Precontact Indian societies generally lacked polities or distinct institutional structures in which secular authority was vested.[13] Politically, traditional Indian identity rested on the extended family, clan (kinship system), or autonomous bands as the key element.[14] More recently, clan rivalry has been accentuated within some tribes due to the reservation system which restricts the independent movement of competing tribal factions. Some tribes, such as the Cheyenne, did have a tribal-level government or council that pre-dated white contact, but most tribes depended on custom rather than a hierarchical structure of authority to govern communal life. *Tribal*-level political identity is, for the most part, a consequence of interaction with whites. However, prewhite Indian identity went beyond political organization and was situated in the symbolic dimensions of "groupness." These symbolic systems also varied between tribes, but religious beliefs, history, shared language, and ties to the land were common elements of Indian nationhood before the European notion of sovereignty was introduced. For example, to the Comanche, the notion of tribe had symbolic meaning but did not function as a political unit. Though some tribes had less developed self-concepts than others, symbolic identification was generally more comprehensive than political identification.

Native media people document these symbolic, participatory practices—including rituals, dances, music, rodeo, and other occasions or activities—that express commitment to the community. The sociologist Robert Bellah and his colleagues write:

> People growing up in communities of memory not only hear the stories that tell how the community came to be…they participate in the practices—ritual, aesthetic, ethical—that define the community as a way of life. We call these "'practices of commitment" for they define the patterns of loyalty and obligation that keep the community alive.[15]

Indigenous directors document these narrative and participatory activities. For instance, an early indigenous film by George Burdeau from the *Real People* series, *Awakening* (1976), profiles Johnny Arlee, Salish, who has supported the cultural revival on the Flathead Indian Reservation since the 1970s. *Awakening* tells of Arlee's quest for personal healing through his renewal of traditional practices such as ritual sweats and solitary contemplation in the mountains. The film also documents Arlee's heightened role as a community leader or, as he says, "a go-between between the young and old." Based on his own personal difficulties, he realized the pain caused to children from broken homes and formed numerous drum groups to help bring kids together. The groups strive to "make the drum sound like one," a task that demands the united concentration of the performers. Young singers and performers learn cooperation as a basis for successful performance. In *Warrior Chiefs in a New Age* (1991), a video made fifteen years later, Dean Bearclaw, Crow, also emphasizes the role of the drum group in passing on generational values. Extended sequences of the video feature an outdoor performance of the Cedar Child Drum Group intercut with shots of children running, playing, and singing and voice-over narration explaining the importance of children as an intergenerational link.

ENACTING COMMUNAL COMMITMENT

The desire for continued intergenerational continuity is tied to a broader concept, that of tradition. Tradition is a difficult concept to define and perhaps to value positively in a contemporary world, where change often seems more highly valued than tradition. In cultures that focus on newness, tradition is constantly in danger of being defined negatively as that which stifles innovation and cultural change. However, it is probably safe to say that religious beliefs are at the roots of tradition in many Native communities. A sense of tradition refers to a coherent belief system that transcends (but does not ignore) the vicissitudes of modern technological and cultural development. Elements of Native belief systems survive within hybrid traditions. One of these is the powwow, which often has the appearance of a performance to outsiders, but which is a hybrid performance and ritual practice that embodies and expresses traditional religious beliefs.

I'd Rather Be Powwowing (1983), produced by George P. Horse Capture and directed by Larry Littlebird, explores the place of powwows in the life of one contemporary Native American, Al Chandler, a member of the Gros Ventre tribe from the Fort Belknap Reservation in Montana. At the beginning of the film, Chandler leaves his rural suburban house in a suit and tie, gets in his late-model van, and drives into work where he is a copier machine technician or "senior technical representative" for the Xerox corporation, a job he has held for many years. This early sequence and shots of the inside of a copy machine Chandler is repairing contrast strongly with images of the powwow he soon attends. Unlike many productions, *I'd Rather Be Powwowing* places powwows in the context of modern life with its emphasis on employment, education, salary, and a rigid temporal system. Leaving the world of work for the world of the powwow evokes a different sense of time. The linear, clockwork time governing the world of work impels us to move faster and faster. As John Collier wrote, after living in this system we may look back and notice "we hardly had time to live at all," in contrast to the traditional Native sense of time that creates a "sense of inner spaciousness."[16] One appeal of powwows is that they establish a different rhythm, a rhythm governed by the drum and the land.

As Chandler loads his powwow outfits into the back of his van and his tipi poles on top, the Indian singing heard on the soundtrack signifies a transition to a different world. This transition continues as Chandler tells his son about his childhood experiences riding up and down the Eastern Montana hills that mark the way to the Rocky Boy Reserve where the powwow is to be held. Many powwows are far from the communities where participants live, but the travel through wide-open country is accompanied by a change of mindset.

> I put it in my mind that I'm going to forget everything: the noisy city, going to work, all of this long driving I do. I think of the good things that are going to happen. I pray that we have a good time and I think of getting dressed, meeting our friends and dancing. When you're at an

Indian dance, you can hear the drum beating and the bells ringing, the movement of people all in harmony. It's a spiritual feeling which you can't really know about it unless you do it. When we get there, we can chant and cook and people are friendly (*I'd Rather Be Powwowing*).

For Chandler the powwow represents "one of the few things we have left that we can do" that produces the sense of "togetherness" with family and friends Indians felt before incorporating the Western economic system into their lives. The powwow ceremony calls to mind the past. Even small details are noticed when they depart from past habits. Chandler comments that we "can't make everything the same as in the past" as he sews parts of his powwow outfit together with thread instead of sinew.

We learn through Chandler's visits with Elders and other families, his buying of Indian goods in tipis, and his preparation for and participation in the ceremonies themselves that powwows integrate Indian culture. For some participants the powwow is a religious event in which they experience a sense of connection: "As you're dancing you feel yourself stand taller and show everything you've got because the creator has given you what you have. And, as you look around, you can see other dancers and they're all feeling that same feeling." Chandler repeatedly describes his feelings as worshipful: "The creator's telling you that this is the right way." After the powwow, participants "say thanks inside for all the good things the creator has given you . . . this is why I'd rather be powwowing." Powwows are a ritual of transformation from the mundane to the spiritual. During the twentieth century, the desire to document and preserve aspects of traditional culture, such as powwows, has motivated many Native American visual artists; this motivation has carried over to Native media producers. Native American directors may find artistic inspiration in personal visions, myths, Native religions, and the performance traditions associated with them. Native Americans often see the clearest expression of collective identity in the traditional participatory arts, dance and music, that serve a religious or quasi-religious function.[17] Many Native Americans, whether Johnny Arlee or Cliff Sijohn in the *Real People* series or Al Chandler in *I'd Rather Be Powwowing*, use the language of religion to explain the importance of Native dance and music. The cultural role of powwows is realized in the connection between performance symbolism and religious feeling.

A docu-drama, *Apache Mountain Spirit* (1985), commissioned by the White Mountain Apache Tribe, confirms the centrality of ceremonial dance to Indian identity. The plot of the drama centers around a young boy, Robert, who has returned to the home of his grandmother after running away from his boarding school. In a state of inner conflict, Robert falls under the influence of Leon, a local hood, as well as the positive influence of his family. A morality tale about hard choices, the video departs from similar productions through its incorporation of dream and vision imagery. Presented as a form of power, dreams and visions occur for a reason: "When the power comes, it is real," but the power has potential for danger; "it's like a rifle, it depends on who is usin' it," says the boy's uncle. In this context of real-life temptations and inner visions, the boy is tested.

An extended sequence in the body of the video documents Robert's vision, set in the historic past. Almost surreal representations of the sacred Crown Dance are intercut with a symbolic hunt for a deer. The location of the deer appeared to the boy in a vision, even though older, more experienced hunters had lacked hunting success for some time. The boy predicts that One Feather will kill the deer but warns the hunters to wait for him before they butcher the animal, which they fail to do. At this point, the narrative cuts to the present where Robert gets caught up in an attempted burglary, backs out at the last minute, and is shot by Leon.

The climax of the video cuts back to a dreamlike vision of an Apache Crown Dance vigil outside the cave where the boy had joined the Apache gods, the *Ga'an*. In this sequence, dissolves—special effects that create sparkling halos around the dancing figures—and firelight illumination, along with the significant power of the hooded dance itself, effectively create an air of compelling mystery, agitation, and spirituality. Set in this context, the dance functions as a powerful form of prayer.

These dance forms and their documentation are an extension of religious ceremony, which acts as an antidote to alcoholism, poverty, and the other problems of contemporary life. One could argue that the transformation which takes place in Indian art or ceremony is a response to negative social pressures: that entering the dancer or painter's state of mind releases a person from social pain and responsibility.

> They (Indians) put on their dance costumes. . . . They look like princes! They're transformed. They can shut off all that poverty, all of their disasters, because that is their moment.[18]

This interpretation of Indians' motives emphasizes the social function of dance as an escape mechanism. However, Indian art, ritual, and performance can be thought of positively as a form of religious transformation. The power of art to transform everyday reality into a more essential psychic or spiritual reality lies at the heart of Indians' own explanations of art's significance. In this context, artistic objects become visionary objects through which artists and performers project psychic intent and spiritual feeling. This interpretation more closely reflects the traditional function of art in Native cultures as a repository of medicine or spiritual presence.[19] The transformational power of some traditional art forms may be quite specific. For instance, the discussion of masks documented in *Eyes of the Spirit* (1983) touched on the power of masks to transform humans into animals and the consistency of belief in the transformative power of masks with a world view that holds that all living things have souls (*inua*). In this world view humans' relationship to nature and animals rests on an acceptance of the possibility of transformation. Traditional Native belief systems express not only intergenerational continuity as a basis of human communities, but a sense of community with the universe itself.

NATIVE MEDIA AND POLITICAL CONSCIOUSNESS

How can these traditionally collective orientations of Indian belief systems blend with the forms of political organization encouraged—or imposed—by non-Native society? Can they be blended at all, or are entirely new conceptual and political identities likely to emerge among Fourth World nations? Traditionally, Native collective identities are based upon symbolic rather than political participation. But historical developments have made political issues of power, control, and authority increasingly central to contemporary Native communities. Several aspects of intercultural contact led to increased political consolidation. Missionaries introduced institutional structures such as churches and schools into Indian communities. These in turn encouraged the development of formal codes of law which included the definition and protection of private property. Intercultural contact also led to the need for negotiation and diplomacy, especially with regard to rights for land. The United States and Canadian governments demanded a structure of authority on the part of aboriginals that would ensure the results of land negotiations. Tribal political roles developed with respect to governmental expectations but also proved legally advantageous to Natives because these roles helped preserve some aboriginal claims to territories. Yet the development of tribes as political, administrative entities may have been at the cost of Native communities' conceptual identities. Since the 1930s, the feeling of "peoplehood" that predated Indian-white interaction has been eclipsed by the notion of the tribe as a political and legal construct. Thus, those same political structures that developed to help preserve land rights may have helped to undermine traditional concepts of the relationship between humans and the land, which did not revolve around the concept of rights. Similarly, other political and economic concepts integral to European cultures such as nation, border, sovereignty, property, territory, natural resource, and so on frame the discourse about land today.

Several films by activist Native directors document Native political issues. *Kahnesatake: 270 Years of Resistance* (1993), directed by Alanis Obomsawin and produced by Wolf Koening for the National Film Board of Canada, is an in-depth account of the takeover of a planned golf course site by members of the Mohawk tribe. The resistance to the actions of the town council of Oka, Quebec, and the Canadian government, along with the armed stand-off and painful negotiations that accompanied this resistance, made international news in the summer of 1990. This film by the Native Canadian director, Obomsawin, situates the contemporary resistance in the context of the Mohawks' centuries-long struggle to retain control of their land. *Kahnesatake* demonstrates the intense anti-Indian feeling found in the community of Oka, the hard-nosed police and military actions undertaken by the government, and the humanity of the resisters themselves. The documentary ends by noting that the land issues which precipitated the entire conflict were not resolved. A major theme of the film, then, is the difficulty of establishing communal control when political discourse is often framed by national governments and by non-Native international media.

One powerful dimension of media is its ability to frame discourse. In order to clearly understand Native media as representation, we must consider the changing definition of Native community in its political sense. For varied reasons, modern Native communities are less clearly definable in terms of *local* tribal, geographical, and spiritual affiliations than in the past. These reasons include the forced displacement of Natives from traditional homelands, the urban migration of indigenous peoples for economic purposes, the participation of Native peoples in foreign wars, the globalizing and nationalizing effects of electronic and print media, the forced and elected education of Natives outside the Native community, and the influx of non-Natives and their activities (spiritual, recreational, political, and so on) into areas that were once inhabited only by indigenous peoples. Thus, media that are representative in the political sense of the term may express the ideas of a global Fourth World political movement as well as more locally defined communities. The Fourth World is a global alignment of indigenous nations within those nation-states that resulted from the colonial period.[20] This emergence of a new movement is both similar to and distinct from the emergence of the idea of a Third World alignment of developing nations in the 1950s which has been problematized in such theoretical discourses as cinema studies under the rubric of "Third Cinema." Over the past forty years, Third World nations have sought increased political, economic, and cultural independence from their colonizers. An obvious distinction between Fourth World and Third World movements is that Fourth World movements are assertions of rights within the borders of existing nation-states. The assumption that we have entered an era of postcolonialism seems less supportable when we examine the ongoing processes of internal colonization that affect indigenous peoples. The question of indigenous self-representation can only arise in the context of neocolonialism; in a noncolonial system, media expressions of Native cultures are simply the expression of a local culture rather than indigenous political representations. Thus, the ways that Native media frame or represent indigenous communities need to be understood in an evolving *political* context.

Indigenous media is at root a struggle over this framing language. Some Native directors seem to address political issues by recontextualizing them within the framework of traditional beliefs about the land. Others counter Euro-American claims using the legal, economic, and political terminology of the West. Of the latter *Lighting the Seventh Fire* (1994), directed by Sandy Johnson Osawa, documents a struggle for land and resource rights. The documentary focuses on the advocacy of Chippewa Indians and opposition by many non-Indians to spearfishing rights on Lac du Flambeau in Wisconsin. This video relates the historical basis of the Chippewa claim to fishing rights and the struggle within the courts to have those rights recognized. The video appears radical because it challenges non-Natives on their own turf, conceptually speaking, in the judicial courts and courts of public opinion about rights. Ironically, the continuing differences over treaty rights, along with the consistent betrayal of treaties in the past, may be the source of the "greatest feeling of unity" among members of various tribes.[21]

By contrast, other documentaries show the continuity of earlier beliefs about the land; videos such as *The Passages of Gifts* (1987), part one from the *Make Prayers to the Raven* series, demonstrate how even Native commercial trappers treat their game in a special ritual fashion designed to show respect to nature. *Circle of Song* (1976) documents the intergenerational importance of hunting for Spokane Indians. Hunting and the preparation for the hunt, which includes the singing of special songs, are ways that cultural values about the land are transferred from father to son. "Songs are given to us from Mother Earth, from the wind and the mountains, from the visions in the clouds, from the animals that walk the earth and the ones that fly in the air, from the old people, and from our hearts."[22]

It is hard to say which of these two kinds of documentaries—those that either explicitly or implicitly challenge non-Native views of the land—is most effective in the long run. But it is true that ties to place, a sense of rootedness and connection, are what seem to be missing from the non-Native discourse about nature. Unfortunately, the idea that Native world views represent a more ecologically sound relationship to the land has become another source of stereotyping. The late twentieth century Green Indian has now taken his rightful place next to the earlier Red Indian. One solution for indigenous peoples, confronted with the stereotypes and misperceptions that arise cross-culturally, is to avoid the natural or "green" connotation of Native beliefs. But the perception of Native views of nature as being mystical holds a degree of accuracy. In many traditional Native cultures, nature is a catalyst for visionary religious experience, a relationship to nature that goes beyond simple concerns for natural preservation. While some non-Natives may be sympathetic to the environmental implications of Native views of the land, many stop short of the visionary, religious understanding of nature found in Native cultures. For many modern Westerners, though nature may be valued, the explanation and experience of nature as a source of place does not really exemplify a *world view*. In traditional Native cultures. this experience of place (and of space) is *the* world view. Indigenous peoples' perceptions of differences between Euro-Americans' and their own understandings of nature emerge as a consistent theme from ethnographic, artistic, and media sources alike. The Native's relation to nature cannot be defined simply in terms of property, though this is what land debates between Natives and non-Natives are often reduced to. Treaties involving land led to legal status for Natives, but the indigenous conception of place predates the era of treaties, and, as such, forms a unique and enduring basis of Native communities' cohesiveness.

ECONOMIC CHALLENGES TO COMMUNITIES

Perhaps the strongest challenge to the indigenous communal experience of place is economic. I have already noted that the idea of property undermines a more encompassing experience of place, but so does the very act of survival in an economy based upon the production and consumption of goods. Due to the interdependent nature of the contemporary global economy, goods are created for export and import rather than for local use. Because contemporary economic interests transcend borders and outweigh the interests of any specific community, it often seems that economic development (or opportunity) is inversely related to specific ties to place. Survival and belonging are oppositional terms in today's global economy, but are traditionally linked in indigenous cultures.

This dependence of capitalism on the fluid movement of goods and readily exploitable human and natural resources has taken its toll on Native communities which were deliberately *contained* at the turn of the century. Even in the earliest days of reservation life, Native communities suffered economic dependency and its attendant resentment, effects that continue in some communities to this day. This is evident in the video *Spirit of Crazy Horse* (1990), made with Native participation, which considers the difference between the "hang around the fort Indians" and those who hope to affect a fundamental change of life through the renewal of traditional cultural practices. The hope is held out that a renewal of aesthetic and ceremonial activities will bridge the gap between those benefiting from the governmental system and those outside the system, represented in the video by full bloods and chemically dependent Indians. Communal participation in dances and feasts and the solidarity it affords have economic as well as cultural consequences. But when financial issues are at stake, even symbolic participation may not create a sense of community unity. The third episode of *The Place of Falling Waters* (1990), which documents internal tribal council disagreement over the use of revenues from a dam built on the Flathead reservation, reveals that consensus through negotiation and persuasion can be just as difficult to achieve within a tribe or council as in the larger society.

The increasing urban migration of Indians is another important economic factor affecting Natives' sense of belonging to a community. Urban migration began in the immediate postwar period as returning Indian soldiers were encouraged to move to cities by the Bureau of Indian Affair's Employment Assistance Program. The current population of urban Natives may be more than 50 percent of the total U.S. Indian population. Though many urban Indians experience the poverty and despair so common to reservation life, a Native American urban working class has gradually emerged. Urban Indians have formed numerous voluntary associations such as singing and dancing groups, sports associations, and Native American churches to promote affiliation and to serve as "identity badges" to the larger community.[23] Economic well-being results from a clear symbolic identity; the identity badges help proclaim a right to economic resources. In addition to the economic function of these cultural expressions, the groups provide a sense of belonging that is often absent in the bland sameness of contemporary urban America. A sequence in the documentary *Winds of Change: A Matter of Choice* (1990), made with a Native advisory board, depicts a successful Indian family from the suburbs of Milwaukee viewing a powwow video at home in their living room. *Winds of Change* explains that through powwows, Indian identity transcends tribal differences. This is especially important in urban environments where members of many tribes live. Urban Indians experience cultural isolation and prejudice. In this context of isolation, powwows express Indianness because they clearly show identity to the larger culture. Native Americans interviewed said that an increase in exposure to the larger non-Indian world leads to a greater appreciation of belonging to Indian groups and communities.

With this discussion of the related issues of economics and urban migration, we have returned to an earlier theme: the role of Native media in intercultural contact and change and the impact of intercultural processes on Native communities. Indian groups progressed through different sequences of cultural contact and change. In general, though, there seems to have been a progression from cultural integration, especially involving material and technological aspects of Western culture, to assimilation.[24] Further integration was inhibited through the use of force by the dominant culture.

ASSIMILATION AND NATIVE MEDIA'S COMMUNITIES

An aspect of Native communities that was acknowledged but downplayed in the documentaries I viewed is the adoption of a cowboy identity by many Native Americans. *Spirit of the Wind* (1976) and *Powwow Fever* (1984) documented the importance of Indian rodeo in some areas of the country. Rodeos are similar to hunting in that preparation for the rodeo is linked to the development of strength of character. Like hunting, participation in the rodeo functions as a transition to manhood and an intergenerational link; rodeoing is often handed down from father to son. Some rodeo events express the oneness of humans and animals, especially the horse, while others are designed around the competition between humans and animals.

But none of the videos fully explored the impact of country and western music, pickup trucks, cowboy dress styles, or the identification of Indians with media images of cowboys. The widespread adoption of a western cowboy identity by Indians has been explained by some theorists as an attempt by Native Americans to fill the cultural void left by the loss of traditional cultural and tribal identities.[25] By contrast, Donald Fixico writes that the adoption of country and western styles has more to do with "practicality" than the loss of cultural identity.[26] In this argument, pickup trucks and cowboy hats better suit environments of the West than traditional native dress and technologies. Even if this position is credible, it still fails to account for the adoption of nonfunctional cultural expressions, such as country and western music, by many Natives. The fact that both Indian and white documentarians largely ignore the widespread adoption of country and western lifestyle and imagery by Natives indicates the desire of directors to emphasize the differences between Indians and the larger, mainstream society. The degree of cultural borrowing from non-Native cultures and its implication for identity formation has not been explored extensively by indigenous media people in the documentaries that I viewed. Perhaps the desire to maintain a separate identity from the larger culture and to retain continuity with the past may be so strong that Native directors have tended to overlook the shifting contours of contemporary Native American identity. A clear challenge to Native directors, then, is to document changes in Native communities that lead to assimilative effects as well as the maintenance of differences. Academic researchers can help in this process by more fully investigating how cultural change is a cross-cultural process that involves both integration and assimilation.

Tourism is another intercultural process that potentially has assimilative effects. Tourism is not necessarily viewed as a negative force in Native communities because of the assumption that it benefits the local economy. However, constructing touristic images for sale to non-Native audiences ultimately has assimilative effects.[27] How can one distinguish between those self-representations that lead to assimilation and those that are authentic representations of difference (or are assimilative, touristic images also "authentic" in their own way)? Do Native-produced films address the cultural and economic impact of tourism from a Native perspective? It seems at this point that there is a reluctance to criticize touristic imagery created by Natives themselves, perhaps because of the association with economic benefits, but more likely because of a reluctance to be highly critical in what remains the fairly small, familial world of Native media.

Pan-Tribal Community

Dependent on borrowed technology, Native media exists at the intersection between traditional outlooks on life and modern technical resources. Native media can potentially extend community beyond the traditional determining factors of physical location and local cultural practices. Yet, instead of displacing traditional communities, new media have allowed for the comparison of differences and commonalities between Native cultures. Most documentaries have focused on the concerns, practices, and beliefs of specific tribes. And indigenous media has, to this point, avoided the homogenizing tendencies of mainstream mass media.

However, as documentaries are viewed more widely by groups other than the ones they are about, as Native directors and producers continue to gather at national forums, and as young talent emerges through centralized training centers, thematic and stylistic commonalities probably will continue to emerge. These common factors may well shape pan-tribal Native American identity in the future, providing another basis for the Native experience of community. This aspect of Native media is similar to the development of independent Asian American media, which relies upon the commonality between members from many cultural backgrounds: Japanese, Chinese, Korean, Vietnamese, Filipino, Thai, Malay, and others.[28] One position with regard to pan-Indianism is that as general identification with Indianness has grown, *local* indigenous culture has declined, accompanied by increased secularization. Pan-Indianism may have led to a more general ethnic identification that eclipses a specific cultural identification, raising the question of whether a conflict between local, tribal, and general Native identification is being expressed in indigenous media. For instance, when discussing the revolutionary nationalistic movements that spread like fire throughout the Third World in the 1950s and 1960s, Franz Fanon questioned the emergence of pan-African and pan-Arabic cultural movements. In his view, only the nation could provide the framework for social change. Pan-ethnic movements detracted from this focus because they tended to ignore the very real social differences between people from different regions of the world in order to foster an international solidarity between members of similar ethnic and cultural backgrounds.

Though the original goal was one of unity, a similar awareness of differences has arisen in Asian American media, where Chinese and Japanese filmmakers have been more active in the movement than more recent immigrants from Vietnam, Laos, Thailand, and other countries. In addition to being an expression of unity, pan-ethnic movements can mask important social differences within a broadly defined group. Reflecting a tension similar to that which Fanon noted in the Third World, Native identity is mediated through local social factors and through international trends in documenting those outlooks. Despite this possible tension, Native media continue to present the concerns, hopes, and beliefs of Native American communities as they attempt to balance the past and present and elements of Indian and non-Indian cultures. It is at the forefront of the struggle for Native American cultural self-determination, which has been pan-tribal in nature at times, and is likely to remain there as long as that struggle continues.

LANGUAGE AND COMMUNITY

While the role of Native media in representing Native communities is becoming more firmly established, is there anything missing from this role as it has developed to this point? One assumption of Native Americans and non-Native scholars is that contemporary media technology has been more readily adopted by traditionally oral indigenous cultures than written forms of communication because it more easily supports oral narrative forms than other communication forms such as extensive written histories.[29] The maintenance of oral communication practices in the face of the loss of Native languages has been a central concern for Native Americans throughout the twentieth century. Recent video documentaries, like *Transitions* (1991), continue to explore the centrality of language and speech to cultural survival. Speech communication forms are central to a traditionally oral culture, including storytelling, oral history, song, and prayer. As with literature, a full accounting of these oral genres would require a book in its own right.

Other videos, including Native American Public Broadcasting's production, *In the White Man's Image* (1992), examine the price of losing language, which was one consequence of the boarding school experience. Collective memory is threatened when languages are lost. In *Transitions*, Fisher and Kipp, both Blackfeet Indians, demonstrate that their tribe feels that the "Mother Tongue [was] gifted us by the maker," and that, as the result of government and religious intrusion, "our Mother grows weaker by the day." Schoolmasters tried to change Indians to the white man's way by using stool pigeons and stern discipline. Older children who had been at the school longer were encouraged to tell on the younger children when they spoke in their own language. As Fisher states, the legacy of boarding schools that emerges from contemporary documentaries is one of "cultural shame," in which the loss of language is part of a "continuum of loss." However, documentaries address a broad, predominantly English language audience and are, themselves, not an ideal medium for the renewal of traditional languages. Thus, while they can serve to register past language loss, they seem inadequate to stop the further loss of Native languages. Perhaps producing more videos or sequences of videos that are in Native languages might help, but this creates the necessity for subtitling, a technique that may alienate younger audiences whom documentarians hope to reach. Subtitling also adds to the cost of documentary production. Thus, the ability of documentary to represent cultural continuity through indigenous languages remains a problem.

NATIVE MEDIA'S SURVIVAL AS A COMMUNITY

Native media people represent familial, local, tribal, and national communities, but they also constitute a community themselves. We just considered the general challenge of language loss. Another serious challenge for the indigenous media community itself is to develop economic viability. Throughout recent history, there has been a need for an economic system in Native communities that allows for indigenous values associated with work, production, and agriculture but that also makes fruitful connections with the non-Native market. In the current economic structure, the question is not whether there will be economic ties to the non-Native community, because inevitably in an interdependent world, such ties will exist. But what will be the quality of those ties? Currently, Native media is overdependent on a system of government funding; what is the long-term effect of depending upon government grants for Native media production?[30] With foundation funding, independents are not forced to raise money within a commercial system, but this arrangement also nullifies the possibility of making money in order to fund new ventures, which a commercial production system would allow.

It seems that one way for Native producers and directors to exert greater control over their visions is through the development of Native-controlled production and distribution systems. Ultimately, this control will depend upon Native American funding of media production. But as an intermediate step

fuller Native participation in organizational roles will result in a greater continuity of vision. The development of Native media production networks may
benefit the development of other successful businesses: local industries, agricultural businesses, educational institutions (indigenous education), Native
medical services, and so on. Currently, the issue of economic viability has not
been resolved within the Native media community itself, so it is hard for Native
media to have a positive effect on other areas of economic development.

Many of the challenges facing Native producers are structural. Further comparative research by scholars into structural aspects of varied independent
media movements and Third Cinema may help Native American producers and
directors analyze the organizational choices available to them. Perhaps the transitions that have been made in some Third World countries, such as in Ghana,
and in African American or Asian American film, can serve as markers for the
development of a Native-controlled production and distribution system. Here
are a few hypotheses about this general evolution that further comparative
research may or may not bear out. Most independent groups of media producers started with government support in a way similar to Native media. This initial funding, fostered in the climate of affirmative action or economic
development, allowed for the growth of a grassroots, critical cinema. The next
challenge has been to achieve continuity by developing a pool of Native talent
and funders willing to sustain the media beyond its critical, activist stage.
Younger filmmakers may not be drawn to the same causes that motivated the
movement's founders, so how can an independent media movement sustain
itself?

It seems that this intermediate stage is often a result of community television and media workshop or media arts centers. These kinds of community
organizations still depend heavily upon government funding, but they provide
a way to pool intellectual and skilled labor and economic resources—of building an infrastructure—that may lead eventually to the development of independent commercial endeavors. However, Native cinema has tended to diverge
from this model for a couple of reasons. First, much of the Native population is
still located in remote rural areas. This is especially true of the Plains and Southwest tribes which have been central players in media production. By contrast,
media arts workshops and community television networks are often centered in
urban areas. Second, these workshops are often tied to major educational institutions such as UCLA where there has seldom been a critical mass of Native film
people active in media education, development, and research at any given time.
Fortunately, Native producers have developed an alternative community framework, the tribal media center model. The Creek, Ute, Salish/Kootenai, Yup'ik,
Inuit, and other groups have sustained media production units at a tribal level.
Sometimes these organizations are tied to low-power, Public Television stations
which allow the tribe to offer a mix of Native and non-Native programming in
its area. In cases where full production or broadcast units have not been established, some tribes have still been able to participate in production by funding
media on a contractual basis. By extension, many tribes are developing web sites

to communicate important issues to a global audience.

While it is fortunate that the tribal media center model has evolved, it may also place limitations on Native media producers. As in any other organization, tribal resources are limited. Funding and precious production time often go first to the areas needed most by educational and governmental institutions: training and instruction, cultural awareness, historical documentation, local news and information, media resource management for instructional purposes, and so on. Projects considered for development may be brought before formal or informal committees to determine whether funding is appropriate based on institutional needs. It is important that tribes continue to support media for a variety of informational and social purposes, but in my view, it is doubtful that the tribal media center will, of itself, be able to catapult indigenous media to the status of a full-blown independent cinema. For instance, it is not often in the specific interests of the tribe to develop contacts with national and international distributors. To the extent that Native producers want to develop a global Fourth World cinema, it seems they must continue to develop resources and venues beyond the tribal level.

Another stage of indigenous media's development has been the attempt to break into public television. This has involved institutional networking, skills attainment, and programming targeted toward a mass audience. While this phase has been important in broadening the scope of Native media, it also has to be considered an intermediate stage for various reasons. First, public television is almost exclusively an outlet for documentary production, which complements some of the original activist and informational goals of Native producers, but does not, I believe, encompass the full scope of Native producers' visions. Second, public television is a relatively young, and by no means secure, institution whose origin only precedes the development of Native media by a decade. Its fate is increasingly uncertain in light of the government's attempt to tighten its spending. And third, public television is a media network in its own right that places restrictions on quality, length, style, and subject matter—which may be unacceptable to Native producers in the long run. As is the case with relying on any other governmental agency, a danger exists that indigenous media will develop into a network of "trust fund babies" if public television remains the primary goal of the movement. In the end, this can only lead to an elitist community of insider producers and directors, cut off from the very audience that indigenous media people may hope most to address.

What, then, has been the formula for successful non-Native independents? It must first be noticed that there are very few producers and directors who can be considered financially successful, so there may, in fact, be no formula. It seems that these filmmakers (here, of course, the director Spike Lee comes to mind) have been able to establish a relationship with the commercial industry, at least for the sake of distribution. These independents also produce a commercially viable product that authentically expresses their experience, a combination that is hard to achieve; their work, in a film such as *Do the Right Thing* (1989), is able to provoke, persuade, enlighten, and entertain. Thus, the development of a Native production system probably depends upon a breakthrough feature film or two. This is not solely for the purpose of establishing a commercially viable product, but to reach and appeal to the broad audience that needs to be exposed to Native points of view. These initial films will probably be produced on shoestring budgets, but if successful, should eventually lead to backing by major funders. In a sense, this discussion is moving in a direction that may prove unpalatable to many Native and other independent producers, since independent media has traditionally developed in opposition to mass-produced television and film. But in order to counterbalance what has been and continues to be the staple of Hollywood representation, indigenous media may need to strive for a broader audience. Ironically, this requires breaking into the very medium that Hollywood has made its specialty—the feature film—and gaining access to the distribution networks to ensure that the film is seen. Finally, when they do break in, successful independents seem to maintain an integrity of vision. This last issue is important, because co-optation is an ongoing process in global corporate culture.

As the economy moves ever more clearly toward being information based, Native communities are striving to ensure that they are not once again marginalized. Information economies transcend specific regions and can help Native peoples overcome the economic deprivation that has inflicted many communities since the development of the reservation system. Economic opportunity seems to have often been inversely related to one's ability to maintain specific ties to place. Do new forms of communication offer a way to overcome the distances associated with regional and economic isolation? New media may allow the development of shared visions without sacrificing specific ties to place, the sense of rootedness that comes not only from living in a particular location over time, but through sharing a common understanding of humans' relationship to nature and cosmological place in the universe with other community members.

Through media (video, film, computing, telecommunications), indigenous peoples can develop a sense of community in imaginative new ways while still maintaining continuity with traditional communication forms and the values that these forms embody. Indigenous media both document traditional forms of symbolic participation—powwows, naming ceremonies, feasts—and emerge as new participatory forms in their own right. Media can change Native political representation processes, as well as the visual representation of Natives, by involving larger segments of the community in political awareness and governance. Ultimately, issues related to the self-governance of Native communities—power, control, authority over one's own destiny—are seated in the authority to represent one's self that forms the essence of indigenous media.

Chronological Filmography

Native Directed

The *Real People* Series. 16 mm, dir. George Burdeau and Larry Littlebird:
  Circle of Song, 1976.
  Circle of Song: Part II, 1976.
  Awakening, 1976.
  Spirit of the Wind, 1976.
  Legend of the Stick Game, 1976.

I'd Rather Be Powwowing. 16 mm. Prod. George P. Horse Capture, dir. Larry Littlebird. WNET-TV, NY, for series "Matters of Life or Death," 1983.

Eyes of the Spirit. Prod. Corey Flintoff and Alexie Isaac, KYUK, Bethel, Alaska, 1983.

Powwow Fever. Indian News Media, Blood Reserve, 1984.

The Honor of All. Prod. and dir. Phil Lucas for the Alkali Lake Indian Band, B.C., Canada, 1985.

Itam Hakim Hopiit. Dir. Victor Masayesva, Jr., IS Productions, 1985.

Ritual Clowns. Prod. and dir. Victor Masayesva, Jr., IS Productions, 1988.

Siskyavi: The Place of Chasms. Victor Masayesva, IS Productions, 1989.

The Place of Falling Waters. Dir. Roy Bigcrane, Thompson Smith, Salish Kootenai College and Native Voices Public Television Workshop, 1990.

Warrior Chiefs in a New Age. Dir. Dean Bearclaw. Native Voices, 1991.

Transitions. Dir. Darrel Kipp, Joe Fisher. Native Voices Public, 1991.

In the White Man's Image. Prod. and dir. Christine Lesiak and Matt Jones, NAPBC and Nebraska Educational TV, 1992.

Kahnesatake: 270 Years of Resistance. Prod. Wolf Koening, dir. Alanis Obomsawin. National Film Board of Canada, 1993.

Lighting the Seventh Fire. Dir. Sandy Johnson Osawa, Upstream Productions, Seattle, 1994.

Native-themed, Advised and/or Coproduced

Hopi: Songs of the Fourth World. Prod. and dir. Pat Ferrero. Independent, 1983.

Seasons of a Navajo. Prod. John Borden, Tony Schmitz. Peace River Films for KAET-TV, Tempe, 1984.

Apache Mountain Spirit. Prod. John and Jennie Crouch, dir. Bob Graham, Kate Quillan-Graham. Silver Cloud Video Productions, 1985.

The Passages of Gifts, Part One. From Make Prayers to the Raven series. Prod. Richard K. Nelson. KUAC TV, University of Alaska, 1987.

The Spirit of Crazy Horse. Dir. James Locker. Frontline, WGBH, PBS Home Video, 1990.

Winds of Change: A Matter of Choice. Prod./writer Carol Cotter. WHA-TV, Madison, PBS Home Video, 1990.

Winds of Change: A Matter of Promises. Prod./writer Carol Cotter. WHA-TV, Madison, PBS Home Video, 1990.

Notes

1. Because of many factors, primarily the economics of media production, the line between indigenous and non-Native documentary is often not hard and fast. For a discussion of production issues in Native media see Steven Leuthold, "Social Accountability and the Production of Native American Film and Video," *Wide Angle*, 16:1–2 (August, 1994): 41–59.

2. Leslie Marmon Silko, "Videomakers and Basketmakers," *Aperture* (Summer 1990): 72–73.

3. Ibid., 72.

4. Ibid., 72.

5. John Woestendiek, "Film at Center of Hopi Riff," *The Philadelphia Inquirer* (Oct. 11, 1990): 14–A.

6. It should be noted that insight into the spiritual life of the Hopi people has been obtained through respectful documentation of their artistic, kinship, and agricultural practices and through the visual presentation of traditional narratives, as in Victor Masayesva Jr.'s videos and the documentary *Songs of the Fourth World*. It is not necessary to violate sacred space in order to gain deep insight into the culture.

7. Several earlier sources have discussed the misrepresentation of Native Americans in Hollywood films. See Gretchen Bataille and Charles Silet, eds. *The Pretend Indians: Images of Native Americans in the Movies* (Ames, IA: Iowa State, 1980); Ralph Friar, *The Only Good Indian...Hollywood Gospel* (New York: Drama Book Specialists/Pubs, 1972); and John O'Connor, *The Hollywood Indian: Stereotypes of Native Americans in Films* (Trenton: New Jersey State Museum, 1980). An examination of Native American responses to their representation in westerns is found in Steven Leuthold, "Native American Responses to the Western," *The American Indian Culture and Research Journal* 19:1 (Spring, 1995): 153–89.

8. Faye Ginsburg, "Indigenous Media: Faustian Contract or Global Village?" *Cultural Anthropology* 6:1 (1991): 97.

9. Eric Michaels, *For a Cultural Future: Francis Jupurrurla Makes TV at Yuendumu* (Melbourne: Artspace, 1987), 17.

10. Ibid., 13.

11. Robert Bellah, et al., *Habits of the Heart* (New York: Perennial/Harper and Row, 1985), 37.

12. Elizabeth Weatherford and Emelia Seubert, *Native Americans on Film and Video*, Volume II, (New York: Museum of the American Indian/Heye Foundation, 1988), 75.

13. Stephen Cornell, "The Transformations of Tribe: Organization and Self-Concept in Native American Ethnicities," *Ethnic and Racial Studies* 11:1 (1988): 28.

14. Jack Forbes, "The Manipulation of Race, Caste and Identity: Classifying Afroamericans, Native Americans and Red-Black People," *The Journal of Ethnic Studies* 17:4 (1990): 1–51.

15. Bellah, et al., *Habits of the Heart*, 154.

16. John Collier, *American Indian Ceremonial Dances* (New York: Bounty Books, 1972): 13–15.

17. For this contrast, see my article, "Native American Art and Artists in Visual Arts Documentaries from 1973–1991," in *On the Margins of Artworlds* (Boulder: Westview Press, 1995): 265–281.

18. Arthur Silberman in Jamake Highwater, *Song from the Earth: American Indian Painting* (Boston: New York Graphic Society, 1976), 197.

19. Ralph Coe, *Sacred Circles: Two Thousand Years of American Indian Art* (Kansas City: Nelson Gallery Foundation, 1977), 12.

20. Noel Dyck, *Indigenous Peoples and the Nation-State: 'Fourth World' Politics in Canada, Australia and Norway* (St. John's, Newfoundland: Memorial University of Newfoundland, Institute for Social and Economic Research, 1985).

21. Vine Deloria, *Custer Died for Your Sins: An Indian Manifesto* (Norman: University of Oklahoma Press, 1969), 50.

22. Cliff Sijohn, *Circle of Song*, (film)1976.

23. Robert Jarvenpa, "The Political Economy and Political Ethnicity of American Indian Adaptations and Identities," *Ethnic and Racial Studies* 8:1 (1985): 36.

24. By *cultural integration*, I mean Native people's adoption of non-Native material and cultural practices in a way that does not threaten the core structures of indigenous cultures. By *assimilation* I mean the absorption of Native peoples into non-Native cultural and economic patterns, which leads to the eventual transformation or disappearance of earlier patterns.

25. Clifford E. Trafzer, *American Indian Identity* (Sacramento: Sierra Oaks Publishing, 1985).

26. Donald L. Fixico, "From Indians to Cowboys: The Country and Western Trend," in *American Indian Identity*, ed., Clifford Trafzer (Sacramento: Sierra Oaks Publishing, 1985).

27. For a sociological analysis of the impact of tourism on one Native community, see Carol Chicago Lujan, "A Sociological View of Tourism in an American Indian Community: Maintaining Cultural Integrity at Taos Pueblo," *American Indian Culture and Research Journal* 17:3 (1993): 101–120. Lujan notes that in Taos Pueblo, which has been inundated by tourists for decades, there has been a concerted attempt to maintain the culture through concealment and secrecy.

28. One objection to the "commonality" assumed to exist among Asian Americans is that it masks the experiential differences of immigrants from many cultures. A similar charge has been leveled against pan-tribalism.

29. Tom Beaver, "Producers' Forum I: Uncovering the Lies," Symposium at Two Rivers Native Film and Video Festival (October 10, 1991, Minneapolis), and Eric Michaels, *For a Cultural Future: Francis Jupurrurla Makes TV at Yuendumu* (Melbourne: Artspace, 1987).

30. A discussion of varied funding sources is found in Leuthold, 1994 (see note 1).

10

Shadow Catchers or Shadow Snatchers? Ethical Issues for Photographers of Contemporary Native Americans

Lee Philip Brumbaugh

CONCERN OVER THE ETHICS of depicting Native Americans in photographs grew out of postmodern critiques of power relations and representation, as well as the rising political and cultural awareness of Native Americans themselves. Native American activism and the Red Power movement preceded Foucault and Derrida, and the latter postmodern authors reflect the concerns already raised by minority and indigenous authors.[1]

At the same time as concern over the rights of indigenous peoples has grown, public interest in Native Americans and the photographic record of their history has also burgeoned.[2] The period from the 1970s to the present has been marked by a spate of books on photographers of Native Americans. On the whole, these books trace an increasing awareness of the representational issues raised by both Native Americans and postmodern critics, although reviewers have accurately pointed out significant areas for improvement.[3]

Collections of photographs by Edward Curtis, the best-known photographer of nineteenth-century Native America, illustrate the evolution of sensitivity to indigenous concerns. Beginning with works whose titles retain the "vanishing race" notion fostered by Curtis (despite his own awareness that it was inaccurate), one moves through time to Brown's still ambiguously titled collection of 1972, *The North American Indians*, which could be taken to imply that Indians, like Curtis, are part of the past (despite the editor's interior contrary statement). Next, Graybill's and Boesen's 1981 title, *Visions of a Vanishing Race*, is perhaps better, for "visions," in contrast to earlier "portraits," could at least imply a false perception. Finally, in the 1990s, Lyman unambigiously titled his Curtis compilation, *The Vanishing Race and Other Illusions*.[4]

I should hasten to add that I do not mean to propose through this anecdotal illustration that the nation—or even the book-publishing industry—as a whole has become thoroughly cognizant of Native American issues, or routinely places ethical concerns above profit. The passage of the Native American Graves

Lee Philip Brumbaugh is curator of photographs at the Nevada Historical Society.

Protection and Repatriation Act, as well as the increasing number of movies (e.g., *Dances with Wolves*) and television shows (e.g., *500 Nations*), which attempt, however imperfectly, to convey indigenous perspectives, also support the idea of a growing awareness of Native American concerns.

The concept of a crisis of representation within anthropology has referred primarily to the literary portrayal of other cultures by ethnographers; however, it has quite literal significance within photography. Few activities by the ordinary outsider raise more concerns among Native Americans than photography. Violation of treaty rights, denial of self-government, and adoptive kidnapping of Native American children are all undoubtedly larger issues, but these are not activities in which very many of us, as outsiders, are directly involved—although we certainly all share responsibility. The appropriateness of photographing Native Americans is an issue faced today not just by museum personnel and anthropologists, but by the ever-growing number of non-Native attendees at powwows and other indigenous events.

In this brief article, I shall examine some of the practical issues involved in photographing contemporary Native Americans, as I personally experienced them in California. Also, for those not already familiar with the subject, I shall try to convey my sense of why Native Americans have a particular ambivalence toward this latest of art media. The present discussion is not intended as a holier-than-thou diatribe. I cannot say that it initially occurred to me that dance groups giving public performances, as both culture sharing and professional engagements, would have any aversion to what our culture calls publicity. My discussion here reflects what I subsequently learned to be the expected cross-cultural photographic etiquette.

Although I have attempted to address certain broader ethical concerns and their historical background, the article is not intended to offer advice to Native Americans, either collectively or individually, about how they should deal with the photography issue. I would not presume to be qualified to offer such advice. The original version of this paper was presented to an audience that included administrators and personnel from museums and public agencies. The present version is similarly intended as an introduction for nonspecialists, or for anyone considering photographing at Native American events for the first time. Many Native Americans and experienced field anthropologists may well find my comments to be little more than statements of the obvious.

From my own experience, I shall describe how a number of central California community leaders are attempting to balance public attendance with the internal spiritual needs of Native participants, often within the same event venue. Again, this approach, which clearly has its own problems, is not presented either as an example of what Native Americans should do, or what other non-Native Americans should expect in their region. The problems faced by Native Americans in dealing with photography and photographers are different in every region and for every indigenous Nation, as well as for each individual. Individual and tribal policies vary accordingly, and it is not appropriate, in my opinion, for outsiders, even well-meaning and interested ones, to attempt to influence Native views about this issue, or to "speak for" Native Americans to other outsiders.

In any photographic situation, rights issues, both for the photographer and for those photographed, can be divided between legal issues and ethical issues. A number of basic legal principles apply to all photography, anywhere in the United States. However, federally recognized indigenous Nations also have the right to make their own legal regulations, which the photographer must obtain from the local tribal offices. Within the general U.S. legal realm (off-reservation), the most relevant laws are probably those related to copyright and privacy.[5] At present, a photographer apparently holds copyright and is free to publish a photograph unless it was taken at a location where the subject has a "reasonable expectation of privacy." For example, from a legal perspective, a photographer can publish a photograph taken in a public location without the subject's permission, but publishing a photograph taken through the window of a home, without the occupants' knowledge or permission, would be illegal. The exception, of course, is public figures, who basically have no privacy rights. These legal privacy and publication rules apply to so-called educational photographs, such as illustrations for newspaper or magazine articles. In this context, *educational* refers to any medium that disseminates information, as opposed to selling products. Photographs used in commercial advertising, by contrast, legally require a subject's written permission and prior determination of financial remuneration to the subject. Photographic ethics deal with nonlegal concerns over possible harm done to others through photography.

In California, as elsewhere, Native Americans sometimes allow public attendance at religious or partly religious ceremonies, both on and off reservations and community rancherias. Media accounts as well as my own experiences suggest that indigenous people within the United States and elsewhere increasingly feel that photographs of sacred ceremonies should not be permitted. Without trying to speak for Native Americans, I believe it is obvious that photography of certain religious rituals is seen as potentially harmful. Since it is not currently possible to bar publication of photographs made in a public place (even on a reservation, if they were originally permitted under tribal law), U.S. indigenous Nations have sometimes banned photography entirely. In California, many dance groups take the more moderate approach of barring photography during the sacred dances and ceremonies but permitting it during the social dances. In such cases, the spokesperson for the dance group usually announces when and when not to take pictures. The same rules apply to everyone present, including Native Americans, so it is not a matter of discrimination.

However, permission to photograph, in the midst of most indigenous Californians (and probably most people in general), does not automatically constitute permission to publish or exhibit. Although in my experience most indigenous Californians will grant permission for any reasonable use of images, they at least would like to be asked, as well as to be offered copies of the photographs and publications. Even though it is not legally required for educational photographs to be taken in a public location, it would be best for any photographer to get written permission for use at the time the photographs are taken, as well as addresses for sending copies. Native Americans often feel that they are not being treated fairly or with respect if these rules are not followed. If photographers grant publication approval to the relatively powerless, they are actually extending a privilege that is not available to the power elite, who are often public figures and thus have no photographic privacy rights. However, the ethical position is, I believe, to follow the wishes of the individual subjects, because it is their perception of harm that matters, not the objective reality, if there is such a thing.

Although banning the use of existing archival photographs might be considered censorship or even a First Amendment violation, Native Americans clearly have the right, like any other group, to control photography of current religious events. Christian churches do not typically permit photography during services, except for special, preapproved purposes. Even if there were no denotation of a power differential, one can see how the whirring and snapping of cameras and the associated tourist atmosphere would not be conducive to religious experience. This, of course, was less of a problem earlier in the century, when only a few people had cameras. On the down side, I would note, banning photography means that the photographic history of Native American religious growth and transformation is no longer being preserved. The old photographs of indigenous ceremonies are just as valuable to tribal historians and Native educators as they are to anthropologists. For example, in California, the early photographs, along with the material collections of museums, have been used by some indigenous groups to help revive the old dance costumes and other material aspects of ceremony. Usually, this has involved a revitalization of existing ceremonies, but in some cases long-discontinued dance styles have been revived. I am, of course, not trying to influence Native Americans in favor of unlimited photography, but merely noting that the old-time permissiveness did have some positive consequences in its period. It is better, today, I think, to have active, healthy traditions that do not need to be revived.

In recent times, there has been an effort to portray anthropologists and museums strictly as cultural appropriators and exploiters of indigenous cultural traditions. In my own view, one of the functions of anthropology museums has always been to educate the public about the beauty and worth of other cultures and their arts. Anthropology museums once followed the nationalistic paradigm that other cultures were only preludes to the glory of Western civilization. But such extremes of museological ethnocentricity have not been the norm for many decades. Those who prefer a monolithic picture of the white oppressor, I believe, tend to ignore the positive contributions of anthropology and museums in promoting the value of non-European cultures.

However, the "bad rap" of museums among Native Americans is not entirely undeserved. Museum curators traditionally have seen little need to consult with members of the cultures they displayed and promoted, and were thus operating—if unconsciously—on the same hegemonic principle that they saw themselves as opposing. This was/is probably not always a matter of Eurocentric arrogance. A sensitive, reflective, and politically correct exhibit is also an exhibit that is more expensive than the traditional arrangement, in which the curator hauls some artifacts up from the basement and slaps a few hastily typed labels on the wall next to them. In many cases, curators would probably have loved to consult with indigenous people about the meaning and significance of the objects or photographs in their collections, but funding for such "new research" was not available. Increasingly, it may not be politically possible to have exhibitions of Native American materials without such consultation, and museums will have to come up with the money required. I believe the new knowledge obtained through such consultation and preserved with the collected photographs and objects will far outweigh any drawbacks of the potential thematic restrictions.

In my experience, the different uses of photography also present different kinds of ethical problems for the photographer. Mass-market publications, for example, often do not allow the photographer final say on captions and may introduce errors or drop out the names of individuals photographed. A typical mass-market caption might read something like, "Maidu women preparing acorn soup." Should one therefore, on ethical grounds, refuse to contribute images to general-audience publications, or can their value in educating the public about Native American issues be seen as outweighing their flaws? In the case of one popular book to which I personally contributed, the text is strongly pro-Native American, but, without the last-minute addition of a few of my contemporary photographs, the publication might have unwittingly furthered the notion that indigenous Californians are extinct.

Certainly the safest approach for the anthropologist working in Native America is to avoid doing photography, unless it is essential to her or his project. Barring that perfect solution, it is crucial to determine indigenous rules and expectations regarding photography. Projects planned and published or exhibited by Native Americans are perhaps the least likely to be controversial. For example, I shot one series of photographs for a well-known Karuk artist and activist, who used them in articles and lectures promoting preservation of spiritual power-quest areas in northwest California.

However, no photographic project is likely to be beyond criticism. Native American groups often are divided (among other ways) between factions termed the "traditionalists" and the "progressives"; the traditionalists favor preservation or revival of the old ways, and the progressives champion European-style economic development over other values. In the case of the GO (Gasquet-Orleans) Road controversy, the progressives saw the economic advantages of a new log-transport road to the coast as more important than the consequent infringement on sacred geography. By providing photographs to the traditionalists, I was, in effect, taking sides in an internal conflict. For a number of reasons, anthropologists tend to align themselves with the traditionalists. First, most anthropologists are more interested in traditional culture than they are in the highly acculturated lifestyles of many progressives. Further, anthropologists tend to be politically liberal to leftist, while indigenous progressives are often perceived as conservative.

Within anthropology, supporting the Native equivalent of the left is usually seen as perfectly desirable and ethical, whereas anthropologists who actively support right-wing causes are typically denounced as unethical. The possibility of finding an indigenous-sponsored photography project that has the support of all tribal factions is remote. In any event, one cannot assume that because a project has Native support or official tribal-office sanction it will be free of controversy or ethical problems.

Photographs for publications that are primarily by or for Native Americans, especially if they do not pay their photographers, are also likely to be received favorably. For example, I have made a number of photographs for *News from Native California*, a nonprofit newsletter for Native Californians and anyone interested in their current activities. In one series, I documented a fund raiser organized by Native Americans to support continued publication of this newsletter.[6]

In another *News from Native California* article, Julian Lange of the Karuk tribe used some of my photographs to illustrate his article on the GO Road protest at Six Rivers National Forest Headquarters in Eureka, California.[7] It is advisable to get written permission from anyone photographed even if the author of an illustrated article is Native American and has permission to do the article. Such permission given to the author may or may not be seen as including the use of photographs.

Donation of photographs to a public archives creates another set of problems. The managers of such archives do not necessarily check with individuals to see if public use has been approved. Ethical considerations often are largely up to the donor. Photographs intended for permanent inclusion in a public archives actually need to be accompanied by more than a simple model release. From an ethical position, one should also obtain letters from tribal councils and religious leaders authorizing publication and other public use of images on behalf of the tribe and its legitimate authorities. Individuals now or in the future may or may not be deemed to have the right to grant permission to use their images. This is especially the case if individuals are involved in ceremonial activity or wearing ceremonial costumes.

The photographer and archivist should not assume that present distinctions between secular and sacred costumes or activities will necessarily hold in the future. For example, in California, the Big Head dance has always been sacred, but there is nothing in the literature to suggest that the Big Head outfit itself used to be considered too sacred to be photographed, as it is today. Posed photographs of individuals wearing the Big Head regalia in the P. A. Hearst Museum collection—dating from the early 1900s—probably were not in any way illicit, but, to my knowledge, there is no documentation with the negatives to show that they were authorized by either the individuals or the appropriate dance leaders and Elders.

Before beginning my concluding discussion, I would like to suggest that the rise of the conservative right should be taken into account in current political debate over control of our public museum collections. Unless all multiculturalists work together, there may soon be no public museums under anyone's control. The far right would be glad to close our public museums, or at least to rid them of any non-Christian elements, but it certainly would not be out of any multi-culturalist sentiments. We should keep in mind that so far as Newt Gingrich is concerned, we are all "enemies of normal Americans."

The uneasiness of Native Americans toward photography, as well as the guilt-tinged, newly discovered ethical concerns of anthropologists, I would argue, can be understood only in their historical context. A number of recent histories of the photography of Native Americans summarize the so-called revisionist view of American history.[8] According to this perspective, with which I am certainly in agreement, a major part of the history of Native America since the arrival of the Europeans has been one of conquest and exploitation by Euro-Americans, based on the numerical superiority of the invaders and the power advantages of their technologies. Photography not only recorded this history but, in some cases, became a tool of it. The early expeditionary photographers saw the indigenous people as part of the natural scene and as curiosities whose images could be sold at a profit to incredulous easterners. After the Western conquest was completed, live examples of the Native personage were displayed and endlessly photographed at a series of expositions and world fairs. Then, as the influence of the Romantic Movement permeated photography, the Pictorialist photographers saw in the indigenous people a vision of a noble but doomed race. For these Romantics, the Native Americans were essentially the New World equivalent of the ancient Greeks, whose more noble civilization inevitably fell before the crass but more powerful imperial order of the Romans. The emotional piquancy of Pictorialist imagery was based on the assumption that their idealized Native subjects would soon be extinct.

When the anticipated racial extinction of the Indian did not arrive but the automobile did, a new wave of tourist photographers descended in person upon the Indian reservations of the West. Their motives as photographers were even less clear than those of their predecessors, signifying perhaps a token of passage, but it is clear that tourist photographers typically had little sense of Native Americans as individual people with rights to privacy and dignity. The ordinary tourist was frequently joined by the anthropological fieldworker, who at this time saw in the more traditional Native Americans an opportunity to approximate visually the precontact lifeways of those they regarded as "primitive." To these insults within the still-photography genre were soon added the full range of negative and racist stereotypes promulgated through the medium of "moving pictures."

The "taking" of photographs by whites has been one of the most recent of a series of disastrous takings, including the taking of Native American lives, the taking of Native American lands, in many cases the taking of their freedom and sovereignty as independent Nations. In my personal experience, I have found the Native Americans are often remarkably forgiving of these rather extreme grievances. When photographers, even anthropological photographers, attempt to redefine the photographic act as a mutually agreed-upon "giving," rather than a "taking," their efforts, even if naive, will often be well received.[9] This attitude of giving, I believe, means more than just handing out free prints; it means accepting Native American limits and conditions for the making and use of photographs. It also means putting in the time and effort to understand and accurately portray each separate culture and each individual being photographed. Still, one must be careful even here. Revisionist history and politically correct accommodation can become one more facet of hegemony and misunderstanding if they involve a rhetorical "speaking for" Native Americans or an assumed contract.[10] Only the views directly expressed by Native Americans and tribal authorities have validity in determining whether photography is an appropriate part of cross-cultural experience.

Notes

1. Jacques Derrida, *Derrida Reader* (New York: Columbia University Press, 1990); Peter Matthiessen, *In the Spirit of Crazy Horse* (New York: Penguin, 1980); Peter Nabokov, ed., *Native American Testimony: A Chronicle of Indian-White Relations from Prophecy to the Present* (New York: Penguin, 1991); Gerald Vizenor, "The Ruins of Representations: Shadow Survivance and the Literature of Dominance," *American Indian Quarterly* 17 (January 1993): 7–30.

2. Alfred L. Bush and Lee Clark Mitchell, *The Photograph and the American Indian* (Princeton, NJ: Princeton University Press, 1994); Paula Richardson Fleming and Judith Lynn Luskey, *Grand Endeavors of American Indian Photography* (Washington, DC: Smithsonian Institution Press, 1993); Ulrich W. Hiesinger, *Indian Lives: A Photographic Record from the Civil War to Wounded Knee* (New York: Prestel, 1994).

3. For the latter, see especially Michael Dorris, "In the Eyes of the Beheld," *Natural History* 103 (November 1994): 24–29.

4. Joseph Epes Brown, *The North American Indians: A Selection of Photographs by Edward S. Curtis* (Princeton, NJ: Princeton University Press, 1972); Florence Curtis Graybill and Victor Boesen, *Edward Sheriff Curtis: Visions of a Vanishing Race* (New York: American Legacy Press, 1981); Christopher M. Lyman, *The Vanishing Race and Other Illusions: Photographs of Indians by Edward S. Curtis* (Washington, DC: Smithsonian Institution Press, 1994).

5. Diane Cochrane, "The New Copyright Revision Act," *American Artist* (April 1978): 2–97.

6. "Songs Against the GO Road," *News from Native California* 4 (August/September 1990): 24–25.

7. Julian Lang, "The NO-GO March," *News from Native California* 2 (July/August 1988): 4–7.

8. The works cited in the second endnote are all examples of this revised view of American history and the photography of Native America. The authors collectively provide expanded discussion of each of the aspects covered in my brief synopsis.

9. William Albert Allard, foreword to John Running, *Honor Dance: Native American Photographs* (Reno: University of Nevada Press, 1985).

10. The present article is not above reproach in this regard, since I freely mix reportage on Native American practices with my personal opinions and those of non-Native American historians. I have, at least, tried to mark the shift each time.

PART V

HEALTH

Since the first days of European contact, health issues have been of central concern to the physical and cultural survival of Native people. Economic and cultural domination, as well as wholesale change in diet, food production, and access to land and resources, contribute to a contemporary world in which Native people suffer from severe health problems and live in relatively unhealthy life situations. When tribes did not live on reservations and took their food from the land, they were much healthier than at present day. In the last century, significant advances in vaccines have helped ameliorate the devastating effects of smallpox, cholera, and other communicable diseases. Nevertheless, confinement to reservations and the general removal from access to traditional plants and animals led to dependency on food provided by government officials, with deleterious effects. As food market systems grew in efficiency, most tribes were increasingly removed from production and consumption of their own food. For example, horticultural pueblos began to produce less food and purchase more from trading posts. Eventually, they became dependent on supermarkets, as the economy of food consumption became commodified. Meanwhile, most Indians remained poor or became increasingly impoverished in the reservation setting and were thus without access both to the means of food production and to the means of food purchase. Further, nutritionally poor food, heavy in starches and carbohydrates, became a staple of Native diets, leading to a variety of health problems such as diabetes.

On reservations, the scarcity of economic opportunity, subjection to extensive external police control, and restrictions on the ability to practice traditional lifestyles have produced massive disruptions in social and cultural life and increased alcoholism, depression, and other social pathologies. Sometimes new cultural institutions like the Native American Church arose to help ameliorate such conditions, but reservation life continues to be characterized by high levels of health risk, low life expectancy, high child mortality, and excessive rates of alcohol and substance abuse. Health issues are of central concern for urban and rural Native communities alike. Diabetes and weight control are especially severe. At least one reservation community reports 100 percent of their population having diabetes, and many young Native children are showing signs of early diabetes symptoms.

Native communities must work to gain more control over their own health care and develop community-based programs that will help prevent substance abuse, diabetes, and other health problems. Like issues of economic and cultural sovereignty, improved health care is crucial to the future survival and vitality of Native cultures. Chapters in this section give both general context and specific examples of health problems and community programs that seek solutions.

11

The Epidemiology of Alcohol Abuse among American Indians: The Mythical and Real Properties

Philip A. May

 BECAUSE OF THE DRUNKEN INDIAN stereotype and other myths often associated with American Indians, it is important to critically examine the detailed evidence that best defines the epidemiology of alcohol abuse among Indians and particular tribal communities. Public health understandings and programs must be based not on myth but on fact. In this paper, twelve major myths, statements, and questions about the nature of the alcohol abuse problem are reviewed. An analysis of current mortality data and an understanding of the extant literature will reveal that many current myths are either false or, at best, half-truths.

The literature on American Indians, at one time rather small, has grown to a substantial body of useful documents. In a bibliography of the relevant Indian alcohol literature published before 1977, Mail and McDonald[1] list 969 works. The number published since 1977 is anyone's guess and a task for future research. One would be safe in assuming, however, that the literature has at least doubled in the last fifteen years. Furthermore, it is evident to those of us in this field that the quality of information and data has improved in some areas. With such an extensive and growing body of literature, there is no excuse for operating on myth and common knowledge. Although not all questions are answered in the literature, many certainly are. The literature needs to be used more by students, scholars, public health workers, health officials, and tribal groups. A critical reading can advance knowledge greatly.

A series of common myths, questions, and statements regarding alcohol and Indians is presented below. Some of these myths have been presented before.[2] They do not seem to go away, even though more evidence is accumulated that speaks directly to them. The evidence for and against various myths and common beliefs is summarized in a very terse fashion in this paper. References cited, however, contain much more detail for the interested reader to consult.

Philip A. May is a professor of sociology and psychiatry at the University of New Mexico. He also is director of the University of New Mexico Center on Alcoholism, Substance Abuse, and Addiction (CASAA).

Is Alcoholism the Number One Health Problem among Native Americans?

That alcoholism is the leading health problem among Indians is probably the most popular and common statement about alcohol and Indians that one hears from laymen and health professionals alike. It is accepted as gospel by many and is seldom questioned or elaborated on in the planning and implementing of alcohol abuse prevention programs. Yet it is a half-truth at best.

In table 1, an analysis of the most recent Indian Health Service (IHS)[3] data from 1986 to 1988 indicates that 17.0 percent to 19.0 percent of all Indian deaths are probably alcohol-related.[4] Similar patterns and data are common in other years as well.[5] These data are quite complete in scope, for they include an estimate of the percentage of alcohol-related deaths from motor vehicle and other accidents, suicide, homicide, and alcoholism/alcohol dependence. Therefore, it is true that alcohol is involved in a very high percentage of Indian deaths—substantially greater than the general U.S. average of 4.7 percent. But the term *alcoholism* can be very misleading. Alcoholism generally denotes only alcohol-dependent or chronic drinking behaviors, which are only part of the problem. In table 1 the data are broken down to compare deaths from behaviors that are generally the result of alcohol-abusive drinking patterns (sporadic, binge drinking) with those that result from alcohol-specific/alcohol-dependent drinking styles (chronic, "alcoholic" drinking). For 1986–88, data show 2,213, or 74.9 percent, of all alcohol-related deaths were from alcohol-abusive causes, while 742, or 25.1 percent, were from alcohol-specific/alcohol-dependent causes (alcohol-dependence syndrome, alcohol psychosis, and chronic liver dis-

Table 1: Estimated Alcohol-Involved Deaths
of American Indians in Reservation States, 1986–1988
and the U.S. General Population, 1987

Cause of Death	Total Indian Deaths (N) x	Estimated % Alcohol-Involved =	Indian Alcohol-Involved (N)	Alcohol-Involved U.S. (N)	Alcohol-Involved from nine IHS areas* (N)
Alcohol Abusive					
Accidents					
Motor Vehicle	1,687	(.65)	1,097	31,389	847
Other	1,278	(.25)	320	11,683	250
Suicide	534	(.75)	401	23,099	302
Homicide	494	(.85)	395	16,962	279
Subtotal	(3,993)		(2,213)	(83,133)	(1,678)
Alcoholic/ Alcohol-Specific**	(742)	(1.00)	(742)	(15,909)	(580)
TOTAL	4,735		2,955	99,042	2,258
Deaths as a percent of total deaths	27.2%		17.0%	4.7%	19.0%

Source: Computed from U. S. Indian Health Service, *Trends in Indian Health* and *Regional Differences in Indian Health.*
* IHS states that data are more complete in nine of their service areas (Aberdeen, Alaska, Albuquerque, Bemidji, Billings, Nashville, Navajo, Phoenix, and Tucson). The far right column only includes these nine areas.
**Alcohol-specific deaths include these causes: alcohol-dependence syndrome, alcoholic psychoses, chronic liver disease and cirrhosis specified as alcoholic.

ease specified as alcoholic). Therefore, one would be more accurate in stating that alcoholism per se is not the leading cause of death among Indians. More accurately, alcohol abuse and alcoholism combine to be the leading cause of mortality.[6]

Alcohol-induced morbidity (sickness) is also a great problem among Indians. Again, though, alcohol abuse and alcoholism combine to cause the illness. In fact, alcohol abuse produces more sickness and injury than do alcohol-specific or alcoholic behaviors. This is also true in mainstream U.S. society.

The importance of these distinctions is great. If public health officials and citizens focus solely on chronic alcoholic behaviors and problems in their planning of intervention and prevention, they will miss the majority (three-fourths) of the problem. Complete alcohol abuse prevention and intervention programs must address the full range of alcohol-abusive and chronic alcoholic behaviors.[7]

DO INDIANS METABOLIZE ALCOHOL DIFFERENTLY OR MORE SLOWLY THAN DO PEOPLE OF OTHER ETHNIC GROUPS?

The most persistent myth about Indians is that they have particular biophysiological reasons for "not being able to hold their alcohol." In fact, not only do non-Indians believe this, but many Indians also believe that their ethnic group has a biological deficit in metabolizing alcohol. One survey among the Navajo asked if Indians have a biological weakness to alcohol that non-Indians do not, and 63 percent of the respondents said yes.[8]

This myth has virtually no basis in fact. Only one study ever reported that Indians metabolize alcohol more slowly than non-Indians,[9] but it was criticized as highly flawed in its use of controls and other methods.[10] All of the remaining studies of alcohol metabolism among Indians have found Indians to metabolize alcohol as rapidly[11] as, or more rapidly[12] than, matched controls who were non-Indian. Furthermore, liver biopsies have shown no discernible difference in liver phenotype between Indians and non-Indians.[13]

Therefore, no basis at all for this myth is found in the scientific literature, and it should not be a consideration in current prevention and intervention programs. Major reviews of alcohol metabolism among all ethnic groups usually conclude that alcohol metabolism and alcohol genetics are traits of individuals and that there is more variation within an ethnic group than there is between ethnic groups.[14] Further, when biophysiologic investigators attempt to explain major alcohol-related behaviors, they generally point to sociocultural variables as the major factors.[15]

ARE INDIAN ALCOHOL-RELATED PROBLEMS UNIQUELY INDIAN?

Certainly some alcohol-related behaviors in which Indians participate seem to be unique in their manifestations. Indeed, this was a major theme of the early literature.[16] But what is often overlooked in practical explanations of Indian drinking behavior is that there are many similarities between Indians and other groups. Further, there may also be common explanations for both Indian drinking and that practiced by other groups.

First, the fact that Indians have high rates of alcohol-related death is influenced by demographic traits. The American Indian population is very young in almost every community. The median age of Indians is in the low twenties over-all[17] and is commonly much lower on some reservations.[18] In 1988, the U.S. median age was 32.3.[19] Young populations tend to have much higher rates of death from a number of alcohol-related causes (e.g., motor vehicle and other accidents, suicide, and homicide) than do populations that are elderly or middle aged. Because of the demography of many Indian communities, one would expect to find higher rates of these problems than in the more middle-aged U.S. mainstream. Conversely, one would also expect lower rates of death from chronic diseases such as heart disease, stroke, and cancer among Indians.[20]

Second, geography plays a role in alcohol-related statistics. Because the majority of Indians still live in rural western states, higher death rates are to be expected due to factors such as higher-risk environments, distance from care, time lag to care, and reduced availability of services.[21] Alcohol-related injuries may be more common in rural western environments. Also, serious injuries (from events such as motor vehicle crashes) often become deaths because of the distance to, and timing of, care.[22]

Third, social, political, legal, and local policies may create conditions that exacerbate alcohol-related problems and rates. The low socioeconomic status of many Indians shapes their behavioral patterns.[23] Also, because most reservations are still under prohibition,[24] drinking styles and patterns are such that higher rates of alcohol-related arrest, injury, and mortality are more likely to occur.[25] Changes in policy similar to those enacted in other groups and societies might eventually produce very different alcohol-consumption characteristics and patterns of alcohol-related problems.[26] In addition, upward changes in social class and education in the future would change drinking and alcohol-related behavior patterns.[27]

Finally, tribal culture or social practices may contain some of the seeds of both problems and solutions. Elevated rates of alcohol-related death from automobile accidents may arise from dangerous cultural practices such as not wearing seat belts and not being licensed and well educated in safety and/or defensive driving.[28] The same can be said of many other subgroups of the U.S. population. Even if a person is driving while intoxicated, he might not become an alcohol-related statistic if he is strapped in by a seat belt. Unpublished data from New Mexico surveys show a lower use of seat belts among the youth of some tribes as compared with non-Indian youth in the same schools. But some tribes have higher rates of belt use than others.

In summary, the explanations of high rates of alcohol-related problems and their solutions may well be found in demographic, geographic, political, and cultural variables that are not necessarily uniquely Indian. Researchers, planners, and others must not overlook these relatively simple and conventional explanations in either their studies of etiology or their designs of solutions.

Is There a Higher Prevalence of Drinking among Indians?

It is often said or implied that a vast majority of Indians drink. Frequently, I have asked audiences at a number of reservations, "What percentage of your adult population drinks?" The response for most sites was frequently "90 percent" or greater. Similar responses about Indians are also common within the mainstream population of the United States.

The evidence in the published literature is quite different from what most people believe.[29] In fact, there is extreme variation in prevalence of drinking from one tribal group to another. Unfortunately, however, only a handful of extant adult prevalence studies have been published. Nevertheless, from these studies one can conclude that adult prevalence is lower in some tribes than the U.S. general averages; in others, it is about the same as or higher than U.S averages.[30] Furthermore, drinking prevalence may vary over time in many tribal communities.

Two prevalence studies among the Navajo in 1969 and 1984[31] indicate that, in both periods, fewer Navajo adults drank at all (31 percent and 52 percent) than adults in the general population of the U.S. (67 percent). But these same studies indicate that Navajo drinking prevalence is increasing.

Two similar studies among the Standing Rock Sioux[32] showed that prevalence was decreasing (69 percent to 58 percent). In 1960, overall drinking prevalence was about the same as in the general population; twenty years later, it was lower than U.S. averages (67 percent).

Studies were also carried out among two other tribes. The Southern Ute and the Brokenhead Ojibwa of Canada demonstrated drinking prevalence rates (80 percent and 84 percent) higher than U.S. averages.[33] The prevalence of adult drinking among Indians, therefore, varies widely from tribe to tribe and over time. Variation over time is also found with Indian youths.[34]

These prevalence studies provided other significant findings as well. Among those who do drink in these tribes, there is a substantially higher prevalence (two to three times) of problem and excessive drinking indicators than among the general U.S. population.[35] Consumption of more than five drinks per situation, as well as experience with delirium tremens (DTs) and blackouts, are much higher in these studies. Therefore, among those Indians who drink, there is a substantial number of problem drinkers who produce a high frequency and variety of problems such as arrests, morbidity, and mortality.

More positive findings are also found in these studies. For example, among Indian males who are in their middle age and older, more have completely quit drinking than among most other groups of U.S. males. Also, in virtually every tribe, a lower proportion of the women drink.[36]

Therefore, the overall prevalence of drinking among Indians is not the most important variable in the epidemiology of drinking. What is more important are the drinking styles, some of which emphasize very problematic behaviors.

Do All Indians Drink in the Same Manner or Style?

Tribal and urban studies have reported various styles of drinking.[37] Most researchers describe two patterns that cause either no or few alcohol-related problems: abstinence and moderated social drinking. But at least two problem drinking patterns are common among subgroups or "peer clusters" in many tribal communities.[38] One is a chronic alcoholic drinking pattern that Frances Ferguson has called "anxiety" drinking.[39] The other is the "recreational" pattern defined by Ferguson and others.

Recreational drinkers are predominantly young (age 15–35) males who are students or relatively new participants in the work world; they drink sporadically for special occasions, at night and on weekends, away from home, and in a celebration or party manner. Some young females also participate in this pattern, but they are less involved and generally for a shorter period of time. This drinking style is not unlike college fraternity drinkers. Indian recreational drinkers are at very high risk for alcohol-related injury, arrest, and death because of the prescence of high blood alcohol levels for a "blitzed" experience. Many people mature out of this pattern, but a disproportionate number of Indians die young from recreational drinking.

Anxiety drinkers, on the other hand, are more typical of the chronic alcoholic. They are downwardly mobile, unemployed, and socially marginal to both Indian and non-Indian society. They are predominantly male, but some females fit this pattern. They tend to drink chronically, whether alone or with other drinking buddies. Anxiety drinkers are commonly found spending long periods of time in border towns or in skid row areas of many western cities.

These two types of problem drinkers produce the alcohol-abusive and alcohol-specific problems described earlier. The recreational drinkers produce many of the accident and suicide deaths, while the anxiety drinkers produce the alcoholism deaths (e.g., cirrhosis of the liver) and a preponderance of the pedestrian-vehicle collision deaths.[40]

In summary, there are a number of drinking styles among Indians that affect the epidemiological patterns and create a challenge for prevention and treatment. There is no one Indian drinking pattern.

Why Are Indian Rates of Death from Alcohol-Related Causes So High?

Many of the answers to this question have already been presented. However, the common, stereotypical answer to this question is that "Indians are like that."

Just as it is said that the "Irish drink because they are Irish," it is said that "Indians drink because they are Indian." The simple, logical extension of this, then, is that high rates of drinking produce high rates of alcohol-related death and other problems. But we have seen that the prevalence of drinking alone does not explain the high rates of alcohol-related death among Indians.

Table 2. Age-Adjusted Mortality (rates per 100,000) from
Alcohol-Abusive and Alcohol-Specific Causes
for American Indians, 1986–1988
and the U. S. General Population, 1987

Cause of Death	Estimated Alcohol-Involved	All IHS Area	All U.S.	Ratio IHS/U.S.	Nine IHS Areas*	Ratio Nine Areas/ U.S.
Alcohol-Abusive Accidents						
Motor Vehicle	.65	57.5	19.5	2.95	75.2	3.89
Other	.25	45.5	15.2	2.99	61.5	4.05
Suicide	.75	17.9	11.7	1.53	22.8	1.95
Homicide	.80	16.9	8.6	1.97	20.1	2.34
Subtotal		(137.8)	(55.0)	(2.51)	(179.6)	(3.26)
Alcoholic/ Alcohol-Specific**	1.00	(32.7)	(6.0)	(5.45)	(45.8)	(7.63)
TOTAL		170.5	61.0	2.79	225.4	3.69

Source: Computed from U. S. Indian Health Service, *Trends in Indian Health* and *Regional Differences in Indian Health.*.
* IHS states that data are more complete in nine of their service areas (Aberdeen, Alaska, Albuquerque, Bemidji, Billings, Nashville, Navajo, Phoenix, and Tucson). The far right column only includes these nine areas.
**Alcohol-specific deaths include the following causes: alcohol-dependence syndrome, alcoholic psychoses, and chronic liver disease and cirrhosis specified as alcoholic.

Recent IHS data (see table 2)[41] indicate that Indians die more frequently than the U.S. averages from motor vehicle accidents (2.95 to 3.89 times higher); other accidents (2.99 to 4.05 times higher); suicide (1.53 to 1.95 times higher); homicide (1.97 to 2.34 times higher); and alcoholism (5.45 to 7.63 times higher). These ratios of Indian to U.S. averages reflect rates, not the actual numbers of deaths. There are three elements of explanation for this different experience. One element can be found in the previous sections, which deal with demographic, social, and political considerations discussed in the literature. The second element of explanation is centered on drinking style. The flamboyant drinking styles that are very common in a number of Indian peer clusters (recreational and anxiety drinkers) emphasize abusive drinking and high blood alcohol levels. Further, heavy drinking peer groups among many tribes encourage, or do not discourage, the frequent mixing of alcohol impairment, risky behavior, and risky environments.[42] Driving while intoxicated, sleeping outside in the winter, aggression, and other unsafe practices are examples of this element.

The mixing of (1) high-risk environments, (2) flamboyant drinking styles, and (3) risky post-drinking behavior combine to elevate Indian rates of alcohol-related death far above those of the general U.S. population. This is true as well with arrest, injury, and other problems for which statistics are recorded.

How is the Drunken Indian Stereotype Perpetuated by a Naive and Uncritical Use of Statistics?

Many authors and speakers on the topic of Indian drinking and alcohol-related problems often cite statistics that do not capture an unduplicated count of the individuals involved in abusive drinking. For example, if one looks at alcohol-related arrest rates, there generally is little opportunity for knowing if the data reflect the experience of a few or a large number of individuals. In Gallup, New Mexico, Ferguson[43] found that 115 alcohol-dependent Navajo males accounted for almost twelve hundred arrests in 1.5 years. A careless or uncritical researcher could report this as twelve hundred Navajo with a problem, rather than one hundred with a chronic drinking problem and repeated arrests.

When working on my doctoral dissertation in Montana, I stumbled across a situation and calculated an overall arrest rate that further emphasizes this point. On one small Northern Plains reservation (less than 3,000 people) the arrest rate was 100,103 per 100,000 from 1970 to 1974.[44] In other words, a literal and naive interpretation would be that every man, woman, and child had been arrested at least once during the five-year period. My, what a criminal place one could imagine with these data! Further, 75 percent of these arrests were for alcohol-specific crimes on a dry reservation. Could this mean that three-quarters of all the men, women, and children are such problem drinkers that they are arrested? Certainly not. It was a situation where a small proportion of the population (mainly males) spent time in a "revolving door" situation. They drank excessively in nearby border towns and on the reservation and were in and out of jail, time and time again. How absurd the uncritical use of aggregate and duplicative data such as these arrest statistics can be! But such data frequently are presented uncritically in newspapers, lectures, and even academic and agency program papers.

The same can be said of morbidity data. One person with a drinking problem can generate literally dozens of visits to a clinic, inpatient admissions, and emergency incidents. IHS data showing a large number of patient encounters should not be taken to indicate the prevalence of the problem. Counts of individuals, not visits, should be used for epidemiological purposes, and, even then, one is dealing only with treated prevalence. For example, in a chart review study of IHS records in the Southwest covering ten years, 21.4 percent of the individuals who visited six IHS general clinic facilities were seen at least once for a mental health or alcohol-abuse problem.[45] This is not a substantially high percentage based on U.S. estimates. The vast majority of inpatient episodes (83 percent) by these individuals, however, were for alcohol and substance abuse, as were 53 percent of outpatient visits.[46] On average, each episode of mental health and alcohol-related illness presented by these individuals accounted for 3.9 outpatient and inpatient visits before the problem was fully dealt with or was cured. Therefore, just from looking at visits, one might conclude that the problems were much more extensive. Thus, morbidity data, like arrest data, can be highly duplicative in counting or estimating problems, even when estimating treated prevalence.

One should always ask, then, "Are the prevalence data that are being presented representative of true prevalence or treated/clinic prevalence?" Or, more importantly, "Are they nothing more than workload data?" Too often, arrest, morbidity, social welfare caseload, and other statistics are merely workload, contact, or activity counts. Unduplicated data, such as random surveys of individuals in the population to document adult drinking, are best for estimating prevalence. Further, school-based youth surveys tell us little or nothing about adults. Mortality data are much better for estimating prevalence, because people die only once. Indian epidemiological information has suffered greatly over the years, because data used have not often enough been unduplicated counts that provide valid measures of prevalence. In populations with a substantial concentration of high-risk, heavy drinkers, this has led to inaccuracy and distortion of the true extent of the problem. Measuring the repetitive, high-risk, and problematic behavior of a subculture of problem drinkers within a tribe, and using it uncritically, can stigmatize the whole tribe.

WHAT IS THE LEVEL OF SEVERITY OF DRINKING AMONG THE ALCOHOL-ABUSING POPULATION?

Within the drinking populations of most Indian communities, a substantial number of people drink very heavily. These people are found in both the recreational and anxiety drinker populations.

More than 70 percent of Indians who die in traffic accidents in New Mexico have been drinking. A University of New Mexico study of all ethnic groups in the state found that American Indian decedents from crashes had very high blood alcohol concentrations (BAC).[47] The average BACs of those who had been drinking and were killed in vehicular crashes in New Mexico were Indian .191, Hispanic .189, and Anglo .128. All ethnic groups, therefore, were averaging levels well above the legal intoxication level (.10). Indians killed in alcohol-related crashes had BACs significantly higher than those of the Anglos but not much higher than those of the Hispanics.[48] A full 85.7 percent of the Indian and 82.5 percent of the Hispanic victims who had been drinking were above the legal limit. This compared with 55.4 percent of the Anglos. Thus, the level of drinking among the Indians and Hispanics who drink is very high, probably indicating similar sociocultural patterns of drinking by certain peer clusters among the two groups.

A comparable pattern of blood alcohol levels exists for Indian decedents from suicide. Among those Indians who die from suicide in New Mexico, 69 percent to 74 percent (depending on the year studied) are alcohol involved, with the alcohol level being quite bimodal. In other words, one-fourth of the victims tend to be completely sober, while three-fourths have very high BACs, as above (work in progress).

Research indicates, then, that those who are members of alcohol-abusing peer clusters in many tribes drink in a manner that produces very high blood alcohol levels. Both suicide and motor vehicle accidents are alcohol related in a majority of cases. These results also support the notion that there is a connection between heavy drinking and risky behavior.

WHAT IS THE RELATIONSHIP BETWEEN CHILD ABUSE, CHILD NEGLECT, AND ALCOHOL?

The one major study that has examined, in detail, the relationship between child abuse and neglect and alcohol use demonstrates clearly that alcohol often is involved. In northern New Mexico, 85 percent to 93 percent of the Indian child-neglect cases and 63 percent of the child-abuse cases involve alcohol.[49] Neglect, abuse, and alcohol problems were found to be part of a complex found in a number of multiproblem families where intergenerational transmission of pathology was present.

A subsequent paper from the above study compares the abuse/neglect sample to a matched group of Indian control families. Alcohol use and abuse was found to have been present in 58 percent of the control homes at one time or another, as compared to 88 percent in the abuse/neglect target groups.[50] This control study concluded that alcohol seems to be a necessary, but not sufficient, condition for child abuse. This is not unlike the relationship with suicide.

IS ALCOHOL ABUSE ONLY A MALE PROBLEM?

Alcohol abuse, in the form of both alcohol-related and alcohol-specific/dependent behavior, takes its greatest toll among Indian males. IHS data from 1986 to 1988 (see table 3) indicate that the number of Indian male deaths from alcohol-related and alcohol-specific causes is much higher (N = 2,705) than for Indian females (N = 951). This is true in every category. Twenty-six percent of male deaths are alcohol involved, whereas 13 percent of female deaths are. Stated another way, in a typical three-year period, 12.3 percent of all Indian deaths are related to alcohol use by males, and 4.3 percent are related to alcohol use by females.

Further, according to the rates in table 3, male Indians fare far worse than U.S. males in general. For example, in a comparison of Indian and U.S. males ages 25–34, the rate for motor vehicle accident deaths among Indians is 2.8 times higher, for other accidents 2.7 times higher, for suicide 1.9 times higher, and for homicide 1.5 times higher; the alcoholism rate is 6.8 times higher.[51]

Indian females, however, do not fare much better in comparison with U.S. female rates. In the same age category (25–34 years), Indian female rates are 3.4, 2.7, 1.4, 1.5, and 12.0 times higher than U.S. females.[52] Thus, Indian females have higher rates of alcohol-involved death than U.S. females in general, and this is true in most age categories and alcohol-involved causes.

Therefore, although the numbers indicate that alcohol-abusive mortality and alcohol abuse are mainly (in numbers) an Indian male problem, Indian females are also at high risk compared to other U.S. women. This should be kept in mind for alcohol treatment and prevention in Indian Country. Indian women who are in the alcohol-abusing categories also have a strong need for attention,[53] especially regarding alcohol-specific causes. The number of female deaths from cirrhosis of the liver (w/alcohol), alcohol dependence, and alcoholic psychosis is one-half the number (46.2 percent) of Indian male deaths from these causes. Chronic alcohol-dependence problems are, therefore, more equally shared among Indian females and males than the other alcohol-related causes of death.

Is Fetal Alcohol Syndrome (FAS) a Major Problem for Indians?

Like many of the problems mentioned above, FAS rates vary greatly from one reservation to the next. Two studies have been carried out on Canadian Indian communities with widespread alcohol abuse, and high rates of FAS have been found.[54] Another study found higher rates of FAS recorded on Indian birth certificates in the United States than among any other ethnic group.[55] One other study found both high- and low-risk communities in the same region,[56] with variance based on differing sociocultural and drinking patterns found in the communities. The range of FAS rates in these studies is from a high of 190 per 1,000 children to a low of 1.3 per 1,000 children. However, studies that were based on the largest populations of Indians who were living in relatively stable reservation communities documented rates only slightly higher than the U.S. estimated rate in the 1980s. The overall Southwestern Indian rate in 1978–82 was 4.2 per 1,000, compared to 2.2 for the United States overall.[57] Further, the U.S. rate for all races may well be underreported.[58]

Bray and Anderson[59] and Chavez et al.[60] suggest that, among Indians, better surveillance and more complete reporting of FAS occurs. This may be true both in the disrupted Indian communities that were highly alcohol abusive and therefore were studied by researchers and also in general birth certificate recording.

Much of the newspaper, popular media, and conference coverage of FAS has been highly dramatic and quite distorted. The figures quoted of "one in three" or "one in four" Indian babies being FAS have no support at all in screening, epidemiologic or scientific studies. This is even true for the small, most highly alcoholic communities such as the one studied by Robinson et al.[61] Furthermore, the

TABLE 3. Estimated Alcohol-Involved Causes of Death for U.S. Indians and Alaska Natives (1986–1988)** and the U.S. General Population by Age, Sex, Rate per 100,000 and Number

	Rates											
Cause of death	15–24 Ind.	U.S.	Ratio	25–34 Ind.	U.S.	Ratio	35–44 Ind.	U.S.	Ratio	45–54 Ind.	U.S.	Ratio
Male												
MV accident	97.0	55.5	1.7	104.7	36.8	2.8	86.2	25.6	3.4	65.7	21.8	3.0
Other accdt	42.5	18.6	2.3	63.5	23.6	2.7	77.1	23.8	3.2	59.9	23.4	2.6
Suicide	40.7	21.3	1.9	49.6	24.8	2.0	30.3	22.9	1.3	21.7	23.8	0.9
Homicide	32.1	21.9	1.5	44.7	23.3	1.9	38.6	17.1	2.3	19.4	12.1	1.6
Alcoholism*	0.8	0.1	8.0	21.8	3.2	6.8	65.5	12.9	5.1	98.6	24.4	4.0
Total deaths for above causes				4307			2705					
% of all Indian deaths				19.6%			12.3%					
% of all male Indian deaths				42.1%			26.5%					
Female												
MV accident	30.7	19.7	1.6	39.5	11.5	3.4	32.2	9.3	3.5	27.8	9.2	3.0
Other accdt	8.2	3.5	2.3	13.1	4.8	2.7	16.9	5.2	3.3	13.3	6.4	2.1
Suicide	6.5	4.3	1.5	8.3	5.9	1.4	9.3	7.2	1.3	5.0	7.6	7.5
Homicide	10.2	6.0	1.7	10.4	6.9	1.5	9.3	4.8	1.9	4.4	3.6	1.2
Alcoholism	1.2	0.1	12.0	16.8	1.4	12.0	25.1	4.2	8.4	57.3	7.6	7.5
Total deaths for above causes				1474			951					
% of all Indian deaths				6.7%			4.3%					
% of all female Indian deaths				20.5%			13.2%					

Source: Computed from U.S. Indian Health Service, *Trends in Indian Health*
* Alcoholism deaths include the following causes: alcohol-dependence syndrome, alcoholic psychoses, and chronic liver disease and cirrhosis specified as alcoholic.
** Includes all Indian and Alaska Natives in all parts of the 32 reservation states served by IHS (total deaths in reservation states 1986–1988 = 21,943.

more disrupted communities studied are not representative of Indian communities in general. In the studies done among Indian populations where culture and society are more intact, FAS rates are much lower. It is no more accurate to project an FAS rate from one or two disrupted, alcohol-abusing communities onto all Indians than it would be to project the rate from an urban, skid row census tract to all of the U.S. population.

In general, the scientific literature points out that FAS is an "equal opportunity" birth defect and can affect any ethnic group where there are sufficient levels of maternal drinking. FAS, to a great degree, depends on the quantity, frequency, and timing of maternal drinking. In many tribes, there are more alcohol-abstaining women than in the general U.S. population. This obviously protects a substantial portion of Indian children from FAS and lowers levels of prenatal alcohol damage. In almost every population ever studied, a very small number of women produce all of the FAS children. This is very true in Indian epidemiologic studies of other problems as well.

Rates						Number		
55–64 Ind.	U.S.	Ratio	65–74 Ind.	U.S.	Ratio	Total Deaths (all ages)	x Est% alcohol-involved	Total alcohol-involved (all ages)
52.2	27.7	2.4	65.6	24.6	2.7	1452	(65%)	944
82.3	30.3	2.7	113.0	42.6	2.7	1139	(25%)	285
12.2	26.6	0.5	16.7	34.8	0.5	546	(75%)	410
13.0	8.8	1.5	12.6	6.2	2.0	521	(80%)	417
95.4	33.1	2.9	79.5	27.0	2.9	649	(100%)	649
18.3	10.2	1.8	17.7	13.7	1.3	577	(65%)	375
22.8	10.6	2.2	43.7	21.1	2.1	358	(25%)	90
4.6	7.7	0.6	2.4	7.2	0.3	107	(75%)	80
4.6	2.5	1.8	1.2	2.8	0.4	132	(80%)	106
50.2	9.4	5.3	20.1	7.3	2.8	300	(100%)	300

FAS prevention, however, has been cited as an extremely promising area for American Indians.[62] In fact, it is apparent that Indians today are very aware of FAS as a problem, and a large number of established FAS initiatives and prevention programs are underway in Indian communities.

CAN PREVENTION PROGRAMS DESIGNED FOR ONE TRIBE BE ADJUSTED AND APPLIED TO OTHERS?

In spite of the unique social and cultural nature of each tribe, prevention and intervention programs designed for one tribe can be used in others. It has often been implied that each tribal community is so distinctive that programs have limited or no applicability across tribal settings. But a detailed knowledge of the particular history, culture, and current epidemiological features of alcohol abuse in a community will allow for fine tuning and adaptation to other, somewhat similar tribes and communities.[63]

Knowing the demographic and epidemiologic features (age; sex ratio; cultural, social, and economic indicators; mortality; morbidity; fertility; and gender-specific drinking patterns) of a community will facilitate the design and implementation of successful programs of prevention and treatment. The problem with some efforts in the past was that local data were not utilized or available, and relevant studies were not always done. Further, when epidemiological understandings are very general or poor and programs are based on myth, failure is more likely. Facts such as those presented in this paper are the building blocks of prevention and intervention. Improvement in the alcohol-abuse dilemma of Indian communities will require a detailed and specific understanding of the characteristics and epidemiology of the population. Indian health professionals have a responsibility to seek out such data and apply them carefully and sensitively.

CONCLUSION

Many of the myths and common understandings about alcohol use among American Indians are gross oversimplifications. As Benjamin Franklin once stated, "Half the truth is often a great lie."[64] If they are to succeed, programs of prevention and intervention must not be built on common mythical understandings but on empirical fact. Unfortunately, facts and detailed truths are not sought or believed frequently enough.

"The truth is sometimes a poor competitor in the market place of ideas—complicated, unsatisfying, full of dilemmas, [and] always vulnerable to misinterpretation and abuse."[65] As this paper has demonstrated, the truth about Indian drinking is indeed complicated and quite different from the myths. But the insights and explanations that emerge from seeking the facts are those that will help create meaningful improvement.

Acknowledgments

The author wishes to acknowledge the clerical support provided by ADAMHA grant T34-MH19101. Special thanks to Virginia Rood and Phyllis Trujillo for their support on this project.

Notes

1. Patricia D. Mail and David R. McDonald, *Tulapai to Tokay* (New Haven, CT: HRAF Press, 1980).

2. Joseph Westermeyer, "The Drunken Indian Stereotype: Myths and Realities," *Psychiatry Annual* 41(1974): 29–36; Joy Leland, *Firewater Myths* (New Brunswick, NJ: Rutgers Center of Alcohol Studies, 1976).

3. Indian Health Service (IHS), *Trends in Indian Health* (Rockville, MD: U.S. Dept. of Health and Human Services, 1991); IHS, *Regional Differences in Indian Health* (Rockville, MD: U.S. Dept. of Health and Human Services, 1991).

4. Philip A. May, "Alcohol Policy Considerations for Indian Reservations and Border-town Communities," *American Indian and Alaska Native Mental Health Research* 4:3 (in press). May, "The Prevention of Alcohol and Other Substance Abuse among American Indians: A Review and Analysis of the Literature," NIAAA Monograph Series (in press).

5. May, "Alcohol Abuse and Alcoholism among American Indians: An Overview," *Alcoholism in Minority Populations,* ed. Thomas D. Watts and Roosevelt Wright (Springfield, IL: Charles C. Thomas, 1989), 95–119.

6. Ibid. See also May, "Alcohol Policy Considerations," and May, "Prevention of Alcohol and Other Substance Abuse."

7. Institute of Medicine, *Broadening the Base of Treatment for Alcohol Problems* (Washington, DC: National Academy Press, 1990).

8. Philip A. May and Matthew B. Smith, "Some Navajo Indian Opinions about Alcohol Abuse and Prohibition: A Survey and Recommendations for Policy," *Journal of Studies on Alcohol* 49 (1988): 324–34.

9. D. Fenna et al., "Ethanol Metabolism in Various Racial Groups," *Canadian Medical Association Journal* 105 (1971): 472–75.

10. Chester S. Leiber, "Metabolism of Ethanol and Alcoholism: Racial and Acquired Factors," *Annals of Internal Medicine* 76 (1972): 326–27; Lynn Bennion and Ting K. Li, "Alcohol Metabolism in American Indians and Whites," *New England Journal of Medicine* 284 (1976): 9–13.

11. Ibid.; John J. Farris and Ben M. Jones, "Ethanol Metabolism and Memory Impairment in American Indian and White Women Social Drinkers," *Journal of Studies on Alcohol* 39 (1978): 1975–78; Farris and Jones, "Ethanol Metabolism in Male American Indians and Whites," *Alcoholism: Clinical and Experimental Research* 2:1 (1978): 77–81; Arthur R. Zeiner, Alfonso Paredes, and Lawrence Cowden, "Physiologic Responses to Ethanol among the Tarahumara Indians," *Annals of the New York Academy of Sciences* 273 (1976): 151–58; James M. Schaefer, "Firewater Myths Revisited," *Journal of Studies on Alcohol* 9 (1981): 99–117.

12. T. Edward Reed et al., "Alcohol and Acetaldehyde Metabolism in Caucasians, Chinese and Americans," *Canadian Medical Association Journal* 115 (1976): 851–58.

13. Bennion and Li, "Alcohol Metabolism in American Indians and Whites"; Douglas K. Rex et al., "Alcohol and Aldehyde Dehydrogenase Isoenzymes in North American Indians," *Alcoholism: Clinical and Experimental Research* 9:2 (1985): 147–52.

14. Peter H. Wolff, "Vasomotor Sensitivity to Alcohol in Diverse Mongoloid Populations," *American Journal of Human Genetics* 25 (1973): 193–99. T. Edward Reed, "Ethnic Differences in Alcohol Use, Abuse and Sensitivity: A Review with Genetic Interpretation," *Social Biology* 32:3–4 (1985): 195–209.

15. Bennion and Li, "Alcohol Metabolism in American Indians and Whites."

16. Richard D. Curley, "Drinking Patterns of the Mescalero Apache," *Quarterly Journal of Studies on Alcohol* 28:1 (1967): 116–31; Theodore D. Graves, "Drinking and Drunkenness among Urban Indians," *The American Indian in Urban Society,* ed. Jack Waddell and O. M. Watson (Boston: Little Brown and Company, 1971), 275–311; John J. Honigmann and Irma Honigmann, "Drinking in an Indian-White Community," *Quarterly Journal of Studies on Alcohol* 5:4 (1945): 575; Honigmann and Honigmann, "How Baffin Island Eskimos Have Learned to Use Alcohol," *Social Forces* 44:1 (1965): 73–82; Jerrold E. Levy and Steven J. Kunitz, *Indian Drinking and Anglo American Theories* (New York: Wiley Interscience, 1974); Nancy O. Lurie, "The World's Oldest Ongoing Protest Demonstration: North American Indian Drinking Patterns," *Pacific History Review* 40:3 (1971): 311–22; Gerald Mohatt, "The Sacred Water: The Quest for Personal Power

through Drinking among the Teton Sioux," *The Drinking Man,* ed. David C. McClelland et al. (New York: Free Press, 1972), 261–75; May, "Explanations of Native American Drinking," *Plains Anthropologist* 22:77 (1977): 223–32.

17. IHS, *Trends in Indian Health.*

18. Enis Baris and Raynold Pineault, "A Critical Appraisal of the Navajo Health Care System," *International Journal of Health Planning and Management* 5 (1990): 187–99. David W. Broudy and Philip A. May, "Demographic and Epidemiologic Transition among the Navajo Indians," *Social Biology* 30 (1983): 1–16.

19. U.S. Bureau of Census, *Statistical Abstract of the United States: 1990* (Washington DC: U.S. Government Printing Office, 1990).

20. Broudy and May, "Demographic and Epidemiologic Transition"; Steven J. Kunitz, *Disease Change and the Role of Medicine* (Berkeley, CA: University of California Press, 1985).

21. Julian Waller, R. Curran, and F. Noyes, "Traffic Deaths: A Preliminary Study of Urban and Rural Fatalities in California," *California Medicine* 101 (1964): 172–276.

22. Philip A. May and Phillip S. Katz, *Motor Vehicle Accidents on the Navajo Reservation, 1973–1975: Health Planning Summary* (Window Rock, AZ: Navajo Health Authority, 1979); May, "Motor Vehicle Crashes and Alcohol among American Indians and Alaska Natives," in U.S. Surgeon General, *The Surgeon General's Workshop on Drunk Driving: Background Papers* (Washington DC: U.S. Department of Health and Human Services, 1989): 207–23.

23. Edward P. Dozier, "Problem Drinking among American Indians: The Role of Sociocultural Deprivation," *Quarterly Journal on Studies on Alcohol* 17 (1966): 72–87.

24. May, "Alcohol Legalization and Native Americans: A Sociological Inquiry" (Ph.D. dissertation, University of Montana, 1976); May, "Alcohol Beverage Control: A Survey of Tribal Alcohol Statutes," *American Indian Law Review* 5 (1977): 217–28.

25. Dozier, "Problem Drinking among American Indians"; O. C. Stewart, "Questions Regarding American Indian Criminality," *Human Organization* 23:1 (1964): 64–76.

26. May, "Alcohol Legalization and Native Americans"; May, "Alcohol Policy Considerations."

27. Levy and Kunitz, *Indian Drinking and Anglo American Theories;* Carolyn B. Liban and Reginald G. Smart, "Drinking and Drug Use among Ontario Indian Students," *Drug Alcohol Dependency* 9 (1982): 161–71.

28. May and Katz, *Motor Vehicle Accidents on the Navajo Reservation.*

29. May, "Substance Abuse and American Indians: Prevalence and Susceptibility," *International Journal on Addictions* 17 (1982): 1185–1209.

30. Ibid. See also May, "Alcohol Abuse and Alcoholism among American Indians."

31. Levy and Kunitz, *Indian Drinking and Anglo American Theories;* May and Smith, "Some Navajo Indian Opinions about Alcohol Abuse."

32. James O. Whittaker, "Alcohol and the Standing Rock Sioux Tribe," *Quarterly Journal of Studies on Alcohol* 23 (1962): 468–79; James O. Whittaker, "Alcohol and the Standing Rock Sioux Tribe: A Twenty-year Follow-up Study," *Journal of Studies on Alcohol* 43 (1982): 191–200.

33. Richard Jessor et al., *Society, Personality and Deviant Behavior: A Study of Tri-ethnic Community* (New York: Holt, Rinehart and Winston, 1968); Lyle Longclaws et al., "Alcohol and Drug Use among the Brokenhead Ojibwa," *Journal of Studies on Alcohol* 41 (1980): 21–36.

34. Eugene R. Oetting and Fred Beauvais, "Epidemiology and Correlates of Alcohol Use among Indian Adolescents Living on Reservations," in *Alcohol Use among U.S. Eth-*

nic Minorities, NIAAA Research Monograph no. 18 (Rockville, MD: U.S. Public Health Service, 1990), 239–67; Fred Beauvais, "An Integrated Model for Prevention and Treatment of Drug Abuse among American Indian Youth"; "Advances in Alcohol and Substance Abuse" (in press).

35. Levy and Kunitz, *Indian Drinking and Anglo American Theories;* Whittaker, "Alcohol and the Standing Rock Sioux Tribe: A Twenty-year Follow-up Study."

36. May, "Alcohol Abuse and Alcoholism among American Indians."

37. Frances N. Ferguson, "Navaho Drinking: Some Tentative Hypotheses," *Human Organization* 27 (1968): 159–67; Levy and Kunitz, *Indian Drinking and Anglo American Theories;* Thomas Beltrame and D.V. McQueen, "Urban and Rural Drinking Patterns: The Special Case of the Lumbee," *The International Journal of the Addictions* 14:4 (1979): 533–48. Liban and Smart, "Drinking and Drug Use among Ontario Indian Students"; Joseph J. Westermeyer, "Options Regarding Alcohol Use among the Chippewa," *American Journal of Orthopsychiatry* 42 (1972): 398–403.

38. Oetting and Beauvais, "Epidemiology and Correlates of Alcohol Use among Indian Adolescents"; Eugene R. Oetting, Fred Beauvais, and Ruth W. Edwards, "Alcohol and Indian Youth: Social and Psychological Correlates and Prevention," *Journal of Drug Issues* 18 (1988): 87–101; Oetting et al., "Indian and Anglo Adolescent Alcohol Use and Emotional Distress: Path Models," *American Journal of Drug and Alcohol Abuse* 15:2 (1989): 153–72.

39. Ferguson, "Navaho Drinking: Some Tentative Hypotheses."

40. Jacqueline Bergdahl, "Fatal Automobile Crashes on and Surrounding the New Mexico Portion of the Navajo Reservation" (M.A. thesis, University of New Mexico, 1991).

41. May, "Alcohol Policy Considerations"; May, "Prevention of Alcohol and Other Abuse."

42. Levy and Kunitz, *Indian Drinking and Anglo American Theories;* Margaret M. Gallaher et al., "Pedestrian and Hypothermia Deaths among Native Americans in New Mexico," *JAMA* 267:10 (1992): 1345–48.

43. Ferguson, "Navaho Drinking: Some Tentative Hypotheses"; Ferguson, "A Treatment Program for Navajo Alcoholics: Quantity," *Journal of Studies on Alcohol* 31:4 (1970): 898–919.

44. May, "Alcohol Legalization and Native Americans."

45. May, "Mental Health and Alcohol Abuse Indicators in the Albuquerque Area of the Indian Health Service: An Exploratory Chart Review," *American Indian and Alaska Native Mental Health Research* 2:1 (1988): 31–44.

46. Ibid.

47. Paul E. Guerin, "Alcohol Related Traffic Fatalities in New Mexico" (M.A. thesis, University of New Mexico, 1991).

48. Ibid.

49. Carol C. Lujan et al., "Profile of Abused and Neglected Indian Children in the Southwest," *Child Abuse and Neglect* 13:4 (1989): 449–61.

50. Lemyra C. DeBruyn, Carol C. Lujan, and Philip A. May, "A Comparative Study of Abused and Neglected American Indian Children in the Southwest," "Social Science and Medicine" (in press).

51. IHS, *Trends in Indian Health;* IHS, *Regional Differences in Indian Health;* May, "Prevention of Alcohol and Other Substance Abuse."

52. May, "Prevention of Alcohol and Other Substance Abuse."

53. May, "Alcohol Abuse and Alcoholism among American Indians"; Kathleen B.

Masis and Philip A. May, "A Comprehensive Local Program for the Prevention of Fetal Alcohol Syndrome," *Public Health Reports* 106:5 (1991): 484–89.

54. Geoffry C. Robinson, Julianne L. Conry, and Robert F. Conry, "Clinical Profile and Prevalence of Fetal Alcohol Syndrome in an Isolated Community in British Columbia," *Canadian Medical Association Journal* 137 (1987): 203–207. Kawado O. Asante and Joyce Nelms-Matzke, "Survey of Children with Chronic Handicaps and Fetal Alcohol Syndrome in the Yukon and Northwest B.C." (Ottawa: National Native Advisory Council on Alcohol and Drug Abuse, Health and Welfare Canada, unpublished report, 1985).

55. Gilbert F. Chavez, José F. Cordero, and José E. Becerra, "Leading Major Congenital Malformations among Minority Groups in the U.S. 1981–86," *MMWR* 37:55-3 (1988): 17–24.

56. Philip A. May and Karen J. Hymbaugh, "A Pilot Project on Fetal Alcohol Syndrome among American Indians," *Alcohol Health Research World* 7:2 (1983): 3–9.

57. Philip A. May et al. "Epidemiology of FAS among Southwestern Indians," *Social Biology* 30:4 (1983): 374–87.

58. Chavez, Cordero, and Becerra, "Leading Major Congenital Malformations."

59. Deborah L. Bray and Percy D. Anderson, "Appraisal of the Epidemiology of Fetal Alcohol Syndrome among Canadian Native Peoples," *Canadian Journal of Public Health* 80 (1989): 42–45.

60. Chavez, Cordero, and Becerra, "Leading Major Congenital Malformations."

61. Robinson et al., "Clinical Profile and Prevalence of Fetal Alcohol Syndrome."

62. May and Hymbaugh, "A Pilot Project on FAS among American Indians"; Philip A. May and Karen J. Hymbaugh, "A Macro-Level Fetal Alcohol Syndrome Prevention Program for Native Americans and Alaska Natives: Description and Evaluation," *Journal of Studies on Alcohol* 50:6 (1989): 508–18; Kate J. Plaisier, "Fetal Alcohol Syndrome Prevention in American Indian Communities of Michigan's Upper Peninsula," *American Indian and Alaska Native Mental Health Research* 3:1 (1989): 16–33; Kawado O. Asante and Geoffry C. Robinson, "Pregnancy Outreach Program in British Columbia: The Prevention of Alcohol-Related Birth Defects," *Canadian Journal of Public Health* 81:1 (1990): 76–77; Masis and May, "A Comprehensive Local Program for Prevention of FAS."

63. May, "Alcohol and Drug Misuse Prevention Programs for American Indians: Needs and Opportunities," *Journal of Studies on Alcohol* 47:3 (1986): 187–95.

64. Quoted in Gordon Caruth and Eugene Ehrlich, *The Harper Book of American Quotations* (New York: Harper and Row, 1988), 559.

65. George F. Kennan quoted in ibid., 559–60.

12

Tobacco, Culture, and Health among American Indians: A Historical Review

Christina M. Pego, Robert F. Hill, Glenn W. Solomon,
Robert M. Chisholm, and Suzanne E. Ivey

INTRODUCTION

IN THE SUMMER AND EARLY FALL of 1992, two of the authors (Hill and Solomon) attended meetings (as evaluators) of the Cherokee Nation's Substance Abuse Prevention Project (CSAP) in the five-county area closest to the tribal complex near Tahlequah in northeastern Oklahoma. The Cherokee CSAP project is supported by a five-year planning grant from the U.S. Center for Substance Abuse Prevention. Based on participant observations at meetings, self-report surveys at local high schools, and self-report survey questionnaires and interviews with adult and youth CSAP coalition members from local communities, the authors determined that tobacco has a distinctive place in the mix of health-harming substances currently used by the Cherokee people. In an evaluative report to the CSAP project in late 1992, the authors (Hill and Solomon) wrote the following:

> As shown in the baseline surveys and interviews, tobacco would appear
> to be the distinguishing drug preferred by Indian-American youth in the
> high schools, as well as by youth in the Cherokee Coalition. . . . Cigarette
> smoking is also common on the part of adult members of the coalition,
> as well as among outside [national] presenters brought in to be role mod-
> els for substance abuse prevention. By contrast, the substance of almost
> exclusive focus in the [CSAP] Project is alcohol.[1]

What is there about tobacco that gives it an apparent "hands-off" exemption in substance abuse prevention programs for American Indians? Are American Indian populations more subject to its use prevalence and harmful effects? Why has tobacco not been recognized as a powerful source of American Indian disease and death, on a par with alcohol and greatly eclipsing other drug problems in this population?

Christina Pego, Chippewa, is an undergraduate student at Dartmouth College in Hanover, New Hampshire; Robert Hill is a professor of pediatrics and Glenn Solomon, Cherokee, is an assistant professor of research, Department of Pediatrics, both at the University of Oklahoma Health Sciences Center, Oklahoma City; Robert Chisholm, Delaware, is a medical student at the University of Oklahoma, Oklahoma City; and Suzanne Ivey, Cherokee, is an undergraduate student at the University of Oklahoma, Norman.

TOBACCO USE AND CONTEMPORARY AMERICAN INDIANS

One of the greatest general health threats that the United States population currently faces is tobacco use. With long-term use, tobacco has been specifically associated with conditions such as cardiovascular disease; lung cancer; chronic obstructive pulmonary disease; cancers of the larynx, bronchus, trachea, and pancreas; as well as fetal and infant morbidity and mortality. Recent studies suggest that substantial dangers are also associated with "secondhand" tobacco smoke, resulting in considerable cost to both families and the national health care system. Smoking, by itself, is responsible for approximately 419,000 U.S. deaths each year.[2] Lung cancer rates continue to rise for both men and women and have surpassed the rates of death caused by other common forms of cancer, including prostate and breast cancer.[3]

Data from the general population indicate that, although smoking is prevalent among all ethnic groups, American Indian rates are consistently the highest.[4] Table 1 shows contemporary reported prevalence rates of smoking among a variety of North American Indian population groupings.[5] These are compared with non-Indian rates in almost half of the listings. Most of the reports summarized in table 1 are based on data collected during the last decade. The data suggest that smoking prevalence rates are especially high among American Indian populations in the northwestern regions of the United States and Canada; they are especially high in reservation areas, where traditional institutions, values, and sentiments are also most prevalent. Recent reports of prevalence rates for smokeless tobacco use (not shown in table 1) reflect a similar epidemiologic pattern; i.e., the highest rates are among American Indians in the Northwest or on reservations.[6] Surprisingly, American Indian prevalence rates are also substantially higher than white rates among those with a college education, according to one listing—a large, national, random telephone survey conducted by the U.S. Centers for Disease Control. This contrasts with substantial research over the years, which has shown a higher prevalence of use associated with lower educated whites.[7]

The significantly higher rates of tobacco use among contemporary American Indians, especially in the more rural, remote, culturally traditional areas, and even among the best educated, suggest that ethnohistorical factors may play some part. Is it possible that tobacco distribution and use patterns in precontact and colonial North America may somehow inform or help explain contemporary prevalence rates, with their long-term, ominous health implications? A common stereotype of this earlier historical period is the bronze-skinned Indian chief, smoking a long-stemmed Indian pipe for pleasure or peacemaking, and generously passing along this wonderful practice to naive, curious, and trusting Europeans. A more cynical image might be that of the sly, smiling cigar store Indian, gracing the entrance of tobacco shops the world over, stolidly foisting "the Indian's revenge" on foolish Europeans. Both these images are vivid, colorful, and appealing, albeit to different groups (based on their ethnic background or political persuasion). More importantly, neither of these images reflects historical reality.

Population Description	Sample Size	Table 1 Percentage Using (By Group)	Associations with Use	Source/Note
U.S. National: Probability sample of adults	300,500	44.5 (Indian men)[a] 26.6 (Indian women) 25.7 ("white" men)	Indians smoked fewer cigarettes per day. Rates were directly related to social class for Indians inversely related for whites.	4
U.S. National: High school seniors, 1976–89	17,000	36.8 (Indian men)[a]	Indian students had highest rate among all ethnic groups.	5 (Bach.)
U.S. National: Indian Health Service reservation areas: Grades 7–12	13,354	20.5 (Alaska area)[b] 10.6 (Other areas)	Students with "below average" grades had highest use rates.	5
U.S. National Youth Survey: 1988–90	102,194	80.0 (reservation 12th graders)[a] 74.0 (reservation 8th graders)	Non-reservation Indian rates were 10% lower. "White" rates were 50% lower.	5 (Blum)
Northwest Territories of Canada: Adults	20,000	70.0 (Inuit)[a] 60.0 (status Indian) 40.0 ("white") 30.0 (all Canada)	Inuit women have the highest rate of lung cancer ever recorded.	5 (Beauv.)
Canadian Artic Youth: Ages 15–19	230	75.0 (Inuit)[a] 64.0 (Dene/Métis) 43.0 (Non-Indian)	None listed.	5 (Millar)
Western U.S.: Blackfeet Reservation of Montana: Adults	463	34.0 (men)[a] 50.0 (women)	None listed.	5 (Goldberg)
North Central U.S.: 7th Graders	4,319	33.0 (Indian)	None listed.	5 (Murray)
Southwest U.S. and U.S. Plains Area: Indian Adults	805	18.1 (S.W. men)[a] 14.7 (S.W. women) 48.4 (Plains men) 57.3 (Plains women)	None listed.	5 (Sugar.)
South Central U.S.: Indian youth	226	54.0 (Navajo)[a]	None listed.	5 (Wolfe)
South Central U.S.: Cherokee tribal area: Youth grades 9–12	974	38.1 (Indian)[a] 25.8 ("whites")	Indian users had lower expectations for college, lower school, religious, and family involvement, and highest rates of alcohol and marijuana use.	5 (Sol.)
South Central Cherokee Nations Industries: Adult sample (mostly women).	144	37.8 (Indian)[a]	None listed.	5 (Hill)

[a] Current use   [b] Daily use

ACQUISITION OF HISTORICAL INFORMATION

Historical information on American Indians and tobacco was acquired through systematic searches of various libraries' literature holdings. Searches were done using computerized bibliographical retrieval systems: Native American Research Information Systems, Medline, Sociological Abstracts, Health, CINAHL, and PSYCINFO. Most work was done in the Native American collection of Bird Library of the University of Oklahoma Health Sciences Center. The University of Oklahoma's Bizzell Library and Western History Collection were also used. John Berry, a reference specialist with the U.S. Food and Drug Administration, Washington, D.C., and now a faculty member at Oklahoma State University in Stillwater, completed additional literature searches and secured access to rare manuscripts. This research made it clear that the earliest history of tobacco use is relatively scarce. More information is available for the period after European traders penetrated the North American heartland.

TOBACCO USE IN HISTORICAL AMERICAN INDIAN CULTURES

The Introduction of Tobacco into European Culture

In table 2, we present a summary of the historical period of American Indian tobacco usage. The first European contact with the custom of tobacco use seems to have come with the first European voyage to the New World.[8] It is said that Columbus encountered tobacco on his first voyage to San Salvador, where his men noted Natives smoking tobacco in the form of cigars. This was the first time any European had seen the plant used for such a purpose. (Appropriately, the word *tobacco* is a Spanish derivation of the Arawak term for cigar.)[9] It was not specified in what context the men saw this tobacco-smoking event, whether it was during ceremonial use and, if so, what kind of ceremony. Smoking was, however, "thoroughly established throughout eastern North and South America at the time of European discovery; and the early explorers, from Columbus on, speak of it as a strange and novel practice which they often find hard to describe."[10] Columbus's men gradually became aware of the social and medical motives behind smoking and of the role that tobacco played in myths and festivals, including pipe ceremonialism. Eventually, they became aware of other variants of tobacco use, including chewing, drinking, licking, snuffing, and use in enemas.[11]

Tobacco was brought to Europe during the early sixteenth century, although it did not receive much attention there until nearly half a century later.[12] When it finally did become popular during the middle of the sixteenth century, it was hailed as a "divine sent remedy" that was capable of curing practically every human ailment. It was prescribed as a treatment for nearly every malaise that affected Europeans. In its initial popularity, the medicinal uses of tobacco were much more well known than the pleasurable ones.[13] A full

Table 2
Summary of Tobacco Use among Indians in the New World

Idea or Evidence	Source/Note
Tobacco use in all its many forms (smoking, chewing, sniffing, drinking, etc.) originated in the New World and was widespread among the hundreds of Native tribal groupings in both North and South America.	14
Some tribes used tobacco strictly ceremonially before European contact; others used no tobacco before European contact.	8, 14, 50
During the precontact period, tobacco may have been smoked less frequently by American Indians than it is today and also less frequently than among Europeans during the colonial period and the years to follow.	10, 14, 50, 68
Pipe smoking (calumet ceremonialism), though a product of American Indian culture, was propogated by French explorers, who may have introduced it to some tribes who were not aware of its existence.	8, 20
Tobacco was often used in ceremonies in ways other than smoking. Smoking tobacco was often not the primary feature of the ceremonies in which it was observed.	8, 14, 20
Tobacco, specifically its active component nicotine, was used medically and in medical ceremonies. It was often used as an analgesic and as treatment for ailments such as asthma, rheumatism, convulsions, intestinal disorders, childbirth pains, and coughs. It was applied to snake and insect bites and was used to treat open wounds because of its presumed antiseptic qualities.	8, 15, 36
The tobacco that spread to Europe and the rest of the world, *Nicotiana tabacum*, originated in South America and was noted for its richer taste and higher potency (i.e., the ability to produce hallucinations and supernatural visions).	15
Kinnikinnik, a mixture of *N. rustica*, bark, and herbs, was often smoked by American Indians rather than pure tobacco because of its milder taste.	8, 20
Tobacco was often used in agricultural ceremonies. There were many rituals concerning its cultivation when it was grown for sacred purposes.	8, 10, 14
Tobacco was viewed as a means of communication with the gods. Tobacco smoke was an important visual symbol of contact with the supernatural world.	8, 14
The harmful effects of tobacco smoking were recognized by some early American Indians.	8
There were gender differences in treatment of tobacco, including the methods for its cultivation. Women generally were not allowed to participate in its cultivation, though they were responsible for other crops.	8, 10
Tobacco was often used socially as a peace offering or to bind agreements.	8, 14

century passed before its recreational use spread throughout the European continent.[14]

Tobacco Species and Location

There are approximately sixty species of tobacco within the genus *Nicotiana*. Among these, only *Nicotiana rustica* and *Nicotiana tabacum* are or ever were in widespread human use.[15] Other species had limited use, including *N. multivalvis*, *N. quadrivalvis*, and *N. bigelovvi* in Washington and Oregon, along the Missouri River, and in California, respectively.[16]

In times prior to European contact, the most commonly used species of tobacco was *N. rustica*. It was used primarily by American Indians in the eastern United States and throughout the Great Plains. *N. tabacum* is the species that was popularly cultivated for commercial use by Europeans.[17] It has been said that *N. tabacum* was initially too strong for North American Indians and that they preferred *N. rustica*.[18] According to an observer of the Mandan in 1843,

> The tobacco of the Whites, unmixed, is too strong for the Indians,
> because [the whites] draw smoke into their lungs; hence [the Indians] do
> not willingly smoke cigars.[19]

Often Native peoples mixed tobacco with other substances such as bark, leaves, herbs, or oil to form a milder substance called *kinnikinnik*, which was smoked ceremonially.[20]

Acquisition and Cultivation

It is difficult to determine by what method American Indians initially came into possession of tobacco. Most researchers conclude that precontact tobacco use originated among the Native peoples of South America, then spread through central America and, later, North America, except for the Arctic, parts of the sub-Arctic, and parts of the Columbian Plateau.[21] Some forms of tobacco grew wild, and others were cultivated. According to Driver,[22] precontact North American Indians on the West Coast gathered tobacco wild for the most part. On the East Coast and the central Plains, they cultivated it for use. As might be expected, a group of intermediate tribes obtained their tobacco through inter-aboriginal trade.

By the end of the sixteenth century, the European penetration of North America had picked up momentum from all directions—and with it a new era of tobacco distribution and use. Tobacco, the "gift" of American Indians to the rest of the world, now came back to them in a new much more potent, abundant form. Most of this reverse diffusion of tobacco came by way of the French fur trade.

Table 3
Diffusion of "Trade Tobacco"
to Selected North American Tribes,
1603–1743

Tribe	Area	Year	Source*
Abnaki	Maine	1608	Parkman
Huron, Wyandotte	New York, Ontario	1608	Goodman
Pequot	New England	1609	Josephy
Kickapoo	Wisconsin	1634	Gibson
Cheyenne	Minnesota	1650	Moore
Salish Confederacy	Oregon and Washington	1656	Josephy
Chickasaw, Choctaw, Osage	Louisiana / Mississippi River	1659	Gibson
Kansa, Ponca, Osage, Omaha, Quapaw	Illinois Confederacy	1680	Unrau
Caddoan et al.	Texas (52 tribes)	1685	Josephy
Taos and Picuris Pueblos	New Mexico	1695	Unrau
Pawnee	Kansas	< 1700	Unrau
Comanche et al.	Louisiana, Texas, Oklahoma	1719	Josephy
Mandan, Cree, Sioux et al.	Montana and Dakotas	1724–43	Sanders
Sauk and Fox, Menominee, Ojibwa	Wisconsin	1731	Gibson

* Note 23

Table 3 shows the approximate chronology of the arrival of French "trade tobacco" to selected American Indian tribes from east to west.[23] The trade tobacco was undoubtedly the stronger variety, *N. tabacum*, imported from commercial fields in Bahia, Brazil.[24] It is interesting to note that the largest part of this tobacco-for-furs trade in the North American heartland encompassed the area where American Indian tribes had, before contact, obtained their aboriginal tobacco from cultivation or intertribal trade.[25] The new dependence on manufactured trade goods—corn, cornmeal, cloth, knives, axes, kettles, awls, beads, and brandy (known as "Ononthio's milk" after the Huron word for the king of France)—established early the situational climate for a dual or parallel tobacco classification system. Aboriginal tobacco was in small supply and was sacred. Trade tobacco was more plentiful in exchange for furs, but it belonged symbolically in the secular, European realm, like Ononthio's milk.

There were several interesting differences in the way aboriginal (*N. rustica*) tobacco was cultivated compared to other nonfood crops—differences that testify to its distinctive, sacred status. In some tribes, women were not allowed to cultivate tobacco.[26] Such a difference suggests a separate cultural meaning for tobacco, since women took responsibility for or shared in the working of most other crops, at least in the eastern half of the continent.[27] Among the Plains tribes, there were tobacco societies. Initiation into their ranks was a prerequisite for the right to sow tobacco.[28] Duties as initiates included the sweat lodge ritual, the selection of medicine, and the planting of sacred tobacco, all of which were executed with the greatest symbolism and care. The Seneca took a different, more naturalistic, approach to its cultivation. They scattered the seeds on the ground and had a religious prohibition against its cultivation.[29]

Historic Ceremonial and Medicinal Use

Tobacco was often used by shamans and in agricultural rites.[30] It was used in the harvesting of crops, to bless the harvest. Such a ceremony linked tobacco and the fertility of the land, a strong psychological bond made still stronger by tobacco-induced altered states of consciousness and supernatural visions.[31] The rising smoke of the tobacco was regarded as a method by which communication with the gods/creator might be facilitated. The Iroquois believed that the smoke carried their petitions to the Great Spirit. The Delaware sacrificed tobacco to ensure success in the hunt. The Crow worshiped the sun, the moon, and tobacco. It was the only thing cultivated to "ensure the continued welfare of the people."[32] Among the Ojibwa/Chippewa, tobacco was placed on a rock to alert the spirit to ward off storms.[33] As stereotypes suggest, tobacco was commonly used to bind agreements between tribes, and it often accompanied invitations to individuals or families. Tobacco was also given as payment to a shaman, obligating him to fulfill the requests of his client.[34]

There was a great deal of ceremony and spirituality involved in the traditional use of tobacco. "In Pawnee ceremonies the pipe was always tamped with an arrow captured from the enemy. It was for-bidden to pack it with the fingers, as the gods might think that the man who did so offered himself with the tobacco and take his life."[35] This example illustrates what power tobacco was believed to have had and its overall, pervasive importance within aboriginal culture.

In addition to its ceremonial uses, tobacco was traditionally employed medicinally by many different tribes. Accounts from tribes from different areas of the country describe tobacco being used in very similar, if not identical, ceremonies. It served as an analgesic and a treatment for ear aches. It was chewed as a remedy for toothaches.[36] Open wounds and the bites of insects or snakes were treated with tobacco because of its presumed antiseptic properties.[37] The Winnebago and the Seminole, along with other tribes, scattered tobacco while repeating prayers to exorcise spirits or ward off the evil influences that caused disease.[38] One Native practice was to blow tobacco smoke into the ear to kill the "Woodland insect" that was believed to cause insanity by drying up the brain.[39] Tobacco was also heralded as a remedy by some for asthma, rheumatism, chills, fevers, intestinal disorders, childbirth pains, and headaches. Scholars note that some reported medical uses may be a result of more recent European uses of tobacco (i.e., reverse diffusion), rather than original American Indian practices. Vogel, author of *American Indian Medicine*, states, "Reports of the therapeutic uses of tobacco by American Indians in the early period are rather sparse compared to the numerous applications of the plant by whites. . . . The more frequent reports of curative uses of tobacco in a late period are subject to the suspicion that they may be due to the example of the whites."[40] It also seems possible that some early healing ceremonies that employed tobacco were not shown to outsiders.

Calumet Ceremonialism

Study of the calumet, an elaborately decorated clay shaft to which a pipe bowl might be attached, seems to be one of the better ways to assess traditional tobacco use. It was different from other pipes in that the calumet was the source of great ceremonialism and was held to be sacred.[41] The earliest Europeans to come into contact with the calumet were the first French explorers in the northern Mississippi Valley.[42] Calumet ceremonialism was probably established in this region, as well as in the Great Lakes region, well before the Europeans reached the area.[43] Author Ian Brown poses the question, "Did such ceremonialism originate in this area and spread with French exploration, or did it exist prehistorically as well?" He states that the calumet (like trade tobacco) was probably spread by the French, because the ceremony "provided balance in a rapidly changing world." The calumet was said to have had the potential to make friends out of mortal enemies and to have provided for peaceful interactions between strangers. Brown suggests that some native groups were oblivious to the existence of the calumet; only through the European practice did they become aware of smoking and calumet ceremonialism.[44]

There seems to be some evidence to indicate that clay pipe-smoking developed with calumet ceremonialism but was not always featured in it. "The earliest renditions of the ceremony are characterized by dancing and much waving of the wands, but smoking, curiously, is not a prime feature in these accounts." With respect to the pipe of the Eastern Woodlands, it is said that smoking may have been important only for the last one thousand years, a relatively recent development but still well before European colonization.[45] The calumet apparently has a history independent of the pipe, in its ceremonial uses.[46] Its significance was once independent of its uses in tobacco consumption and ceremonialism. The pipe bowl, however, eventually achieved its fame as the choice method for smoking tobacco in both the sacred and the secular realms. The union of calumet ceremonialism and tobacco proved to be a very powerful combination for Europeans and American Indians alike.[47]

Europeans may not have understood the ceremonial acts they witnessed and thus may have undermined or underestimated the significance of the acts.[48] "Western observations tend to be ambiguous and contradictory . . . since most remarks are chance descriptions by Euro-Americans who often did not realize the significance of Native activities."[49] Misinterpretation by Euro-Americans of American Indian sweat lodge rituals as spa-like hygienic practices (rather than spiritual healing ceremonies) is another, more contemporary example.

Hedonistic Tobacco Use Minimal in Precontact Period

Several sources from early periods support the idea that hedonistic smoking was minimal among American Indians and that they smoked only in moderation for medicinal or spiritual reasons. For example, in observing the Narragansett in 1643, Roger Williams noted the Natives' practices of cultivating tobacco and the purposes for which they used it, including medicine.[50] As for their smoking habits, he said, "I never see any take so excessively as I have seen men in Europe."[51] Pawnee use of tobacco prior to European contact was strictly sacred and ceremonial.[52] The same is said of the Zuni, according to the observations of the wife of an Indian agent. The Ojibwa/Chippewa, as well, are noted for strictly ceremonial use of tobacco prior to European contact.[53]

Of the Montagnais-Naskapi people who lived north of the Huron in Ontario, it is said that they did not receive tobacco until after European contact.[54] Once tobacco was introduced into the society, it became a sacred object. The Ojibwa/Chippewa people also maintain that they were unaware of "true tobacco" (i.e., *N. tabacum*) before European contact.[55] This observation gives further credence to the idea that Euro-American men were sometimes responsible for the propagation of tobacco's influence in modern American Indian society.

An examination of the early smoking practices of some tribes such as the Northern Paiute of the Great Basin reveals that the early Native peoples understood tobacco much better than did the Europeans and later Americans, even after a few hundred years' use. Smoking was practiced only by men; "young boys would not smoke because they were afraid it would impede their ability to pursue game."[56] This suggests that, although tobacco did have spiritual importance in their lives, its powerful physical effects as well as relative scarcity proscribed its use for individual pleasure.

Contemporary Ceremonialism

Tobacco continues to play a requisite role in at least two contemporary religious healing ceremonies with deep roots in the past: the Peyote religion (or Native American Church) and the Plains Sun Dance. Both ceremonies have been the subject of many scholarly publications, and each has had its ritual features described extensively.[57]

The Peyote curing ceremony, based on ingestion of the hallucinatory peyote cactus plant, dates back to pre-Columbian times in northern Mexico and, like indigenous tobacco, slowly spread to numerous North American tribal areas over the following centuries.[58] The standard ritual, according to LaBarre, is "an all-night meeting in a tepee around a crescent-shaped earthen mound and a ceremonially-built fire; here a special drum, gourd rattle and carved staff are passed around after smoking purifying ceremonies, as each person sings four 'peyote songs.'"[59] In modern times, commercial tobacco (such as Bull Durham) was often traditionalized by rolling it into corn husk cigar-like cigarettes and smoking it in association with prayers. LaBarre's ethnographic description of a "Kiowa-Comanche type rite," representative of most Plains tribes (who were at the center of North American peyote diffusion), includes the following references to tobacco:

> Living beyond the habitat of peyote, all Plains tribes have to make pilgrimages for it or buy it. The journey is not ritualized, but there is a modest ceremony at the site: on finding the first plant, a Kiowa pilgrim sits west of it, rolls a cornshuck cigarette and prays, "I have found you, now open up, show me where the rest of you are. I want to use you to pray for the health of my people. . . ."[60]
>
> After the ceremony is considered begun . . . the leader . . . takes out this cedar incense bag, gourd, tobacco, etc. and arranges them conveniently near him. The first ceremony is smoking or praying together. The leader makes himself a cigarette of Bull Durham with cornhusk "papers" dried and cut to shape, and passes the makings clockwise to the rest, including women. His own made, the fireman presents the smoke-stick [a smoldering coal attached to a slender, decorated handle] to the leader . . . and this too is passed to the left. While all smoke the leader prays: . . . "Be with us when we pray tonight. Tell your father to look at us and listen to our prayers." He holds his cigarette mouth end toward the peyote and motions upward that it may smoke as he prays. . . . All pray silently

to . . . "earth creator" or "earth lord," and older men may add their prayers aloud after the leader. Then following the leader, all snuff their cigarettes in the ground and place them on the west curve of the altar, outside, or at either horn; the fireman may gather those of women, old people or visitors.[61]

The above ethnographic descriptions, recorded in the 1930s, suggest religious cultural continuity with an earlier time. Like the generic shaman of old, the leader of the Peyote ritual uses tobacco smoke, with prayer, to enhance the health of the group.

The Plains Sun Dance ceremony, based on the ritual of piercing the male chest, is perhaps even more generic in a religious sense than the Peyote ceremony. It appeals to the Great Spirit (through prayer and personal sacrifice) for tribal purification, health, wisdom, and renewal,[62] as well as for the curing of specific individuals.[63] As with the Peyote ceremony, tobacco smoking is woven into most phases of the four-day ritual Sun Dance ceremony. While the tobacco receptacle is different (pipe instead of cigarette), the meaning of the ceremony and the place of tobacco in it are very similar. Artist-ethnographer Thomas Mails took part in numerous Sun Dances conducted during the 1970s by the Sioux of the Rosebud and Pine Ridge Indian reservations in South Dakota. His references to the use of tobacco include the following:

> When the lodge is finished, the leader enters it and offers pinches of tobacco to the winged powers of the earth, and to the place where the sun goes down and from where the living water comes that we will use in our ceremony. . . . After this, kinnikinnik, the sacred tobacco is placed in the pipe bowl and a pinch of tobacco is offered to the power of the north, from which comes strength and purification; then to the east which sends peace and light for the eyes and the mind; then to the south, which is the source of life and growth; and finally to the west, which gives rain and nourishment. . . .[64]
>
> [Later] The helper now offers the pipe to the six directions. Then he lights it, takes a few deep puffs, and blows the smoke out so that he can rub it all over his body. He then hands the pipe to the man at his left. . . . The pipe is sent sunwise . . . until it comes back to the leader. . . .[65]
>
> Thus the holy men say that the pipe itself has power to transport power, and it is sacred for it came from god. . . . Those who use the pipe with reverence to seek enlightenment regarding sacred things will receive special help. For when the pipe is understood, smoked and pointed to the other sources of power as one prays, it becomes the very channel through which their power flows from them to the petitioner.[66]

In getting a description from a Sun Dance leader regarding the second day of the ceremony, the ethnographer asks about fasting: "Do your pledgers [those who will be pierced] really go, as you do, without food and water for the entire four days?" The leader answers,

They can smoke but they are not to take water or food. Men smoke because the act is associated in the Indian mind with ceremonies, and the spirits have never told me to deny the men commercial cigarettes.[67]

Thus the line between the sacred pipe tobacco (kinnikinnik) and commercial cigarette tobacco has become blurred.

CLINICAL OBSERVATIONS CONCERNING TOBACCO USE AMONG AMERICAN INDIANS

Again, the early historical record suggests that tobacco was smoked by men of most North American tribes both aboriginally and after contact, but only rarely to excess. A 1908 work makes the statement that "it (tobacco) is never the cause of any sickness."[68] This may imply that none of the morbidities currently associated with tobacco use (e.g., lung cancer, emphysema) occurred, or they occurred in very small numbers or were not recognized as such. One can then speculate that, although American Indians in most areas did cultivate, trade for, and smoke tobacco, their use of the substance was in relatively small amounts, largely for ceremonial purposes, and did not result in a significant number of incapacitating morbidities.

Current medical research seems to lend credence to this notion. Results of recent studies indicate that cancer is only now becoming a significant health problem among American Indians.[69] Ironically, researchers once claimed that American Indians were immune to cancer.[70] The sharp increase in modern prevalence rates seems to suggest that heavy smoking is a newly acquired habit for some native groups, such as the Navajo population in the Southwest, although history proves conclusively that the use of tobacco is not a novel practice in the region. As an increasing number of American Indians have adopted the habitual use of commercial tobacco, the prevalence rates of cancer in certain tribes has risen steadily throughout the century, until now they approximate or even surpass the rates for non-American Indians.[71]

DISCUSSION AND CONCLUSIONS

As a group, American Indians currently have the highest prevalence rate of tobacco use in the United States. This fact has even been recognized by the U.S. government in National Health Objective No. 3.4 of the *Healthy People 2000 Report*: namely, reduce the prevalence of smoking among American Indians and Alaska Natives to 20 percent or less, compared to a reduction goal of 15 percent or less for the general population.[72]

Despite this recognition of the gravity of tobacco use prevalence in American Indian communities, substance abuse prevention efforts have often given priority to alcohol and other drugs. Anecdotal evidence suggests that this has been the general norm for early CSAP efforts nationwide, especially those involving American Indian populations. The question remains, Why has tobacco been given relatively "protected" status in the national war against death and disability among American Indians?

A review of historical literature on tobacco use by pre-Columbian American Indian groups of varying levels of social organization (bands, tribes, chiefdoms, nation-states), suggests a long-term, extensive, substantial but highly varied pattern of acquisition and use by geographical region. However, the commercial development and manufacture of tobacco and its preferred paraphernalia (cigarettes, clay pipes, wooden pipes) for world consumption were carried forward later, during the seventeenth century, by Europeans and Euro-Americans—with the most potent nicotine species (N. *tabacum*) imported from South American fields. This rediffusion of commercial tobacco back into Indian populations, beginning with the French fur traders and ending with the Second World War, may have given rise to a new distinction between two types of Indian tobacco use: sacred, which was mostly still acquired and used for religious ceremonial purposes in the old, traditional way; and secular, provided by and through the acculturation and assimilation of American Indians into Euro-American society and used for individual, hedonistic purposes, in the modern way. During the past half-century, the distinction between sacred and secular tobacco has become blurred. Traditional sacred tobacco is seldom grown and thus is unavailable for religious ceremonies. More and more American Indians clearly have become addicted to commercial Euro-American tobacco—especially cigarettes. Moreover, tribal governments or their affiliates in many parts of North America have become the modern traders of commercial tobacco in Indian country establishments called "smoke shops." The "Indians' revenge" against Europeans for the loss of life, land, and livelihood has been turned into a revenge against their own people for profit. What began many centuries ago as a way to control the gods now symbolizes a loss of control to the power of addiction and tobacco corporations.

Contemporary examples of the blurred distinction between sacred tobacco and commercial tobacco are (1) the preference for Bull Durham in Peyote ceremonies of the Native-American Church, described above; (2) the use of commercial cigarette tobacco (with the paper removed) at a recent (1993) Sun Dance organized by members of the Oklahoma Cheyenne tribe, observed by one of the authors (Solomon); and (3) an American Indian pilgrim's passionate stuffing of a pack of Camel cigarettes through a wire fence holding the sacred white buffalo calf in Wisconsin, observed by one of the authors (Hill), during a 1994 broadcast of the Cable News Network (CNN). These ethnographic vignettes suggest a fairly wide distribution of this trend, although further ethnographic and other empiric substantiation clearly is called for.

Based on the findings of this study, the authors recommend a return to the distinction between sacred and secular tobacco in American Indian communities—especially with regard to substance abuse prevention programs. Symbols are important. Sacred tobacco might again be defined as that cultivated by members of the tribe, specifically for ceremonial use. Secular tobacco, cultivated and manufactured by Europeans and Euro-Americans for commercial profit, should be avoided. Like Ononthio's milk, commercial tobacco is a threat to the health and well-being of all American Indians exposed to its toxins. Because of the harmful effects of secondhand smoke on family members, especially children and the elderly, tobacco addiction has more in common with alcohol addiction than has been generally recognized. Both are health-harming threats to individual addicts as well as their families. Both have negative economic consequences for individuals and families, especially those at the bottom end of the economic spectrum. Both have negative impacts on vocational performance and productivity at work due to increased use of health services and increased absenteeism. Moreover, the use of one is highly predictive of the use of the other. In the authors' recent study of Cherokee adolescents, the "any use" prevalence congruence of alcohol and tobacco was greater than 80 percent.[73]

A major limitation to a study such as this is its dependence on anecdotal or secondary historical sources, whose data were gathered for purposes other than those pursued here. Thus this study may have led to wrong or unwarranted conclusions. On the other hand, these explorations may also have opened an avenue for further study. The authors would like to know much more about the cultural meaning of tobacco in different American Indian social contexts, and why tobacco's prevalence of use rates are consistently higher than those of other North American ethnic groups. It is clear that such research, based on a recognition of great cultural differentiation in contemporary North American society, is essential to an improving health status for all Americans.[74]

Acknowledgments

Support for this effort was provided by the Cherokee Nation of Oklahoma, Tahlequah, Oklahoma; the Cheyenne and Arapaho Tribes Incorporated, of Concho, Oklahoma; the Native-American Center of Excellence Consortium of the University of Oklahoma; the U.S. Center for Substance Abuse Prevention, Washington, D.C.; the Mentorship Program of the Oklahoma School of Science and Mathematics, Oklahoma City; and the U.S. Indian Health Service, Oklahoma City office. The authors also wish to thank Dennis Wiedman, John Moore, Renard Strickland, Tenona Kuhn, and Reba Solomon for bibliographic and ethnographic assistance.

Notes

1. Robert F. Hill and Glenn W. Solomon, *Baseline Description of Youth and Organizational Process: Report to the Oklahoma Cherokee CSAP Project* (Tahlequah, Oklahoma: The Cherokee Nation, 1992), 49.

2. Constance Horgan, *Substance Abuse: The Nation's Number One Health Problem: Key Indicators for Policy* (Waltham, MA: Brandeis University, Institute for Health Policy, 1993), 32.

3. Ibid.

4. Center for Disease Control, "Cigarette Smoking among American Indians and Alaskan Natives–Behavioral Risk Factor Surveillance System," 1987–1991, *Morbidity and Mortality Weekly Report* 42:45 (1992): 861.

5. J. G. Bachman, J. M. Wallace, and P. M. O'Malley, "Racial Ethnic Differences in Smoking, Drinking, and Illicit Drug Use among American High School Seniors, 1976–1989," *American Journal of Public Health* 79 (1991): 634; Robert W. Blum, B. Harmon, and L. Harris, "American Indian-Alaska Native Youth Health," *Journal of the American Medical Association* 267 (1992): 1637; Fred Beauvais, "Comparison of Drug Use Rates for Reservation Indian, Non-Reservation Indian, and Anglo Youth," *American Indian and Alaska Native Mental Health Research, The Journal of the National Center* 5 (1992): 13; L. A. Gandette et al., "Cancer Incidence by Ethnic Group in the Northwest Territories, 1969–1988," *Health Reports* 5 (1993): 23; W .J. Millar, "Smokeless Tobacco Use by Youth in the Canadian Arctic," *Arctic Medical Research* 49 (1990): 39; H.I. Goldberg et al., "Prevalence of Behavioral Risk Factors in Two American Indian Populations in Montana," *Preventive Medicine* 7 (1991): 155; D. M. Murray, C. L. Perry, and C. Oafs, "Seventh Grade Cigarette, Alcohol, and Marijuana Use: Distribution in a North Central vs. Metropolitan Population," *The International Journal of the Addictions* 22 (1987): 356; J.R. Sugarman et al., "Using the Behavioral Risk Factor Surveillance System to Monitor Year 2000 Objectives among American Indians," *Public Health Reports* 107 (1992): 451; M. D. Wolfe and J. T. Carlos, "Oral Health Effects of Smokeless Tobacco Use in Navaho Indian Adolescents," *Community Dentistry Oral Epidemiology* 15(1987): 230; Glenn W. Solomon et al., "Cultural Involvements and Substance Use of Oklahoma Cherokee Adolescents," *Clinical Research* 42:1 (1994); Robert F. Hill et al., "Cultural Correlates of Health among the Oklahoma Cherokees: CSAP Project Data," (Unpublished paper, 1994).

6. G. Boyd, "Use of Smokeless Tobacco among Children and Adolescents in the United States," *Preventive Medicine* 16 (1987): 402; E. D. Glover, M. Laflin, and D. Flumerg, "Smokeless Tobacco Use among American College Students," *Journal of American College Health* 38 (1989): 81; R. J. Hall and D. Dexter, "Smokeless Tobacco Use and Attitudes toward Smokeless Tobacco among Native-Americans and Other Adolescents in the Northwest," *American Journal of Public Health* 78 (1988): 1586; Bonnie Bruerd, "Smokeless Tobacco Use among Native School Children," *Public Health Reports* 105 (1990): 196.

7. Center for Disease Control, "Cigarette Smoking among American Indians and Alaskan Natives," 861.

8. Joseph C. Robert, *The Story of Tobacco in America* (Alfred A. Knopf, New York, 1949), 1.

9. Ibid.

10. Ralph Linton, "Use of Tobacco among North American Indians," *Anthropology Leaflet* 15 (Field Museum of Natural History, Chicago, 1924), 1.

11. Jordan Paper, *Offering Smoke: The Sacred Pipe and Native American Religion* (Moscow, ID: University of Idaho Press, 1988), 8.

12. Robert, *Story of Tobacco*, 4.

13. Ibid.

14. Jordan Goodman, *Tobacco in History: The Cultures of Dependence* (New York: Routledge, 1993), 67.

15. Louis Seig, *Tobacco, Peacepipes and Indians* (Palmer Lake, CO: Filter Press, 1971), 1.

16. Ibid.

17. Paper, *Offering Smoke,* 4.

18. Ibid.

19. Seig, *Tobacco, Peacepipes and Indians,* 18.

20. Ian W. Brown, "The Calumet Ceremony in the Southeast and Its Archaeological Manifestations," *American Antiquity* 54:2 (1989): 313.

21. Seig, *Tobacco, Peacepipes and Indians,* 5.

22. Harold E. Driver, *Indians of North America* (Chicago: University of Chicago Press, 1961), 90.

23. Francis Parkman, *Francis Parkman's Works,* New Library Ed., 12 vols. (Boston: Little, Brown, and Company, 1897–1912), cited in Edward J. Payne, *The History of Nations: Colonies* (New York: P. F. Collier and Sons, 1907), 80; Goodman, *Tobacco in History,* 132; A. M. Josephy, Jr., ed., *The American Heritage Book of Indians* (New York: Simon and Schuster, Inc., 1961), 166; A. M. Gibson, *The Kickapoos* (Norman: University of Oklahoma Press, 1963), 7; John Moore, personal communication, 18 December 1994; Josephy, *American Heritage,* 166; Gibson, *The Chickasaws* (Norman: University of Oklahoma Press, 1965), 7–14; W. E. Unrau, *The Kansa Indians* (Norman: University of Oklahoma Press, 1965), 55; Josephy, *American Heritage,* 57; Unrau, *The Kansa Indians,* 55; Josephy, *American Heritage,* 53; J. E. Sanders, *The Fur Trade in the Upper Missouri* (Norman: University of Oklahoma Press, 1965), 47; Gibson, *The American Indians: Pre-History to the Present* (Washington, DC: Heath, 1980), 120.

24. Goodman, *Tobacco in History,* 162; Gibson, *The Kickapoos,* 7.

25. Josephy, *American Heritage,* 60.

26. Linton, *Use of Tobacco,* 4.

27. Driver, *Indians of North America,* map 8.

28. Seig, *Tobacco, Peacepipes and Indians,* 22.

29. Linton, *Use of Tobacco,* 4.

30. Seig, *Tobacco, Peacepipes and Indians,* 22, 26.

31. Goodman, *Tobacco in History,* 32.

32. Seig, *Tobacco, Peacepipes and Indians,* 22.

33. Goodman, *Tobacco in History,* 31.

34. Ibid., 31, 32.

35. Linton, *Use of Tobacco,* 22.

36. Virgil J. Vogel, *American Indian Medicine* (Norman: University of Oklahoma Press, 1970), 127.

37. Goodman, *Tobacco in History,* 29.

38. Vogel, *American Indian Medicine,* 31–32.

39. Ibid., 128.

40. Ibid., 383.

41. Seig, *Tobacco, Peacepipes, and Indians,* 14–16.

42. Brown, "The Calumet Ceremony in the Southeast," 311.

43. Ibid.

44. Ibid., 314, 316.

45. Ibid., 313.

46. Linton, *Use of Tobacco,* 24.

47. Ibid.

48. Paper, *Offering Smoke,* 6–7.

49. Ibid.

50. Joseph D. McGuire, "Pipes and Smoking Customs of the American Aborigines

Based on Material in the U.S. National Museum," *Report on the National Museum,* Elliot City, Maryland (1897), 417.

51. Ibid.

52. Seig, *Tobacco, Peacepipes, and Indians,* 20.

53. Ibid., 34–35.

54. Ibid., 34.

55. Ibid., 35.

56. Ibid., 38.

57. Weston LaBarre, *The Peyote Cult* (Norman: University of Oklahoma Press, 1989); Leslie Spier, "The Sun Dance of the Plains Indians," in *Anthropological Papers,* ed. Clark Wissler, vol. 16 (New York: American Museum of Natural History, 1921), 451–528; Dennis Wiedman, "Big and Little Moon Peyotism as Health Care Delivery Systems," *Medical Anthropology* 12:4 (1990): 371; Omer C. Stewart, *Peyote Religion: A History* (Norman: University of Oklahoma Press, 1987); Thomas E. Mails, *Sundancing at Rosebud and Pine Ridge* (Sioux Falls, SD: Center for Western Studies, 1978).

58. Driver and Massey, *Indians of North America,* map 3.

59. LaBarre, *The Peyote Cult,* 7.

60. Ibid., 43.

61. Ibid., 48.

62. Mails, *Sundancing at Rosebud and Pine Ridge,* 102.

63. Ibid., 47.

64. Ibid., 90.

65. Ibid., 92.

66. Ibid., 101.

67. Ibid., 208.

68. Areš Hrdlička, "Physiological and Medical Observations among the Indians of the Southwest United States and Mexico," *Smithsonian Institute, Bureau of American Ethnology Bulletin* 34 (Washington, DC: U.S. Government Printing Office, 1908), 173.

69. J. Horm and S. Burhansstipanov, "Cancer Incidence, Survival, and Mortality among American Indians and Alaskan Natives," *American Indian Culture and Research Journal* 16:3 (1992): 25.

70. Ibid.

71. P. A. Nutting, W. L. Freeman, and D. R. Risser, "Cancer Incidence among American Indians and Alaskan Natives," *American Journal of Public Health* 83 (1993): 1587.

72. Public Health Service, *Healthy People 2000: National Health Promotion and Disease Prevention Objectives, U.S. Department of HHS, PHS, DHS* (1991), Publication No. 91-50212 (Washington, DC: U.S. Public Health Service).

73. Solomon et al., "Cultural Involvements and Substance Use."

74. Robert F. Hill, J. Dennis Fortenberry, and Howard F. Stein, "Culture in Clinical Medicine," *Southern Medical Journal* 83:9 (1990): 1071.

13

Cancer Control Research among American Indians and Alaska Natives: A Paradigm for Research in the Next Millennium

Martin C. Mahoney and Arthur M. Michalek

 WHILE CANCER WAS AN UNCOMMON OCCURRENCE among American Indians and Alaska Natives at the turn of the century, it currently ranks as the second leading cause of death among these populations.[1] American Indians and Alaska Natives (AI/ANs) compose a minority group which includes more than two million members. AI/ANs are dispersed throughout each of the fifty states, with the largest numbers located in Oklahoma (252,420), California (242,164), and Arizona (203,527).[2]

American Indians and Alaska Natives, also referred to as Native peoples, tend to be younger than the majority population, with a median age ten years younger than that for the general population (AI/AN median age is 24.2 years versus 34.4 years for U.S. whites).[3] Life expectancy among AI/ANs is seventy years compared with seventy-five years in the general population. In addition, AI/AN populations exhibit higher rates of poverty (32 percent of AI/AN versus 13 percent U.S. all races) and unemployment (16 percent AI/ANs versus 6 percent U.S. all races) and lower rates of educational attainment (65 percent of AI/ANs high school graduates versus 75 percent U.S. all races; 9 percent of AI/ANs college graduates versus 20 percent U.S. all races). More than 70 percent of American Indians reside in places other than reservation areas, with estimates that 50 percent and more reside in urban areas. At present, there are more than five hundred federally recognized tribes, each with a unique and diverse cultural identity resulting in somewhat unique health concerns. As a result, each tribe has unique cultural and health concerns.

The Indian Health Service has been charged with providing and coordinating medical care, including cancer control activities, to AI/ANs residing within

Martin C. Mahoney, M.D., Ph.D., is chief resident in the Department of Family Medicine at the University of Buffalo. He is also a faculty member of the Roswell Park Cancer Institute. Arthur M. Michalek, Ph.D., is the director for educational affairs and dean of the Graduate Division for the Roswell Park Cancer Institute, where he is also professor of epidemiology. Both are members of the NCI Network for Cancer Control Research among American Indian and Alaska Native Populations.

the thirty-three reservation states. Even in communities with IHS facilities, it is estimated that less than half of eligible Natives utilize IHS services.[4] Since passage of the Indian Self-Determination Act in 1975, tribal groups have been encouraged to operate and manage their own health programs directly. A small urban Indian health program is maintained by the IHS; however this particular program represents just 2 percent of the IHS budget compared with estimates that 54 percent to 68 percent of the AI/AN population resides in urban areas. It is worth noting that IHS does not possess sole responsibility for AI/AN health care and seeks to incorporate support from federal and state agencies.

Data from a variety of sources, including regional, state, and community-

	AMERICAN INDIANS: (New Mexico)		ALASKA NATIVES*	
	Cancer Incidence 1988–1992 (site—ratio**)	Cancer Incidence 1988–1992 (site—ratio)	Cancer Incidence 1988–1992 (site—ratio)	Cancer Incidence 1988-1992 (site—ratio)
males	prostate—0.41	prostate—0.68	prostate—0.33	
	colon & rectum—0.32	colon & rectum—0.36	colon & rectum—1.38	colon & rectum—1.16
	kidney—1.30		kidney—1.58	kidney—2.63
	lung—0.18	lung—0.14	lung—1.03	lung—0.94
	liver—4.03	liver—3.03		
		stomach—1.87	stomach—2.83	stomach—3.15
				nasopharynx—38.67
females	breast—0.27	breast—0.31	breast—0.68	breast—0.58
	colon & rectum—0.33		colon & rectum—1.72	colon & rectum—1.54
			kidney—2.83	kidney—2.31
			lung—1.16	lung—1.38
		pancreas—1.06		pancreas—2.21
	ovary—1.08	ovary—0.89		
	corpus uteri—0.47	cervix uteri—3.20	cervix uteri—2.11	
	gallbladder—5.28	gallbladder—(unable to calculate)		

TABLE 1

*Alaska Native Health Service.
**rate ratio=age-adjusted incidence rate among American Indians or Alaska Natives/age-adjusted rate among white, non-Hispanics. Based on note 7

level data, suggest that cancer has emerged as an increasingly important health problem affecting the health status of American Indians and Alaska Natives in the United States.[5] Interestingly, historical scientific publications dating to the late nineteenth century and early twentieth century make reference to the paucity of malignant disease within Native communities.[6]

Site-specific cancer rates among American Indians and Alaska Natives often exceed comparable rates in the general population. This observation might be overlooked if only overall rates are considered. For example, for the period between 1988 and 1992, the rate ratios for cancer incidence among American Indians (in New Mexico) were 0.41 and 0.51 among males and females, respectively, relative to non-Hispanic whites.[7] Cancer mortality data for this period reveal rate ratios of 0.57 and 0.69 among American Indian males and females, respectively. Between 1988 and 1992 cancer incidence rate ratios among Alaska Natives (in Alaska) were 0.77 and 0.98 in males and females, respectively. Rate ratios for cancer mortality in this group were 1.04 and 1.25 among males and females, respectively. As illustrated in table 1, closer inspection of these data reveal incidence excesses among American Indians for cancers of the kidney, liver, and gallbladder, and among Alaska Natives for cancers of the colon and rectum, stomach, kidney, lung, and cervix uteri. Mortality excesses were noted among American Indians for cancers of the stomach, liver, gallbladder, and cervix uteri, while Alaska Natives exhibited excesses for deaths resulting from cancers of the colon and rectum, stomach, kidney, nasopharynx, and pancreas.

Similar excesses for cancer incidence and cancer mortality among American Indians and Alaska Natives have been noted.[8] Data from the Indian Health Service[9] demonstrate several regions where cancer mortality exceeds that experienced by the general population, including Alaska and areas of the Midwest (for instance, the Billings, Aberdeen, and Bemidji service areas).

Survival information, based on Surveillance Epidemiology and End Results data from New Mexico and Arizona, illustrate that American Indians demonstrate the poorest survival among any racial group for all sites combined and for eight of ten leading cancer sites.[10] Following a cancer diagnosis, American Indians demonstrate an overall relative survival of 35 percent compared to 50 percent among whites. Ratios of cancer incidence to cancer mortality (1988–1992) were generally low among American Indian males (rate ratio of 1.59) and females (rate ratio of 1.81), as well as Alaska Native males (rate ratio of 1.65) and females (rate ratio of 1.94). Lower incidence-to-mortality ratios are considered to demonstrate high case fatality, although this observation might also be attributable to racial misclassification on death registration records.[11] Although several hypotheses have been put forth in an attempt to explain these marked differences in survival, exact reasons for poorer survival remain obscure.

Detailed descriptions of cancer patterns among American Indians and Alaska Natives have been published previously.[12] These reports have presented Native cancer patterns at the state level and within selected tribal communities.[13] Efforts to consolidate findings from multiple data sources have proven challenging.[14]

Issues

Cancer is a major health problem for American Indians and Alaska Natives. American Indians and Alaska Natives should be made aware that cancer is a growing health concern.

American Indians and Alaska Natives have among the poorest survival rates from cancer of all racial groups. Specific cancers occur at unusually high rates among American Indians and Alaska Natives and warrant special attention.

Communications barriers often exist among American Indians and Alaska Natives, health care providers, and research scientists.

Cancer prevention and control intervention efforts and research on American Indians and Alaska Natives require a continuing evaluation program accountability.

Variability in incidence rates for certain primary cancer sites among American Indians and Alaska Natives provides an opportunity to investigate cancer etiology and cancer prevention strategies (state plan only).

TABLE 2

FUTURE DIRECTIONS

Marked differences have been identified in disease frequency and outcomes among racial/ethnic groups. In the *Healthy People 2000* document,[15] the Public Health Service developed objectives to improve the overall health status of all peoples, with special emphasis on disparities among minority groups, including American Indians and Alaska Natives.

The Special Populations Studies Branch of the National Cancer Institute has sustained the ongoing activities of the Network for Cancer Control Research among American Indian and Alaska Native Populations since its inception in 1990. It is the mission of this network to reduce cancer morbidity and mortality to the lowest possible levels and to improve cancer survival through culturally sensitive research. This network has struggled with developing approaches to promote and facilitate cancer control activities in Native communities.

In 1992, the AI/AN Network released a National Strategic Cancer Plan for federal agencies (for example, Centers for Disease Control and Prevention, National Institutes of Health, Agency for Health Care Policy and Research, Public Health Service, Indian Health Service, Office of Minority Health, Office of Disease Prevention and Health Promotion) to enhance the awareness of the cancer problem among Native populations. This was followed in 1994 by a Strategic Plan for State Public Health Agencies.[16] Both plans are organized around a framework of selected issues as identified in table 2. Action items and outcome measures relevant to each issue, as well as specific types of cancer control research, are contained in the respective strategic plans. The cancer control research needs of American Indians and Alaska Natives appear in these plans.

Selected elements from these plans are referenced below along with the authors' call for action. These items of greatest relevance will be presented. It should be noted that these items and responses were developed by the Network for Cancer Control Research among American Indian and Alaska Native Populations. Network membership is represented by fifteen individuals, at least two-thirds of whom are of American Indian or Alaska Native descent. Thus these plans represent the collective thoughts of individuals who are not only expert in the field but are sensitive to the cultural context in which this research must be conducted. Each of the issues shown in table 2 have been paraphrased below.

Accurate Surveillance Systems

1. Underreported incidence and mortality from cancer and other inaccurate cancer data on American Indians and Alaska Natives should be recognized by federal agencies and state public health agencies. The process of data collection should be corrected to prevent misleading and erroneous conclusions.

2. The overall quality of cancer data should be carefully reviewed; statistical data should attempt to address racial misclassification, diagnostic errors, and other sources of inaccuracies.

Proposed Action: Methodological concerns about various databases have complicated precise interpretation of available data on cancer patterns among AI/ANs. Extant surveillance data are generally a blending of multiple regional and/or community-based data sources; no national database is available. For example, data commonly cited by the National Cancer Institute Surveillance, Epidemiology and End Results program are not generalizable since they are based largely on data from New Mexico, as well as limited areas in Arizona. In other areas of the country, racial misclassification in vital records results in inaccuracies in surveillance data. Problems with denominator data include undercounts of Native respondents to census surveys and inconsistent responses to items requesting information on race. IHS data are based on encounters with a "user population" (i.e., individuals who have used IHS facilities within the last two years) from predominantly rural areas limited to thirty-three reservation states. Thus, there is an urgent need for investigators across the country to work with Native populations in their region to develop more accurate surveillance systems.

Public and Professional Education

1. State and federal public health agencies should support public education to increase awareness of cancer as a threat to the health of American Indians and Alaska Natives through policy development, increased communication, and the commitment of staff and financial resources.

2. These agencies should support professional education of scientists, health professionals, and care givers to enhance their awareness of cancer in these indigenous populations.

3. Investigators should also be sensitive to their role and the tribal community's perception of their research. Success can only be achieved if tribal members

are engaged as *active* members of the research team. This benefits the researcher with insight into community norms and benefits the tribe by sharing research skills that the involved tribal members may transfer to other projects of benefit to their communities.

Proposed Action: Health agencies should demonstrate their commitment to these populations through policy development, the commitment of staff and financial resources, and the hiring of AI/AN professionals to guide these efforts. Support for the training of Native researchers should be provided. Community development strategies designed to empower local communities in educational efforts should be promoted.

Research Needs

1. The reasons for the poor cancer survival rates among American Indians and Alaska Natives require examination.

2. Etiologic research should focus on cancers both common and uncommon to American Indians and Alaska Natives.

3. Federal and state health agencies should fund research to identify cancer risk factors prevalent among American Indians and Alaska Natives.

Proposed Action: The disproportionate rates of gallbladder, gastric, nasopharyngeal, and pancreatic cancers argue for focused etiologic research aimed at reducing high incidence and mortality rates. Tribal differences in rates for more common cancer sites also warrant further investigation. Analyses should consider associations with genetic, nutritional, and environmental risk factors as well as care-seeking behaviors related to prompt diagnosis and treatment.

Moreover, the study of rare tumor types in populations at higher risk may yield insights that will be of benefit to all populations. Equally important, the etiologic study of cancers uncommon in Native populations may yield clues to prevention that may be directly transferable to other populations.

Data on cancer risk factors are limited to specific tribal groups and/or geographic regions. More comprehensive and specific risk-factor data would aid in the interpretation of cancer patterns as well as assist in the development and implementation of intervention programs targeting risk reduction and behavior modification.

Enhanced Communication

1. The unique relationship that exists between the United States government and American Indian and Alaska Native nations, tribes, and communities must be recognized as this relationship directly affects the delivery of health care.

2. State and federal agencies should maintain an ongoing dialogue regarding health problems among American Indians and Alaska Natives.

3. Federal and state agencies need to acknowledge the cultural diversity of American Indians and Alaska Natives and recognize how they differ from the rest of the United States population.

Proposed Action: Whenever possible, collaborative approaches to cancer control projects should be considered. Researchers need to recognize and acknowledge cultural distinctions present within Native communities. The failure to acknowledge these cultural differences may serve as a barrier to prevention, early detection, and treatment of cancer in these populations. This again argues for the inclusion of and ownership by the Native community rather than the historical role of exclusion.

Evaluation and Dissemination

1. Cancer prevention and control interventions in place among American Indians and Alaska Natives should be appropriately evaluated with the assistance of federal and state agencies when necessary.

2. The development of community partnership and program ownership between tribal communities and federal and/or state health agencies should be advocated.

3. Information regarding successful intervention efforts and models for replication in other American Indian and Alaska Native communities should be disseminated and replicated through cooperative endeavors with public and private resources.

Proposed Action: Shared ownership and effective communication would improve community cooperation with future cancer prevention and control efforts and provide feedback to both the community and researchers about benefits to subjects from participating in interventions. In all cases, American Indians and Alaska Natives should be fully informed about cancer prevention and control projects and actively involved as members of the research team. Prior written approval and consent should be obtained from the appropriate tribal governmental bodies before these programs are initiated. Appropriate Institutional Review Board clearance need also be granted by the IHS.

Cancer Prevention

1. Efforts to examine the low risk of specific cancers (e.g., breast, lung, prostate) among some American Indians and Alaska Natives should be supported at the federal and/or state level.

2. The unusually low incidence rates demonstrated by some Native groups relative to incidence patterns in the general population may provide important insights into methods to prevent these cancers in other communities.

Cancer Control Interventions for AI/ANs

Limited data are available concerning cancer control activities accessible to American Indian and Alaska Native communities. To address this knowledge gap, three national surveys investigating cancer control programs for American Indians and Alaska Natives were recently completed by Network members.[17] These surveys were focused at three organizational levels in an attempt to assess comprehensively cancer control activities offered by state public health agencies, tribal health departments, and urban Indian clinics.

A cross-sectional survey of state chronic disease program directors was completed in 1992 to elucidate the extent of cancer prevention and control programs for AI/ANs directly supported by state public health agencies.[18] Forty-four percent of the directors reported that cancer was as important or somewhat more important than other health problems among AI/ANs. However, more than one-half of the respondents did not know whether there had been any change in AI/AN cancer rates. The extent of AI/AN cancer control programs supported by state public health departments was limited.

The second survey examined the perceptions and priorities ascribed to cancer among directors of tribal health departments.[19] Compared to other health problems, cancer was rated as "somewhat more important" or "much more important" by 45 percent and 21 percent of health directors from Alaska Native and American Indian tribal groups, respectively. This survey also revealed that cancer represents a single disease entity among several health issues which confront Native peoples at a community level. Among Alaska Native health directors, cancer ranked behind alcohol and injuries in relative importance. American Indian tribal health directors ranked cancer fifth behind diabetes, alcohol, heart disease, and injuries. Thus, despite statistics which support the importance of malignant disease among AI/ANs, the presence of other diseases should not be overlooked.

To ascertain the extent of cancer control programs for American Indians resident in urban areas, a survey of IHS urban clinics was undertaken.[20] While 71 percent of urban health clinic directors felt that cancer incidence was stable or increasing, 25 percent indicated that they were unfamiliar with incidence patterns. Similarly, 67 percent of urban clinic directors reported that American Indian cancer mortality was stable or increasing, while 33 percent did not know incidence trends. Only 21 percent of respondents felt cancer was as important or more important than other health problems. As a health problem, cancer was ranked fifth among seven health problems by urban health directors. Most urban clinics reported sponsoring programs for smoking control, as well as breast and cervical cancer screening services.

In aggregate, information from these three surveys provides a comprehensive overview of the limited cancer control programs directed toward AI/AN populations. In addition, findings from these surveys underscore a need to better sensitize health professionals and tribal leaders to the cancer problem in Native communities.

SUMMARY

Secular trends in cancer incidence and mortality demonstrate steadily increasing rates among Native populations. Our limited knowledge concerning cancer, let alone health in general, among Native populations is based primarily on the experience of reservation populations. Little research has focused on urban populations despite that fact that most American Indians reside in urban areas.

Recent papers have reported marked disparities across a variety of health status measures,[21] including increased trauma rates,[22] among urban AI/ANs. The historical void of cancer-related information in Native communities is further attested to by findings from a recent bibliometric analysis.[23] The reader is directed to a special issue of *Cancer* for detailed descriptions of research projects involving these populations.[24]

Currently, Native Americans are at greater risk of death than the U.S. general population for causes such as tuberculosis, diabetes, liver disease, pneumonia, accidents, homicide, and suicide.[25] During the course of only several decades, AI/AN populations have experienced dramatic changes in diet, environment, lifestyle, and occupation, as well as the inherent stresses of assimilation, cultural estrangement, and integration of traditional values. Combinations of these factors have resulted in shifts in competing causes of death and increased longevity. As a result, more Natives are achieving ages at greatest risk for developing cancer. The instance of cancer in Native American populations has been transformed from the oddity it was at the beginning of the century[26] to a common occurrence.

Responsibility for maximizing the health status of American Indians and Alaska Natives will rely upon a cooperative approach by tribal groups along with the proactive involvement of federal and state public health agencies. Implementation of a comprehensive cancer control research program for American Indians and Alaska Natives will require government resources, at both the federal and state levels, as well as funding from private and nonprofit organizations where available. The authors hope that this overview might serve to stimulate enhanced cancer control efforts involving American Indians and Alaska Natives, including projects which both assess and expand cancer control services as a means of addressing this important health issue.

Acknowledgments

The authors wish to thank the members of the Steering Committee of the Network for Cancer Control Research among American Indians and Alaska Native Populations for their guidance, insights, and support.

Notes

1. Department of Health and Human Services, Public Health Service, Indian Health Service, *Trends in Indian Health—1996* (Rockville, MD: DHHS, PHS, IHS, 1996).

2. Department of Commerce, Office of the Census, *1990 U.S. Census* (Washington, DC: U.S. Government Printing Office, 1992).

3. Ibid. Subsequent statistics in this paragraph are also taken from the *1990 U.S. Census*.

4. Linda Burhansstipanov and Connie M. Dresser, *Native American Monograph No. 1: Documentation of Cancer Research Needs of American Indians and Alaska Natives*, National Cancer Institute, NIH Publication No. 93-3603 (Bethesda, MD: National Institute of Health, 1993).

5. Anne P. Lanier, Janet Kelly, Bonnie Smith, et al., *Alaska Area Native Health Service* (Anchorage, AK, December 1993); *Trends in Indian Health and Native American Monograph.*

6. James W. Hampton, "The Heterogeneity of Cancer in Native American Populations," *Minorities and Cancer,* ed. Lovell A. Jones (New York: Springer-Verlag, 1989).

7. Barry A. Miller, Lawrence N. Kolonel, Leslie Berstein, John L. Young, Jr., G. Marie Swanson, Dee West, Charles R. Key, Jonathan M. Liff, Claudia S. Glover, George A. Alexander, et al., eds., *Racial/Ethnic Patterns of Cancer in the United States 1988–1992,* National Cancer Institute, NIH Pub. No. 96-4104 (Bethesda, MD: National Institute of Health, 1996).

8. Burhansstipanov and Dresser, *Native American Monograph.*

9. U.S. Department of Health and Human Services, Public Health Service, Indian Health Service, Office of Planning and Program Evaluation and Legislation, Division of Program Statistics, *Regional Differences in Indian Health, 1995* (Rockville, MD: PHS, IHS, 1995).

10. John W. Horm, and Linda Burhansstipanov, "Cancer Incidence, Survival, and Mortality among American Indians and Alaskan Natives," *American Indian Culture and Research Journal* 16:3 (1992): 27–28.

11. See Miller, et. al. *Racial/Ethnic Patterns of Cancer.*

12. Martin C. Mahoney and Arthur M. Michalek, "A Meta-Analysis of Cancer Incidence among North American Native Populations," *International Journal of Epidemiology* 20 (1991): 323–27; Martin C. Mahoney and Arthur M. Michalek, "A Bibliography of Cancer among American Indians and Alaskan Natives, 1966-1994," *Alaska Medicine* 37 (1995): 63–74; Anne P. Lanier, Janet J. Kelly, Bonnie Smith, Annette P. Harpster, Harvey Tanttila, Claudette Amadon, Dennis Beckworth, Charles Key, and Anna M. Davidson, "Alaska Native Cancer Update: Incidence Rates 1989-1993," *Cancer Epidemiology, Biomarkers & Prevention* 5 (1996): 749–751. Also see notes 1, 4, and Lanier, note 5.

13. Ibid.; Mahoney and Michalek, "Meta-Analysis of Cancer Incidence"; Lanier, "Alaska Native Cancer Update."

14. Mahoney and Michalek,"Meta-Analysis of Cancer Incidence"; Mahoney and Michalek, "Bibliography of Cancer."

15. Indian Health Service, U.S. Department of Health and Human Services, *Healthy People 2000: National Health Promotion and Disease Prevention Objectives* (Washington, DC: IHS, 1990).

16. Network for Cancer Control Research among American Indians and Alaska Native Populations, "Cancer Prevention and Control Research among American Indians and Alaska Natives: A Strategic Plan for State Public Health Agencies," in Burhansstipanov and Dresser, ed., *Native American Monograph* No. 1; also see chapter 12.

17. Martin C. Mahoney and Arthur M. Michalek, "Provision of Cancer Control Services to Native Americans by State Public Health Departments," *Journal of Cancer Education* 9 (1994): 145–147; Martin C. Mahoney, Arthur M. Michalek, Mia Papas, Martha Tenney, and Linda Burhansstipanov, "Tribal-based Cancer Control Activities Among Alaska Natives: Services and Perceptions," *Alaska Medicine* 38 (1996): 59–64, 83; Martin C. Mahoney, Arthur M. Michalek, Linda Burhansstipanov, Martha Tenney, and Nat Cobb, "Urban-based Native American Cancer Control Activities: Services and Perceptions," *Journal of Cancer Education* 11 (1996): 159–63.

18. Ibid., Michalek and Mahoney, "Provision of Cancer Control Services."

19. Michalek and Mahoney, et al., "Tribal-based Cancer Control Activities."

20. Michalek and Mahoney, et al., "Urban-based Native American Cancer Control Activities."

21. David C. Grossman, James W. Krieger, Jonathan R. Sugarman, and Ralph A. Forquera, "Health Status of Urban American Indians and Alaska Natives: A Population-based Study," *Journal of the American Medical Association* 271 (1994): 845–50.

22. David C. Grossman and Jonathan R. Sugarman, "Trauma among American Indians in an Urban County," *Public Health Report* 111 (1996): 321–27.

23. Martin C. Mahoney and Arthur M. Michalek, "A Bibliometric Analysis of Cancer among American Indians and Alaska Natives, 1966–1993," *Alaska Medicine* 37 (1995): 59–62,77.

24. Native American Cancer Conference III, "Risk Factors, Outreach and Intervention Strategies," *Cancer* 78:7 (1996).

25. *Trends in Indian Health—1996.*

26. Aleš Hrdlička, "Diseases of the Indians, More Especially of the Southwest United States and Mexico," *Washington Medical Annual* IV (1905): 372–94. Also see Hampton, "Heterogeneity of Cancer."

PART VI

ENVIRONMENTAL ISSUES

Native American cultural life has traditionally been deeply connected to the environment. Spiritual views and languages show great respect for the interconnectedness of humans, plants, animals, and the world. Most tribes have rituals and teachings that emphasized humans' dependence on animals and plants for subsistence. In many tribal teachings, the animals willfully sacrificed themselves to the people so that they would have food to live on. In return for the gift of life, the animals expected humans to treat them with respect, and by doing so ensured that the spirit of the animal or plant would be preserved and reborn again. In this way, the taking of animals and plants did not exploit and deplete the environment. As long as the people showed their respect and thanksgiving for the plant and animal spirit-beings taken for sustenance, the people ensured the rebirth and replenishment of the plants and animals. Only when the people failed to fulfill their ritual obligations did the spirits of the plants and animals withdraw their blessings and sacrifices for the benefit of humans. Then the people suffered from the loss of animals willing to give themselves up for food.

Colonialism and the impact of European economies forced massive change in the relationship among Native peoples, the land, and the plants and animals. The fur trade is one primary example of the dynamics of the domination and disruption of Native resource use and relationship to the environment. It is argued by some historians and economists that soon after Europeans introduced fur trade into Northern America, many Indians overexploited game to supply furs to European traders in exchange for metal goods, guns, ball powder, and other goods. Yet many, if not most, Indians remained tied to the ethic of preserving the ritual and physical balance among humans, plants, and animals. The consequences for disturbing this balance led to impoverishment and failure in game hunting. The demand for furs in Europe out-stripped the supply of beaver furs and deer skins. Left to their own resources, Native teachings would inhibit Native Americans from overexploitation of game resources. However, inclusion into the world economic systems and the reduction of traditional resource and land base for self-sufficient production of food and goods created situations in which the demand for furs overstepped local supplies, and thus disrupted ethics of balance and sustainability.

Contemporary Native Americans live in a world of markets and resource exploitation in which Native land base and resource control has been drastically reduced. In this context, economic survival is often pitted against spiritual teachings and resource conservation, and tribes are faced with difficult and divisive decisions. Still, many tribal communities continue to observe the ethic of spiritual parity with the plants, animals, and other animate beings. For example, during the 1970s, the Northern Cheyenne rejected millions of dollars of up-front money and royalty payments in exchange for coal development on their reservation because they believed that such development threatened the political and cultural integrity of their community. Economic development on many Indian reservations will only succeed if community members feel that such activity does not disrupt spiritual relations and ties to living beings.

Because environmental issues are so central to Native ways of life and health on all spiritual, cultural, political, and economic levels, there have been much activity and struggle for environmental justice. Further, a vast body of Native knowledge about the environment has been marginalized or simply ignored. While Native communities have sometimes succeeded in forming strategic alliances with mainstream environmentalist groups, ignorance of Native conditions and perspectives has often placed Native people at odds with these environmentalist agendas. The chapters in this section address some of the major ecological problems Native people face today and examine the multifaceted relationships of Native people to the environment, governments, local and global economies, and the agendas of mainstream environmentalism.

14

Friendly Fire:
When Environmentalists
Dehumanize American Indians

David Waller

 ENVIRONMENTALISTS DISAGREE with animal liberationists over how to repair the relationship between human beings and other species. While this often comes as a surprise to those not deeply involved in either movement (or those like me who identify with both movements), the fact is that the agenda and values of each group sometimes contradict those of the other. For the purposes of this paper we can summarize the basic, conflicting intuitions of environmentalists and animal liberationists as follows: Environmentalists often argue that human consumption of animals is natural, and what is natural is permissible, and therefore human consumption of animals is permissible (hereafter this will be referred to as the naturalistic argument). Animal liberationists often argue that pain and death are evil, and that it is incumbent upon humans to eliminate evil to the extent that they can; therefore, it is incumbent upon humans to eliminate the pain and death that accompany the consumption of animals.[1]

In arguing against the vegetarian plank of animal liberation, some environmentalists have tried to strengthen the naturalistic argument with an appeal to the example of indigenous cultures in general and Native American cultures in particular. In this paper I will examine and criticize this strategy. However, I am not concerned here with defending animal liberationism. Rather, I would like to show how these arguments reveal—unintentionally, I am sure—an unflattering view of Native Americans and are damaging to Indians of the past, present, and future. It is my contention that environmentalists who argue by appealing to American Indian cultures tend to (1) characterize Indians of the past as non-cultured, (2) characterize Indians of the present as culturally contaminated or nonexistent, (3) "disappear" important concerns of contemporary Indians, and (4) trivialize American Indian cultures. This critique is not to be construed as a denial of the power of American Indian cultures as models of environmental

David Waller recently completed his doctoral degree in philosophy at the University of Massachusetts, Amherst.

consciousness. Nor does anything written here against this particular line of argument imply the falsehood of the environmentalists' belief in the permissibility of animal consumption (the fact that an argument is unsound or dangerous does not mean that its conclusion is false).

The bulk of this paper addresses arguments made by J. Baird Callicott, perhaps the most famous of the current generation of environmentalist philosophers. Callicott certainly must be given credit for environmental philosophy's attaining some measure of respectability within the philosophical profession. He also has exhibited a sincere and sustained interest in indigenous cultures.[2] Furthermore, and most relevant here, his philosophical clarity gives us a chance to analyze the most lucid presentation of the kind of argument under discussion. I believe that this naturalistic argument is the implicit foundation of more obtuse New Age appeals to Indian culture. Therefore, after a lengthy examination of Callicott's argument and a quick look at a more recent presentation by philosopher Ned Hettinger, I will briefly analyze the New Age version. The paper closes with some thoughts on the reduction of American Indian cultures by non-Indians.

THE MAIN ARGUMENT—"SAVAGERY" VERSUS "CIVILIZATION"

In his famous essay "Animal Liberation: A Triangular Affair,"[3] Callicott argues that we must follow Aldo Leopold's prescription to reevaluate "things unnatural, tame, and confined in terms of things natural, wild, and free," and that this

> means, among other things, the reappraisal of the comparatively recent values and concerns of "civilized" Homo sapiens in terms of those of our "savage" ancestors. . . . Savage people seem to have had, *if the attitudes and values of surviving tribal cultures are representative*, something like an *intuitive grasp* of ecological relationships and certainly a morally charged appreciation of eating [my emphases].4

Callicott concludes that this reappraisal will reveal that the most morally responsible diet consists of wild animals and wild plants—i.e., the traditional food of hunter-gatherer societies.[5] Achieving that diet and lifestyle requires, according to Callicott, "a shrinkage . . . of the domestic sphere; . . . a recrudescence of wilderness and a renaissance of tribal cultural experience."[6]

I have found that it is helpful to arrange even the most straightforward argument semiformally; such an arrangement helps me to bring to the surface and distinguish one from another the assumptions imbedded in the premises of the argument. Here is such an arrangement of Callicott's argument:

> 1. We should reevaluate things unnatural, tame, and confined in terms of things natural, wild, and free.
> 2. If (1), then (2b) we should reevaluate the values and concerns of "civilized" human society in terms of the values and concerns of "savage" human society.

3. If (2b), then (4).

4. Therefore, we should eat wild animals and wild plants.

Let's consider each premise in turn. In statement 1 (and thereafter), Callicott is not simply suggesting, by the expression *reevaluate in terms of,* that natural things become the units in terms of which we measure the value of unnatural things. After all, whether you evaluate, in the closing days of 1994, the American dollar in terms of the Mexican peso (6) or the peso in terms of the dollar (1/6), you still get the result that the dollar was roughly six times as valuable as a peso. What Callicott means, of course, is that a natural thing x is more valuable than an unnatural thing y—perhaps to the degree that x is more natural than y. Continuing in this train of thought, a wild thing is better than a tame thing (perhaps we should assume an "all other considerations being equal" condition), and a free thing is better than a confined thing (all other considerations being equal). By *better* or *more valuable* I mean (as I am sure Callicott does) *intrinsically better* or *of greater intrinsic value* (intrinsic value being the kind of value that is not determined by usefulness). So, when comparing the intrinsic values of wolves and poodles, we get the result that wolves, which are wild, free, and natural, are of greater intrinsic value than poodles, which are tame, confined, and unnatural, because wildness is better than tameness, freedom is better than confinement, and naturalness is better than unnaturalness. We should probably note that an operating assumption implicit in the premise is that our evaluations have been upside-down, so to speak. We have been assuming not only that poodles are better than wolves, but that tameness is better than wildness, confinement better than freedom, and unnaturalness better than naturalness. The reevaluation Callicott is calling for requires a transposition of those evaluative assumptions.

The assumption in the second premise is that human society can be divided into two kinds, "civilized" and "savage." Making that division is tricky. On the face of it, the premise implies that the values and concerns of civilized society are unnatural, tame, and confined, whereas the values and concerns of savage society are natural, wild, and free. Now, what it would mean for a value to be *natural* I am not at all sure. Perhaps what Callicott means is that the things (and qualities) that civilized society values are unnatural(ness), tame(ness), and confined(ness). Or perhaps he means that, since savage society is more natural than civilized society, its values and concerns—whatever they might turn out to be—are better and should be emulated by the civilized. Since it might be fair to say that what it values and is concerned with defines, in part, any given society, the last two proposed interpretations might be practically equivalent: civilized society values and is concerned with things that are unnatural, tame, and confined; savage society values and is concerned with things that are natural, wild, and free.

The assumption in the third premise is that whether a human society values and is concerned with things that are natural, wild, and free is a function (in part) of the extent to which wild animals and wild plants are eaten by members of that society. Callicott believes that a hunting-gathering culture (which values and is concerned with eating wild animals and wild plants) is more natural, more wild, and more free than an agricultural, vegetarian culture (a culture that values and is concerned with eating domesticated plants) and therefore is better. I am not sure whether the "freedom" to which Callicott refers translates, in the case of humans, to anything like political freedom. More likely, the three words *wild, natural,* and *free* are simply evocative expressions referring to a single property.

What that single property might be is a difficult question, and one that Callicott perhaps needs to address more directly. Without clarification on this point, it is difficult to evaluate the plausibility of the first premise. However, for purposes of this critique it might be just as well to indulge our intuitions. The argument has problems, in premises 2 and 3, that are more directly relevant to my concerns here. Assuming that there is a tenable distinction between civilized and savage societies, does the Leopoldian preference for the natural over the unnatural translate into a prescription to adopt the diet of the so-called savage?

There does seem to be a problem with drawing the distinction in terms of each society's values and concerns. After all, civilized society must be concerned with and value things natural, wild, and free inasmuch as these are the raw materials for manufacturing things unnatural, tame, and confined. Civilized society might value such things intrinsically but sacrifice them in order to manufacture things of instrumental value. It might be more to the point to drop the references to the "values and concerns" of people and instead just speak of the *people* or *groups of people* or *cultures* themselves. This alters the argument somewhat, but I believe it is a change that Callicott would not consider unfair, for he also writes,

> Leopold's prescription . . . does not stop . . . with a reappraisal of nonhuman domestic animals in terms of their wild (or willed) counterparts; the human ones should be similarly reappraised.[7]

What makes Callicott's proposal so interesting is that he is suggesting not only that we should become more wild than we are, but that we once were more wild and some of us are more wild than others. These wilder people serve as models that the rest of us should emulate. So who were/are these wild counterparts in terms of which we human domestic animals should be reappraised?

CALLICOTT REVIVES THE NOBLE SAVAGE

Remarks of Callicott's such as the following in Part IV ("American Indian Environmental Ethics") of *In Defense of the Land Ethic* indicate that he would offer up Native American cultures as examples of the kind of "savage" societies (or "surviving tribal cultures") we should emulate:

> I thus represent a romantic point of view; I argue that the North American "savages" were indeed more noble than "civilized" Europeans, at least in their outlook toward nature.[8]

Callicott regards Native Americans, and indigenous peoples generally, as natural, wild, and free phenomena of the sort that Leopold approves, and he regards their environmental practices as exhibiting "traditional patterns of human-nature interaction."[9] With this in mind, we can reformulate 2b to read, "We should reevaluate Euro-American culture in terms of Native American cultures" (although any indigenous group will do). This reevaluation will entail the devaluation of agriculture and the rejection of vegetarianism.

I will offer two rather simple and even uninteresting criticisms of Callicott's naturalistic argument.[10] I hope that it will be evident that the criticisms succeed so easily precisely because of the superficial conception of Native Americans invoked by Callicott. The next section of this paper begins with an analysis of that conception.

First, our revision of 2b entails at least one important and questionable assumption: Callicott is, in effect, asking us to buy into assumptions reminiscent of the Tylor-Redfield "classical, unilinear evolutionary paradigm of culture":

> Two relevant corollaries of this theoretical posture are, first, that contemporary nonliterate nonWestern societies are "primitive" in the literal sense that their cultures closely resemble the cultures directly ancestral to contemporary civilizations and, second, that there exist universal features that characterize all cultures at a given stage of development.[11]

Callicott and co-author Overholt do not make clear what they think of this paradigm.[12] In any case, Callicott's argument would seem to demand that we consider as our model of humans' proper ecological niche a specific kind of human culture that cannot, I argue, claim the title of being the first, the original, human culture—at least, not without evidence, which I do not think is forthcoming anytime soon. Were the original humans big game hunters? Three problems here are the sparseness of the fossil record, the difficulty of deciding who will count as that first human culture, and the difficulty of figuring out which patterns of behavior (so far as they could be determined from the evidence) were natural and which were unnatural innovations of culture; the success of Callicott's argument depends on this latter distinction and on being able to classify any human activity as either one or the other. If the original humans were actually herbivores and meat-eating was introduced as a cultural innovation, then we must drop the reference to Native Americans (due to the hunting tradition) in the revised 2b, and 3b becomes "We should eat nothing but wild plants." There is no reason to suppose that it is more probable that humans always ate other animals. On the contrary, throughout our biosphere's history, hominids have been notoriously ill equipped to bring down almost any sort of animal, large or small. It is a fair empirical question to wonder whether human hunting began with the development of certain social structures and/or tools (weapons). It is no good speculating that perhaps (as seems likely) the original humans, like today's chimpanzees, ate easy prey like ants; this supposition will not support the kind of big game hunting that Callicott wants to defend. The latter activity may just be an unnatural augmenting of the former—the "fact" that humans ate ants would not justify the eating of anything else, if we stick to the assumptions of Callicott's naturalistic argument. The question of who will count as the first humans (Homo sapiens, Homo erectus, Homo habilis, a species of Australopithecus, or someone in between?) and the question of whether hunting was a cultural innovation become even more problematic in light of Callicott's liberal views (with which I agree) regarding where (i.e., among which sorts of animals) culture exists:

> In the more flexible, more rapidly changing processes of cultural evolution information is inherited by means of social communication, which among animals may take many different forms. Predatory animals, for example, very often teach their young to hunt by demonstrative methods. Facial gestures, body language, and vocalization convey important "cultural" information among primates.[13]

Even if we grant Callicott the point that such a culture can be identified somewhere in the human past, premise 3 of his argument is still weak. We would not have a model of proper human ecological behavior outside of those areas in which the species originated. An ecological niche is not just a diet; a creature's ecological niche is better thought of as a hyperdimensional volume in which the dimensions describe not only what the creature eats but also the geographic and temporal locations of this and all the rest of its activities. So, for example, if we buy into the concept (I do not, but Callicott must) of a "proper" ecological niche, then we find that a giraffe cannot fill its proper ecological niche in North America because it has none in that particular place—it does not belong, so to speak, even if it could survive there. Similarly, human behaviors at a given place and time will not serve as a model for such practices at all places and all times. To use a science-fictiony example: Suppose that there is abundant life on Mars, and people want to go live there. What is the morally responsible diet for humans on Mars, if we take *morally responsible diet* to mean, after Callicott, "the diet that the *first* humans ate?" Obviously, the answer is not Martian animals, nor is it Martian plants. The bottom line is, anything humans do on Mars will of necessity be completely ecologically innovative—and the same was true of the first Maori to sail to New Zealand six hundred years ago. If Callicott's argument were to succeed, then it would prove too much—not only would we be morally obligated to stick with the diet of our ancestors, but we would be morally prohibited from emigrating. Hence, not only would the Maori have been wrong, perhaps, to hunt the Moa to extinction,[14] but they would also have been wrong to eat anything outside of their traditional eastern Polynesian diet, and wrong even to have left home.

Why do I offer these simple criticisms based on merely biological considerations? Because Callicott's argument is weighted down by two assumptions that together make it the case that he cannot help but approach the Native American as an almost strictly natural phenomenon upon which to construct an easily refuted naturalistic argument against vegetarianism. He weds the Leopoldian formulation of the problem of environmental ethics, a war of the natural versus the cultural, with the assumption that the American Indian environmental experience is a purely natural experience unmediated by the complications of culture.

How to Construct a Savage

As noted above, Callicott portrays indigenous peoples as possessing a sort of intuitive grasp—versus rational or scientific knowledge—of their environment. Callicott devotes part of his book to Native American thought, but how does he describe the content of that thought? The answer is indicated by the title of one of his essays: "American Indian *Land* Wisdom"[15] (my emphasis). Callicott invites us to consider certain conceptualizations of nature as definitive of the indigenous person's experience as an indigenous person. Nowhere does he make this more clear than in his suggestions for tackling what he calls "the uncertainties of the descriptive ethnological approach to the verification of the hypothesis that there *existed* some sort of environmental wisdom among traditional American Indians"[16]—emphasis (mine) on the past.

His first suggestion is that we investigate historical documents that lie as close as possible to the "documentary horizon" (Native Americans' first appearance in written history). This method is based on two assumptions: (1) Native American wisdom is exhausted by certain definitive conceptualizations of nature, and (2) Native encounters with nature are more limited now than they were in the past. These assumptions in turn suggest the conclusion that Native wisdom is trapped in the past—hence Callicott's endorsement of the historical approach, which is predicated on the further assumption that readier access to Native American wisdom is available through European invaders of centuries ago (the source of any documents at the horizon) than through Native Americans living today.

Callicott's second suggestion[17] is that we analyze Native American languages. There is no denying the immense value of linguistic analysis to cross-cultural philosophical enterprises, but Callicott, by narrowly focusing on native encounters with nature, cheats himself out of the potential that lies within this technique.

> Overholt and I undertook a reexamination of Hallowell's analysis of Ojibwa semantic categories with an eye to applying them to the question of an Ojibwa land wisdom. According to Hallowell, the formal Ojibwa linguistic distinction between animate and inanimate (analogous to gender distinctions in Romance languages) does not correspond to scientifically informed Western intuitions. For example, some stones (flint), certain kinds of shells (the megis shell of the Midewiwin, for instance), thunder, various winds, and so on, as well as plants, animals, and human beings fall into the animate linguistic class. Further, the category of person, according to Hallowell, is not coextensive with the category human

being in Ojibwa semantic distinctions as it is in English and other modern Western languages. Animals, plants, stones, thunder, water, hills, and so on may be persons in the Ojibwa linguistic organization of experience.[18]

Callicott then points out that this personhood of nonhuman entities is naturally attached to their being included in social relations and hence being of ethical concern. But certainly these considerations will not suffice for an understanding of Native American environmentalist ethics, nor will they go very far as an explanation of why those ecological attitudes and practices are so different from those of Euro-America. True, Euro-American philosophy and culture emphasize the necessity of personhood for inclusion in the sphere of moral concern (hence, those in the slave trade found it morally convenient to deny that Africans have souls). However, it is all too evident that my acknowledgment of your personhood is not sufficient to guarantee my treating you equitably nor even of my believing that I should (hitmen, rapists, child labor exploiters, etc., do not usually need to be persuaded that their victims are not persons).

Callicott repeats this error in his comments on Lakota culture:

> To speculate briefly on other Plains cultures, if the Lakota world view familiar to everyone from *Black Elk Speaks* survives critical scrutiny, then the Sioux pictured nature as more like a vast extended family than a congeries of societies. Such a world view appears to be corroborated by the Lakota mythic materials collected in the 1890s by James R. Walker. *An environmental wisdom is certainly immediately inferable from such a representation* [my emphasis] but it would not be very precisely described as an ethic. One's familial duties, it seems to me, go beyond ethics. Ethics suggests, at least to me, a formality inappropriate to intimate familial relations.[19]

Callicott characterizes his remarks here as "brief speculation," but, according to the method he employs in explicating Ojibwa environmentalism, his work on Lakota environmentalism is almost done. If we do not need an account of Ojibwa interhuman ethics in order to understand Ojibwa environmentalism (we need only know that nonhumans can be persons, too), then we should not need an account of Lakota (human) family relationships in order to understand Lakota environmentalism (we need only know that nonhumans can be family members, too).

Callicott's descriptions of native "land wisdom" suffer from a lack of content, and I believe that this lack arises in part from a failure to share with his readership the material (and especially the social) contexts in which native environmentalist beliefs and practices appear. I am no sociologist, but I suspect it would be a similarly hopeless task to understand Western environmental destruction without investigating Western interhuman relationships, including economic relationships and their competitive structure. I suspect that the same holds true for the environmental destruction in eastern Europe; one would have to understand the dynamics of interpersonal relationships (including economic relationships), concepts of interpersonal rights and obligations, the traditional Marxist attitude toward nature, and the dynamics of bureaucracy. If we focus exclusively on a culture's conceptualizations of nature, then—and it seems ironic—we can only pretend to understand that culture's relationship with the environment.

Perhaps all I am doing is pointing out an oversight of Callicott's. However, I suspect that Callicott would deny this and deny that material considerations are essential in these kinds of investigations (although he does admit now and then that they are useful). He explicitly subscribes[20] to Stephen Tyler's conception of culture:

> It is assumed [in cognitive anthropology] that each people has a unique system for perceiving and organizing material phenomena—things, events, behavior, and emotions (Goodenough, 1957). The object of study is not these material phenomena themselves, but the way they are organized in the minds of men. Cultures then are not material phenomena; they are cognitive organizations of material phenomena.[21]

Hence, all of the cognitive anthropologist's eggs are in the taxonomical basket. No doubt I should leave it up to the anthropologists to decide what makes a culture a culture, but I cannot restrain a naive urge to question the fruitfulness of any project that aims to understand a culture primarily through what comes down to (at least in the case of Callicott) linguistic analysis. If an anthropologist downplays the material experiences of a culture, how much can she communicate to us when she attempts to explain how those material phenomena are organized in the minds of the participants in that culture?

Parenthetically, we can see a similar problem haunting claims such as the following in Overholt's and Callicott's book *Clothed-in-Fur and Other Tales: An Introduction to an Ojibwa World View*:

> [Ojibwa] narratives certainly reflect and affirm a fundamentally economic relationship between human persons and animal, plant, and mineral persons. Animals, plants, and minerals are not, however, rightless resources, as is the case in Western economic assumptions. They are as it were trading partners with human beings, and are pictured as profiting, from their own point of view, from exchange with human beings.[22]

No one who has read or heard these Ojibwa narratives will deny the contrast with Western economic assumptions, but neither can we deny a similar contrast between some traditional English and German narratives (just break open a copy of Grimm's) and Western economic assumptions. The information about a culture that is available in a culture's narratives, when not supplemented with knowledge about the material existence of the members of that culture, is limited. Speaking for myself, I do not find the Ojibwa narratives so different from some of our own in the appearance of animal persons, the moral content, and the use of the narratives in "the child's enculturation by elders."[23] Perhaps this point is exemplified in the fact that an audience of Ojibwa listeners reacted positively, rather than expressing puzzlement, when John Rogers, Chief Snow Cloud, regaled them with the story of Red Riding Hood.[24] Furthermore, it is difficult for the uninformed reader to know just how the moral lessons within the tales might differ (in this case, with respect to ethics and the environment) from the moral lessons in English and German tales. It seems to me that knowing the moral of a story one has never heard before requires at least some idea of the direction in which the storyteller is inclined to go. It is easy, I think, for a non-Indian to find morals in Indian stories not very different from those told in non-Indian society. This should not be mistaken for a claim that the Ojibwa regard their tales in the same way Euro-Americans regard, say, the story of the "Three Billy Goats Gruff." Whether the Ojibwa stories are regarded as fact or fiction and whether that distinction is of any consequence to the listeners are examples of the deep and interesting questions that remain. I only suggest that the tales by themselves are not terribly strong evidence for the foreignness of Ojibwa culture nor even for an Ojibwa environmental ethic—although I do believe that, once someone knows more about the actual living conditions and material relationships of the Ojibwa, he or she will be convinced on both counts.[25]

I conclude that Callicott's arguments and investigative methods contribute, albeit unwittingly, to an image of Indians as natural beings whose ways are easily understood and imitated due to the absence of the complications of culture.

A VARIATION ON THE NATURALISTIC ARGUMENT

The strategy of urging a naturalistic argument for hunting and then appealing to the example of American Indians sees another, more recent, incarnation in an article by Ned Hettinger in *Environmental Ethics*.[26] Here we have another example of environmentalists' overemphasis on Indians' ecological image at the expense of their social image. Hettinger's argument is based on the naturalistic principles of Holmes Rolston III and, formalized, goes something like this:

> 1. If human ancestors had not hunted animals and eaten meat, humans would not have evolved.
> 2. If (1), then (2b) hunting animals and eating meat affirm human nature.
> 3. If (2b), then (4).
> 4. Therefore, hunting animals and eating meat are morally obligatory.

Hettinger's argument has some difficulties in common with Callicott's, including an undefended emphasis on relatively recent hunter-gatherer cultures (not all of our ancestors ate meat—there was no meat in the primordial sludge). Also, Hettinger's argument, like Callicott's, gives the past carte blanche in determining the moral acceptability of future behavior: If the underlying assumption of the argument is to be taken seriously, then we should not wear shoes either. Also, Hettinger would have to accept vegetarianism as morally obligatory for people in the thirtieth century if the intervening generations decide to go veggie. Less flippantly, since most of the current generation of African Americans would not exist without the institution of slavery, consistency with premises 1 and 2 would lead us to the unacceptable conclusion that slavery affirms their nature, and therefore (the third premise tells us) we have a duty to continue that tradition.

Again, though, Hettinger tries to bolster the naturalistic argument by appealing to the example of American Indians. He tells us that, just as non-Indians cannot value their humanity while rejecting the killing and eating of animals, they also cannot "value the culture of Native American [P]lains tribes while rejecting their tradition of killing buffalo for food, clothing, and shelter." The appeal hints that animal consumption is the be-all and end-all of Plains cultures. Besides overlooking the fact that non-Indians might appreciate the context in which Plains hunting traditions occur,[27] it slights other aspects of Plains culture that deserve appreciation, such as political structures, the extended family, communitarian values, and general ethical principles.

HOW TO BECOME A NEW AGE SAVAGE

The naturalistic argument is just one way in which some environmentalists have simplified Indian cultures in order to argue for the permissibility of animal consumption. That argument also serves as the foundation for another strategy, which is to suggest that non-Indians who wish to consume animals simply borrow ritual or the attitudes associated with ritual. This seems to be the approach advocated by Karen Warren,[28] Nel Noddings,[29] Dolores La Chapelle,[30] and Pulitzer Prize-winning deep ecologist Gary Snyder. Snyder does the deep ecology movement a great disservice when he rides on the spiritual gravy train with an eclectic collection of non-Western traditions and peddles them out of context, New Age style. An excellent example of this is the essay that accompanies the following poem:

Song of the Taste
Eating the living germs of grasses
Eating the ova of large birds
    the fleshy sweetness packed
    around the sperm of swaying trees
The muscles of the flanks and thighs of
        soft-voiced cows
    the bounce in the lamb's leap
    the swish in the ox's tail
Eating roots grown swoll
        inside the soil
Drawing on life of living
    clustered points of light spun
        out of space
hidden in the grape.

> Eating each other's seed
> > eating
> ah, each other.
> Kissing the lover in the mouth of bread:
> > lip to lip.[31]

This homage to burgers, lamb chops, and oxtail soup apparently derives its inspiration from "people who live entirely by hunting, such as the Eskimo, [who] know that taking life is an act requiring a spirit of gratitude and care, and rigorous mindfulness."[32] But the eroticization of flesh-eating that continues in the essay following the poem is completely divorced from any considerations of context or differences in needs between Eskimos in Alaska and Iowans in the grain belt:

> How to accomplish [an understanding of nonharming as an approach to all of living and being]? We can start by saying Grace. . . . To say a good grace you must be conscious of what you're doing, not guilt-ridden and evasive. So we look at the nature of eggs, apples, and oxtail ragoût. What we see is plenitude, even excess, a great sexual exuberance. . . .

Snyder's uninhibited disclosure of his feelings for the meat on his table is admirable. But do these feelings, or this disclosure, magically transport him into a native context? Snyder's essay reminds me of a couple who recently married. The ceremony took place in a vegetable and flower garden. They wore intricately designed clothes that they made for the occasion. Their vows were from an Omaha Indian wedding ceremony. Their friends read poems and performed music in a day-long ceremony incorporating still more elements of Native American culture. The affair had a very earthy, green-friendly sensibility. Then, for lunch, they roasted a whole pig on a spit.

At such moments the hollowness of New Age culture sounds like thunder. The general view seems to be that some crystals, poetry, and nods to women and indigenous peoples will suffice to give a ceremonial stamp of approval to the consumption of animals (sort of like going to a notary public, only much more expensive, as anyone who has been in a New Age store knows). I agree with Dolores LaChapelle that ritual is or should be an important part of our lives. However, I am disturbed by the uncritical and naive way in which ritual and the attitudes associated with ritual are usually discussed in connection with animal consumption.[33] The mere presence of ceremony does not legitimate indigenous peoples' consumption of animals anymore than going through a funeral ritual would legitimate burying someone alive. A ritual is just one part of an entire context in which some action is appropriate. I am not living in an Eskimo-like context, and the borrowing of their rituals in order to somehow associate myself with their culture will not suffice to establish the propriety of my borrowing their diet. Indeed, Henry S. Salt anticipated Snyder more than one hundred years ago when he wrote,

> It does not follow because an Eskimo, for example, may appropriately

wear fur, or a Red Indian feathers, that this apparel will be equally becoming to the inhabitants of London or New York; on the contrary, an act which is perfectly natural in the one case, is often a sign of crass vulgarity in the other.[34]

Worse than the gap in the argument, the assumption that the borrowing of Indian ceremonies will suffice to excuse the consumption of meat contributes to the erasure, in the minds of non-Indians, of the complex historical and social positioning of Native cultures. Again we are left with the implication that the characteristic activity of Native Americans—or the only activity of theirs worthy of our attention—is the killing and consuming of animals.[35]

SOME THOUGHTS ON THE GENERAL PROBLEM

Just before Thanksgiving break, a student in my Introduction to Ethics class defended her upcoming turkey dinner with the following remark: "But the Indians do it." This fixation on Native Americans' ecological activity—when those cultures receive any attention at all—is all too common among Euro-Americans. Typically, non-Indians possess images of that activity: The phenomenon of subsistence hunting of buffalo by Plains cultures is widely known, and of course there is the "weeping Indian" image of the 1970s environmentalist campaign. We also have images of the Native relationship with white America: the first "Thanksgiving," the Little Big Horn, Wounded Knee, leaders like Chief Joseph and Sitting Bull, and, yes, even John Wayne movies. Such images—whether veridical or dangerously mythological and even racist—of these two facets of the Native American experience almost exhaust the non-Indian's conception of all that is Indian. For many non-Indians, the Indian is a two-dimensional cartoon. What is missing, or at best uncommon, is a third kind of image: that of Native American relationships with each other. While there are a few icons such as the "chief," the "squaw," the "papoose," and the "brave," there is a paucity of images—real or imagined—of activity and attitudes within the community.

It is easy for a distortion of, or overemphasis on, the first image to arise in the absence of the third. A classic case was that weeping Indian television ad of two decades ago: A Native American man in traditional dress surveys environmental havoc. A tear runs down his cheek. The image should be ambiguous, but it is not. It should cause us to consider both the destruction of his environment and the destruction of his people, but it does not. We should think for a moment that he might be weeping in memory of all the cultural destruction that was predicated on land theft and environmental recklessness—the destruction of people and interpersonal relationships, the disease, the genocide, the boarding school terrorism, alcoholism, unemployment, the theft of language—but we do not. No, we see immediately that the Indian weeps because white people do not pick up after themselves. This advertisement represents the way in which environmentalism has marginalized the Indian.

SUMMARY

I hope I have shown that environmentalists have been doing no favor to Native American cultures by referring to them to bolster naturalistic arguments against animal rights. I hope I have shown that those kinds of arguments tend to dehumanize Native Americans and trivialize Native cultures by implying that the ecological experience exhausts the Native experience. I hope it also will be evident at this point that, by obsessing over the "original" or "authentic" Indian, environmentalists have tended to imply that contemporary Indians are not "real" Indians, thus contributing to the (perceived) disappearance of contemporary Indians and their social, political, and economic issues.

Environmentalists are right to reach out to American Indians, and indeed original peoples throughout the world, for help in discovering less destructive ecological ideas and practices. However, we must not accept their aid and then cause their issues and their cultures to become the first casualties in our fight against environmental irresponsibility.

Acknowledgments

I would like to thank Hank Theriault and Joseph Yeh for comments and suggestions.

Notes

1. The following sources are recommended for those interested in learning more about the dispute: J. Baird Callicott, "Animal Liberation: A Triangular Affair," *Environmental Ethics* 1 (1979): 71–81; Mark E. Sagoff, "Animal Liberation and Environmental Ethics: Bad Marriage, Quick Divorce," in *Earth Ethics: Environmental Ethics, Animal Rights, and Practical Applications,* ed. James P. Sterba (Englewood Cliffs, NJ: Prentice Hall, 1995), 166–72; H. J. McCloskey, *Ecological Ethics and Politics* (Totowa, NJ: Rowman and Littlefield, 1983); John Rodman, "The Liberation of Nature?" *Inquiry* 20 (1977): 83–145; Joni Seager, *Earth Follies: Coming to Feminist Terms with the Global Environmental Crisis* (New York: Routledge, 1993); Jim Mason, "Why Those Who Would Save the World Cannot," *The Animals' Agenda* 15 (September/October 1995): 5, 44–45.

2. See his *Earth's Insights: A Survey of Ecological Ethics from the Mediterranean Basin to the Australian Outback* (Berkeley: University of California Press, 1994).

3. Reprinted in J. Baird Callicott, *In Defense of the Land Ethic: Essays in Environmental Philosophy* (Albany: State University of New York Press, 1989), 15–38. Further references to Callicott are to this volume.

4. Ibid., 34.

5. Ibid., 36. "Second best is eating from one's own orchard, garden, henhouse, pigpen, and barnyard. Third best is buying or bartering organic foods from one's neighbors and friends."

6. Ibid., 34.

7. Ibid.

8. Ibid., 177.

9. Ibid., 94.

10. I will forgo the point that many indigenous cultures practice agriculture (corn, for example, has been bred for so many centuries that its origins in the wild are a matter of some dispute among botanists). Callicott would no doubt argue that indigenous cultures that practice agriculture are not as natural as those that do not.

11. Thomas W. Overholt and J. Baird Callicott, *Clothed-in-Fur, and Other Tales: An Introduction to an Ojibwa World View* (Washington, DC: University Press of America, 1982), 5.

12. On page 9 they write, "From the biological point of view there are no necessarily universal cultural characteristics distributed species-wide, nor necessarily any distinctly primitive cultural universals as the panprimitivists suppose." The context, though, makes it unclear whether they are expressing their own view or that of Dobzhansky.

13. Overholt and Callicott, *Clothed-in-Fur*, 8.

14. Assuming that they did, and that they did not have a good reason for doing so.

15. Callicott, *In Defense of the Land Ethic*, 203–19.

16. Ibid., 212.

17. The third and fourth suggestions include the use of "nostalgic memoirs" and "disciplined and methodical modern ethnographic reports." Again, the emphasis is on the past—on "the *reconstruction* of an American Indian attitude toward nature" (ibid., 179—my emphasis).

18. Ibid., 214.

19. Ibid., 216.

20. Overholt and Callicott, *Clothed-in-Fur*, 20.

21. Stephen Tyler, *Cognitive Anthropology* (New York: Rinehart and Winston, 1969), 3.

22. Overholt and Callicott, *Clothed-in-Fur*, 155.

23. Mary B. Black-Rogers, introduction to ibid., xv.

24. John Rogers (Chief Snow Cloud), *Red World and White: Memories of a Chippewa Boyhood* (Norman: University of Oklahoma Press, 1974), 124–25.

25. The lack of a more holistic appreciation of Native American society endangers even the kind of direct cross-cultural research that Richard Brandt engaged in for his book *Hopi Ethics: A Theoretical Analysis* (Chicago: University of Chicago Press, 1954). Brandt makes an error that complements Callicott's: He goes directly to the source—the Hopi themselves—but with no appreciation of the general metaphysical and evaluative principles underlying their ethical judgments. Hence he does not know what to make of the apparent Hopi (as well as Navajo) disregard for domesticated sheep and dogs (circa 1954) when Hopi respect for animals and nature was otherwise evident. Consequently, he cannot help but see a contradiction where there is none.

26. Ned Hettinger, "Valuing Predation in Rolston's Environmental Ethics: Bambi Lovers versus Tree Huggers," *Environmental Ethics* 16 (Spring 1994): 3–20.

27. The principles of vegetarianism and animal liberation are qualified by most proponents to take into account a variety of contextual issues—for example, immediate necessity.

28. Gary Snyder, "The Power and the Promise of Ecological Feminism," *Environmental Ethics* 12 (1990): 125–46.

29. Comment on Donovan's "Animal Rights and Feminist Theory," *Signs: Journal of Women in Culture and Society* 16:2: 418–25.

30. Bill Devall and George Sessions, "Ritual Is Essential," in *Deep Ecology: Living as if Nature Mattered* (Salt Lake City, UT: Gibbs M. Smith, 1985), 247–50.

31. Gary Snyder, "Song of the Taste" (and an untitled essay), in Devall and Sessions, *Deep Ecology*, 12.

32. Ibid., 12–13.

33. Including LaChapelle's example of ceremony in connection with the consumption of salmon.

34. Henry S. Salt, *Animals' Rights: Considered in Relation to Social Progress* (Clarks Summit, PA: Society for Animal Rights, 1980), 83. *Animals' Rights* was first published in 1892.

35. For more reasons why deep ecologists should steer clear of the New Age movement, see Ward Churchill, "Sam Gill's *Mother Earth*: Colonialism, Genocide and the Expropriation of Indigenous Spiritual Tradition in Contemporary Academia," *American Indian Culture and Research Journal* 12:3 (1988): 49–67. Other critiques of the use of Indian cultures by philosophers include Greta Gaard's "Ecofeminism and Native American Cultures: Pushing the Limits of Cultural Imperialism?" in *Ecofeminism: Women, Animals, Nature,* ed. Gaard (Philadelphia: Temple University Press, 1993), and Andy Smith's "For All Those Who Were Indian in a Former Life," in *Ecofeminism and the Sacred,* ed. Carol J. Adams (New York: Continuum, 1993). See also Annie L. Booth and Harvey M. Jacobs, "Ties that Bind: Native American Beliefs as a Foundation for Environmental Consciousness," *Environmental Ethics* 12:1 (Spring 1990): 27–43.

15

Ecological Risk Assessment and Management: Their Failure to Value Indigenous Traditional Ecological Knowledge and Protect Tribal Homelands

Jeanette Wolfley

INTRODUCTION

A TRIBAL LAND BASE or homeland is the sine qua non of sovereignty. Tribal territories form the geographical limits of each tribe's jurisdiction, support a residing population, are the basis of the tribal economy, and provide an irreplaceable forum for cultural vitality based on religious practices and cultural traditions premised on the sacredness of land. Today, fully functioning Indian Nations possess four distinct yet interwoven and interdependent attributes of sovereignty: secure land base, functioning economies, self-government, and cultural vitality.[1] Some describe these attributes as geographic and political independence. In short, the tribes' land bases are the linchpin to tribal existence and autonomy as sovereign nations.[2] Moreover, a priority implicit in Indian land tenure is maintaining a homeland in which both present and future generations of the tribes may live and flourish, since tribal individuals and families reside on secure land bases which have supported and nourished their ancestors for thousands of years past and continue to be the core and integral foundation of tribal existence.

For most indigenous tribal peoples of the United States,[3] creation stories, songs, prayers, and traditional ecological knowledge and wisdom teach us to visualize and understand the connections between the physical environment, the spiritual values that create and bind a tribal community, and the social welfare of the community. We are taught a system of values that induces a profound respect for the natural forces which give life to the complex world of which we are but a small part. The wisdom and knowledge that indigenous people possess of the ecosystems and their homelands is based upon millennia of observation, habitation, and experience, all using a balance of human interaction and intervention with the environment. It is the traditional ecological knowledge—an interactive natural world science—which has preserved many tribal homelands in pristine condition and protected the many medicines and foods for

Jeanette Wolfley is a member of the Shoshone-Bannock Tribes of the Fort Hall Reservation in Idaho. She is an attorney practicing in the areas of federal Indian law and environmental protection and adjunct professor in the Indian Studies Program at Idaho State University.

generations. This traditional ecological knowledge held by indigenous peoples of the United States will continue to be the beacon for tribal ways of life to guide us into the next century.

In sharp contrast, the majority of the mainstream non-Indian people in the United States have lost their sense of reliance on nature for survival and therefore have lost their respect for the world we inhabit. Many non-Indians no longer possess the stories, songs, and prayers that helped them see their connections to the natural world and the impact of their actions. Essentially, the relationship among the spiritual world, the physical world, and the social world has disintegrated, having become, instead, a world of exploitation and commodification of natural resources for economic gain. The stories, songs, and prayers have been replaced by a kind of institutionalized science and technology that attempt to justify the manipulation, contamination, and deterioration of the environment. With the advent and wholesale embracing of an institutionalized science and technology, can non-Indians imagine why preserving biological diversity is something deeply connected to who and what we are in the world? And what can tribal people do to decolonize the institutional supposition that indigenous values and knowledge have no place at the table to begin to solve the ever-pressing environmental dilemma facing the United States and the world?

This article discusses the critical role that indigenous ecological knowledge can and should play in protecting and preserving ecosystems and tribal communities. Cultural values and diversity are as urgent as biological diversity and must inform scientific methods of valuing lands, resource ecosystems, and human rights. Cultural knowledge must be considered equally in evaluating and planning for future projects and activities impacting tribal rights and resources. This article explores the threats to tribal homelands and treaty rights and explains the role tribes should play in their protection. This article also seeks to present a tribal perspective of ecological risk assessment and risk management by identifying and suggesting three major areas which the federal agencies must address to start to protect tribal homelands and resources. This article, however, is no substitute for direct consultation with Indian tribes and communities. Risk assessment cannot be undertaken and risk management cannot be adequately implemented without tribal input.

RISK ASSESSMENT AND RISK MANAGEMENT

Federal and state governmental officials and decisionmakers resolve national and local environmental and/or waste-management issues by performing risk assessments[4] and risk management[5] on an ongoing basis. Risk assessment is viewed as the preferred tool to consider systematically and explicitly issues affecting the environmental decision-making process. In short, risk assessment is a scientific and technical process. It uses scientific information derived from past experience or other scientific information to evaluate quantitatively or qualitatively the potential consequences and risk associated with a given situation, action, or alternative. Risk management is the ranking of different risks, development of strategies to eliminate or mitigate the risks, decision on which risks are to be eliminated or mitigated, and implementation of selected strategies.

TRIBAL HOMELANDS AND OFF-RESERVATION RIGHTS

Any discussion of ecological risk assessment and risk management and their impact on tribal homelands must be premised on an understanding of tribal land tenure in the United States and off-reservation treaty-guaranteed rights. There are 557 federally recognized Indian tribes in the United States.[6] Tribes and individual tribal members in the lower forty-eight states own approximately 56.6 million acres of land,[7] which roughly amounts to only 3 percent of the original tribal land base.[8] Alaska Natives, pursuant to the Alaska Native Claims Settlement Act, own another 44 million acres.[9] At least half of the 1.9 million tribal people in the United States live on or adjacent to one of 310 reservations.[10] The size of tribal reservations ranges from the largest landholding of approximately 15 million acres (the Navajo Nation) to others of about 100 acres.[11]

Since the beginning of federal-tribal relations, Indian tribes have fought in war, in Congress, in courts, and in public forums to maintain an existence apart from the majority. Indeed, the United States' promise of separatism in perpetuity was a fundamental premise underlying the treaty negotiations with the tribes of the lower forty-eight states.[12] Although tribes did not want to give up their lands, tribes across the country relinquished millions of acres of land in exchange for assurances of a retained homeland of a smaller size in which they would remain free from federal and state interference and the intrusions of non-Indian settlers. In many respects, the promise of tribal sovereignty has survived only because of the separatism made possible by the retained tribal land base.

This tribal separatism withstood the most devastating attack by Congress in the late 1800s under the General Allotment Act of 1887, also known as the Dawes Act.[13] Under the allotment policy, Congress attacked the basic tribal practice of holding land in common. For tribes whose reservations were allotted, the basic approach was to take land out of tribal ownership and divide it into parcels for allotment to individuals. Congress ultimately repudiated this allotment policy when it enacted the Indian Reorganization Act in 1934, but, by the end of the allotment era, Indian tribes and individuals held only a third of the land that the tribes had held in 1887.[14] Viewed from the late twentieth-century perspective, the General Allotment Act can be seen for what it was—an attempt to carry out cultural genocide against indigenous people.[15]

The pressure to exploit the remaining tribally owned lands is ever present. Private enterprise and the federal government covet the vast Indian land resources, which includes 6.3 million acres of commercial timberland,[16] 43 million acres of range land, and 3 million acres of agricultural land.[17] Approximately one-third of the low sulfur coal in the western states, more than one-half of all uranium deposits, and 20 percent of all known U.S. reserves in oil and natural gas are located on tribal homelands.[18] More recently, tribal lands also have been viewed as sites for waste disposal.[19]

Under the same treaties that reserved tribal homelands, tribes also reserved and were guaranteed access to crucial off-reservation hunting, fishing, and gathering rights on lands ceded by the tribes to the United States. Some of the major law cases have involved fishing in the Pacific Northwest[20] and the Great Lakes,[21] and inland fishing and hunting in the Midwest.[22] Tribal off-reservation treaty rights have also been recognized in at least seven states.[23] The court cases have made clear that numerous treaties and agreements secure rights to harvest fish and game that are different from those held by non-Indian citizens generally, and that while the states can regulate the exercise of Indian hunting and fishing rights, they can only do so in limited circumstances.

The treaty resources now stand vulnerable to the development and pollution that plagues nearly every sector of the United States. Throughout the country, there are numerous instances of tribal lands and water resources contaminated with pollution originating from off-reservation sources. Moreover, treaty rights to take wildlife and gather foods and medicines, while integral to maintaining a traditional economy and fulfilling a promise of separatism, are quickly fading largely because of the destructive actions of the majority, industrial society. Rampant development, the construction of dams and flooding, mining, and the continuing storage and transportation of nuclear waste adjacent to reservations are increasingly destroying wildlife habitats and pushing species into extinction at an accelerating rate. Even in cases in which wildlife remains available for Native use, health risks associated with contamination of the flesh from toxins present in the habitat are mounting.

The federal government is often involved in off-reservation activities through its role as manager of vast tracts of public lands and resources located off-reservation. Much of the public lands ceded by indigenous people passed into the public domain and became national forests, national parks, and range land. A variety of federal agencies[24] play a role in regulating private activities such as grazing, mining, recreation, oil and gas production, and timber harvesting, all of which seriously impact tribal rights. Other federal agencies manage natural resources such as water and wildlife that are vital to tribal people.[25] Many of the lands, resources, and sites upon which tribal people have lived for thousands of years are now in peril due to environmental degradation. In many instances, federal agencies bear responsibility for these threats through their actions in managing public lands and regulating polluting activities, managing shared water and wildlife resources, and approving new development on federal lands. For example, the federal government has engaged in nuclear weapons testing near reservation lands inhabited by the Western Shoshone Nation in Nevada. And for years, the Department of Energy engaged in open dumping of highly radioactive waste at the Hanford site, located along the banks of the Columbia River near the boundary of the Yakama Indian Nation's reservation.[26] This waste has found its way into the Columbia River, a major waterway to the Pacific Ocean.[27] In addition, another federal agency, the U.S. Army Corps of Engineers, operates a line of dams along the Columbia River that kills up to 95 percent of the migrating salmon.[28] Indeed, for the first time in the memory of tribal people of the Pacific Northwest, there are not enough harvestable fish to support even the most basic cultural needs.

The various approaches to ecological risk assessment and management developed and employed by the federal agencies are critical areas to tribal people. As we move into the twenty-first century, these approaches will substantially determine the future ecological viability of our separate land bases and the subsistence rights guaranteed under treaties and agreements executed more than a century ago. Risk assessment methodologies and risk management of environmental and natural resources will determine in many instances the future of traditional Native existence. The myriad of ecological risk assessment approaches and decision-making strategies will guide governmental regulation and management of federal lands. This will have significant environmental consequences for tribal people as they work to influence the federal government's responsibility over resource development such as oil and gas production, mining, logging, and storage and processing of nuclear waste. The impact is particularly evident for tribes that reside in states which have a large percentage of federal land, and for the tribal nations that reside in states which have enormous sections of federal lands managed by the by Department of Energy and Department of Defense.

TRIBAL ROLES IN ECOLOGICAL
RISK ASSESSMENT AND MANAGEMENT

Indian tribes are significantly absent from ecological risk assessments and risk management. Usually, these assessments and management strategies do not mention the impact that certain federal, state, local, and private sector activities will have on tribal homelands or treaty-guaranteed hunting, fishing, and gathering rights. Indeed, most risk assessment analyses are void of any mention of tribal governments, Indian lands, treaty rights, or tribal cultural values. Instead, the standard approaches identify decision-making officials in federal, state, and local governments, as well as private-sector leaders in commercial, industrial, and private organizations, but omit or exclude representatives from tribal government whose reservation lands and/or aboriginal territories include the areas being assessed.

Indian tribes have the power to regulate persons and property within their territorial boundaries to fully protect their homelands. This tribal power stems from three sources: inherent tribal authority, treaties and executive orders, and federal statutory delegation of authority to tribes.[29] In general, tribal governments retain inherent sovereign powers to regulate conduct of tribal members and non-members that threatens or directly affects public health and safety or the economic security of the reservation community.[30] This jurisdiction includes activities that degrade the environment.

Tribes are in the best position to regulate and to be intimately involved in risk assessment, environmental activities, and management affecting tribal lands and natural resources. Accordingly, Congress has supported tribal efforts to do so in amendments to various federal environmental statutes.[31] Indeed, states have never been granted authority by Congress to regulate conduct of Indians or non-Indians relating to environmental regulation within reservations.[32] Thus, as recognized by Congress and the courts, Indian tribes can adequately preserve, protect, and perpetuate the rights and resources under tribal control for all people located on their treaty-guaranteed homelands.

President Clinton's directive of April 29, 1994, sets the tone for his administration's approach to Indian affairs. In a memorandum to heads of executive departments and agencies, President Clinton required all federal agencies and departments to implement their programs in a "sensitive manner respectful of tribal sovereignty," and set forth several principles to guide agency dealings with Indian tribes.[33] These principles include: (1) operate within a "government-to-government relationship" with tribes; (2) consult "to the greatest extent practicable" with tribal governments prior to taking actions that affect them; (3) "assess the impact" of federal actions on "tribal trust resources" to "assure that tribal government rights and concerns are considered during the development of such plans, projects, programs, and activities"; and (4) take "appropriate steps to remove any procedural impediments" to working with tribes. These policies direct the dealings between tribes and federal agencies on environmental issues such as the development of ecological risk assessment guidelines and approaches and implementations by decisionmakers.

The current ecological risk assessments and risk managers are totally inconsistent with the established case law, congressional, and executive policies relating to tribal involvement in the protection of environmental quality. Most agencies such as the Department of Energy, Department of Defense, Forest Service, and Bureau of Reclamation undertaking risk assessments disregard the policies to work with tribes on a government-to-government basis, to recognize tribes as the primary decisionmakers for environmental matters on reservation lands, and to encourage tribal, state, and local cooperation in areas of mutual concern. Indeed, tribes are the most appropriate nonfederal parties for making decisions and carrying out program responsibilities affecting Indian reservations, their environments, and the health and welfare of the reservation populace.

Tribal governments should be included in risk management and be included in the dialogue between federal risk managers and risk assessors. Additionally, in order to effectuate the government-to-government relationship fully, federal agencies must communicate with tribal governments regarding ecological risk assessments, thoughtfully consider tribal concerns, recognize and give due respect to tribal governments' efforts to incorporate tribal values in risk assessments, and adequately design alternative approaches that protect tribal lands, resources, and treaty rights. The administration's strong policy of government-to-government relations directs agencies to form a tribal working group on ecological risk assessment and management to gain tribal knowledge and expertise on the issue and to formulate decision-making approaches that fully protect and preserve the treaty-guaranteed reservations and resources.

TRADITIONAL TRIBAL CULTURAL VALUES IN RISK ASSESSMENT AND RISK MANAGEMENT

The modern-day risk assessment and risk decision-making process purports to estimate acceptable harm to a given species, food web, population, or ecosystem. Accordingly, conducting an ecological risk assessment in areas affecting tribal homelands or ancient tribal boundaries involves a basic understanding of a large regional ecosystem. However, the understanding of such a large and complex ecosystem impacting tribal people under existing approaches is limited to institutional technological knowledge. For example, under the current scientific approach, numbers and studies are plugged into models and frameworks of risk assessment by people who may never view the particular site or ecosystem where the proposed activity will occur or toxin will be released. Thus, only a few activities can be measured or estimated that will affect tribal communities. The approaches consider very few consequences in an artificial, isolated environment and in controlled experiments based on method assumptions and date-set characteristics, which do not analyze the range of impact on each other or the impact on ecological and cultural attributes. Finally, the modern-day risk assessment processes are set on a short time scale and assess a limited geographic area.

In stark contrast, at the heart of tribal cultures and other indigenous cultures of the United States is the inseparability of the health and welfare of the tribal people and the natural, ancient, indigenous environment, encompassing all other organisms and their habitats. Most indigenous peoples in the United States understand that the environment is a harmonious blend of what is known as science and management. Indeed, tribal communities have persevered for centuries because so many have knowledge of the natural, spiritual, and ecological world and understand and respect the interconnectedness among humans and all other living things. Additionally, tribal people possess a culture-based knowledge of ecosystems that has evolved and accumulated over thousands of years and is continually tested and improved for the lasting maintenance of the tribe's existence. The collection and use of this complex knowledge of the physical world—including values, histories, stories, ethics, and the culture of indigenous ways of life—is an integral part of any tribal decision-making process.[34]

The incorporation of values, meaning what we believe in and care to achieve, is essential to risk assessment and risk management processes. From the Native American perspective, the values embodying our cultural and religious beliefs are necessary in any engagement process with other distinct cultural groups for the purpose of conflict resolution in risk assessment and risk management. Not all tribal cultural values are quantifiable, nor must they be quantified in order to obtain recognition in ecological risk assessments and risk management.[35] The time has come for federal agencies to develop and institute systematic procedures and interactive processes to make the values explicit, by direct and indirect means, and communicable to improve the proposed risk assessment and risk management decisions.

Tribal cultural wisdom can assist in the ecosystem characterization and context of species interdependence, particularly within the naturally proper boundaries of the ancient Native landscape. In the absence of predisturbance/experimental field data, traditional tribal knowledge associated with a particular scenario can be employed to discern the spatial and temporal distribution of endemic ecological components under characterization. True characteristics of the ecosystem can affect the ultimate nature and distribution of the stressors[36] and may only initially be estimated through site-specific tribal cultural knowledge. Local microbial communities and environmental fate processes can transform the chemical stressors, the remaining of which can in turn influence the level of exposure of the ecological components[37] of concern. Without a formal process for the incorporation and integration of the cultural and scientific values essential to the exposure characteristic phase,[38] risk assessments cannot meet the obligation of optimally utilizing all available means to determine the long-term ecological risks. Examples of the characteristics of the ecological components that affect their exposure to the stressors are the habitat needs, food preferences, reproductive cycles, and seasonal activities such as migration and selective use of indigenous natural resources.[39] Thus, the cultural and traditional resources of indigenous peoples can be immediately brought to bear on the exposure-information gathering and processing phase under mutually agreed upon formal engagement conditions.

Characterization of exposure and ecological effects often requires the application of statistical methods. Given the complexity and uncertainty extant in the information about potential impact on the indigenous native landscape by the introduced stressors and the method assumptions, the data cannot be fully trusted to the interpretation based on the controlled experiments and limited scientific analyses. Statistical significance does not always reflect biological and ecological significance, and profound ecobiological changes may not be detected by statistical tests or manifested in any measurable way. The employment of tribal elders' wisdom and traditional knowledge of the key variables pertinent to the native landscape can assist in the evaluation between statistical and ecobiological significance, and in the assessment of the level of intrinsic uncertainty.[40]

A decision process that is inclusive of and interactive with Native cultural values will result in greater trust in the decisionmakers by tribal governments and the public. Consequently, federal agencies can more effectively deliberate why one alternative is chosen and why other alternatives are not. Additionally, conceptual ideas for incorporating cultural value models should be explored by federal agencies.

Such decision-making processes of mutual, respected engagement with Native cultural values exist. For example, in 1994 the Yakama Indian Nation instituted a project with the Department of Energy-Hanford site in Washington to incorporate and integrate the use of tribal and cultural knowledge and values into the decision-making process for Department of Energy activities affecting the Yakama Indian Nation. This project, known as the Holistic Engineering Project, blends the institutional perspective with the technological and cultural/tribal points of view.[41] Similarly, the Confederated Tribes of the Colville Reservation in Washington have developed a decision-making process known as the Holistic Resource Management Model.[42]

ECOLOGICAL RELEVANCE

Generally, three principal criteria inform the selection of assessment endpoints (what to protect): (1) their ecological relevance, (2) their susceptibility to the known or potential stressors, and (3) whether they represent management goals. In other words, ecological relevance and susceptibility are essential for selecting assessment endpoints that are scientifically valid. Importantly from an indigenous perspective, what is missing from an ecological relevance discussion is the recognition and inclusion of cultural values and the operational approach of tribal traditions. In short, the standard ecological-relevance approach is too limited, and, without the proper assessment endpoints, the risk to a given ecosystem may be seriously misrepresented, which could lead to major adverse impact or misguided management. Any discussion with regard to ecological relevance endpoints that assist in sustaining a natural structure or reflect the structure of the community ecosystem or landscape must consider that tribal people possess ancestral territories or ancient boundaries which go far beyond their present-day reservation political boundaries or ecosystem. Ancient tribal boundaries or ancestral territories are relevant to the ecological risk assessment because they recognize the time-tested relationship between the natural resources and the regional subsistence culture, that is, all endemic species and their associated habitats corresponding to the indigenous way of life under investigation.

The historically interactive and adaptive nature of Native biodiversity prior to the introduction of modern technology and economic exploitation is self-evident. However, the tribal spatially mediated and time-tested culture cannot be properly understood within the political boundaries of the present homeland in accordance with traditional wisdom and scientific knowledge. Therefore, in order to accomplish a meaningful ecological risk assessment, the federal reviewing agency must consider the proper spatial domain (regional subsistence culture) of the affected tribe with the potential impact to be defined by the ancient and aboriginal boundaries of the tribes. Indeed, tribal cultural resources, which include foods and medicines of the tribes, demonstrate that a fragmented network of habitats and endemic species cannot continue to exist without the preservation of the associated patterns of interdependence and diversity well documented in the oral traditions of tribal people.[43]

Additionally, most endpoint discussions fail to recognize that risk can occur when tribal communities have lost their traditional land base because of a hazardous materials accident or when new technologies are sited in culturally sensitive areas such as tribal lands or aboriginal territories. The consequences can be devastating. The loss of treaty homelands or the use of traditional sacred lands can lead to the risk of irreversible cultural extinction for some communities. As explained, the tribal land base is the linchpin to tribal sovereignty because it serves as the center for economic stability and cultural vitality. If tribal lands or places are contaminated or damaged, habitation may be restricted or eliminated which will result in the Indian tribe losing its political powers to control and regulate the activities occurring on its homelands. Moreover, the tribe will be unable to preserve and protect adequately its membership's general health, welfare, and safety. Loss of tribal culture and identity may occur because tribal identity depends heavily upon the sociocultural ties that link individuals, families, and groups to specific tribal territories and lands.[44]

PRIORITIZATION OF SPECIES

Tribal traditions recognize that all species are connected and impact each other in a complex natural web of life. Consequently, all species are treated with equity and cultural recognition, and therefore we cannot prioritize one species over another by the standard biodiversity conservation, for instance, measuring the genetic distance between the classified species within a region. Generally, tribal values support the idea of multispecies risk analysis within the context of a traditional information system, which respects the functional relationship between species, and between species and the hierarchical organization of species. The tribal value for the sustenance of all life in the ecological web must share the risk of extinction on each and every species interactively. The procedure for evaluation of such interrelated risks consequently would reflect the Native cultural value system and assume adaptive and online characteristics.

Ecological risk assessments often employ systematic biology and genetic distance measures to determine the priority of species for conservation. For example, risk assessors identify or analyze the potential "cascade of adverse effects" and "series of effects among a diversity of organisms" which implies the hierarchical structure of species and processes of interrelationships.[45] While tribal cultural values are not in direct conflict with the scientific research of conservation priority and the mathematics of biodiversity, tribal people express the deep and singular concern of the presumed human superior ability and intelligence to decide which species and process are ultimately most relevant to the protection and preservation of life, ecological health, and lasting welfare for all. Given the very limited and short existence of scientific knowledge in the life history of all species, and that scientific fallibility is the premise for technological progress, the tribal cultural value system challenges the assumed superiority of the human race in its search for a balanced solution to preserve the natural

resources, in this case using ecological risk assessment as the main consideration.[46]

To avoid the possible escalation of conflict between the different value systems within the ecological risk assessment processes and risk management decision making, tribal governments, tribal Elders, and other indigenous people
should promote a moderate and equitable approach by first establishing and
institutionalizing the formal dialogue and engagement process between Native
peoples who possess distinct cultural value systems. Accordingly, the conservation genetics or prioritization of species question will be addressed in the manner cognizant of the relative importance of each and every species rather than
the less than perfect and self-destructive power of the human species.

CONCLUSION

Since first entering into treaties with the United States, Native nations have
waged a two-hundred-year struggle to maintain an autonomy against an
encroaching majority society. Now at the threshold of the twenty-first century,
the future of tribal existence for many indigenous communities is imperiled.
The tribal way of life that remains intrinsically connected to the natural environment and dependent on the continued integrity of the land and resources
faces an ecological crisis of unprecedented magnitude. Due to the unique nature
of tribal land tenure and tribal culture, tribes cannot simply relocate to new
areas when their lands become contaminated, their water polluted, or their
wildlife resources decimated as a result of ecological abuse by the non-Indian
sector. The mobility and transience that provide short-term solutions to members of the majority society do not provide options to tribes when their way of
life is threatened or destroyed.

This article has suggested a fundamental means by which the federal government can begin to meet its federal trust responsibility of protection—the
institutionalization of risk assessment and risk management that incorporate
time-honored, traditional indigenous knowledge of the environment. Federal
agencies have a unique opportunity to design ecological risk assessment
approaches that can fully value tribal homelands and resources and support the
existence of tribal lifestyles in this country. The development of such approaches
and management should serve as a focal point of future dealings between tribal
communities and the federal government, and will be a fundamental challenge
for federal agencies to overcome the years of reliance solely on science and technology to inform their decision making. This challenge, however great, is
implicit in the promise of Native separatism that underlies the vast cessions of
land made just over two centuries ago.

Even beyond this challenge, the introduction of tribally held cultural values
to the majority society, which seems at a loss to secure a sustainable future for
its own coming generations, will confer immeasurable benefits to non-Indian
society. And, finally, the recognition and acceptance of such tribal wisdom and

knowledge is only the beginning. There must be a continuing federal dialogue with tribes, resolution of existing issues, resources provided to tribal communities, and meaningful consultation with tribes in order to fully preserve the creation for all.

Acknowledgments

I would like to express my deep appreciation and thanks to members of the Intertribal Risk Assessment Committee who critiqued drafts of this article and offered helpful suggestions and advice. The Intertribal Risk Assessment Committee members include: Mary Fadden (St. Regis Mohawk); Germaine White (Confederated Salish and Kootenai); Dean Canty (Catawba Indian Nation); Vietchau Gio Nguyen; Russell Jim (Yakama Indian Nation); Heather Westra (Prairie Island Indian Community); Robert Holden (National Congress of American Indians); Ted Howard (Shoshone-Paiute); Toney Begay (All Indian Pueblo Council); and Claudeo Broncho (Shoshone-Bannock Tribes).

Notes

1. For a comprehensive discussion of these attributes of tribal sovereignty, see Mary Christina Woods, "Indian Land and the Promise of Native Sovereignty: The Trust Doctrine Revisited," *Utah Law Review* (1994): 1,471.

2. Charles F. Wilkinson, *American Indians, Time, and the Law* (New Haven: Yale University Press, 1987), discusses land base as the linchpin to other attributes of tribal sovereignty.

3. For purposes of this article, the term *indigenous peoples* refers to people descending from the original inhabitants of the Western Hemisphere who have maintained distinct languages, culture, or religion from time immemorial. Most consider themselves to be custodians, not owners, of the land and other cultural and natural resources. See Russell L. Barsh, "Indigenous Peoples, an Emerging Object of International Law," *American Journal of International Law* 80 (1986): 369, 373–75.

4. *Risk assessment* is defined as "the systematic, scientific characterization of potential adverse effects of human and ecological exposures to hazardous agents or activities. Risk assessment is performed by considering the types of hazards, the extent of exposure to hazards, and information about the relationship between exposures and responses, including variation in susceptibility. Adverse effects or responses could result from exposures to chemicals, microorganisms, radiation, or natural events." The Presidential/Congressional Commission on Risk Assessment and Risk Management, "Risk Assessment and Risk Management in Regulatory Decisionmaking," *Final Report*, Vol. 2 (1997), 2.

5. *Risk management* is defined as "the process of identifying, evaluating, selecting, and implementing actions to reduce risk to human health and to ecosystems. The goal of risk management is scientifically sound, cost effective, integrated actions that reduce or prevent risks while taking into account social, cultural, ethical, political, and legal considerations," ibid.

6. The number of federally recognized Indian tribes as of June 1997 was provided by the Office of the Assistant Secretary for Indian Affairs, Department of Interior, Washington, D.C.

7. David H. Getches, et al., *Cases and Materials on Federal Indian Law*, 3d. ed. (1993): 20.

8. Valerie Talisman, "Environment Key to Native Survival," *Ethnic Newswatch* (May 31, 1993): 14.

9. Getches, et al., *Cases and Materials on Federal Indian Law*, 20.

10. Ibid., 8, 13, 15.

11. Ibid., 8–9.

12. Wilkinson, *American Indians, Time, and the Law*,18.

13. Act of February 8, 1887, ch. 119, 24 Stat. 388, codified as amended at 25 U.S.C. Sections 331–34, 341–42, 354, 381 (1988).

14. Act of June 18, 1934, ch. 576, Section 1, 48 Stat. 984, codified at 25 U.S.C. Section 461 (1988). Of the 1.38 billion acres of tribal lands in 1887, only 48 million acres remained in 1934. Felix S. Cohen, *Handbook of Federal Indian Law* (Charlottesville, VA: Michie Company, 1982), 138.

15. See Rennard Strickland, "Genocide-at-Law: An Historic and Contemporary View of the Native American Experience," *Kansas Law Review* 34 (1986): 713.

16. Getches, et al., *Cases and Materials on Federal Indian Law*, 20.

17. Ibid., 22.

18. Ward Churchill and Winona LaDuke, "Native North American: The Political Economy of Radioactive Colonism," in *The State of North America: Genocide, Colonization and Resistance*, ed. M. Annette Jaimes (South End Press, Boston, MA, 1992), 241.

19. Pamela A. D'Angelo, "Waste Management Industry Turns to Indian Reservations as States Close Landfills," *Environmental Report* (BNA) 35, at 1607 (Dec. 28, 1990): 21; Valerie Talisman, "Stuck Holding the Nation's Nuclear Waste," *Race, Poverty & Environment* (Fall 1992): 6; "Nuclear Waste: On the Reservation," *Economist* (Oct. 3, 1992): 30.

20. See, e.g., *United States v. Washington*, 384 F. Supp. 312 (W. D. Wash. 1974), affd. 520 F.2d 676 (9th Circuit, 1975), *cert. denied*, 423 U.S. 1086 (1976); *Sohappy v. Smith*, 302 F. Supp. 899 (D. Or. 1969), affd., 529 F.2d 570 (9th Cir. 1976).

21. See, e.g., *United States v. Michigan*, 471 F. Supp. 192 (W. D. Mich. 1979), affd., in part and rev'd in part, 653 F.2d 277 (6th Cir.), *cert. denied*, 454 U.S. 1124 (1981).

22. See, e.g., *Lac Courte Oreilles Band v. Voight*, 700 F.2d 341 (7th Cir.), *cert. denied*, 464 U.S. 805 (1983), on remand, 775 F. Supp. 321 (W. D. Wis. 1991).

23. Idaho, Montana, Michigan, Minnesota, Oregon, Washington, and Wisconsin.

24. These federal agencies include the U.S. Forest Service, the National Park Service, and the Bureau of Land Management.

25. The agencies responsible for management of these resources include the U.S. Fish and Wildlife Service, the National Marine Fisheries Service, the U.S. Army Corps of Engineers, and the Bureau of Reclamation.

26. From 1955 to 1959, federal workers at Hanford dumped more than 30 million curies of radioactivity directly into the Columbia River. Paul Koberstein, "Hanford's Tank 103–C Potential Chemical Nightmare," *Oregonian*, July 23, 1992.

27. Ibid. From 1943 to 1966, the Department of Energy dumped an additional 444 billion gallons of radioactive waste into open trenches and 178 underground storage tanks, many of which are leaking. See also, Churchill and LaDuke, "Native North America: The Political Economy of Radioactive Colonialism."

28. See John Daniel, "Dance of Denial," *Sierra* (Mar.–Apr. 1993,): 64, 66–67.

29. See *United States v. Mazurie*, 419 U.S. 544 (1975); *Montana v. United States*, 450 U.S. 544 (1981).

30. Ibid.; *Nance v. EPA*, 645 F.2d 701 (9th Cir.), *cert. denied*, 454 U.S. 1081 (1981).

31. See the Safe Drinking Water Act, 42 U.S.C. Sections 300f–300j-12 (1988); Comprehensive Environmental Response, Compensation, and Liability Act, 42 U.S.C. Sections 9601–9675 (1988); the Clean Water Act, 33 U.S.C. Sections 1251–1387 (1988); and the Clean Air Act, 42 U.S.C. Sections 7400–7642 (1988).

32. See *Washington Department of Ecology* v. *EPA*, 752 F.2d 1465 (9th Cir. 1985) upholding EPA's refusal to accept the state's application to regulate on-reservation activities involving hazardous waste.

33. William J. Clinton, "Memorandum for the Heads of Executive Departments and Agencies, Government-to-Government Relations with Native American Governments," *Federal Register* 22,951, May 4, 1994, 59.

34. See, e.g., Wolfley, J., et al., "A Process for Developing and Implementing the Methodology for Collecting Data to be Used in and for Tribal Decision-Making," Shoshone-Bannock Tribal Risk Assessment Forum, Pocatello, Idaho (June 1996).

35. See E. Tso, et al., "Risk Assessment In Indian Country: Guiding Principles and Environmental Ethics of Indigenous People," ibid.

36. The term *stressor* is defined as "any physical, chemical or biological entity that can induce an adverse response," in "Framework for Ecological Risk Assessment," United States Environmental Protection Agency, Risk Assessment Forum, Washington, D.C. (Feb. 1992), 38.

37. *Ecological component* is "any part of an ecological system, including individuals, populations, communities, and the ecosystem itself," ibid., 37.

38. The *exposure characterization phase* or *characterization of exposure* is a "portion of the analysis phase of ecological risk assessment that evaluates the interaction of the stressor with one or more ecological compounds. Exposure can be expressed as co-occurrence, or contact depending on the stressor and ecological component involved," ibid., 37.

39. R. Jim, G. Nguyen, and B. Barry, "Introducing Native Landscape Ecology to Hanford Cleanup," *Proceedings of the Vienna International Conference on Radioactive Waste Management and Environment Remediation*, eds. S. C. Slate and S. V. Johnson, ASME.

40. See G. Nguyen, "A Cultural Value System Based on Native Landscape Ecology," Nez Perce Tribal Risk Assessment Forum, Clarkston, Idaho (October 1996).

41. See R. Jim, and B. Barry, "The Yakama Indian Nation Holistic Engineering Project: A Novel Integrated Risk Management System Approach to the Cleanup of the Hanford Site" (Papers presented at Department of Energy meetings, 1994); P. Kurstedt, et al., "The Environmental Trilogy Project: Balancing Technical, Institutional, and Cultural Perspectives to Environmental Management," ibid.

42. Confederated Tribes of the Colville Reservation Holistic Resource Management, "Planning Today for Future Generations" Nez Perce Tribal Risk Assessment Forum.

43. See D.L. Hawksworth, *Biodiversity: Measurement and Estimation, The Royal Society* (London: Chapman & Hall, 1995).

44. See, S. Curtis, "Cultural Relativism and Risk Assessment Strategies for Federal Projects," *Human Organization* 1 (Spring 1992): 51.

45. *Cascading adverse effects* means that the interrelationship among entities and processes in ecosystems results in the potential for cascading adverse effects: As one population, species, process, or other entity in the ecosystem is altered, other entities are affected as well, often adversely.

46. See S. Blackmore, "Knowing the Earth's Biodiversity: Challenges for the Infrastructure of Systemic Biology," *Science* 274 (1996): 63–64; R.H. Crozier and R.M. Kusminski, "Genetics Distances and the Setting of Conservation Priorities," *Conservation Genetics*, eds. V. Loeschcke, et al. (Birkhauser Verlag, Basel, Switzerland, 1994), 227–237.

16

Uranium Is in My Body

Rachel L. Spieldoch

THE NAVAJO PEOPLE PERCEIVE the world as an interconnected whole. This applies to religion, concepts of health, and their view of themselves in relation to the world. In effect, a disruption in one part of their lives creates a disharmony in the overall system. This disruption not only creates stress on the individual but threatens the Navajo fabric of life.

In the late 1940s and 1950s, the Navajo fabric of life was disturbed by the ill effects of uranium mining. With the rise of the Cold War, the United States government opened uranium mines in the Four Corners area of the Navajo Nation and remained the sole purchaser of uranium for defense purposes from the late 1940s to the early 1960s. During this period, the government offered higher paying jobs to local Navajo people in return for uranium. The Navajo were unaware of the dangers associated with uranium mining and radon daughters. In contrast, the federal government was hardly naive about the situation when it allowed thousands of Navajo people to face hazards to their health and their lives in the pursuit of the rich resources underneath reservation lands. The hazardous conditions in the mines eventually led to lung cancer and respiratory diseases that cause severe disability or death.

Navajo people were sacrificed for economic growth. Many early uranium miners died without compensation as a direct result of radiation exposure. The government viewed these people as expendable. Currently, almost fifty years later, widows and surviving miners are still fighting for compensation. The United States government, which has a trust responsibility to Native Americans, ignored its duty to warn and protect the Navajo uranium miners from hazards. This experience reminds the Navajo people that terms such as *deculturation, ethnocide, termination,* and the *Vanishing American* are not dead concepts.

"I wonder if the ground has anything to say? . . . The Great Spirit in placing men on earth, desired them to take good care of the ground and to do each other no harm,"[1] says one Navajo tribal member. In 1947, Navajo miners entered the black holes blasted into the earth in search of uranium. These mines lacked proper ventilation, light, and water supplies. In fact, many Navajo workers

Rachel L. Spieldoch is a student at the University of Wisconsin, Madison, majoring in molecular biology and biochemistry.

quenched their thirst in these mines by drinking from "hot" puddles on the mine floor. They ate their lunches in the dust-filled mines and brought their work clothes home to be washed with their families' laundry. Houses were built from radioactive materials. The workers' children often played in the uranium tailings. In a study conducted by Susan Dawson with the Department of Sociology, Social Work, and Anthropology at Utah State University, forty-eight Navajo people who had worked in uranium mines for an average of thirteen years reported that at no time were they informed of the dangers of radiation.[2] These early uranium miners, their wives, and their children were all exposed to radiation.

Perhaps the company best known for neglect of uranium miners was Kerr McGee Corporation. Spurred by the advice of the Bureau of Indian Affairs and the promise of higher wages, the Navajo Tribal Council approved an agreement with the Kerr McGee Corporation in 1952. Although wages averaged $1.60 per hour, two-thirds of the off-reservation rate for miners, it was a substantial amount for Navajo people, and they grabbed at this improved financial opportunity for their families. In addition, royalties were not a consideration; the agreement provided only for flat rates.

In 1952, a federal mine inspector reported that the mine's ventilation system was not in operation. The inspector returned in both 1954 and 1955 and reported similar conditions: The fans and ventilation blowers were not working adequately to provide a safe environment for miners. In 1959, the radiation levels in the Kerr McGee shaft allegedly had reached ninety times the "permissible" limit.[3] More than seventy-one acres of uranium tailings were abandoned at the mining site in early 1980. Uranium has a half-life of 4.5 billion years.[4] However, it is not the uranium itself that is most dangerous but the radon daughters, which result from uranium decay and actually have a much shorter half-life, approximately thirty minutes. The radon daughters quickly become attached to solid surfaces such as dust particles and are ingested by the miners and others in the vicinity of the contaminated areas. Once ingested, the particles are internalized and delivered to the lungs.

Although the situation with Kerr McGee in Shiprock, New Mexico, exemplifies abusive and inhumane treatment of Navajo people, this experience does not stand alone. Unfortunately, the atrocities at Shiprock represent common treatment for the majority of Navajo uranium miners during this time in history. Maltreatment in uranium mines was not well publicized because the mines were primarily controlled by the federal government, which did not want to bear the burden of public scrutiny.

During the late 1940s and the 1950s, uranium was sought more than all other metallic minerals combined. Uranium mining promised billions of dollars for the federal government and the national economy. Not only did the government effectively own all uranium for most of the period between 1947 and 1971, but it aggressively encouraged production during this time. On the Navajo Reservation, the government demonstrated indifference toward its 1868 treaty with the Navajo Nation by failing to protect the people from life-threatening conditions in and near the mines. Enormous quantities of uranium tailings were negligently dumped into local water tributaries used by the Navajo, their live-stock, and the people in neighboring communities. Uranium was abandoned in piles near mine sites, left ripped from the earth in "National Sacrifice Areas"[5] not fit for human sustenance. The Navajo people were faced with the destruction of their land, the poisoning of their bodies, and the unraveling of their religious fiber. As one Navajo stated, "There is no center anymore, the sacred tree is gone."[6] The facts are embarrassing for the United States government. Safety standards were not implemented until 1971, thirty-five years after the initiation of uranium mining, despite already published literature concerning the effects of radiation on human lives.

As early as the mid 1500s, miners of uranium-bearing ores in the Erz Moun-tains of east-central Europe were reported to have an unusually high frequency of lung disease, which became known as "bergkrankheit," meaning mountain sickness. In 1913, Arnstein reported that of 665 Schneeberg uranium miners, 40 percent died of lung cancer. In 1932, Pirchan and Sikl reported that 53 per-cent of uranium miners in Joachimsthal Czechoslovakia between 1929 and 1930 had died of lung cancer.[7] By the 1940s, the hazards associated with ura-nium mining were well accepted by the scientific community. Nevertheless, ura-nium mining began in the Four Corners region of the United States.

Once the uranium mining was well underway in 1949, the United States Public Health Service (PHS) conducted a study to assess the risks to uranium miners. For the first time, researchers could isolate uranium as the sole cause of illness, without cigarette smoking as a limiting factor. The majority of Navajo people did not smoke, and as a population they had demonstrated a low fre-quency of lung cancer prior to this time. This study clearly indicated that the miners were exposed to extremely high levels of radiation and silicate dust. By 1951, the PHS and the Atomic Energy Commission (AEC) realized that mechanical ventilation to remove the dust concentration in mines could greatly reduce health hazards. The results of the study also showed that incidence of lung cancer was much higher than expected. In 1957, the U.S. Public Health Service proposed "1 Working Level"[8] as the standard for control of radon daughter exposure, and this standard was adopted by the American Standards Association in 1960.[9] However, the lack of attention to these standards became a mockery to all of the uranium miners who died. In fact, the PHS announced at this time that it still had insufficient knowledge to establish exposure standards. By 1962, 68 percent of uranium mines were found in excess of the recommended level. During the mid-1960s, ventilation surveys showed that many uranium mines were still relying on natural draft pressure or nonfunctional mechanical ventilation systems with inoperative blowers for ventilation. Four years later, only 44 percent of uranium mines in the United States had reduced radiation levels to the recommended limit.[10] During this time, new activist groups such as NIOSH, MESHA, and MESCA expressed Navajo discontent and supported the imple-mentation of safer work environments and compensation for uranium miners.

One of the most documented epidemiologists on this topic, V. E. Archer, reported in 1964 both a significant excess of lung cancer mortality and an increase in debilitating respiratory diseases such as pulmonary emphysema, fibrosis, and chronic bronchitis. In 1967, F.E. Lundin discovered sixty-two deaths related to lung cancer among white underground uranium miners in contrast with 10.02 expected.[11] He and Archer concluded that an exposure of 120 Working Level Months (WLM) appeared to double the normal lung cancer incidence among uranium miners. Shockingly, the WLM of early uranium miners was frequently above 1,000 WLM and could reach as high as 3,000–4,000 WLM.

As research advanced, it was found that lung cancer associated with radioactive exposure is often the small, undifferentiated cell type. In the late 1960s and early 1970s, a scientist named Saccomanno reported an association between radon daughter exposure and increased incidence of bronchogenic tumors of small cell undifferentiated histology among miners with WLM as low as 40–200.[12] In a demonstration of how drastically political attitudes contradicted scientific facts, the Federal Radiation Council concluded in 1967 that "the data is not sufficient to indicate an association between exposure to radon daughters and the subsequent development of lung cancer when cumulative exposures are less than 1000 WLM."[13] Finally in 1971, the U.S. Department of the Interior declared four WLM as the standard exposure to radon daughters. This standard assumed that a thirty-year exposure would yield an upper danger limit of 120 WLM, thus *only* doubling the risk for lung cancer. Dr. Hornung, chief of the Statistical Services Section at the National Institute for Occupational Safety and Health in Ohio, stated during the 1990 congressional hearings that "*no* totally safe level of radon exposure is assumed. Each additional WLM of exposure above naturally occurring background will produce an increment in lung cancer risk. Therefore, one must speak in terms of acceptable risk rather than a totally safe level of exposure."[14]

The message conveyed is that the federal government, in an effort to benefit economically, intentionally neglected its responsibility to educate Navajo Indians about the health and safety hazards associated with uranium mining. The federal government, the Public Health Service, and the Atomic Energy Commission would have to have been completely uneducated about the situation in order to have possessed a legitimate lack of awareness of the potential dangers. Traditional Navajo people believe that material wealth is an indication of false status; in this situation, the opposite seems true for the United States government.

Prior to the Congressional hearing in 1990, compensation for uranium miners was nonexistent unless the worker contracted the disease while actively working in the mines. For example, New Mexico has several provisions that clearly make it difficult or impossible for early uranium miners to receive compensation. First, a claim cannot be filed unless a written notice was given to the employer within thirty days of the onset of illness. For many miners, this deadline was passed before they became aware of their entitlements. Second, a claim must be filed within one year of the onset of illness. Many individuals found it very difficult, if not impossible, to collect all the necessary paperwork and records to file a claim by the deadline. The businesses were shut down years ago, and the names of employers and managers have been forgotten. Third, countless miners contracted cancer or respiratory disease ten or more years after working in the mines, but there is no compensation for illnesses that develop so long after the miner last worked. Although these provisions are specific to New Mexico, similar problems arise with the compensation laws for early uranium miners in other states of the Four Corners Region prior to 1990.

In the fall of 1990, Congress passed the Radiation Exposure Compensation Act. Forty-three years had passed since the uranium miners' first exposure to radiation. The majority of people instrumental to the reasoning behind this act are no longer alive. Their medical records are gone, their families are gone, their land is destroyed. These people cannot be compensated for their losses. Although a proposal for this act was first presented in 1979, eleven years had transpired before the law was passed. Under the law, miners or their beneficiaries are entitled to $100,000 in compensation if they (1) worked in the uranium mines in New Mexico, Arizona, Colorado, or Utah between 1947 and 1971, (2) were exposed to two hundred or more WLM of radiation, and (3) contracted lung cancer or another serious disease. An afflicted miner who worked for three years or more in one or more uranium mines prior to federal standards in 1971 is potentially eligible for benefits under this act. The eligible survivors of each miner are entitled to the benefits unless it is established that, at the time of death, such miner was not partially or totally disabled due to radiation-induced or dust-induced latent disease.[15]

The Radiation Exposure Compensation Act makes an important statement in history. The federal government offered a public apology for the maltreatment of early uranium miners. However, after the law passed through the Department of Justice, the ideology behind compensation was lost as fraud against the federal government became a basis for political paranoia. The original congressional intentions for the act were greatly misinterpreted during implementation. As a result, strict rules and regulations disqualified many uranium miners.

In an inspection report, the U.S. Department of Justice wrote that, between April 1992 and March 1993, the unit received 2,634 compensation claims. Out of all of these, only 585 claims were approved. Two hundred sixty-two claims were denied and 1,787 claims were left pending.[16] Although the Radiation Exposure Compensation Act was a move in the right direction, it contained numerous deficiencies and left many problems unresolved. For example, the act does not cover families that lived near the mining area but whose members were not miners. Just like the miners, these people ingested the dust-filled air, their children played in the uranium tailings, and their homes were built from radioactive materials. In addition, when the mechanical ventilation systems were finally implemented, they were not engineered to protect surrounding communities. The dust that was blown out of the mines to improve the safety of the workers was diffused into the air of the nearby community.

Perhaps an even larger concern is that compensation has not been provided for uranium millers, who were exposed to uranium in many different stages of development. At the mills, uranium oxide (U_3O_8) was stockpiled, crushed, sampled, ground, and leached to extract the uranium.[17] The final concentrate, often termed *yellow-cake,* remained on the clothing, hands, and hair when the workers went home. The government has not provided compensation to these workers because it claims that not enough studies have been completed concerning hazards to millers. Past studies should be sufficient evidence that radiation, in any form, is extremely hazardous.

Although many early uranium miners have been diagnosed with specific work-induced diseases such as silicosis, they are not eligible for compensation because they are not disabled. If the government accepts its responsibility for having caused illness in a certain group of people, then it should also provide benefits to individuals with medically related ailments who are not necessarily disabled.

Finally, the federal government made the mistake of relating nonrespiratory diseases such as fibrosis and silicosis to radiation exposure. According to Dr. Samet, an expert on pulmonary medicine at the University of New Mexico, "nonrespiratory disease linked to radiation exposure is medically inappropriate. Silica causes silicosis; radon exposure does not cause silicosis."[18] It seems apparent that there were no doctors around when the compensation act was written. Silicosis, fibrosis, and other dust-induced respiratory diseases are not connected to radiation. Therefore, the compensation act should not use radiation exposure levels to determine benefits for workers with nonmalignant respiratory diseases.

Passage of the Radiation Exposure Compensation Act implies that the federal government sympathizes to some degree with early Navajo uranium miners and is willing to compensate them for their suffering. However, along with complications and exclusions in the actual wording of the act, interpretation and implementation have become another political mess that delays and negates compensation. The intent of the act has been twisted and made so stringent that many Navajo people are having difficulty applying for benefits. According to Dr. Abel, head of the Indian Health Service's pulmonary clinic, "one miner had a cardiac arrest in our office. Ironically, he was coming in for paperwork. Paperwork seems to be more of a problem than anything else."[19] The three areas of greatest conflict in interpreting and implementing the act are records, medical supplies, and regulations.

According to the law, each claimant must present a complete medical history in order to receive compensation. Unfortunately, almost fifty years after the Navajo miners were poisoned with illness-causing substances and radiation, the medical and work records of many of these individuals remain lost or incomplete. It seems ironic to disqualify someone from receiving compensation because the federal Indian Health Service cannot find the correct documents. The National Institute of Occupational Safety and Health, which was responsible for keeping lists of all mine workers, also has incomplete records.

Adding to the confusion is the fact that physicians often have misdiagnosed the miners' illnesses. Proper medical facilities for correctly diagnosing mine-related diseases often are not available. Tests such as MRI for detecting fibrosis and Beta reading tests for detecting silicosis are extremely expensive and are not available on or near the reservation. Without MRI, silicosis and fibrosis are difficult and sometimes impossible to distinguish. Apparently, several miners traveled to the

Mayo Clinic in Minnesota to have MRIs done for their compensation paperwork. Unfortunately, even after all this energy is expended on paperwork, chances remain slim that compensation will be received.

The government will not budge to help these Navajo people when records or medical tests are not available. To simplify the compensation process, the act ought to eliminate the required diagnostic distinction between silicosis, fibrosis, and pneumoconioses and instead should define nonmalignant respiratory disease as "any occupationally caused restrictive respiratory disease."[20] In this manner, the benefit of the doubt would be given to the Navajo people.

Most important, regulations mandated by the Department of Justice now have superseded the original agreement passed by Congress. In order to receive compensation for nonmalignant respiratory diseases such as silicosis or pneumoconioses, the miners are required to have accumulated all of their exposure on the reservation. This regulation was derived from the direct passage in the act that "miners with silicosis must work on the reservation."[21] Although this passage does not necessarily imply that all mining must be performed on the reservation, Navajo individuals who ingested less than the required number of WLM on the reservation but accumulated more than the requirement at several mines both on and off the reservation are ineligible for compensation. In addition, the required radiation exposure standard for compensation is two hundred WLM. As mentioned earlier, after thirty years in a uranium mine with an average exposure of four WLM per year, the worker will have accumulated 120 WLM, which more than doubles his risk of lung cancer. The 200 WLM requirement is extremely high and prevents many sick people from qualifying for benefits.

Finally, although attitudes toward smoking are largely negative today, smoking was hardly uncommon in the 1940s and 1950s. For the Navajo uranium miners who smoked, the risk of lung cancer from a combination of radon daughter exposure and cigarette smoking is multiplicative. However, under the Radiation Exposure Compensation Act, Navajo uranium miners who smoked are required to have a higher level of radon daughter exposure, and thus a higher risk of cancer, before becoming eligible for compensation. Further, a man who smoked three packs a day for thirty years and a man who smoked one pack a day for one year are both considered smokers by law and are subject to the same compensation limits.[22]

Although lost or incomplete medical records, inadequate medical facilities, and ambiguous regulations are the most blatant obstacles to compensation in the current legislation, the number of complications becomes almost infinite when each claimant's situation poses a different set of problems. Additional complications arise from the required certification of medical records and a thirty-day deadline for returning requested documents. Spousal compensation can be complicated by the fact that many Navajo couples had traditional marriage ceremonies, which are not regarded as legitimate by the federal government.

Uranium mining in the 1940s and 1950s had a terrible effect on the water resources, the usable land, and the lives of the people. Already many of the miners' children have developed cancers at a young age. Today the Navajo must choose between death from hazardous exposure or deculturation through relocation. Many are uneducated and unaccustomed to life outside the reservation. They do not know how to survive in an urban environment. If they leave their land and are forced into an economic and social structure incompatible with their own, the religious threads of their lives are broken and their culture shatters: "The creator has planted me here on this earth. This is all one body—humans, geese, animals, grasses, rain. My roots go way down deep and can't be pulled out. If we relocate, we sell our prayers and that will be the end of us."[23] The International Convention on Suppression and Punishment of the Crime of Apartheid prohibits "deliberate imposition on a racial group or groups of living conditions calculated to cause its or their destruction as a whole."[24]

According to Mark Zannis and Robert Davis, "the welfare system is a form of pacification. Combined with political and physical repression, it keeps people alive at a subsistence level but blunts any attempt at revolt while turning them into captive consumers of industrial products."[25] Continuing government hand outs can only promise a bleak future for Native American culture. Past efforts by the government to deal with the "Indian situation" suggest that self-sufficiency is not acceptable without assimilation. Historically, the federal government has attempted to contain and stifle Indian livelihood in order to maintain control over government-to-government relations. Federal documents suggest a weaker sovereign accepting the protection of a stronger sovereign without extinguishing its own sovereignty. In reality, however, the incidents surrounding uranium mining on Indian lands reveal a weaker government exploiting its resources and labor in an effort to survive economically. From this perspective, mining developers view Native American values as an obstacle to be overcome.

Almost half a century ago, uranium miners stole from the earth's core for the economic benefit of the federal government. Fifty years later, many of these individuals are dead, but the consequences of the experience are still being felt by the survivors. One scholar regards the trust relationship between Native Americans and the federal government as "racial discrimination and unfettered U.S. power disguised as moral duty."[26] Ronald Reagan's statement in 1988 that "maybe we should not have humored Indians in their primitive lifestyle—maybe they should have been made citizens like everyone else,"[27] proves that ignorance about Indian history still thrives in our society. Some people—people with political power—still regard the concepts of termination and ethnocide as viable despite the struggles of Native Americans for their rights. Native Americans must become educated about energy politics so that they can protect themselves in the future.

Native Americans are not going to vanish. Although the losses to Navajo land and resources resulting from uranium mining cannot be recovered, recognition and respect as a sovereign nation should be attainable. A gap of understanding exists between Native Americans and the United States government. If this gap continues to grow, the deaths of early uranium miners will have been in vain, and the lessons of history will be left untold. While Native Americans must continue to fight for self-determination and the preservation of their culture, the

U.S. government also must strive to recognize and protect Native American rights. Both parties must work together for a better future for Native Americans and for the enrichment of all people.

Notes

1. Todd Howland, "U.S. Law as a Tool of Forced Social Change: A Contextual Examination of the Human Rights Violations by the United States Government against Native Americans Big Mountain," *Boston College Third World Law Journal* 7 (1987): 61–96.

2. U.S. Senate, Committee on Energy and Natural Resources, Subcommittee on Mineral Resources Development and Production, "Impacts of Past Uranium Mining Practices: Hearing, March 13, 1990," *One Hundred First Congress: Second Session on the Impacts of Past Uranium Mining Practices: Shiprock, NM, 101-683* (Washington DC: U.S. Government Printing Office, 1990), 147.

3. M. Annette Jaimes, *The State of Native America: Genocide, Colonization, and Resistance* (Boston: South End Press, 1992), 247.

4. J.K. Wagoner, "Uranium: The United States Experience, A Lesson in History," *Exhibit 1: One Hundred First Congress,* 84.

5. Jaimes, *The State of Native America,* 253.

6. A Navajo made this statement in the 1985 film documentary *Broken Rainbow,* 70 min., Earthworks, 1985.

7. Wagoner, "Uranium: The United States Experience," 1.

8. One Working Level (WL) is equal to any combination of radon progeny in 1 liter of air that results in the release of 1.3×10^5 MeV of potential alpha energy. R. J. Roscoe et al., "Mortality among Navajo Uranium Miners," *American Journal of Public Health* 85:4 (1995): 535–40.

9. U.S. Senate, *One Hundred First Congress,* 9–11.

10. Ibid., 62.

11. F. E. Lundin, Jr. et al., "Mortality of Uranium Miners in Relation to Radiation Exposure, Hard Rock Mining and Cigarette Smoking: 1950–September, 1967," *Health Physics* 16 (1969): 571–78.

12. Wagoner, "Uranium: The United States Experience," 75.

13. Federal Radiation Council, "Report No. 8 Revised, Guideline for the Control of Radiation Hazards in Uranium Mining," *Staff Report of the Federal Radiation Council* (September 1967), 20.

14. U.S. Senate, *One Hundred First Congress,* 23.

15. U.S. Senate, Committee on Labor and Human Resources, "Oversight of the Radiation Exposure Compensation Act: Hearing, June 5, 1993," *One Hundred Third Congress: First Session on the Oversight of the Radiation Exposure Compensation Act: Shiprock, NM, 103-619* (Washington DC: U.S. Government Printing Office, 1993), 4. *Radiation-induced disease* includes lung cancer, bronchogenic cancer, cancers involving the respiratory or the lymphopoietic system, and any other disease that the secretary concludes is radiation-induced. The term *dust-induced latent disease* includes pulmonary fibrosis, silicosis, corpulmonale, and any other disease resulting from employment as a uranium miner. U.S. Congress, *Congressional Record: Proceedings and Debates of the 96th Congress, First Session September 27, 1979* (Washington DC: U.S. Government Printing Office, 1979), 134.

16. Ibid., 74.

17. U.S. Senate, *One Hundred First Congress*, 79–80.

18. U.S. Senate, *One Hundred Third Congress*, 19.

19. Ibid., 14.

20. Ibid., 7.

21. Ibid., 16.

22. Ibid., 12.

23. Trebbe Johnson, " Indian Wars in the Nuclear Age: The Navajo-Hopi Land Dispute," *Amicus Journal* 8 (1986): 23.

24. Howland, "U.S. Law as a Tool of Forced Social Change," 81.

25. Jaimes, *The State of Native America*, 245.

26. Howland, "U.S. Law as a Tool of Forced Social Change," 78.

27. President Ronald Reagan made this statement during his 1988 visit to the former Soviet Union (*Frontline*, Boston, WGBH, 58 min., 1988).

INDEX

The following typographical conventions used in this index are: f and *t* identify figures and tables, respectively, *n* identifies a note.

320 / Index

ACKOWLEDGMENTS

SNYDER, GARY. SONG OF THE TASTE, FROM REGARDING WAVE, © 1997 BY GARY SNYDER. REPRINTED BY PERMISSION OF NEW DIRECTIONS PUBLISHING CORPORATION.

The following articles are reprinted from the *American Indian Culture and Research Journal*, by permission of the American Indian Studies Center, UCLA, © Regents of the University of California:

AMERICAN INDIAN IDENTITIES: ISSUES OF INDIVIDUAL CHOICES AND DEVELOPMENT. Devon A. Mihesuah (22:2, 1998)

THE CRUCIBLE OF AMERICAN INDIAN IDENTITY: NATIVE TRADITION VERSUS COLONIAL IMPOSITION IN POSTCONQUEST NORTH AMERICA. Ward Churchill (1999)

ABORIGINAL WOMEN AND SELF-GOVERNMENT: CHALLENGING LEVIATHAN. Katherine Beaty Chiste (18:3, 1994)

THE GOOD RED ROAD: JOURNEYS OF HOMECOMING IN NATIVE WOMEN'S WRITING. Beth Brant (21:1, 1997)

CONTEMPORARY TRIBAL CODES AND GENDER ISSUES. Bruce G. Miller (18:2, 1994)

THE POWWOW AS A PUBLIC ARENA FOR NEGOTIATING UNITY AND DIVERSITY IN AMERICAN INDIAN LIFE. Mark Mattern (20:4, 1996)

SOUTHWESTERN OKLAHOMA, THE GOURD DANCE, AND "CHARLIE BROWN" originally printed as "CHARLIE BROWN": NOT JUST ANOTHER ESSAY ON THE GOURD DANCE. Luke E. Lassiter (21:4, 1997)

CULTURAL IMPERIALISM AND THE MARKETING OF NATIVE AMERICA. Laurie Anne Whitt (19:3, 1995)

NATIVE MEDIA'S COMMUNITIES. Steven Leuthold (21:2, 1997)

SHADOW CATCHERS OR SHADOW SNATCHERS? ETHICAL ISSUES FOR PHOTOGRAPHERS OF CONTEMPORARY NATIVE AMERICANS. Lee Philip Brumbaugh (20:3, 1996)

THE EPIDEMIOLOGY OF ALCOHOL ABUSE AMONG AMERICAN INDIANS: THE MYTHICAL AND REAL PROPERTIES. Philip A. May (18:2, 1994)

TOBACCO, CULTURE, AND HEALTH AMONG AMERICAN INDIANS: A HISTORICAL REVIEW. Christina M. Pego, Robert F. Hill, Glenn W. Solomon, Robert M. Chisholm, and Suzanne E. Ivey (19:2, 1995)

CANCER CONTROL RESEARCH AMONG AMERICAN INDIANS AND ALASKA NATIVES: A PARADIGM FOR RESEARCH NEEDS IN THE NEXT MILLENNIUM. Martin C. Mahoney, Arthur M. Michalek (22:1, 1998)

FRIENDLY FIRE: WHEN ENVIRONMENTALISTS DEHUMANIZE AMERICAN INDIANS. David Waller (20;2, 1996)

ECOLOGICAL RISK ASSESSMENT AND MANAGEMENT: THEIR FAILURE TO VALUE INDIGENOUS TRADITIONAL ECOLOGICAL KNOWLEDGE AND PROTECT TRIBAL HOMELANDS. Jeanette Wolfley (22:2, 1998)

URANIUM IS IN MY BODY. Rachel L. Spieldoch (20:2, 1996)

ABOUT THE EDITOR

DUANE CHAMPAGNE is a professor in the UCLA Department of Sociology, director of the American Indian Studies Center, and editor of the *American Indian Culture and Research Journal*. He is author of many articles and book chapters in sociology and American Indian studies. Dr. Champagne's main research interests are in social change among American Indians, change in macro institutions, historical comparative sociology, contemporary American Indian issues, and theory. Professor Champagne is author of *Political Change and Social Order: Constitutional Governments Among the Cherokee, Choctaw, Chickasaw and Creek* (Stanford University Press, 1992) and *American Indian Societies: Strategies and Conditions of Political and Cultural Survival* (Cultural Survival, 1989) and is editor of several volumes including *The Native North American Almanac* (Gale Research Inc., 1994). Professor Champagne has served as consultant for Native American Studies programs at several universities including the University of California, Berkeley; the University of New Mexico; Black Hills State University; SUNY-Oswego; and the University of Ohio.